Schoenhut Dolls

A Collector's Encyclopedia

by Carol Corson

Published by  Hobby House Press, Inc.
Cumberland, Maryland 21502

ACKNOWLEDGEMENTS

Many books have a list of people whom the author thanks for their help. Books on collectibles are completely dependent on the willingness of collectors to share their treasures with the rest of the world. The people who generously opened their collections and their homes for the visit of a complete stranger, and gave generously of their time, their knowledge, and an ear to test ideas on (as well as a bed to sleep in) are numerous. Without them this simply would not be a book and I am deeply grateful to:

Blossom Abell, Evelyn Ackerman, Ed and Peggy Bealefield, Charles and Barbara Buysse, Vicky Candido, H.B. Christianson, Louise H. Christoffers, S.K. Coburn, Evelyn Jane Coleman, Ella and Larry Corn, Marjorie Darrah, Dorothy M. Dixon, Margaret Dowling, Diane C. Dustir, Helen Feuerstein, Jan Foulke, Howard Foulke, Carl and Mary Hansen, Gail Hiatt, Dolores Hoover, Dot and Bud Hutton, Donna Kaonis, D. Keith Kaonis, Fredrick E. Keller, Sara T. Kocher, Winnie Langley, Marie Lehmann, Becky Lowe, Jay Lowe, Frank J. Mahood, Meriel Marlar, Dorothy A. McGonagle, Carol A. McKee, Harry R. McKeon, Anna McQuilken, Becky and Monty Moncrief, Roxanne LeMay Morison, Phyllis Schoenhut O'Hare, Betty O'Sullivan, Quentin O'Sullivan, Gloria Osborn, Barbara E. Pio, Marianne Ripley, Carolyn H. Roush, Richard Saxman, Jane and Henry Schlosser, Virginia Schoenfeld, Mrs. Norman Schoenhut, William F. Schoenhut, Sherryl Shirran, Helen Sieverling, Nancy A. Smith, Regina A. Steele, Eleanor P. Swanson, Fredericka Tate, Joan Timmins, Lois Townsend, Billie Nelson Tyrrell, Vida and Gus Van Lennep, Richard Wright, Ruth Zimmer, Ruth Zimmerman, Robert Zimmerman, Zips Toys to Go, Richard Duffy and Geyer McAllister for permission to use old articles and ads from *Playthings* and Eric Rubin for his searching out materials.

I would also like to thank Keith Kaonis and especially Howard Foulke for their help in patiently going over the basics of photography with me and, in Howard's case, going over work I had done to help me improve the quality.

A special thanks to Joan Timmins, who helped me "punch it up" and keep it simple, and David Greenberg and Sue Scirica who took me from an italic fountain pen to a computer so that I could really write this book.

Finally thanks to the Schoenhut family, especially William F. Schoenhut and his cousins Phyllis S. O'Hare and Eleanor P. Swanson for sharing family stories and pictures with me, and Ruth Zimmer who showed me the first company doll catalogue years ago and thereby triggered the hunt.

Front Cover: 17in (43cm). This superb example of Doll 16/301 is the Flower Girl from *The Wedding Party. Becky and Jay Lowe Collection. See page 92 for further information.*
Title Page: 19½ (50cm). This lovely bride from *The Wedding Party* uses the Graziano head design 300. *Becky and Jay Lowe Collection. See page 193 for further information.*

Back Cover: (Top) This baby is 13in (33cm) from toe tip to top of head when lying down. *See page 196 for further information.* (Bottom left) 16½in (42cm) 16/306 doll. *See page 63 for further information.*
(Bottom right) 16¼in (41cm). This example of Doll 16/306 has beautifully molded eyelids with charcoal lid lines. *Gail Hiatt Collection. See page 63 for further information.*

Additional copies of this book may be purchased at $39.95
from
HOBBY HOUSE PRESS, INC.
900 Frederick Street
Cumberland, Maryland 21502
or from your favorite bookstore or dealer.
Please add $6.25 per copy for postage.

TABLE OF CONTENTS

DEDICATION

To my niece and nephew Samantha and Sean Corson, who taught me the joy of the Schoenhut Circus and to the students of Plymouth Meeting Friends School and Germantown Friends School, who have taught me, and continue to teach me every day.

Doll 16/310 all original.
See The "Classic"
Period Part I

INTRODUCTION

There are many ways to "read" this book about Schoenhut dolls, so here is a guide to help you pick and choose what interests you. I am an incredibly curious person and as I have collected Schoenhuts over the last 15 years, I have had lots of questions, many of which were raised by reading other people's writings and listening to other collectors talk. I decided to turn to the most reliable information I knew, prime source material. I searched through original Schoenhut Company catalogues as well as Company advertising and for the first several years I avoided any secondary source material except to check it for accuracy against what I found in the prime source material. Next I moved to contemporary secondary source material, that is articles written about Albert Schoenhut and the A. Schoenhut Company during the lifetime of Albert Schoenhut himself. After this I turned to articles written about the company during its existence and ending with the *Philadelphia Record's* feature by Robert Reiss, accompanied by three photographs, on the auction held by the trustees on Wednesday, February 26, 1936.

Oral history research was begun with the first meeting of the Schoenhut Collector's Club, held in Lancaster, Pennsylvania, in October of 1986. The meeting was attended by three of Albert Schoenhut's grandchildren, William F. Schoenhut (son of William G. Schoenhut), Harry E. Schoenhut Jr. and Phyllis Schoenhut Roundtree O'Hare (children of Harry E. Schoenhut who had headed the company's Art Department from 1912 to 1930). William F. Schoenhut recalled earning extra pennies as a child doing simple "piece work" in a back room of the factory after school. More importantly he had actually worked at the company as an adult for two years. As the meetings were structured so that people were encouraged to join in "from the floor" with any additional information they might have about the topic presented at any seminar, we were soon flowing with all sorts of informational bits from what kind of paint the company used (different makes of oil enamel, but often Benjamin Moore) to answers to why a doll's paint will suddenly pop off? (The gesso under the enamel absorbs moisture from the atmosphere when the surface is crazed or broken and it expands, popping the enamel surface off, or the wood is trying to reassert its original shape and is becoming "unpressed.")

I am grateful for the writings of other collectors. They increased my enjoyment as well as my knowledge. I have always chosen to use the information found in primary source materials, whenever there has been a conflict in "facts." I have also deliberately omitted information which I could not substantiate with primary source material. In spite of all the care taken, there will be errors. My apologies are offered for them.

All the time I continued to see, study, photograph, and best of all play with the wonderful dolls and toys produced by this Philadelphia toy company that sold its products in Europe, Australia, South Africa, South America and all over the United States for over 60 years.

In a period when Germany was the toy capital of the world, Schoenhut was selling its toys to Germany. This seems to be because of a blending of two cultures. Albert Schoenhut was a product of a German apprenticeship and training. When he came to this county at 17, he already knew how to make wooden toys. He immigrated to a nation bursting with opportunities for a skilled worker. He also came into a strong first and second generation German community well established in a section of the city of Philadelphia near the Delaware River and north of Market Street. Philadelphia was a major toy making center in the second half of the 19th century. (Ludwig Greiner has the historical honor of holding the first American doll patent, 1858, for an improvement on a doll he had apparently been making in Philadelphia for 20 years.) This community provided the support a young man would need to get established. The country provided a social structure fluid enough for him to grow to head what may have been the largest toy company in the world. Albert Schoenhut adopted Philadelphia's passion for quality. His toys sold abroad because he did not compete with the German market for cheap goods; he created his own market abroad for quality toys.

As I have presented parts of the project in slide programs, I have had many reactions. Some people tell me it is exciting. Several men have told me they expected it to be boring because it was about dolls and they collected the Circus and they were delighted to find they enjoyed it. Needless to say, I love hearing things like that; but I have also heard that "It was too long and you ought to drop all those numbers." Now it is up to you to enjoy this any way it pleases you. Forget all those model numbers if they bother you. Although some of you may find the history as fascinating as I do, many will want to skip the history and enjoy the variety of faces on the dolls in the pictures. Pick and choose what interests you. If you are able to feel some the joy of the Schoenhut doll, the goal of this book will have been accomplished.

SCHOENHUT COMPANY HISTORY
Part I

Albert Schoenhut was born in Goeppingen, Germany, on February 5, 1849, the seventh child (fifth son) of Friederick Wilhelm Schoenhut and Eberhardina Christianna Faber Schoenhut. He was part of the third generation of a toy making family. He served an apprenticeship in a commercial house there before coming to America at the age of 17. He came to Philadelphia, Pennsylvania, under the sponsorship of John Doll, whose son John T. Doll later became the toy buyer for the John Wanamaker Department Store. Albert came to Philadelphia at an ideal time. There was a thriving German community whose society members not only celebrated their heritage with festivals, but whose business community helped new members to get established. There were also a number of paper and fabric mills and wood was cheap and plentiful. The city was, at the time, a major center for the growing "novelties," doll and toy industry. Albert took a job with John Deiser & Sons, 1030 Germantown Avenue, which specialized in rocking horses and other wooden toys.

It was during the six-year period that he worked for John Deiser & Sons that Albert wrestled with the fragility of the toy pianos which were made with glass rods glued on string. A percussion instrument with glass pieces seems a contradiction in terms. Albert designed a piano based on a glockenspiel principle, using flat metal bars struck by hammers. He later added small metal spacers to hold those bars in place. This made it very difficult for an accident to dislodge the keys and helped keep the piano in tune. The result was a remarkably sturdy instrument that, time has shown, lasts for generations.

On January 30, 1870, Albert married Emilie Langbein. The bride had been born in Philadelphia and was not quite 19 years old. Their first child, a son named Albert Frederick, was born on March 25, 1871.

Albert Schoenhut founded his company in 1872 in order to manufacture his piano. The original place of business was in one room of a small building, at 2221 Trenton Avenue in the Kensington section of Philadelphia. The young family lived at 1066 Dauphin. His first order was received from Strasburger, Pfeiffer & Company, New York. His wife is reported to have worked with him in the business. At first the piano in its various models was the only product.

The company, which began on such a small scale, went through its first enlargement, within the original building, two years after its founding. An entire building at 2337 Frankford Avenue was leased in 1875. The sign on the building, as shown in a picture in the collection of the Historical Society of Pennsylvania and Albert Schoenhut's listing in Gopsill's *Philadelphia City Directory*, states that the company made metallophones as well as pianos. In January of 1877 the company moved to 621 Aramingo and the family, which now consisted of daughters Emilie Louise (born January 3, 1874) and Caroline (born January 26, 1877), as well as Albert F., moved to 618 East Adams. These locations are difficult to verify on the actual map of Philadelphia today as the city has renamed and renumbered many of the streets over the years; however, the Trenton Avenue address still exists, and all appear to have been within a few blocks of each other.

By the late 1870s the piano had found a market and other percussion instruments were added to the line. Schoenhut made glockenspiels, metallophones and xylophones. The first two had polished steel bars and the latter was made with maple or rosewood bars. The maple bars were for children to play. The rosewood xylophones were almost three times as expensive for the same number of keys and were designed for orchestra use. The sizes on all these instruments ranged from an eight bar simple scale to a 37 bar three-octave chromatic instrument. Albert alternated his listing in the city directories, from year to year, between "toys" and "musical instruments." This continued through 1890, after which he settled on "toys."

In 1879 Albert again expanded the factory by adding 623 Aramingo to his property. As the buildings were already connected, he had only to open up and connect the insides. At about the same time he added the word "Novelties" to the sign fastened to the factory roof. Albert took advantage of the desire for imaginative play and provided "equipments" for children who wanted to pretend to be policemen, firemen, soldiers, etc. These equipments consisted of hats, breast plates, play fire axes, popguns, badges and every other conceivable "bit" to make the play more realistic. These props were made of light-weight wood and papier-mâché. In 1881 the company became Albert Schoenhut & Co. when Albert took on a partner, Frederick Sting. This partnership lasted through 1889, during a period of steady growth.

A fairly large assortment of military type toys were quickly added. The guns which shot a variety of ammunition such as sticks, corks, rubber balls, paper and percussion caps would hardly pass today's product safety standards. Some even came with a 12in (31cm) iron bayonet. Play swords were manufactured as well.

In 1886 the company had outgrown its quarters again and it moved to 2215 East Adams Street, just two blocks from the original factory. The family, which had three more sons (Gustav Adolph, born March 1, 1879; Theodore Carl, born July 15, 1881; and William George, born December 8, 1883) moved to a home nearby at 2335 East York Street.

During the next decade vocophones and shooting galleries were added to the line, as well as cannons, caissons and forts. The vocophones were instruments made out of paper fabric and wood composition to look like those found in a brass band. The parts were not movable. The "player" hummed into the instrument to make the tune, and with other players, the harmony as well. It appears to have worked like a kazoo. It was suggested that the players be chosen to have a voice range of the real instruments so that the proper effect could be achieved.

The last two sons were also born to the family during this period. Harry Edison was born on October 1, 1889, and Otto Franklin was born on November 24, 1891. In 1889 the family moved for the last time to a handsome three and a half story home at 2209 Cumberland Street. The house was two blocks north of the factory, which expanded to 2217 Adams and then began to move south along Sepviva Street as well as west on Adams, taking over properties in the 2100 block of East Adams as it grew over the next 18 years.

Illustration 1. The second location of the A. Schoenhut Co. at 2337 Frankford Avenue, Philadelphia. Albert is thought to be the man with his arm up on the door. Pianos and metallophons are carefully stacked to show off the company's products. Photograph from the *Collection of The Historical Society of Pennsylvania.*

Illustration 2. This picture has been previously identified in other books as being located on Adams Street, but the directory for the City of Philadelphia for 1883 locates the A. Schoenhut and Co. (and Co. stood for partner Frederick Sting) at 619, 621 and 623 Aramingo and the address is on the sign which now has added the word Noveltys (sic) to Toy Pianos. This picture also shows the Schoenhut float for the German-American Bicentennial Celebration in October 1883. The entire company personnel appear to be in the picture. The children on the float are probably young Schoenhuts — Harry and Otto are not born yet. Albert had a large collection of walking sticks and canes, and as he needed one himself, it has been said that he made a point of hiring workers who had mild physical disabilities. *Photograph from the Collection of The Historical Society of Pennsylvania.*

7

In 1892 the 2215-2217 Adams building's height was increased to five stories. It also extended north through to Letterly Street. An extensive line of sailboats, with a patented iron keel design which kept them upright during rough play and oil-based enamel paint which allowed them to float on Fairmount Park's ponds without losing color, as did the imported water-base painted boats, was successful enough to warrant its own color catalogue.

By this time Albert F. Schoenhut had joined his father in the company, as did each succeeding son. It was clear that all the boys were expected to join the firm and each was trained to take specific roles. The roles apparently were not simply dictated by company needs. Albert seems to have been aware of his sons' abilities. Although Harry is reported by both his children to have wanted to be a surgeon, he is also said to have been constantly drawing as a young child. His daughter, Phyllis, who was only seven when Harry left the company and went into the hosiery business, says that her father often drew, painted and modeled in clay for his own pleasure long after the business need for it was gone.

By the 1890s Schoenhut was already manufacturing items made basically for store displays. He had several mechanical figures, including a Father Christmas, for department store windows. He also produced a 42in (107cm) fully-jointed wooden figure to best show off his popular costumes. These figures were jointed at the neck, shoulders, elbows, wrists, hips, knees and ankles. The joints were "mortise and tenon" style and allowed the figures to take many realistic poses. The heads were produced in six distinctive, character styles and were purchased separately so that they could be changed at will. The company also produced figures that were spring-jointed. These figures, the best known of which are the Palmer Cox Brownies, were jointed at the shoulders and elbows only. The spring-joint allowed them to hold their arms in a set position much more firmly than a non-spring joint would have. This made them particularly suitable for displays in hard to reach places where the shifting of slipped arms would have been a major project. All this means that the A. Schoenhut Company was making spring-jointed and multi-jointed figures before 1900, and it was only a short step to combine the two.

A photograph of the A. Schoenhut Company from 1872 to 1901, given to the Historical Society of Pennsylvania by grandson George Schoenhut, shows the prosperous company on the brink of its next great period of growth. In the upper center part of the composite picture is the original Trenton Avenue factory and a small picture of the young Albert Schoenhut. On either side of it are drawings of the current factory now covering 2154-2160 Adams Street and the office and "warerooms" at 2215-2217 Adams Street complete with its famous weather vane figure of Santa in his sleigh on top of the highest corner tower. All three buildings have American flags flying over them. The large central part of the picture is a photograph of the 1901 Company which shows Albert Schoenhut, already beginning to resemble Santa Claus, and all six of his sons in business suits. Harry E. (11 years) and Otto F.(9 years) have short pants with their double breasted suit jackets and long stockings. This picture is a clear indication of how Albert viewed his company's past, present and future.

On February 5, 1902, Fritz K.T. Meinecke, a German citizen living in Philadelphia, applied for a patent for a toy animal, which by design of the parts and the use of heavy elastic would hold a great many different positions. He assigned this patent from the time of its application to Albert Schoenhut of Philadelphia. The family story is that Mr. Meinecke came to Albert Schoenhut with a model and asked him to buy it. Albert is said to have offered to purchase the use of the figure, paying a royalty on it. This allowed the potential for Mr. Meinecke to make a great deal of money if the toy sold well, but Meinecke wanted his money immediately and thus sold the entire invention outright. This was the beginning of the Humpty Dumpty Circus which was to expand Schoenhut sales to four continents. Readers are referred to the excellent book *Schoenhut's Humpty Dumpty Circus From A to Z* by Evelyn Ackerman and Fredrick E. Keller; ERA Industries, Los Angeles, California, 1975, for a most complete and well-researched history of the toy that dominated the history of the company for the next 30 years and was still in production at the end in 1935.

The tremendous success of the Circus caused the company to once again expand its space. In 1905 the factory was listed at 2154 to 2166 Adams Street with the office and warehouse still located at 2215 and 2217 East Adams Street. In 1907 an additional story was added to the warehouse. According to a 1908 article in *Playthings*, a fire late that summer destroyed that floor and $70,000 in stock was lost; however, through extra work the company filled all its orders by Christmas.

In 1908 a new building was constructed covering a space of 60 by 150 feet and six stories in height. The construction of this, the final building, involved the taking over and demolition of ten row houses. It incorporated a central driveway between Adams and Boston Street into a giant courtyard around which the new building was constructed. This allowed all workrooms access to natural light on two sides through huge windows around the outside of the building and also around the inside courtyard. Carriages could be driven inside the "doughnut" from an entrance on Sepviva. The factory had its own power plant across Boston Street, next to the old Hackett Elementary School and its own lumber yard on Amber, above Venango next to the rail line. The company now advertised itself as "The Largest and Best Equipped Toy Factory in the World" and with over five and a half acres of floor space and more toys coming out of it than ever, it probably was!

The Rolly Dolly was brought out in 1908. A novel and particularly sturdy version of an old toy, it was also a success story. By this time four of Albert Schoenhut's sons had joined the firm. An article in *Playthings* written that year lists their positions as follows: Albert F. (at 39 years) was treasurer and general manager; Gustav A. (29) was the "superintendent of the manufacturing department;" Theodore Carl (27) was listed as being "in charge of the mechanical and electrical department;" and William George (24) was an assistant to his eldest brother Albert and was "supervising the cost department." Harry (18) and Otto (16) were still in high school but the article states that Harry was expected to join the factory later that year.

In April 1909 Theodore Roosevelt set sail to Africa on a trip sponsored by the Smithsonian Institution. Teddy himself was a colorful character and Albert Schoenhut lost no time capitalizing on his popularity. By July of 1909 "Teddy's Adventures in Africa" was on the market so that as "the whole World eagerly awaits the daily reports from Africa of our **Great American Hunting Party**" children could act out the latest happenings. The initial company brochure, from which the previous quote was taken, has seven different action scenes set up in front of panels of scenery (which were also available for sale). It presents the "Adventures" as additions to the Circus and from the beginning this wonderful toy was available by the piece as well as in a variety of sets. It appears in the 1910, 1911 and 1912 company catalogues, but it is no longer available by 1914. The animals that were designed to go with the set became part of the Circus line. The scenery continued to be offered in the 1914 catalogue, as back-

Illustration 3. From left to right: William George, Caroline, Theodore Carl, Albert Frederick, Harry Edison with his mother Emilie, Gustav Adolph, Emilie Louise, Albert Schoenhut and his youngest son Otto Franklin. Circa 1895. *Courtesy William F. Schoenhut.*

ground for "The Big Game Hunter," a series of flat target animals to be shot at with a "neat little spring gun" that fired wooden cartridge-shaped darts.

While most of the figures and animals were based on the design of the Circus there was an important new design that caused Albert Schoenhut to apply for another patent. He wanted to make the figures of the American hunting party able to sit on horseback, kneel behind a rock, "take pictures" with a miniature wooden camera, and sight a gun (available for 70¢ per dozen). He applied for in 1909, and received on January 17, 1911, a patent for a spring-jointed doll figure. "Teddy," and members of his American hunting party, when found undressed, show in their knees a miniature version of the spring joint that was to become the hallmark of Albert Schoenhut's next great invention, the Schoenhut Doll.

Illustration 4. This Schoenhut Brownie is 38in (97cm) tall and was on display for years at the Cliff House in San Francisco. His spring-jointed shoulders still allow him to hold his arm up very well. He probably was restored years ago, as his owner says that old pictures of the Brownies at Cliff House show that they had become quite faded. *Photograph by Yvonne L. Baird. Yvonne L. Baird Collection.*

Illustration 5. The Schoenhut Company was awarded the "First Premium Silver Medal and Diploma" for this exhibit by the National Export Exposition on the recommendation of the Franklin Institute in 1899. It is packed with the company's products at that time. Above the entire display is a Palmer Cox Brownie Band. Inside the display are other Brownies — The Policeman and a Dandy. On the back wall are uniforms, guns, wagons, metallophons, glockenspiels, and pianos. Inside on the floor are the multi-jointed character figures dressed as soldiers, sailors, policeman, and a fireman. Three large mechanical figures — a clown, a black man and a 42in (106cm) gnome which run by clockwork for about four hours, which moves the eyes and mouth. The signs are supplemented with German language signs because Schoenhut was exporting his toys to Europe and later to South Africa, South America and even Australia. *Photograph from the Collection of The Historical Society of Pennsylvania.*

Illustration 6. *From the Collection of The Historical Society of Pennsylvania.*

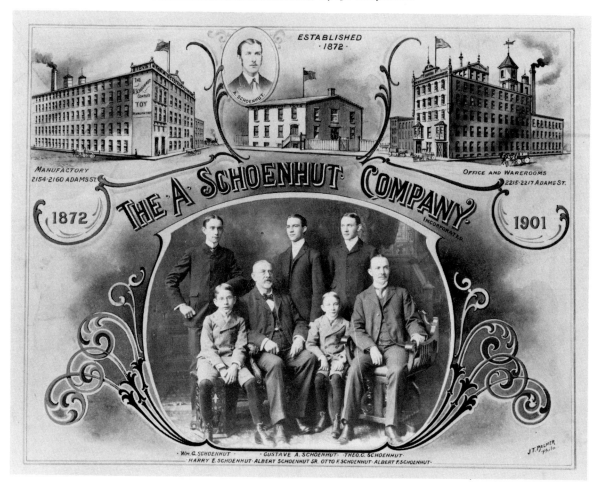

Illustration 7. This early "studio shot" of Albert Schoenhut with his wonderful new Humpty Dumpty Circus pieces may have been made for a press release on the great success of the toy. *William F. Schoenhut Collection.*

Illustration 9. The 1908 factory taken from the intersection of East Adams Street (now East Hagert) on the right and Sepviva Street (on the left). The main door is now in the corner tower. The growth along Adams Street simply took in a number of old buildings, while on the Sepviva side the new building has a large entrance which allowed wagons to drive right through to the center courtyard. The factory was noted for its use of natural light. The rooms had large banks of windows on two sides. *Photograph from the Collection of The Historical Society of Pennsylvania.*

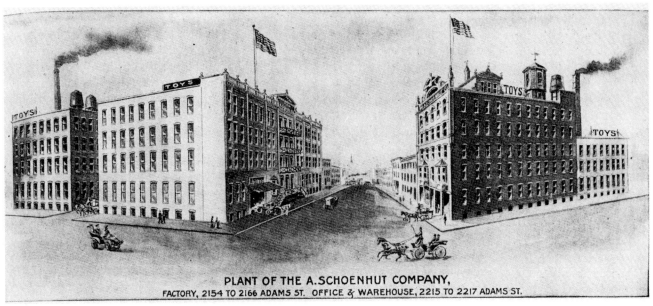

PLANT OF THE A. SCHOENHUT COMPANY,
FACTORY, 2154 TO 2166 ADAMS ST. OFFICE & WAREHOUSE, 2215 TO 2217 ADAMS ST.

Illustration 8. This ad from the February 1905 issue of *Playthings* shows the expansion of the factory on the left to fill the entire 2100 block of East Adams Street. The factory is two large buildings. Artistic license has been taken with the placement of the office and warehouse which is really a half block closer to the viewer and not on the corner but near the middle of its block. That building still stands.

Photograph from The "SCHOENHUT DOLL" Catalog of 1914 showing the natural light available in final doughnut shape factory designed which incorporated the drive between two earlier buildings and turned it into a central courtyard.

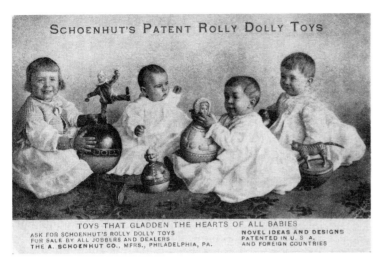

Illustration 10. This postcard advertisement for the new Rolly Dolly is typical of the company's use of family members in catalogues and promotions. The children and infants are, left to right: Dorothy Schoenhut (daughter of Gustav A.), Frieda M. (daughter of William G.) and two pictures of George W. (son of Theodore C.). The picture dates from late 1908. *Courtesy Marie Lehmann.*

Illustration 11. This small Teddy's Adventures in Africa just begs to be played with. The original box bottom had scenery on the inside, but this set also came with a roll of its own scenery for set-ups. The miniature spring joint in Teddy Roosevelt's knee enables him to ride a horse as well as to kneel and sight a rifle. Albert Schoenhut applied for a patent for these joints in 1909. The patent would have covered this 8in (20cm) figure but clearly specifies the entire doll which came out two years later. *Becky and Jay Lowe.*

Illustration 12. Studio shot of a young boy (probably a Schoenhut grandchild) playing with circus figures. The boy's suit and the animals' painted eyes date this picture to circa 1915-1918. *Courtesy Becky Moncrief.*

THE GRAZIANO 'YEAR'
— MAY to NOVEMBER 1911

"At Last!! Everybody predicted 'SCHOENHUT' would do it — and he did," began a full-page advertisement in January 1911's issue of *Playthings*, the journal used by manufacturers of toys to reach the retail stores that sold their products. The ad further announces all the benefits of "The Schoenhut Doll." It states that the doll is patented in the United States and foreign countries and that samples and prices will be ready by May 1, 1911. The only picture is a portrait of Mr. Albert Schoenhut, Sr.

This full-page announcement must have been quite intriguing to the trade, and it is interesting to note that the doll was fully patented before the first picture (let alone sample) was shown.

In the March 1911 *Playthings*, a two-page spread of pictures of the first dolls was presented. There was a minimum of text to this unusually large ad. The dolls are simply shown in interesting poses, both dressed and undressed. The action in the poses is emphasized. This set the stage for how different these dolls would be from other dolls of the period. Several of the doll heads bear a remarkable similarity to the Kämmer and Reinhardt model 101 and, just as Kämmer and Reinhardt presented their dolls, it is shown as both a boy and a girl. A carved haired boy is similar to Gebrüder Heubach's model 7622 and a Swaine and Company model of the same period.

In the same copy of *Playthings*, the trade news section of the journal shows another picture of six of the dolls dancing in party clothes. In the background are two other dolls in traditional German festive clothing providing music for the dance. The picture covers the entire top one-third of page 136 and under it is a column and a third of a press release by the Schoenhut company with a complete description of the doll and all its features. It also lauds Albert Schoenhut himself and his many fine products.

May 1911 brought another full-page ad, stating that the "'Schoenhut Doll' Catalogue and Price List is now ready." There were three pictures, all from the 1911 doll catalogue and all showing the dolls in active positions. The ad lists the other Schoenhut products briefly and says that the 1910 catalogue may be used to order them as the line and prices remained the same. Clearly 1911's creative energies were put into developing the doll which had its own separate catalogue for six years. Also included in the ad was the first picture of the paper shield-shaped tag identifying the Schoenhut All Wood Perfection Art Doll. This tag apparently both predates and postdates the metal pin found on some dolls dating from around 1915.

The early group pictures showed the dolls relating to each other like real children. This emphasized the dynamic part of playing with the dolls which makes them appealing to both toy lovers and doll collectors. It also makes one Schoenhut not enough.

Because the major appeal of the dolls was their durability, it was possible to own one Schoenhut doll and never need a replacement. Not many children had more than one or two dolls at a time. A new one might come at Christmas to replace one smashed in an accident. With the invention of the new sturdier dolls came a new advertising policy stressing the play value of the doll to the developing child's mind. The character doll movement, part of a larger philosophical movement affecting how childhood was viewed, emphasized dolls that were portraits of real children. Not only did they look like real children, but Schoenhut allowed them to interact like real children. To have them relate as real children do, a child needed more than one. Early advertising stressed that the dolls would last for generations; however, they also frequently mentioned that over time a parent might like to provide their child with several of these remarkable dolls to extend their child's play possibilities. The company stressed, from the beginning, the use of these dolls as window displays to sell not only the dolls but other people's products. They were also suggested for use as models in art classes and to demonstrate exercises in gym classes.

June 1911 brought another full-page ad with three different pictures from the 1911 catalogue to entice the buyer. This ad has a description of the use of the stand in posing the doll as well as two pictures of the dolls "relating" to each other and a delightful picture of two Schoenhut granddaughters (identified as cousins Dorothy and Frieda by William F. Schoenhut, Frieda's brother) making clothes for five Schoenhut girl dolls.

According to family stories told to me by William F. Schoenhut, and told to Marion Ball Poe by Dorothy Schoenhut, Dorothy's little brother, Norman, provided the push for the development of an unbreakable doll when he broke three of Dorothy's bisque headed dolls trying to make them ride his pony, "Blitz." Their father, Albert's second son, Gustav Adolph, brought Dorothy a sample doll, and announced that here, at last, was a doll her little brother could not break. Norman is reported to have asked, "How do you know?" to which his father replied that he had taken it to the fifth story of the factory and dropped it out the window to the central courtyard below. It received only a bumped nose. Norman is said to have rushed upstairs with the doll and thrown it out the second story window to "test" it. (See *Schoenhut Treasures* by Marion Ball Poe, published through a grant from the Ball Family in the *United Federation of Doll Collectors Silver Anniversary Convention Souvenir Book 1974* and as a separate booklet.)

About the dolls themselves: The initial child dolls were all 16in (41cm) tall. The infants were 15in (38cm). These sizes are easy for children to handle. The doll body had only one difference from the dolls made from late 1912 on. Originally the stocking was not tied to a groove cut in the leg just above the knee. Instead, the doll had a small nail sticking out of the back of its thigh. There was a grommet hole at the top of the back of the stocking which could be hooked on to the nail to hold up the stocking. A child might easily scratch himself on these nails and adding a metal grommet must have been more expensive than tying the stocking up with a ribbon garter.

The other main manufacturing difference is that the earliest "carved hair" dolls seem to have hand carving in the finishing process. They do not have the "blur" or gap in the carving caused where the hot mold halves met. Some examples seem to have a roughness or tool marks where the hairline meets

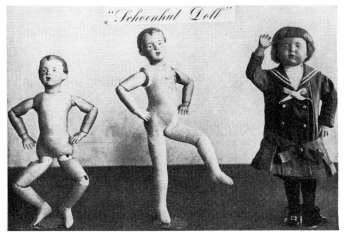

Illustration 13a. *Playthings*, March 1911, page 44. Doll 200 shown nude and "undressed" in a union suit and stockings. These poses show the balance and flexibility of the Schoenhut doll. Doll 400 on the right shows a fully dressed version (based on K*R 101) in the bulky boy's clothing presented in the first year of Schoenhut doll production. There are trousers under the sailor-style coat.

Illustration 13b. *Tootsie Wootsie* in all three styles as presented in the 1911 catalogue.

Illustration 14a. *Playthings*, March 1911, page 45. The dancers are all Doll 302, based on Kämmer and Reinhardt's 101. By the time the catalogue was released in May, the company brushed her hair back and up in a simple knot. Note elaborate cotton and lace dresses.

Illustration 14b. Dolls 302, 202, 302 and 400 further demonstrate the flexibility and realistic poses possible as well as more samples of early clothing.

the face, as well as around the eyes and mouth. Another difference is in the paint used. The earliest dolls appear to have very thin paint with no gesso underneath. The flesh, which is quite pale, does not "pop" as easily as the later heavier paint, but it wore off easily with repeated washings and where it was bumped there is no base coat under smaller bashes, only bare wood. The company responded very quickly to either complaints or its own observations. In 1912 it announced that they were now using a better paint that would stand up to both play and cleaning.

The initial dolls' heads appear to have been designed by M. Graziano, as was reported by Eleanor St. George in *The Dolls of Yesterday*, copyright Charles Scribner's Sons 1948, and reconfirmed by George Schoenhut 40 years later. There were four "carved hair" girls, four "carved hair" boys, eight wigged girls, four wigged boys and two "infants."

The text of the catalogue stressed the suitability of dolls for boys and showed a picture of George (Theodore's son) and his cousin, Norman, playing with boy dolls along with some circus toys. (In fact, you will notice that, Norman is the only child appearing in the catalogue who does not look enthusiastic over the unbreakable doll.) Even in this first year there were not quite as many boy models as there were girl models and the proportion of boys to girls dropped from late 1912 on.

The numbering system of the "undressed dolls" is easy to follow and remains consistent throughout the production of Schoenhut dolls. Basically it consists of a size number in inches (which was always 16 for the child dolls and 15 for the "infants" in this first year). This size number was separated by a slash from the model number. The hundred digit of the style number told you instantly whether you were referring to a "carved hair" child or a wigged one and whether the doll was a boy or a girl. Thus the 100 series was reserved for "carved hair" girls, the 200 for "carved hair" boys, the 300 for wigged girls and the 400 for wigged boys. During the first full year of production, until the "Classic" line came in April 1912, different doll model numbers (such as 300 and 301) might stand for the same face with different wig styles. The doll models were as follows.

The 100 Series — "Carved Hair" Girls

Doll 100 is a sweet, round-faced girl with a slightly pointed chin. She has a slightly pouty look emphasized by the modeling of her upper eyelids and temples. Although in photographs she appears to be modeled on Kämmer and Reinhardt's 101 *Marie*, which was designed in 1909, in reality she is quite different. Her face and chin line are much rounder and her nose is larger. She has small intaglio eyes rather than the flat painted eye of Kämmer and Reinhardt. She also has a chin-length bobbed hairstyle with bangs and a nicely carved or molded side swirl which makes her hair curl under on the ends. Doll 100 survived the first major design change in the fall of 1911. She appears to have been made until April of 1912, when the Classic Line came out. Thus she may be found with the very thin, pale early paint as well as the warmer flesh tones introduced after November 1911.

Doll 101 is an original model. She is a laughing girl doll. Her narrow intaglio eyes are squeezed by their well-carved pouchy lids so that her grin involves all the muscles of her face. Her smile is broad, and she has four prominent teeth showing. These are, by their size, "second teeth," indicating that the doll represents a child of eight to ten years of age. Her eyes were not only intaglio carved, their depth was emphasized by a ring of darker color around the outside edge of the iris. The first catalogue shows that this outer iris ring, an extra decorating step, was a part

of most of the Graziano dolls. She has single-stroke eyebrows. She is dynamic. She has character and personality, but she is not pretty.

The first catalogue pictures clearly show this doll with both light and dark painted hair. There seems to have been no way to specifically request hair color in the "carved hair" dolls; but a variety of color apparently existed. Her hair is the same straight bob style that doll 100 has. It has good "comb marks" which appear to be hand carved.

The flesh paint is a pale pink with a flat finish. The cheek color of these earliest dolls is a soft pink rather than the orange tone used later. Her hair was finished in a thin high-gloss enamel. The hair on these early dolls, particularly the blonde ones, is translucent and extremely thin. The high gloss, which shows clearly in the 1911 catalogues and advertisements, may have been achieved by adding a coat of varnish on top of the hair tint.

The very character that makes Doll 101 so appealing to the collector made her unappealing on the market. She must have been too extreme for children, or at least for the grownups that purchased dolls, for her design was radically changed by November 1911, giving her a production run of about six months. She is thus very rarely found, and I have only seen two examples (one of them a picture from the late Ralph Griffith's Collection) thus far. An advertisement found in the November 1911 *Ladies' Home Journal* shows the transitional model 102, indicating that the first design changes had already taken place.

Doll 102 was a rather sweet and slightly stolid youngster with her heavy long hair swept up into a "knot" on the top of her head in the same style as the Schoenhut Circus Lady Riders and Acrobats. Her hair has a good deal of modeling but not the individual comb marks of doll 101. The two examples that I have been able to photograph show the hand finishing of these early models. One is actually almost an inch taller than the other because of the higher top knot carved on her head. Both dolls are undamaged and the difference is in their making, rather than in restoration done on them. Doll 102's face is round, her eyebrows are single stroke and her outlined irises are small, but her lids are not as pouchy as those of doll 101. She has a pleasant and curious look with a good deal of quiet self-assurance about her. She also appears to be an older child. She is sometimes found dressed as an adult; however, she was sold by the company as a child. It seems necessary to add that collectors attach a name to this doll. Because the company did not use this name in any of their catalogues or advertising, I have omitted it on purpose, in the belief that the doll was originally known only by its model number and that she acquired the name from collectors in later years. Her number was reassigned to a new design by November 1911. Known examples of this doll have had brown and dark blonde hair and blue eyes.

Doll 103 is a very peaceful looking girl of about ten. Her "pageboy-style" hair looks as though her mother set it in rags as it falls in soft corkscrew curls well below her earlobes. The bangs in the front are uneven and brushed in small separated pieces. Examples have been found with blonde as well as brunette painted hair. She has larger eyes with well-modeled lids. Her irises are also outlined in a darker shade giving her eyes a good deal of depth. Unrestored examples found have single-stroke eyebrows. She appears to have lasted about six months as well, as her number was reassigned to a completely new design at the end of 1911.

200 Series — "Carved Hair" Boys

Doll 200 is a sweet faced boy who bears a strong resemblance to Gebrüder Heubach's mold #7622, as well as to an

Illustration 15. Dorothy Schoenhut already looks worried about her little brother Norman who does not yet appear to be ambulatory, but already shows his outgoing personality. Circa 1909. This picture was given by Dorothy to her cousin Eleanor Swanson and appears by her courtesy.

Illustration 16. Labeled "Norman A. Schoenhut" and "January 1913," this picture shows Norman at age five with his Schoenhut Calvary Horse. This, along with two similar pictures, appears in the 1914 illustrated Schoenhut catalogue. *Courtesy Eleanor Swanson.*

Photo of grand-daughters Dorothy Schoenhut (whose need for a doll her brother, Norman, couldn't break was the inspiration for the Schoenhut Doll) and her cousin Frieda, who was given the other K*R 101 on which Graziano modeled the early wigged dolls 302 and 400. From the *Illustrated Catalogue ... Dolls The A. Schoenhut Company 1911*.

Photo of grandsons George Schoenhut and his cousin Norman (the only child who doesn't look delighted with the new unbreakable doll). From the *Illustrated Catalogue ... Dolls The A. Schoenhut Company 1911*.

Illustration 17. The enlargement of Doll 16/100 does not show the outlined iris common to the rest of the Graziano line. This is how she appeared in the original catalogue.

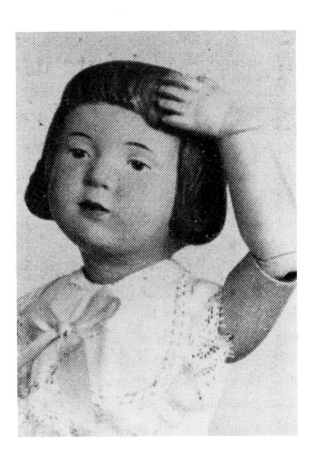

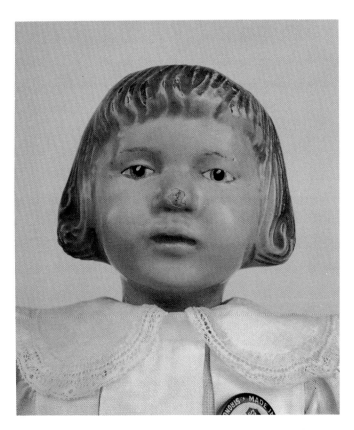

Illustration 18. This Doll 16/100 is in excellent condition and appears all-original as well. Her pale coloring and single stroke eyebrows date her to this first period. *Photograph by Monty Moncrief. Becky Moncrief Collection.*

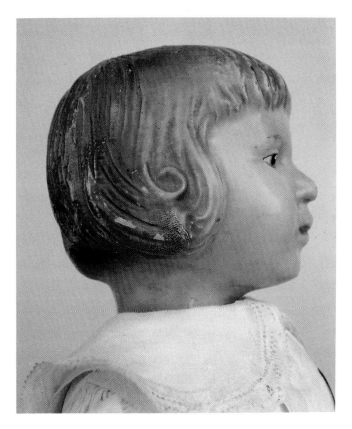

Illustration 19. The profile of Doll 16/100 shows the asymmetrical curls (more like swirls) in her hair. There is a smoothness and lack of detail above the temples which may indicate early hot press finishing. *Photograph by Monty Moncrief. Becky Moncrief Collection.*

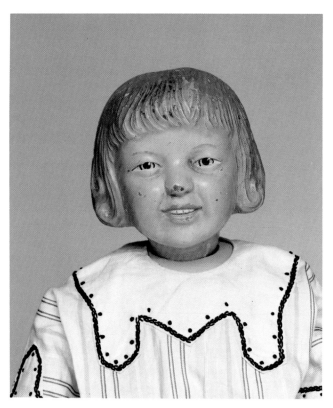

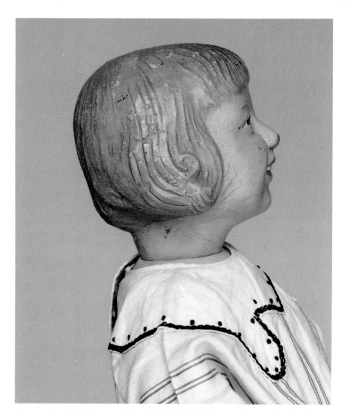

Illustration 20. 16in (41cm). Doll 16/101 from 1911 Catalogue. Designed by M. Graziano. Her four teeth are quite prominent. "Squinty" eyes are typical of 1911 dolls. She has pouchy eyelids accented with a dark brown upper lid line. Clear, light blue irises are rimmed in darker blue. Her teeth are carved and accented with pink paint between them.

Illustration 21. The profile of Doll 16/101 shows signs of having been molded. Her face is smooth. There is, however, wood debris at the hairline on the right side and there is at least some carving involved. Her features are higher in her face than those of a young child and her prominent teeth are those of an eight to ten year old before face development catches up with her.

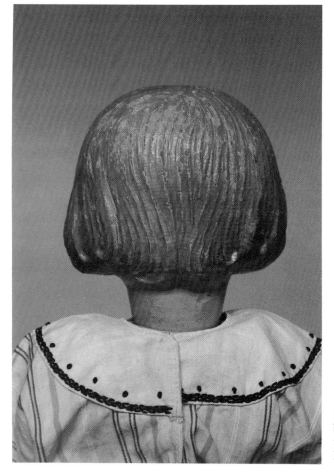

Illustration 22. The back of Doll 16/101 shows strong hair modeling with hair turning forward on the ends from the rear center. Her hairstyle is identical to that of Doll 16/100.

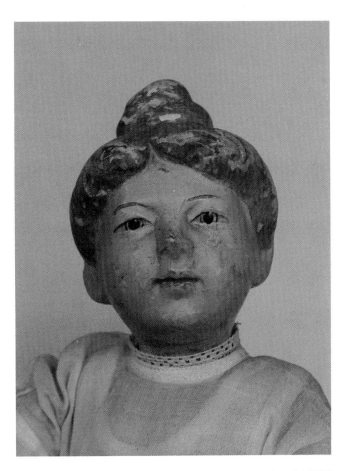

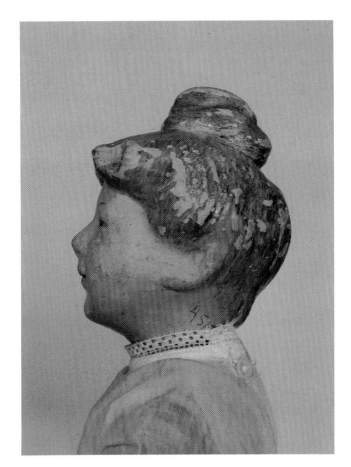

Illustration 23. 17in (43cm). This charming example of Doll 16/102 appears curious and alert. She is a honey blonde with a high top knot, and single stroke eyebrows of the same color. Her upper eyelids are lined with black and her light blue irises are outlined in darker blue. This doll's thin coat of paint has a fair amount of wear but it does not diminish her special appeal. Her hair is parted just off center and piled loosely on top of her head. *Dorothy Dixon Collection.*

Illustration 24. Doll 16/102 has a sharply pointed nose and a firm chin.

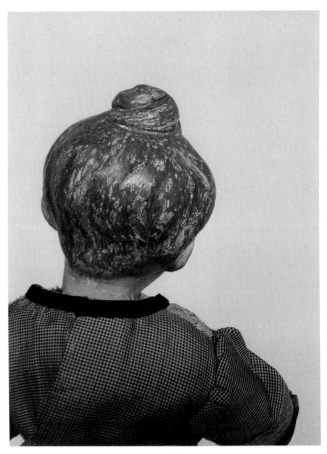

Illustration 25. This brunette example of Doll 16/102 is an inch shorter than the blonde one due to differences in her hair modeling. Her early dress is similar to an example in the 1911 catalogue. The back of her head shows the modeling of the mass of her hair but not individual "comb marks." *Private Collection.*

Illustration 26. These two Graziano design Dolls 16/102 are quite different in their carving and decorating. The one on the left is 17in (43cm) due to her higher topknot. Her irises are outlined in darker blue and her hair is blonde. The blue eyed example on the right has no outline on her iris and her brown hair has a smaller knot on top. *Dorothy Dixon Collection (left). Private Collection (right).*

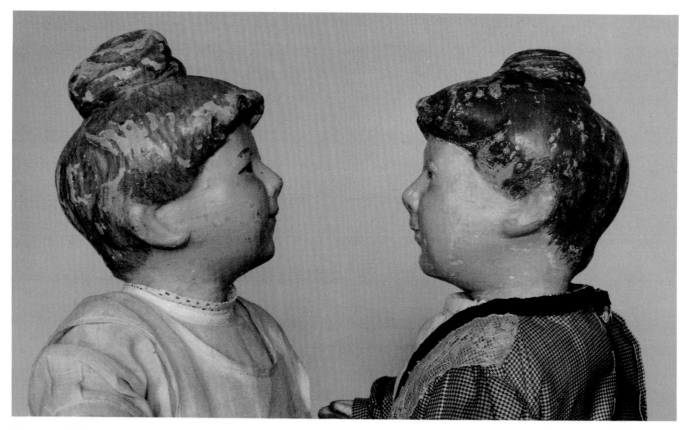

Illustration 27. The profiles of the two examples of 16/102 show differences in hair modeling and the amount of "comb marks" used. There was a good deal of hand work on these first dolls.

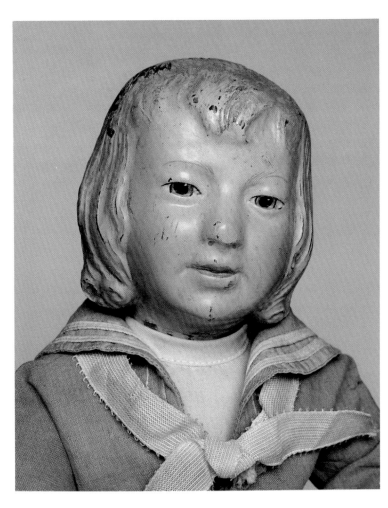

Illustration 28. 16in (41cm). Doll 16/103 as designed by Graziano is a peaceful looking, older child.

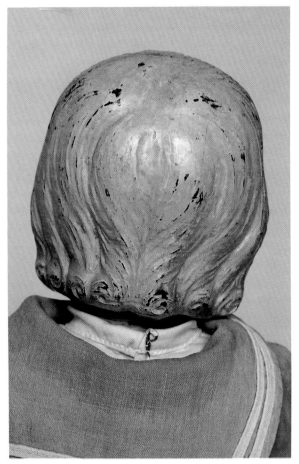

Illustration 29. Doll 16/103's hair is longer than the other "carved hair" girls. The wave is pronounced and the curls look as if her mother set her hair with socks.

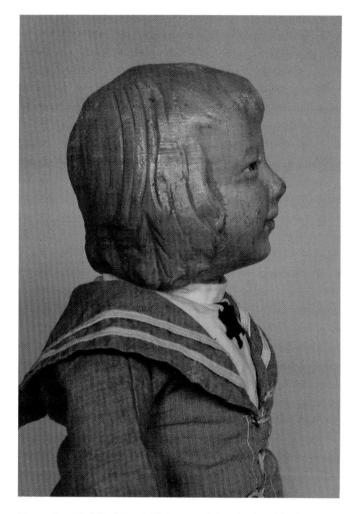

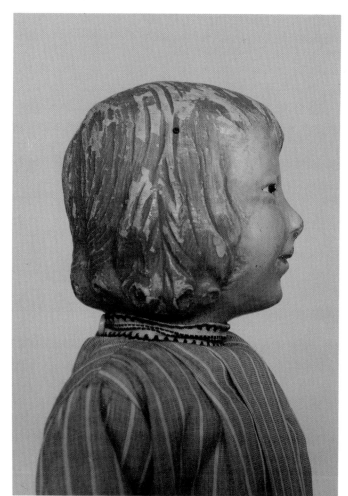

Illustration 30. 16in (41cm). This example's paint is original and while her face shows the rougher carving of the earliest dolls. Her profile is strong and not blunted by nose wear. Her dress is factory-original and in this outfit she was sold as model #504. The "shield" is a replacement made many years ago. *Dorothy Dixon Collection.*

Illustration 31. 16in (41cm). This example of Doll 16/103 is in very good shape for such an early doll. Where there is wear, the bare wood shows through as there is no gesso undercoat on these first year dolls. Her profile is clearly defined as that of an older child. There is hand carving on the side of her hair. The small dark nails on the sides of her hair held her silk bows in place. *Private Collection.*

unnumbered character boy by Swaine and Company. He has a softly rounded face with high chubby cheeks, a short nose and slightly separated lips. His hair is short (a little shorter than the Heubach mold) and curly. His eyes are intaglio carved with a dark brown lash line on the upper lid. He has single-stroke, widely spaced eyebrows. I have not yet found an example of this doll with its blue irises outlined in a darker shade of blue. Doll 200 survived the original design change which occurred at the end of 1911, but probably was not produced much beyond 1912 when the company had perfected its own designs and no longer was tempted to use German designs.

Doll 201's face was apparently modeled on Kämmer and Reinhardt's 114. He has a very pouty face. His eyes, however, are deeply intaglio carved with an outlined iris. He also has strongly detailed wavy hair parted on the left side. Examples found to date have blonde or very light brown hair and blue or brown eyes. He survived the November 1911 change, but may have been out of production as early as June 1912. He then surprises us completely by reappearing in the 1930 catalogue in the line described as "Kindergarten" dolls. These are probably old stock refurbished rather than an entirely new production. Examples of this doll found with "suntanned" skin and the decal mark on the back of their shoulders may date to this brief reissue period.

Doll 202 appears to be an original model. He makes a wonderful partner, or twin doll, for 103 as they both have similar wavy hair, the same pleasant face and decorative features. Their profiles also seem to be the same. The example found from this period shows the clearest signs that the doll heads, in the very beginning, were hand-carved finished rather than molded. Doll 202 survived into the next period, with the new hydraulic hot mold finishing process, but does not show up in advertising after the new line appeared in the spring of 1912.

Doll 203 is a smiling doll whose entire face shows his glee. He has a strongly modeled character face with small squinting eyes and pouchy eyelids. His grinning mouth shows four prominent teeth of an older elementary school child. He has strongly modeled wavy hair with carefully detailed curly tendrils at the ends, but much of his hair does not have the comb marks of the later models of this doll. His irises are outlined in a darker shade. He is definitely an original. One example has been found with strong comb marks in his hair indicating that it was finished with the newer molding process. Doll 203's design was significantly modified to look younger and less calculating by the end of 1911. So he is, in his original form, very rarely found.

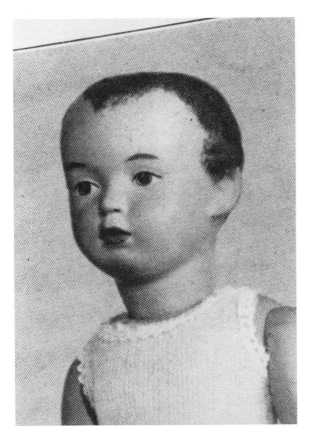

Illustration 32. This close-up of the head of the Doll identified as 16/200 is taken from the original 1911 Doll Catalogue. The hair and eyebrows appear to have been enhanced in the original photography.

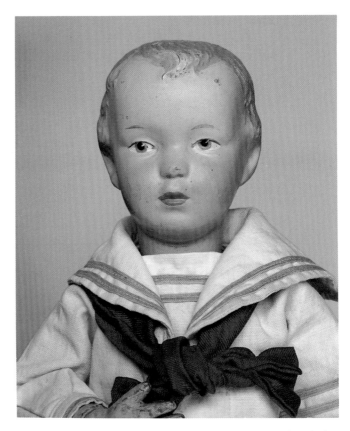

Illustration 33. 16½in (42cm). This Doll 16/200 has the pale coloring and single stroke eyebrows of the earliest dolls. The highlight eye dot is off-center, which is typical of the earliest Graziano dolls. He has the incised mark.

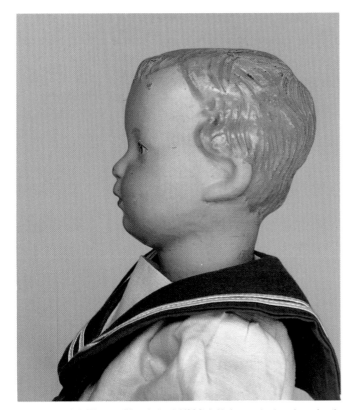

Illustration 34. The profile of the 16/200 doll shows the handcarving in the comb marks above his ears. He has stocking grooves cut in his thigh, as well as the early coloring, thin glossy hair paint and single stroke eyebrows of the earliest dolls. This mixture of features dates him to the end of 1911.

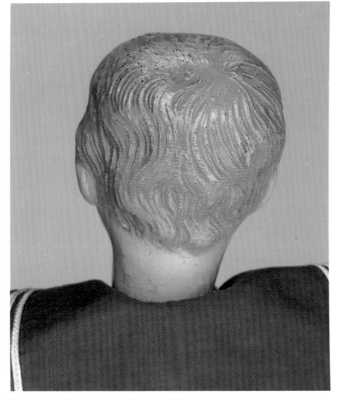

Illustration 35. The back of Doll 16/200 shows the wavy hair which has small curls at the nape of his neck.

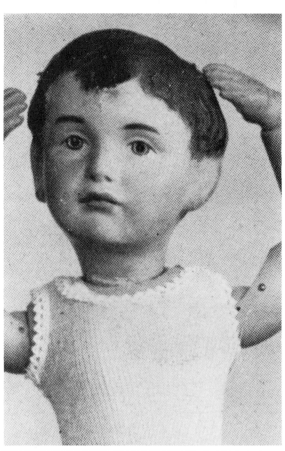

Illustration 36. This enlargement of Doll 16/201 clearly shows that Schoenhut company pictures were retouched to strengthen them for printing in the catalogue. His outlined irises are unusually strong.

OPPOSITE PAGE:
Illustration 37. 16in (41cm). This example of Doll 16/201 is factory-original in a percale shirt and "Boy's Blue over-all suit" (#603). He is from the end of the first six months as he clearly shows the signs of the hot press mold finishing that came in to use at that time. He also has the dark mouth and accent dot painting at the eyes and nostrils that was used briefly at this time. He has the incised mark between his shoulders.

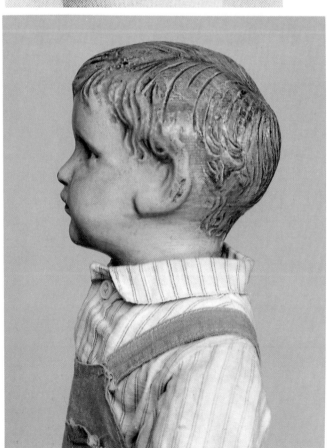

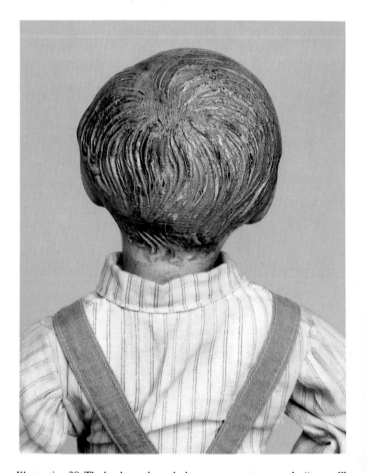

Illustration 38. This profile of Doll 16/201 shows the hand carving used over the blur in modeling caused where the two halves of the mold met. He also appears to have a little hand work around his eyes.

Illustration 39. The back comb marks became very strong on the "carved" hair dolls with the use of the hydraulic heated press which put the wood under a great deal of pressure and resulted in strong detail particularly when the molds were new.

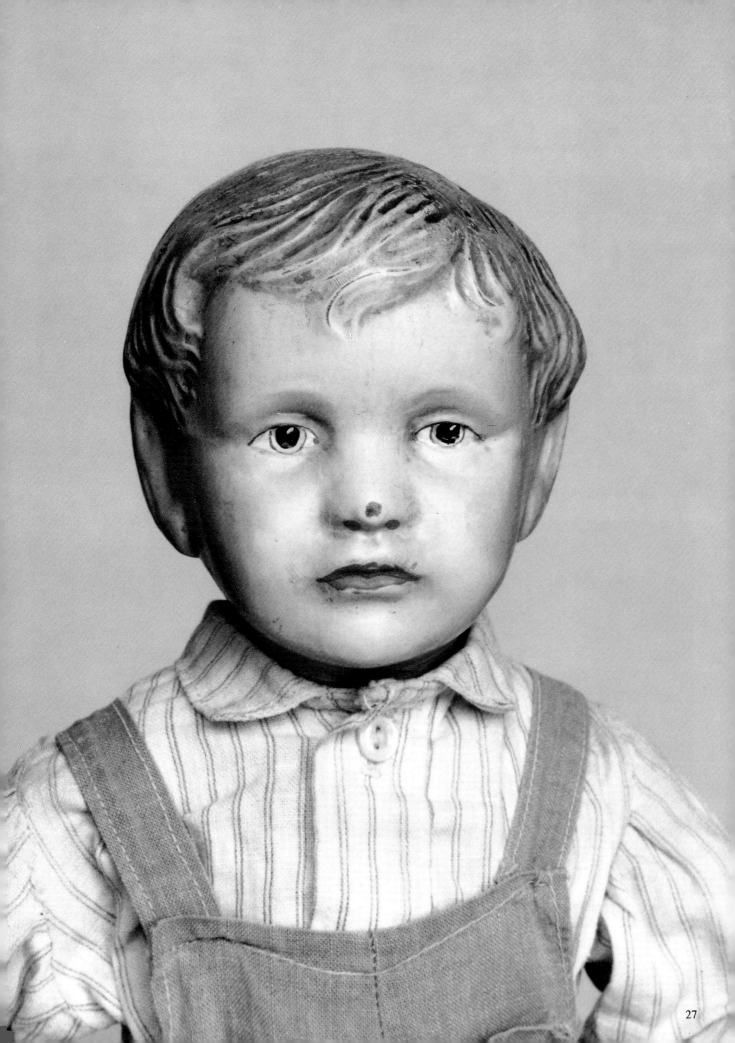

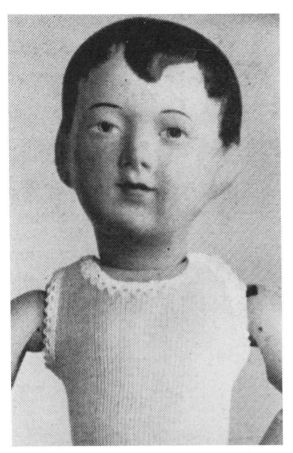

Illustration 40. This enlargement of Doll 16/202 from the 1911 catalogue shows his outlined iris and blue eyes. His hair and eyebrows appeared darkened for clarity.

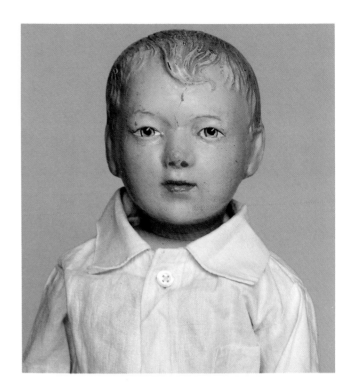

Illustration 41. 16in (41cm). This boy's eyes are light blue with a narrow royal blue outline and the typical Graziano off-center highlight dots. They are intaglio with charcoal brown translucent upper lash lines and bright orange pink tear ducts. He has nicely molded eyelids. He has tool marks, particularly at the hairline. His single-stroke eyebrows are dark gold. He has a deep pink mouth and nostril dots and a fine red line between his lips. His skin is a matte light pink shade and his blush is almost all gone. His shiny translucent blonde hair has a distinctive curl on its forelock. These earliest dolls appear to have hand painted hair rather than airbrushed.

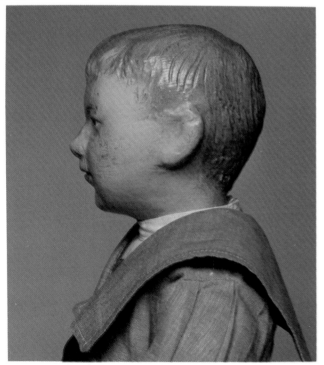

Illustration 42. 16in (41cm). The paint on this fine example of Doll 202 is completely original. It is so thin that bare wood shows under the few small bumps. The handcarving shows around his eyes and nose. The grain of the wood shows clearly. His mouth and accent dots are a strong clear pink. His outfit is factory original #803. The handcarving particularly where his hairline meets his temples is very clear in this boy. He has glossy translucent blonde hair.

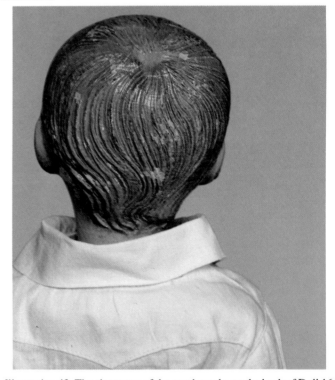

Illustration 43. The sharpness of the comb marks on the back of Doll 16/202's hair may only have been achievable with the hydraulic hot press mold. It is very difficult to tell how much of these early Grazianos were finished by hand and how much by machines.

28

Illustration 44. The original catalogue picture shows no comb marks in this smiling boy's hair. His whole face grins with pleasure. He is identified as Doll 16/203 in this 1911 catalogue.

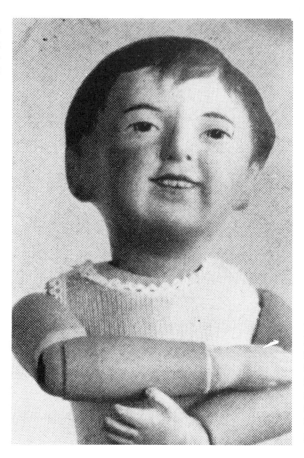

Illustration 45. 16in (41cm). This Graziano Doll 203 is quite rare as are the other first dolls that did not carry into the next period. His teeth and the depth of his smile are accentuated by the decoration of his mouth and eyes. *Private Collection.*

Illustration 46. The profile of Graziano Doll 203 shows almost no "comb marks" in his hair. His four prominent teeth and the placement of his features in his face indicate that he is an older elementary school child. His very large ears are typical of Schoenhuts. He has the incised mark and no stocking groove.

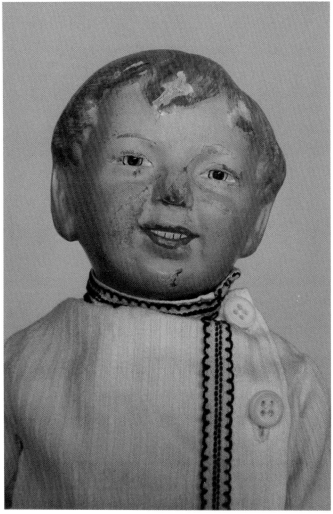

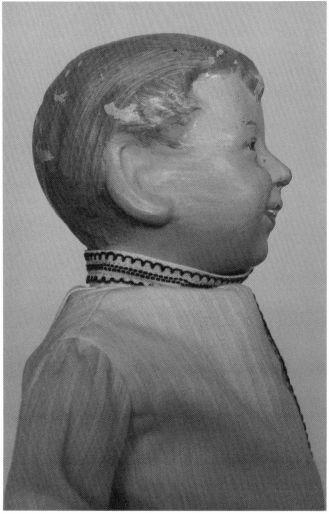

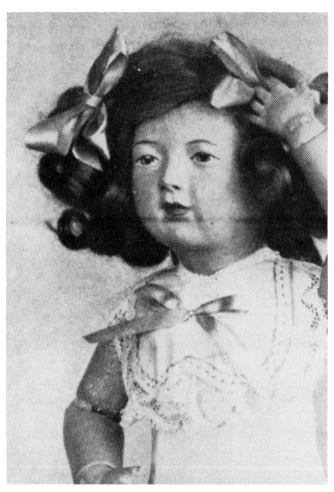

300 Series — Wigged Girls

Although there were eight models of wigged girls offered in the original catalogue some of them appear to have had the same faces with different hairstyles. Therefore the faces that seem to be alike will be treated together. Further research, as more examples of these early dolls are found and can be examined, may prove this theory incorrect.

Doll 300 and Doll 301 appear to have the same face. It is round, with small eyes and a flat appearance. In profile the doll has a medium-sized sharply pointed nose and a firm chin. This profile appears to be the same as that of Doll 102, and in fact, they may be wigged versions of 102. Because all these dolls are very difficult to find and are scattered across the country, a side by side comparison has been impossible to make. Her ears are large but are usually hidden by her wig. She appears to have had at least some hand carving in her finishing.

Doll 300 has a long curl wig held away from her face with ribbons on either side. The wigs are listed as assorted in "blonde and light brown shades."

Doll 301 has a short straight bobbed style wig with bangs. It is parted on the left, and her top hair is held on the right side with a silk bow. Her wig was also assorted blonde or light brown. There was no provision in the 1911 catalogue for a customer to indicate which color was preferred. This choice came later.

Doll 302 has a pointed chin and strongly modeled eyelids. She appears to be based on Kämmer and Reinhardt's mold 101. Her eyes are strongly intaglio, however, which is not so of the Kämmer and Reinhardt model. An example of her has been found with a light red decorating line which further emphasizes her lid crease. Her chin shows the bone which has a slight flat spot on the point. She does not have the slight double chin of the Kämmer and Reinhardt doll, and her nose is not as upturned, but the resemblance is stronger than the few differences.

Doll 302 was presented with a long, straight haired wig, parted on the left side, which seems to be caught up behind her head and fastened with a ribbon bow.

Dolls 303 and 305 are original designs which appear to have the same face with different hairstyles. These are smiling girls with eyes crinkled in laughter and four large teeth showing. Their eyes appear to have their irises outlined in a darker color. They seem to be wigged versions of dolls 101 and 203; however, the lips on these wigged dolls are thinner and wider than those of the "carved hair" ones. These dolls were significantly redesigned to look younger and less strongly character by November 1911. I have not yet found examples of these dolls.

Doll 303 had a short side-parted bobbed hairstyle with no bangs. It is tied with a ribbon on the doll's right side.

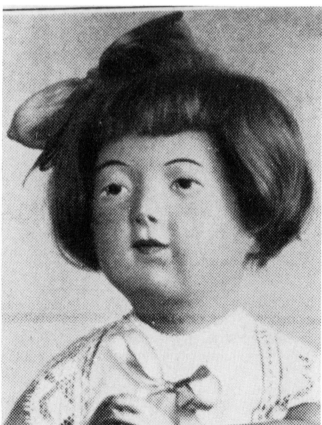

Illustration 48. Doll 16/301 appears to be the same face as Doll 300 with a different hairstyle.

OPPOSITE PAGE:
Illustration 49. 16in (41cm). This face appears with a long curl wig as #300 and with this bob as #301. She has small eyes, the iris of which is outlined in a darker blue. Her face is round and rather flat. The wood grain shows and the roughness of her modeling indicates she may have been hand carved finished rather than hot press molded as the later dolls were.

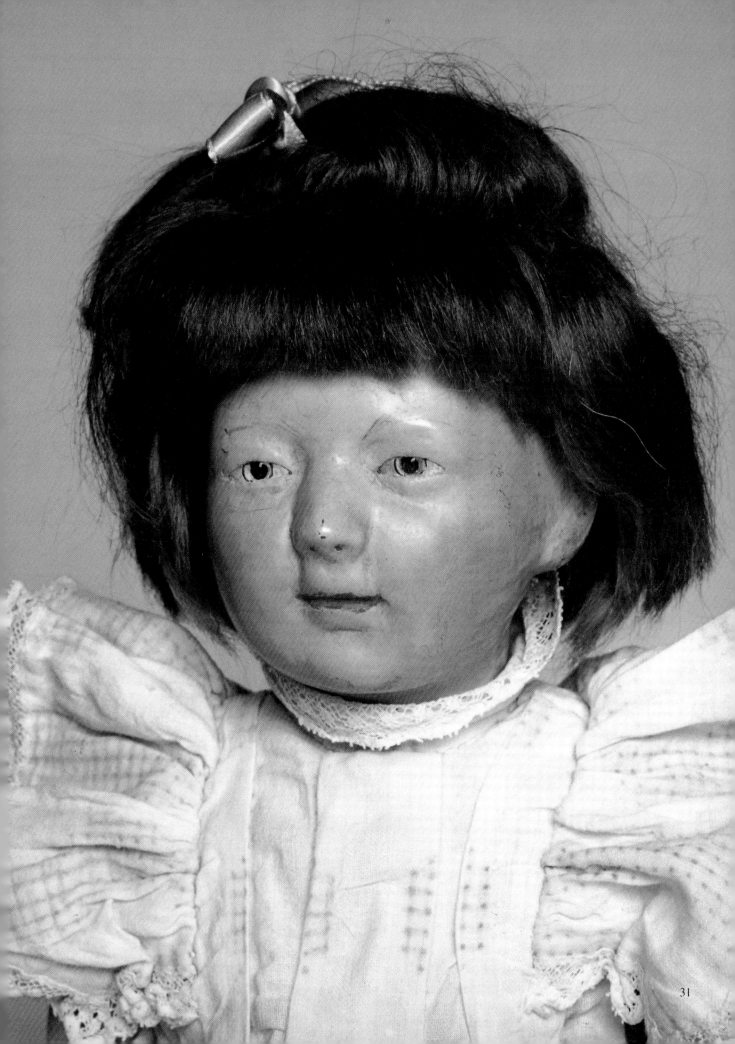

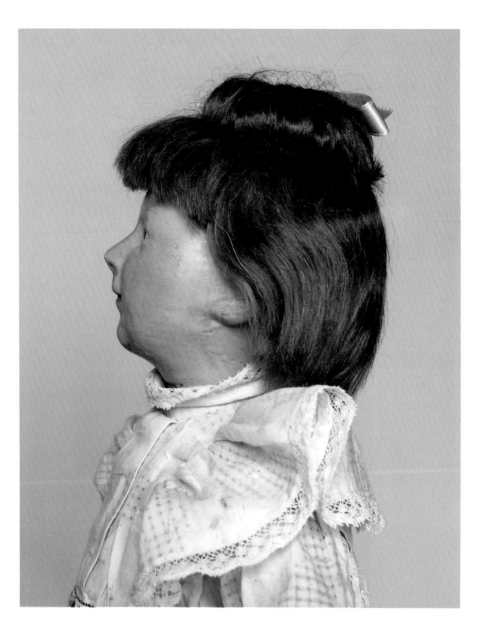

Doll 305 was offered with a thick long wig, parted in the middle, which was put in two braids that were curled over her ears and fastened with bows.

Dolls 304 and 306 are original designs which appear to have the same faces. These dolls share a very unusual head shape. The head has a fairly low forehead with very large ears which stick out on both sides of her head. Her eyes are considerably larger than those of most of the other Graziano models. Her nose is prominent, her upper lip is long and her chin is well defined. An example with very little original paint left and no wig, the first impression is that she makes a perfect "extraterrestrial." Having described all her outrageous details, she is, in fact, arresting in her beauty when the total doll is considered. This is the portrait of a real person and not a cute doll-like idealization. Her modeling is outstanding. She has unusually large intaglio eyes with outlined irises. Her eyelids are well defined, as is the eye socket. Her nose is slightly upturned. She has a long, well-defined philtrum. Her lip edges are also defined in the modeling. While she has a closed mouth her lips are separated with the upper lip more prominent in profile. Her chin line is only slightly pointed and her cheeks are high. She appears to be looking up at someone and might be about to speak. This face disappeared from the line by the end of 1911 and, like several of the Graziano designs, is very rarely found.

Doll 304 has a long wig which was parted in the middle and braided into two braids that were wound around her head and fastened above her ears with bows. This hairstyle shows her unusually prominent ears rather than trying to hide them.

Doll 306 has long curly hair, parted in the middle and held with a bow on the right side. Her long curls cover her ears.

Doll 307 appears to have a round face with a much more "doll-like" face than the other models. Her lips are slightly parted with four upper teeth showing. Her cheeks seem to be quite prominent. Her eyebrows are much heavier than those of the other dolls. Also she has smooth convex eyes like a glass-eyed doll! These eyes are decorated with a darker ring outlining the iris and there is a shine to them as though they were varnished after painting. In spite of the statement that all the dolls were designed on real children she seems most like a wooden version of the typical "dolly faced" German bisque doll.

Doll 307 had a straight, short bobbed hairstyle, without bangs, which was parted on the left and pulled across her forehead and held on the right with a bow. This model continued to be made with some modification through 1916. Her outstanding feature is that she is proof that the firm made smooth-eyed dolls as early as they made intaglio eyed ones.

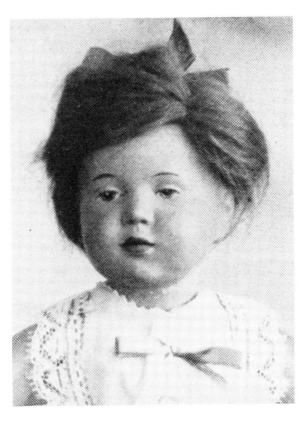

Illustration 51. This doll 16/302 appears to be modeled on Dorothy or Frieda Schoenhut's K*R 101. She has intaglio eyes with narrowly outlined irises. Her eyelid molding is stronger than the K*R examples and her chin line a little less so.

Illustration 52. 16in (41cm). This rare example of Doll 16/302's intaglio blue eyes have darker outlining. Her dark red and gray — blue plaid dress is factory original (#708). *Dorothy Dixon Collection.*

Illustration 53. The profile of 16/302 shows her pointy chin and round cheeks. This doll continued into the "transition" period but is not found in any 1912 advertisements for the "new" line.

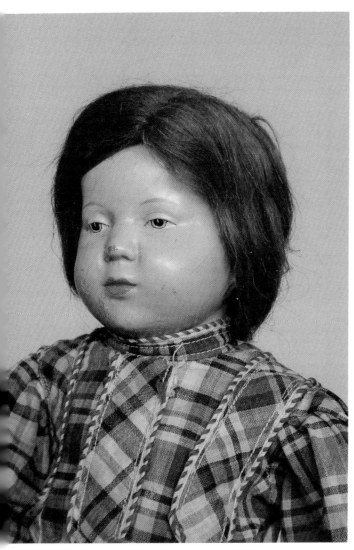

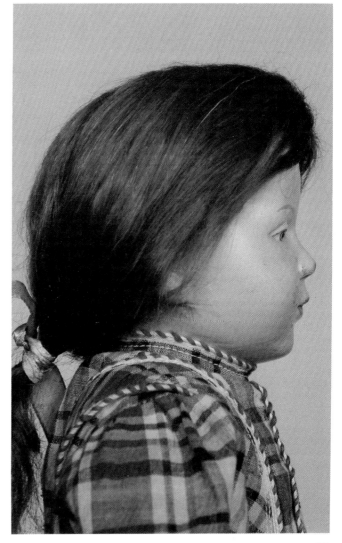

Illustration 54. A comparison of one example of Schoenhut Doll 16/302 (on the left) with her inspiration, Dorothy Schoenhut's K*R 101, which shows that the Schoenhut doll was modeled on the German doll with only slight differences. Both have well modeled upper eyelids, but the Schoenhut's are heavier and in this example are accented with a light red line painted in the crease. Her eyes are smaller and heavily incised with a raised white eye dot. Their depth is achieved by the carving and outlining the light blue iris with darker blue paint. The K*R has a flat eye surface and achieves its depth by shaded paint on the iris. The Schoenhut's nose is less upturned at the end. Her chin line comes to a simple point with less bone definition and without the clear double chin of the K*R model. The K*R 101, on the right, is from the *Eleanor P. Swanson Collection.*

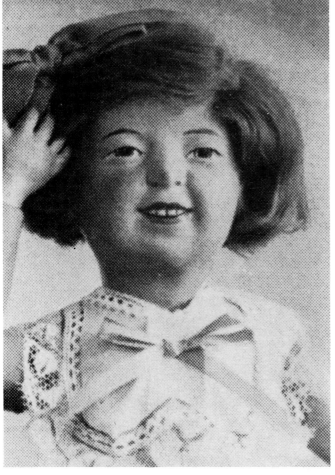

Illustration 55. Doll 16/303, as shown in the original catalogue. Her narrow eyes, four prominent teeth and single stroke eyebrows are typical of all of Graziano's smiling dolls.

Illustration 56. This enlarged picture of Doll 16/305 shows that only her hairstyle distinguishes her from Doll 16/303. Unfortunately, I have not yet found examples of either of these dolls to photograph.

Illustration 58. Doll 306 has the same large eyes, long face, strong nose and sweet expression as Doll 304. This example's lips are not painted as wide and full as 304's, but she seems to be the same face model.

Illustration 57. Doll 304 has her hair braided around her head showing off her spectacular ears.

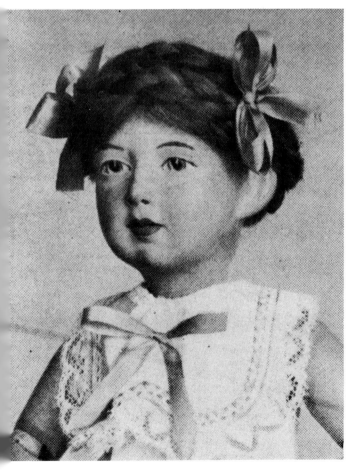

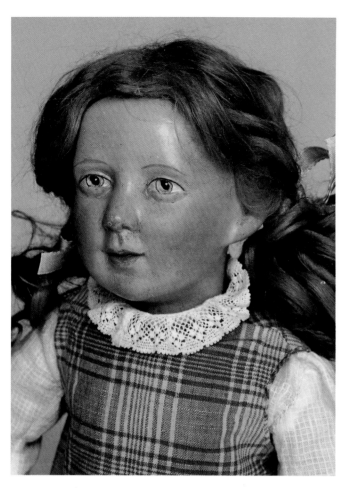

Illustration 59. 16in (41cm). With her long curl tosca mohair wig pulled back with ribbons to show her unusual ears, this example becomes a compromise between the 304 and 306 hairstyles. Her eyelids are particularly strongly modeled as is her philtrum. She has the incised mark in between her shoulders.

Illustration 60. The profile of the 16in (41cm) girl doll shows a strong, straight nose with a very slight uptilt at the end, her prominent upper lip and the deep carving between her lips. She has a firm chin as well.

Illustration 61. Doll 16/307 appears to be a "dolly face" doll. Her eyes are smooth with the iris outlined in a darker color and the highlight dots painted off the top center of her iris. Her eyebrows are considerably heavier than the other first year dolls. Her eyes appear shiny and may have had varnish applied on top of the paint in order to simulate glass eyes. I have never found Doll 16/307 either in her Graziano form, or in the "Classic" form, which was made through 1916.

Doll 400 appears to be modeled on Kämmer and Reinhardt's mold #101. He is the boy version of Doll 302. An example studied had slightly less heavy eyelids and single colored irises, but it is clearly the same model. Both examples shown (one in this chapter and another in the next) are from the second six months of Schoenhut doll production and the variations in details that exist between them may be due to the strike of the hot mold used to "finish" the surface of the roughly carved doll heads and some additional hand carving done on the earliest dolls. This is further emphasized by the different artists applying the paint. This is a very sweet doll, as is its German counterpart. He appears to be more concerned than actively pouting.

Doll 401 appears to be the male version of Doll 300/301. His round face and pointed nose are the same. He appears to have had small eyes with the irises outlined and single-stroke eyebrows. His wavy, short bobbed hair was parted on the left and brushed across his brow. He is extremely difficult to find, as he appears to have been made for only six months. His model number was reassigned to a completely different doll by November of 1911.

Only after I "blew up" (photographically speaking) the faces of the undressed dolls in the catalogue did the differences in dolls 401 and 403 become apparent. Adding to the confusion is that apparently the distinctive wigs of these two dolls were switched with each other in the factory dressed versions. Thus, when dressed by the factory the doll with the face of 401 had a shoulder-length pageboy style wig with short straight bangs across his forehead. He was dressed in a ("Little Lord Fauntleroy") royal blue velveteen suit with short pants, a short jacket and a white lawn blouse trimmed with embroidery and ruffles. His outfit was completed with a velveteen hat to match and white stockings and shoes.

Doll 402 is the wigged version of the "grinning" child as a boy. His eyes are often described as "squinty." He has a broadly smiling mouth with four "second" teeth. His grin is carried out in every muscle of his face. With these earliest smiling children there is a clear impression that they are not "sweet" and as live children they would have been a real "handful" to adults and might have been quite good at terrifying younger children. This design was revised in the beginning of the "Transition" period at the end of 1911, making him very difficult to find.

Doll 403 appears to have been the male version of 304/306. He has the same prominent ears and well-modeled eyelids. He also has the thin pink paint, outlined iris and single-stroke eyebrows found on unrestored examples of the Graziano line. He had an extremely short production run, probably no longer than six months, as his number was assigned to another design by the end of 1911. He was offered with a thick, long pageboy style wig with its curled ends brushing his shoulders. He has full, even bangs across his forehead. If found nude, most collectors would see him as a girl with a "Rembrandt style" wig.

When sold dressed, Doll 403 was presented with the same side-parted wig found on the undressed doll 401 and was dressed in a white sailor suit with long pants and red trim and tie. He also seems to be presented with a short straight bob with bangs and dressed in a "White Linene Russian Suit with blue collar and trim."

The confusion created by the dressed versions of these dolls may have been caused by the need to get the whole line on the market in a fairly short period of time. In fact the company may have settled on a consistent face and hairstyle combination by the time they began filling orders for the dolls. If face 401 and 403 were switched, it seems unlikely that anyone would have been aware of it, as in the catalogue the differences are hard to spot, although it is very easy to see in studying the actual dolls.

Among the dressed dolls in the catalogue are two wigged girls and one wigged boy who are not found among the undressed line. This seems to be the only place to mention them. They were all based on Kämmer and Reinhardt's model 114. The girls came with two different hairstyles.

The first had long straight hair, parted in the middle and braided on both sides of her head. The braids were crossed over the top of her head and held with two silk ribbon bows. She was dressed in a plaid dress with braid trim, and had white stockings and black oxfords. An example is found in the Dorothy Dixon Collection.

The other girl has a long curl wig, parted in the middle and held off her face with bows. She was dressed in a waistless gingham check overdress with a separate guimp.

The boy had a wavy side-part bob. He was dressed in a white shirt, white linene knee-length pants and a red cloth jacket with brass buttons. He also had a large white linene hat with a silk ribbon around the crown. This outfit continued to be made by the company for years.

All three of these dolls became part of the undressed doll line as of November 1911. The only way to distinguish these earliest examples from the ones that appeared in the next period is the outlined iris which apparently was a part of the decoration of the earliest examples, but not of the later ones.

The Graziano infant dolls are covered in the chapter on Infants.

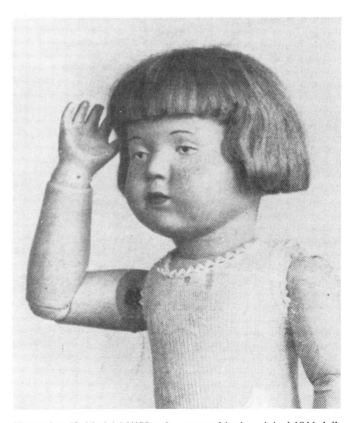

Illustration 62. Model 16/400 as he appeared in the original 1911 doll catalogue. Interestingly, his irises do not appear to be outlined although those of his girl counterpart are. It is possible that a few of these earliest dolls did not have this feature.

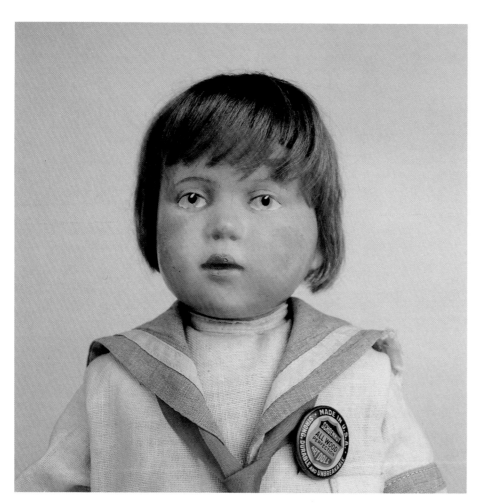

Illustration 63. This exquisite example of Doll 16/400 is particularly sweet and more than slightly anxious. His artist has made his eyes open wider by pulling the color down onto the lower lid and placing the upper lashline on top of the molded upper lid. His upper lip is also painted fuller than usual. He has single-stroke light brown brows and his original tosca mohair wig. His coloring may date him to the end of 1911 or even the beginning of 1912. *Photograph by Monty Moncrief. Becky Moncrief Collection.*

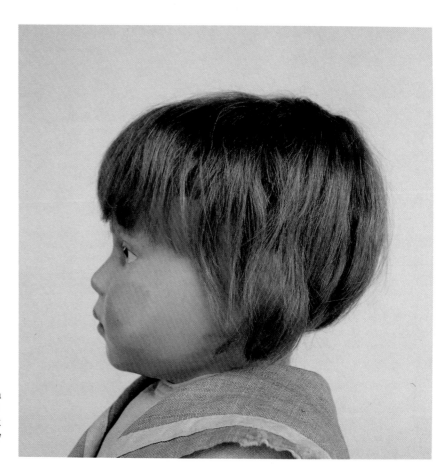

Illustration 64. The profile of Doll 16/400 shows a nose that is a little less upturned than his K*R 101 counterpart. It also shows the heavy round cheek modeling. *Photograph by Monty Moncrief. Becky Moncrief Collection.*

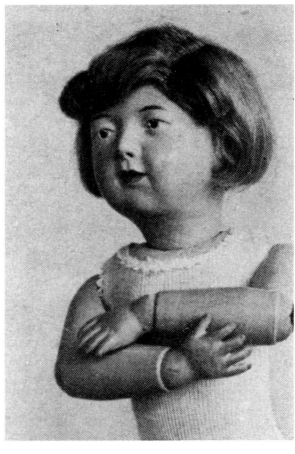

Illustration 65. Catalogue picture of Doll 16/401.

Illustration 66. 16¾in (42.5cm). This example of Doll 16/401 not only has most of his original paint intact, he has his original tosca mohair wig. He has a pointy nose, but not quite as pointy as the girl (301) version that we have seen. This appears to be due to the difference in hand finishing common at this time. His eyebrows are single stroke and light brown. His smaller eyes have the outlined iris. The red lips have their original paint and are like other examples of dolls that appear to be from the fall of 1911. *H.B. Christianson Collection.*

Illustration 67. Since the wig of Doll 16/401 was loose I could not resist taking this shot to show the shape of his head. The sheen on his face appears to be from varnish which may have been added at some point with the intention of preserving his paint.

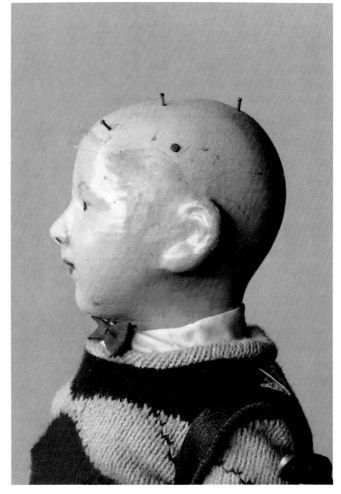

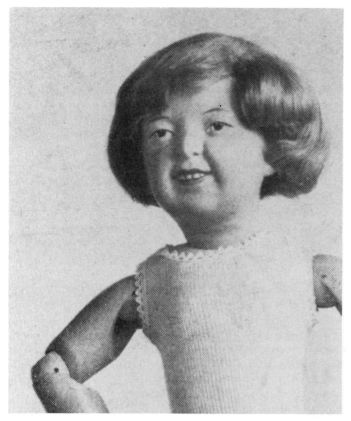

Illustration 68. Catalogue photograph of Doll 402.

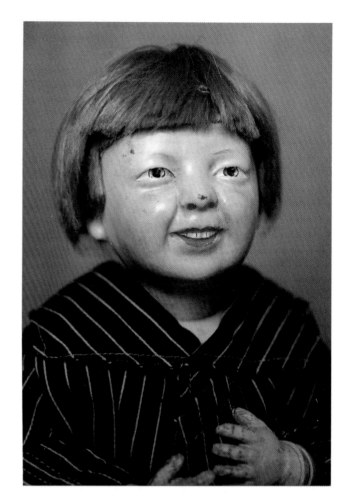

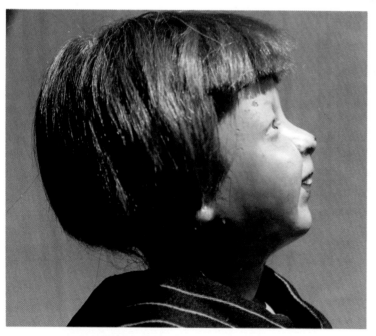

Illustration 70. The profile of Doll 16/402 shows teeth that stick out beyond his lip line like 16/203. His nose is fairly short but very straight and his chin is softly rounded. *Helen Sieverling Collection.*

ABOVE:
Illustration 69. 16in (41cm). This is a terrific example of a rare 16/402 doll made for only six months at most. He has outlined irises in his narrow eyes and a deep smile that takes in his whole face. He has painted separation marks on top of his four large and prominent upper teeth, which may have been done to give the impression of more and smaller teeth of a younger child. His wig is a fine mohair. It appears to be a replacement but is definitely in the Schoenhut style. *Helen Sieverling Collection.*

Illustration 71. A comparison of Graziano Dolls 16/101 and 16/402 show differences in modeling around mouth and decorating, even though they are basically the same face. The 16/402, on the right, has an upper lip that is tighter and his lower lip has a more pronounced dip which is in the carving not just the painting. These earliest dolls may be lathe carved and hand finished rather than steam press molded which accounts for the differences in them. The 16/402, on the right, is from the *Helen Sieverling Collection.*

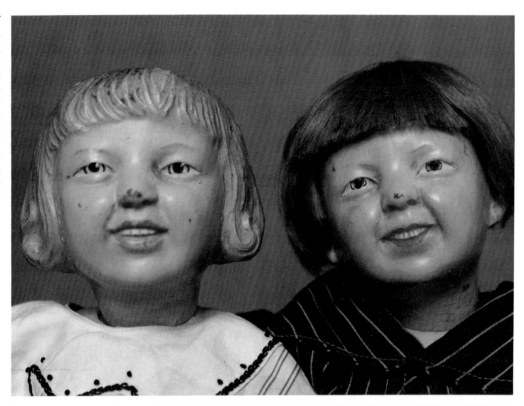

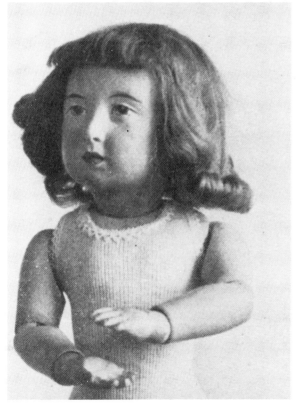

Illustration 72. Doll 16/403 as shown in *Illustrated Catalogue Dolls The A Schoenhut Company.* "1911" is handwritten on cover. Inside, the catalogue says "39 years in business as Manufacturers of Toys and Novelties," confirming the 1911 date.

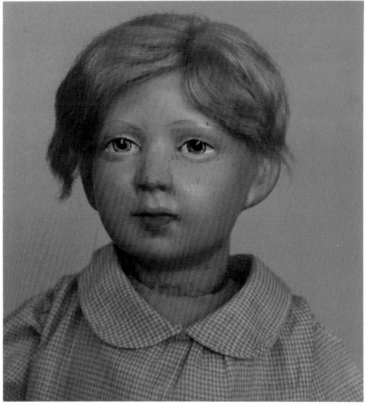

Illustration 73. 16in (41cm). This 16/403 is one of the very rare Schoenhut dolls. He was no longer in the line by November 1911, giving him a production of about six months. He is distinguished by his lower lid modeling and long upper lip as well as by his large protruding ears (which show nicely under his fine strawberry blonde mohair wig). He has the pale skin color, strong rose accents at eye dots, nostrils and lips, as well as the glossy single-stroke eyebrows of the earliest dolls. This is the only example of this face, either as a boy or a girl, that I have been able to find unrestored. The paint is in fine shape and clearly shows the decoration details of the Graziano period. His profile is the same as Dolls 16/304 and 306. *Sherryl Shirran Collection.*

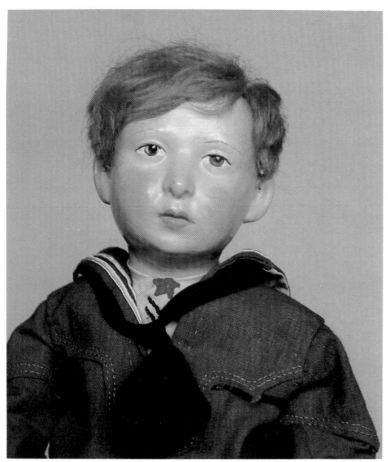

Illustration 74. 16in (41cm). Doll 16/403. Although this doll has had restoration work by doll artist Martha Thompson, he is completely charming. His blue outlined iris eyes have been preserved. The red mohair wig is rougher to the touch than Schoenhut wigs and is probably a replacement. Many Schoenhut collectors would not have a restored doll but this one is a real winner and is likely to be appreciated by many. *Dorothy Dixon Collection.*

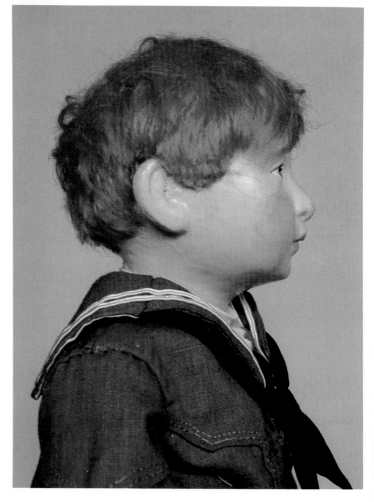

Illustration 75. The strong profile of Doll 16/403 with the incredible ears, for which this doll is known, makes this model a real standout. These dolls come off as beautiful despite the huge ears and the prominent nose. They vanished from the catalogue after six months.

THE TRANSITION PERIOD
— NOVEMBER 1911 to SPRING 1912

The earliest Graziano design dolls must have had a mixed reception because the design of the heads began to change almost immediately. By November of 1911 a company advertisement in *The Woman's Home Companion* showed the number 102 design that collectors love, with a carved center part and the hair brushed back into braids that are wound around her head. Also shown in this advertisement were a revised 303 design and a doll which appears to be the new 404 model. All dolls were 16in (41cm) high and had the early style leg with no stocking groove. The undressed girls in this period were still in a chemise ("slip"), shoes and stockings. The union suit for girls apparently dates to the spring of 1912 when the "Classic" Line appeared.

The most dramatic change in the new dolls was their much younger faces. The original Graziano dolls have the large second teeth (where they show) and more mature faces of eight to twelve year old children. The only exceptions are the designs that were based on the characters of Kämmer and Reinhardt and the two infant dolls, *Schnickel-Fritz* and *Tootsie Wootsie*. Even the babies have "old" faces and are often found dressed as children rather than true infants.

The other major difference from the earliest Graziano dolls is the finishing process. The dolls from all the periods apparently were "roughed out" on a lathe. The patterns were set and the actual machine held from two to four heads depending on the size, at this point one size only. In the initial six month period, by examining actual dolls, it seems that the finishing was largely (if not entirely) hand done. The dolls have obvious hand carved details, particularly in the hair of the "carved hair" dolls. The dolls are not smooth in the areas of the eyes, nose, mouth or where the hairline meets the face. This is true of the wigged dolls as well as the "carved hair" ones.

Examples from the Transition Period show considerable differences in the finishing details. There is a "blur line" above the ears of the "carved hair" dolls. This smooth area often has hand-carved hair details over it. The facial features are smoother, with an almost "glass" smooth quality to the skin, and there are no longer any rough edges and debris around features or hairlines. These changes indicate that the hydraulic press finishing began at this time. The heads continued to be roughed out on a lathe with a cutting pattern. They were then finished by a hydraulic-powered press in an extremely hot mold which pressed the wood quite smooth and literally burned off the rough edges. William F. Schoenhut, a grandson who worked in the company, recalls that the pieces finished this way frequently had scorch marks on them. The finished product was quite smooth, and fine "comb marks" could be shown in the hair. Where the sides of the molds met; however, there was a resulting blur or loss of detail in the "carved hair" dolls, and during this period, that detail was added by hand. The resulting smoothness and added detail was a distinct improvement. The younger faces that came out with the new process ensured considerable success for the new line.

The improvement was furthered when the company, responding to customer comments, as well as its own observations, changed the paint finish as well as the decorating details in 1912. The new paint was applied over a gesso coat, giving even more smoothness with less wood grain showing. The enamel was more natural in color and a little tougher. Therefore, when a minor bang happened, there was still a layer of flesh colored paint under the bash instead of bare wood showing. This made the smallest chips less obvious. The new paint also stood up better to washing, in moderation. The decorating changes include a change from single-stroke eyebrow painting to multi-stroke and feathered brows as well as warmer orange blush and a richer orange-pink lip and accent color.

Over the years collectors have discovered that the few Graziano dolls which have not had their paint washed or worn off seem less likely to have their paint spontaneously pop off. The thin layer, once bashed, leaves bare wood exposed, but it seems to hold onto the wood better during humidity changes. Wood which has been placed under tremendous pressure also tends to swell slightly as it tries to revert to its original unpressed state. The first heads, which apparently were not molded, do not go through these changes in the cell structure.

Undated, but apparently coming out at the end of 1911, is a large (13in by 11in [33cm by 28cm]) six-page brochure sent to retail customers who had written to the company because the dolls were not yet available in their area. The original Graziano design dolls are in the photographs of dolls showing all the positions in which they could be posed. Seven of the original "tableaus" of dolls in action and children playing with them, from the 1911 catalogue, are also shown. The two largest pictures are of all the dolls offered for sale at that time, both dressed and undressed, and they show several dramatic model changes.

Some of the new models are based on the Graziano designs, but they appear to have younger and "sweeter" faces. Some actual dolls from this brief period have the paler, thinner flesh color and pinker cheek coloring of the first dolls and the hair paint still has a glaze of varnish on it. They may have the early leg style with no stocking groove as well. Later examples, possibly from early 1912, have the new tougher paint and more natural coloring as well as the stocking groove cut into the thighs. All the dolls found have the impressed mark on the back of the shoulders. The design changes during this period appear to be many in a short period of time.

It is probably at this point that a Mr. Leslie is reported to have been hired as a doll designer on the recommendation of Charles Graffly, teacher of Harry Schoenhut. We have not yet found contemporary written evidence of Leslie's work, but he has been confirmed as a designer for the firm by family members who worked for the company when it was active.

This brochure is a great find because it allows us to identify and date dolls that have been previously thought to have been "not in any catalogue." The prices quoted, in the brochure, are by the single doll, rather than by the dozen, but the price per doll is identical to those of the 1911 wholesale catalogue. This is one indication that the prices in the Schoenhut catalogues are

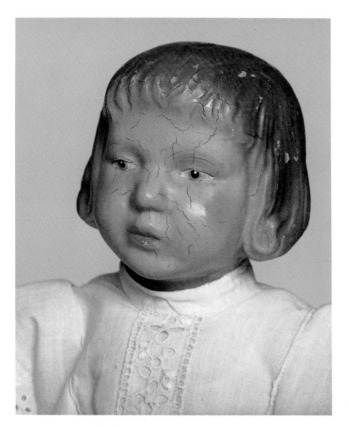

Illustration 76. 16in (41cm). This Doll 16/100 is interesting because she is an example of factory repainting, possibly in multiple layers. She has the vibrant colors of some of the later dolls and her modeling has lost some of its crispness as it has been filled in with paint. The crazing in the center face is probably caused by the thickness of the paint. The paint seems to be holding. Where it has chipped on the lower lip, a slightly fuller and pinker earlier lower lip has been revealed.

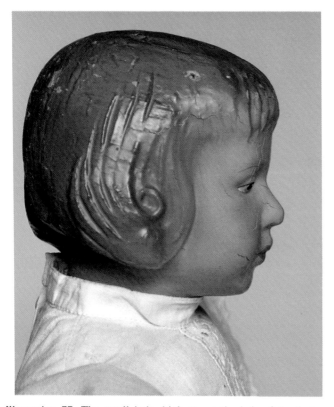

Illustration 77. The small hole, high up on the hair of the factory repainted doll, is where her original hair bow was attached.

retail rather than wholesale and that the retailer ordering from the company simply took a discount, the size of which depended on the retail value of what he bought.

The Transition Dolls continue to be offered in the 16in (41cm) size only, while the infants, who have lost their names and retained their numbers, are still 15in (38cm). The term "transition" to describe these dolls is purely my own and has no historical validity. The models offered in this period are as follows.

100 Series — "Carved Hair" Girls

Doll 100 remains basically the same. Both the dressed and undressed versions have a silk bow nailed to the right side of her bob. Later versions (if you can call early 1912 examples of Schoenhuts as "later") have a groove cut above the knee onto which the stocking was tied. The dressed version of this doll is still listed as 501 as the company had not yet developed the easier, if longer, numbering system that offered more variety of choice.

Model 101 has changed dramatically. While she is still a smiling doll, her eyes are rounded and do not smile as much as her mouth. Her hair is now parted on the left side, and the top hair is pulled back and to the right side where it is held up high with a carved bow. The rest of her hair falls straight down into a tapered bob style. She has six smaller and less prominent upper teeth, and her features are placed lower in her face which makes her appear to be younger than the Graziano child. She is a very alert and curious looking child.

This new 101 model is a little taller than the earlier version (17in [43cm]). She has the thin pale pink paint of the original dolls and a good deal of hand carved detail in her hairstyle. The hair paint is also thin and appears to be covered with a high-gloss varnish. Her eyes still have their light blue irises outlined in a darker blue just like the Graziano model. Her legs have the nail on the back of the thigh to hold up the grommeted stocking.

Doll 102 has also gone through a dramatic change. She now appears to be the "girl with the braids" that is such a favorite with collectors. In the brochure she appears to have the heavy braids beginning on the side of her head. Her hair also appears to be offered in two shades, one the rich dark reddish-brown of the later dolls and the other a lighter brown or dark gold. The pictures are in black and white, and no hair colors are mentioned in the text about the carved hair dolls, but the tonal differences of the examples shown are definite. Doll 102 has two silk bows tacked to the sides of her head. Because I have not found an example of this model that is clearly from this period, it is impossible to accurately describe the differences between this version and the "Classic" 102s. It seems probable that her eyes may have had the iris outline of the earliest dolls and that her skin tone was the same. She probably had hand-carved detail in her hair. I am willing to hazard a guess that the braids on the back of her head, in those examples from the end of 1911, may be quite skinny and have no "carved" bow. This guess is made because the ribbon bows on the sides of her head make a "carved" bow on the back unnecessary, and the next two models (dolls 103 and 104) which have strong similarities to 102 have the same ribbon bows on the sides of their hair and two thin braids neatly crossed behind their heads.

Doll 102 has a soft, round face with slightly separated full lips, a short nose and a slight double chin. She is very sweet looking. While she has the dependable look of Graziano's 102, she does not have her look of alert curiosity.

Doll 103 is another new model and not a modification of the Graziano 103. Her face is rounder, having a slight double chin and the features are placed lower in her face. She appears to have

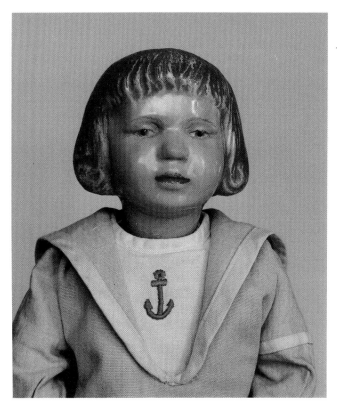

Illustration 78. This beautiful example of Doll 16/100 is from the "Transition period." Her modeling is less sharp than some, but her coloring is typical of the earliest dolls. The paint surface is smooth and she has less grain showing. *Nancy A. Smith Collection.*

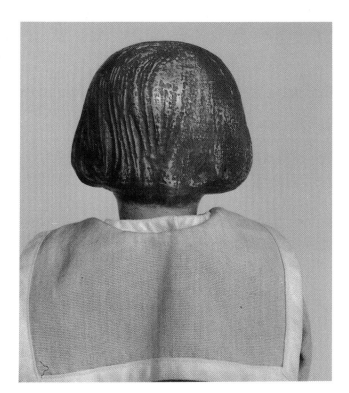

Illustration 79. The back of Doll 16/100 shows her short hair with considerable modeling, but light finishing comb marks. *Nancy A. Smith Collection.*

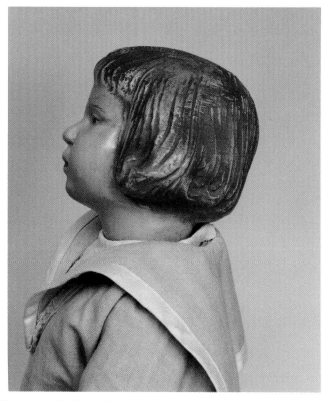

Illustration 80. The profile of Doll 16/100 shows less comb marks than shown in other examples. The grooves in the side of her appear to be hand carved. *Nancy A. Smith Collection.*

the same lower face as 102. She has thick wavy hair parted in the middle and brought back in "wings" on the sides of her head. Her hair is neatly braided into two fine braids which are crossed behind her head. The heaviness of the front hair is in sharp contrast with the fineness of the resulting braids. She has ribbon bows tacked to the sides of her hair. In the eight examples that I have been able to study, none have had the iris of the eye outlined. However, all of the examples have also had the stocking groove cut into the thigh, and it is possible that the earliest examples have the earlier form of eye decoration.

Examples of Doll 103 have been found with a caramel shade of blonde hair and with dark reddish-brown hair. They have been found with brown eyes as well as blue eyes. Again the variety of hair color is indicated in the brochure's pictures but not in the text. Her eyebrows may be single-stroke or feathered.

Doll 104 appears to be another hair treatment with a similar face to 102 and 103. This time the hair is very fine, smooth and straight. The comb marks are soft and fine to accentuate the thinness of her hair. There is additional hand carving on the hair particularly above the ears. The doll's smooth hair is drawn down, as well as back, on the sides of her head and braided into two fine braids that are crossed behind her head. This gives her face a longer and thinner look than the previous two models although her profile has the rounded features and slight double chin of 102 and 103. The Amish look to her hairstyle is in contrast to the ribbon bows tacked on the sides of her head. The fineness of the front of her hair seems totally in keeping with the thinness of the resulting braids.

The other outstanding feature of the one example I have found is her eyes. They are large and round. Her blue irises are sharply outlined in a deeper blue, and she has unusually large pupils which is a feature found in very young children. The modeling of the eyelids is clear. Her high smooth forehead also emphasizes her youth.

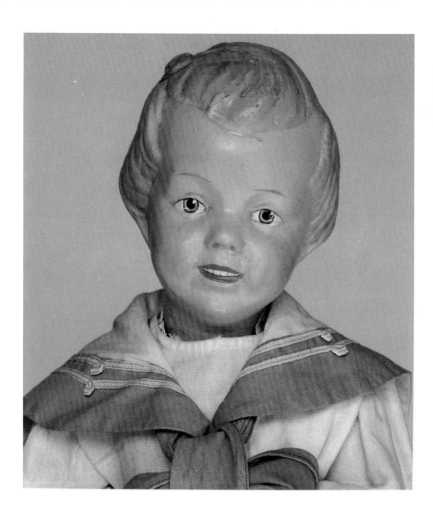

Illustration 81. 17in (43cm). This "Transition Model" 16/101 is from late 1911. Her design is attributed to Mr. Leslie. Note that her rounded eyes retain the dark blue ring around the iris. Her hair shows much molding with the strand across her forehead accented by paint. She has very pale skin, translucent blonde hair with a shiny (perhaps varnished) surface and single stroke eyebrows.

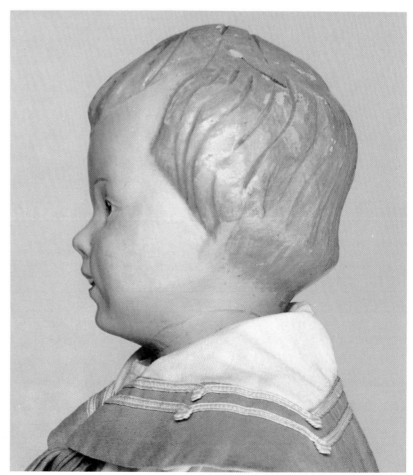

Illustration 82. Hand carving on her hair adds to the strength to Doll 16/101's modeling. She has no stocking groove cut in her thigh, but she clearly shows signs of having been through the new hydraulic hot press process.

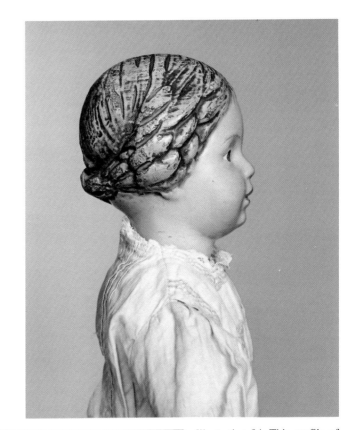

Illustration 83. 16¼in (41cm). This example was chosen for the "Transition" chapter because her factory-original dress is shown in early 1912 advertising so we know that she is an early 102. Her hair shows hand-carved details across the top of the head and on the sides. There is, however, no sign that she had silk ribbons tacked to the side of her head. She has lightly modeled upper lids and nice temples.

Illustration 84. This profile of the "Transition" Doll is of a much younger child than Graziano's 102. She has a short nose, slightly open lips, a round small chin and a second chin behind it. Her features are placed low on her face.

Illustration 85. 16in (41cm). This example of Doll 16/102/ 504 can be dated to the end of the "Transition" or the beginning of the "Classic" period by her factory original two-piece blue chambray "Peter Thompson Dress," which now has the front fastened (with hidden buttons under the panel) blouse which makes it easy to dress and undress her. She has good eyelid and temple modeling. Her lips and accent dots are a medium pink and the center of her mouth has been accented in red. She has a soft orange blush which began to be used in early 1912. Her brown brows are softly feathered and she has dark brown upper lid lines. She has the impressed mark. *Photograph Courtesy Yvonne L. Baird. Yvonne L. Baird Collection.*

47

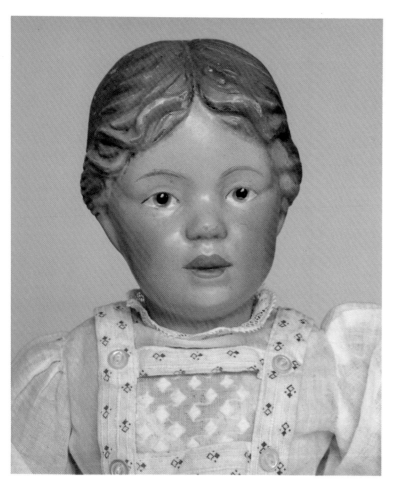

Illustration 86. 16½in (42cm). This Doll 16/103 has light blue intaglio eyes. Her caramel blonde hair is strongly modeled. Her coloring is late (Spring 1912) "Transition" which carried into the Classic Period. This model however was out of production by June 1912. She has the incised mark on her back. The flesh under her eyes and at her temples has nice modeling. Her upper lids are barely indicated. She has blonde multi-stroke brows. Her lips are fuller than most examples of this model.

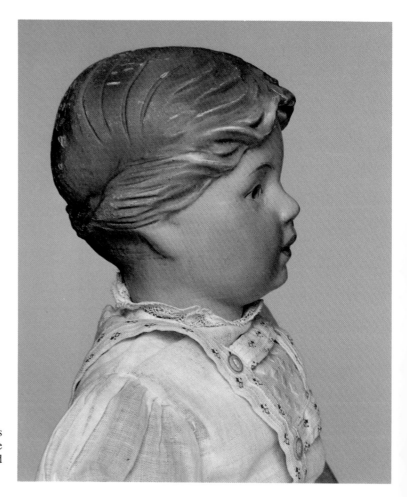

Illustration 87. This is the same profile lower face as Models 102 and 104 from this period. The hand carving adds to the depth of her hair and obscures the mold mark on the sides and top of her hair.

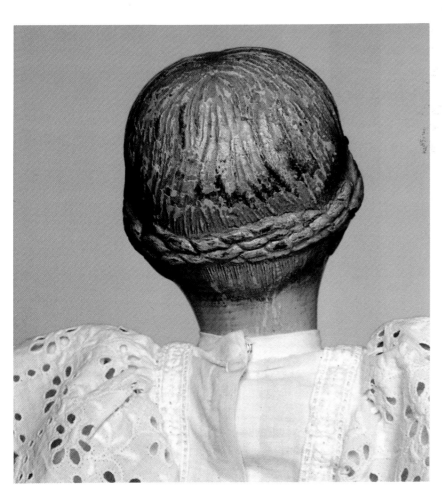

Illustration 88. 16¼in (41cm). This example of Doll 16/103 has the pale coloring of the earliest dolls and the dark lips of the transition period. The comb marks on the back of her hair are quite clear.

Illustration 89. 16in (41cm). This fine example of Doll 16/103 is all-original in dress 503 from the factory. She has nicely modeled upper eyelids with brown lid lines over blue intaglio eyes with pronounced raised highlight dots which are now placed at the top center of the eye. Her heavy blonde hair has a good deal of hand carving. She has early pale skin and single-stroke blonde eyebrows. Her mouth, nostrils and tear ducts are pink. There is a light red accent line between her lips and she has a slight orange blush on her cheeks. Even her pale blue hair bows appear to be original. She has the impressed mark. *Gail Hiatt Collection.*

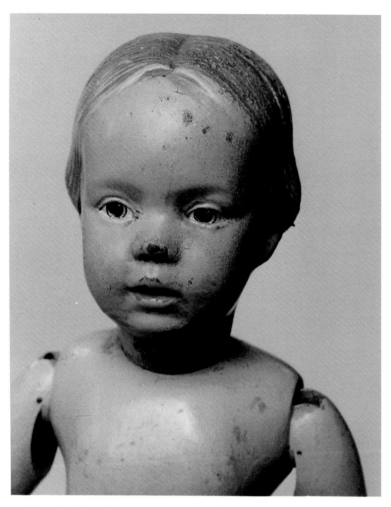

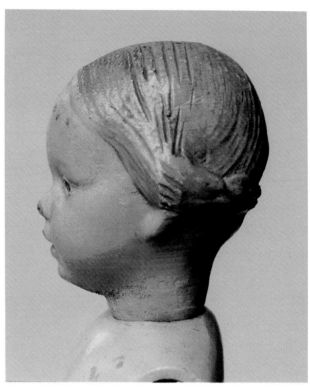

Illustration 91. Doll 16/104's profile is rounded and soft and her hair is smooth and fine. Note the hand-carved detail from the center part down and in the grooves over her ears. Her profile is identical to Doll 102. She is a blue-eyed blonde. From the tones in the original brochure she appears to have been produced as a brunette as well. *Marianne Ripley Collection.*

Illustration 90. 16¼in (41cm). This example of Doll 16/104 has everything special. Her paint is completely original and she has very little wear. Her eyes have the unusually large pupils of a young child. Her eyebrows and eyelids are nicely modeled. The smooth close hairstyle emphasizes that her features are low on her face and her forehead is high and smooth. Her eye highlight dots are off-center, as are those of the Graziano dolls. Also her irises are outlined, but she is one of the earliest Leslie models. *Marianne Ripley Collection.*

Illustration 92. The back of the head of the 16/104 Doll is very consistent with the fineness of her hair in the front and sides. She has the incised mark between her shoulders. *Marianne Ripley Collection.*

Illustrations 93, 94, and 95. 15¾in (40cm). This Doll 200 has the oranger color of a later time. The paint is factory original and he is a nice example of an early brown eyed doll. The coloring seems later and he may be a good example of a factory repaint. *Dorothy Dixon Collection.*

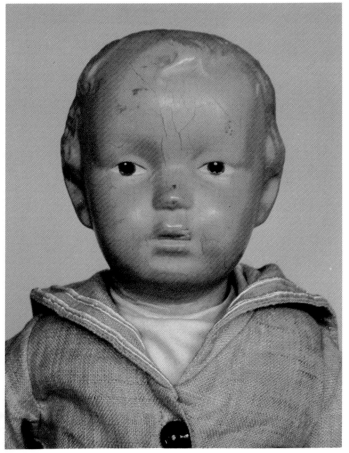

200 Series — "Carved Hair" Boys

Doll 200, which appears to have been modeled on a Gebrüder Heubach molded hair boy #7622, as well as a similar boy produced by Swaine and Company, was still in production at this time. He is slightly smaller than he was, and his finish is smoother. He has more natural coloring as well.

Doll 201, a truly pouty child which was based on Kämmer and Reinhardt's model 114, was still in the line. His hair shows finer comb marks as well as the smoother finish of the hydraulic press. The "blur" above his ears has hand-carved detail over it. Earliest examples have some wood grain showing, the pale pink skin tone and the outlined irises of the earliest dolls. Later versions of this doll have a strong orange tint to their complexions and a dark line between the lips with very slight lip tint. They also have the stocking groove. Although this doll, which was apparently out of production by the end of 1912, reappears briefly for the 1930 "Kindergarten Line." Some of these "orange" examples have original clothing which date them to the 1912 period. It is possible that these have been factory repainted during the later period as the paint on them is heavy and often crazed but appear to be real Schoenhut work.

Doll 202, with his peaceful, mature face, was still available. He has also changed. His features are now finished in the heated mold and are thus smoother. He is also slightly smaller than his earlier brother and has the "improved" paint. His design, however, is the same as that of the Graziano doll, and he has not been redesigned to look younger. Comparing examples of Doll 202 from the first and second six-month periods of production

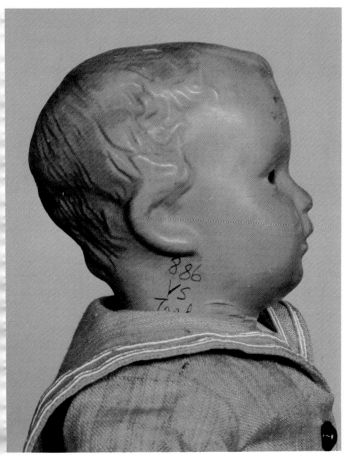

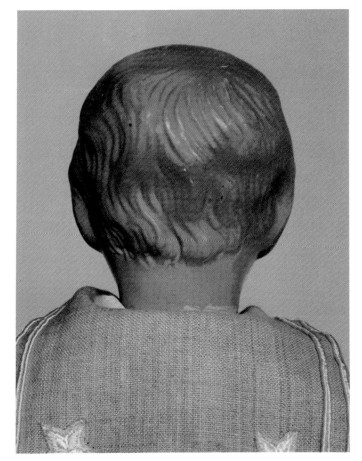

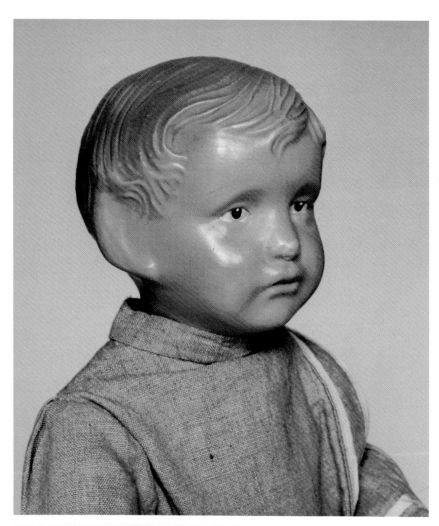

Illustration 96. 16in (41cm). This example of Doll 16/201 has the suntanned look of a later period and may be a late factory refurbishing of a "Transition Doll." His clothes are original and appear to date from about 1912. His blue Russian suit may be very well made at home or may be a factory suit as yet not found in a catalogue. His red stockings and high laced boots are also early. His nose tip shows old repair as it has changed color over time. The rest of him is clearly factory done.

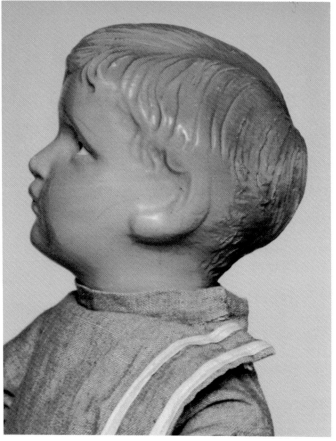

gives the clearest picture of the differences between dolls made by Graziano and those from this "Transition" Period. Although no photograph illustrates this as clearly as studying them in person, you will be able to see these differences in the accompanying pictures. Doll 202 was gone from the line by April of 1912, less than a year after it first appeared.

Doll 203 is a greatly revised design based on the Graziano original. His smiling mouth has six smaller teeth. He has dimples in both cheeks. His eyes are larger and rounder, and his features are set lower in his face, adding to his younger look. This is a happy doll but appears less calculating in his mischievousness. His design continued through the first five-year "Classic" Line.

Doll 204 is an entirely new doll and was to become one of the Classic Line. In many ways he is similar to Doll 202. He has a serious look, perhaps a bit more anxious than peaceful. His short hair is brushed forward in a similar fashion with a wavy forelock on his forehead. His face is rounder with the features placed lower on it. He has a small dimple in his chin. His rounder eyes complete the impression that he is clearly younger than the children designed by Graziano.

Illustration 97. In the profile view of the 16/201 boy it can be seen that the tendrils around his face are nicely modeled. There is a lack of clarity in the modeling where the molds met.

Illustration 98. 16in (41cm). Despite the roughness in his original modeling, this example of Doll 16/202 shows fewer tool marks than the original Doll 202. The back of his hair is particularly strongly modeled. These comb marks are very fine and are the result of the new hydraulic hot press finishing process.

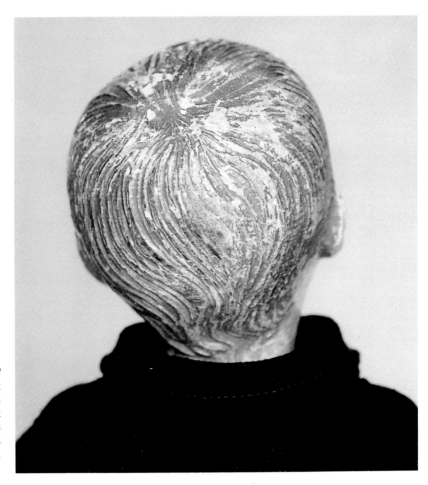

Illustration 99. 15in (38cm). This "Transition Doll" 16/202 is a perfect example of the change that occurred at this time. His color is richer and warmer. Where he has a tiny nick on his eyebrow, a flesh colored undercoat shows through, rather than bare wood. The surface is very smooth. He may have been subjected to steam press finishing. He has blue eyes with no outlining on the iris. *Nancy A. Smith Collection.*

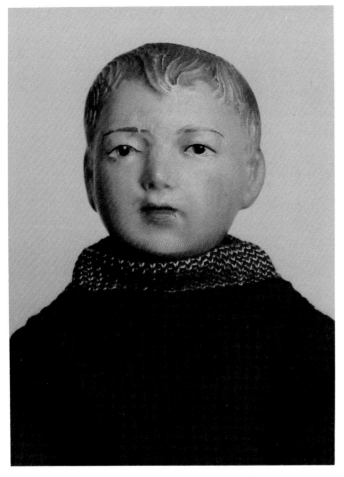

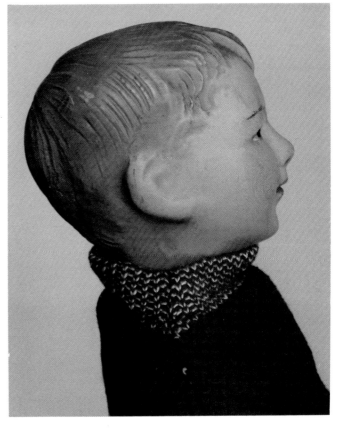

Illustration 100. In profile this "Transition Doll" 16/202 still shows some hand carving in the hair but not the tool marks around the face that the earlier example shows. *Nancy A. Smith Collection.*

53

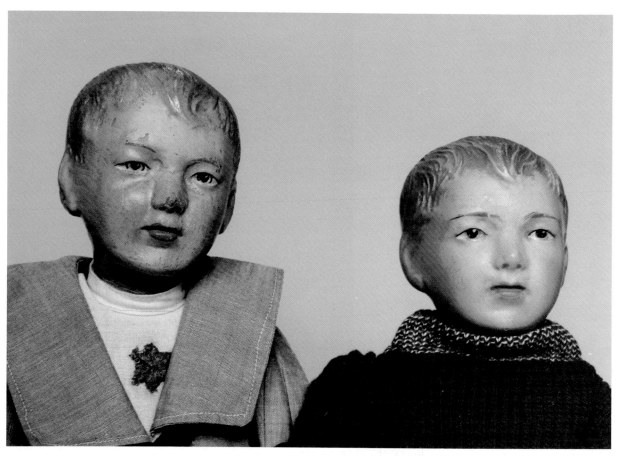

Illustration 101. Comparison of Graziano Doll 16/202, on the left, and "Transition Model" 16/202, on the right, shows the much rougher surface of the earlier model, which has many signs of hand carving. Other differences included a lighter pink paint which is quite thinly applied to the 1911 Graziano doll. He also has no undercoat and where his paint is nicked bare wood shows. The mouth paint is redder and the cheeks are a true pink. *Nancy A. Smith Collection* (doll on right).

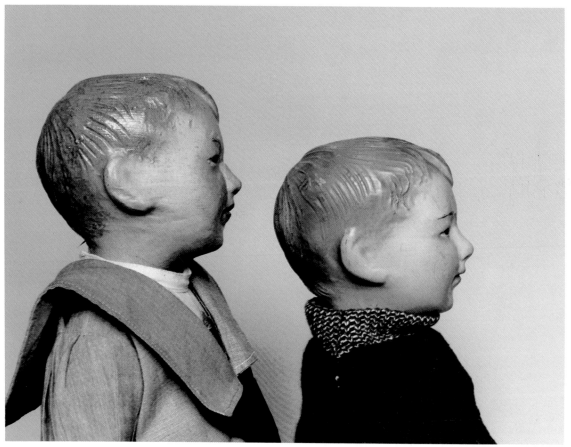

Illustration 102. In profile the "Transition Model" shows a less pointy nose and a deep line between the lips. His paint covers the wood grain. He is clearly smaller than the earlier model and is very attractive. The "Transition Model," on the right, is from the *Nancy A. Smith Collection.*

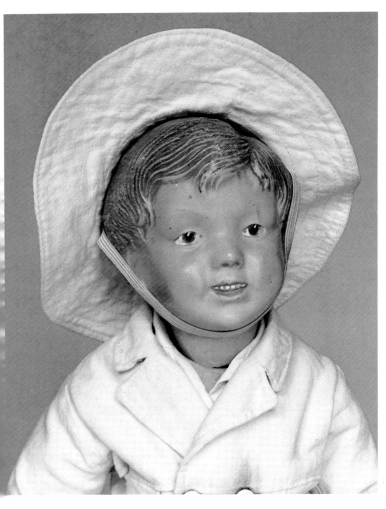

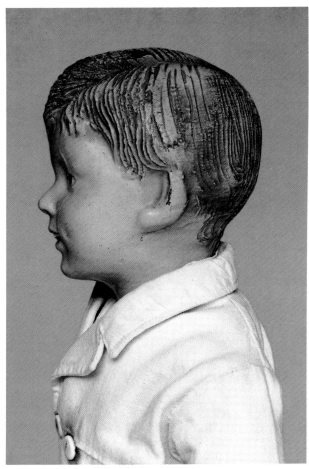

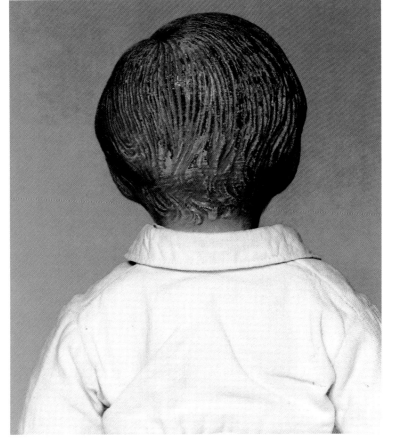

Illustration 103. 16in (41cm). This example of Doll 203 is dated to the "Transition Period" by his original factory-made Norfolk suit (model 16/605) which appeared in its double breasted form in 1912. He has the impressed mark.

Illustration 104. With his hat removed you can see the stronger hair modeling and the placement of his features lower on the face of Doll 203 than his earlier Graziano counterpart. Comparing these two versions of Doll 203 shows how Leslie was able to use the Graziano designs and adapt them to a younger child. Note the cheek dimple.

Illustration 105. The back of the hair of the Leslie doll is just as carefully modeled as the front. He even has ends curling at the nape of his neck.

Illustration 106. 16in (41cm). This nice early example of Doll 16/204 has particularly sharp modeling around his eyes. His pale skin and deep rose mouth and accent dots are typical of this period. He retains a soft blush on his cheeks and above his eyes. He has a small chin dimple.

Illustration 107. 16in (41cm). Doll 16/204 was a new design that came out in November 1911. He is similar to, but clearly younger, than Model 202. The eyelid and mouth modeling are particularly nice on this example. He even has a small chin dimple.

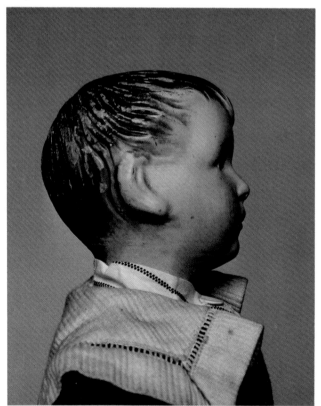

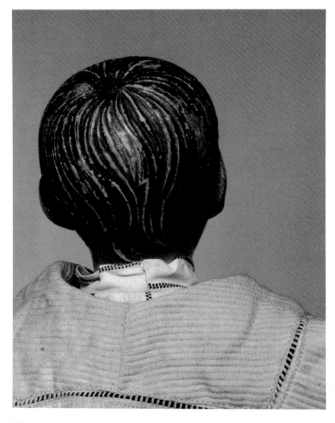

Illustration 108. Doll 16/204's rounded profile and lower features are those of a younger child. Additional carving of the hair hides the blur that occurs where the mold pieces meet.

Illustration 109. The back of this Doll 16/204 shows the strong "comb" marks typical of Schoenhut dolls.

300 Series — Wigged Girls

There are the same number of wigged girl models as there were in the initial catalogue, but many design changes have occurred.

Doll 300 is now the doll with the round face and a dimple in her chin that was to continue in production through 1923. Her eyes are larger and rounder than the Graziano model but still narrower than most of the other models in the Classic Period. Her hairstyle is a heavy, long curl wig, parted in the middle with no bangs and with ribbon bows holding it out of her face on both sides. One example has been studied that has the earlier non-grooved leg. Her face modeling is the same as that found in the Classic model 300. The details of eyelid creases and philtrum are unusually crisp. The paint is the thin, pale flesh color of the earliest dolls, and the wood grain shows through. The lips are a deep pink which is found on other early Transition examples, but the blush is a deeper, slightly more orange color which came into use at this time. The lip painting is a little fuller and softer on the earliest of these dolls making her a pretty child. Close inspection reveals that she has the same lower face and profile as the new "carved" hair boy 204.

Doll 301 is another entirely new doll. She is the classic model complete with her short bobbed hairstyle with bangs that continued to be produced through 1924. Her face has a rectangular shape with a soft round chin line, a short upturned nose and a slight double chin. Undressed, she has the 1911 slip rather than a union suit. She was offered with "blonde or brown" hair, as were all the wigged dolls. Her lower face has a remarkable similarity to the new 102, 103 and 104 models.

Doll 302 remains as one of the dolls apparently modeled on Kämmer and Reinhardt's model 101. Her heavy wig, parted in the middle, is in two long braids which are doubled just behind her ears. An example of her has been found with most of the paint gone which showed traces of iris outlining on her sharply carved intaglio eyes and a red line painted in her eyelid crease. She had stocking grooves in her legs indicating that she was from the later end of the Transition Line.

Dolls 303 and 305 still have identical smiling faces with different hairstyles. These dolls also have revised faces. The eyes have been rounded. They now have the six smaller teeth of a younger child. She has a strong profile with full high cheeks, sharp nose and pronounced chin. There are cheek dimples and a softer face line with a less overwhelming character look that was likely to be more appealing commercially.

Doll 303's short, neat bob with no bangs is parted on the left and held on the right side with a silk bow. Doll 305 has her long hair in two braids coiled in "snails" over her ears and held with neat bows high on the sides above her ears.

Dolls 304 and 306 are now the dolls which appear to have been based on Kämmer and Reinhardt's 114. These models were in the 1911 catalogue but were then sold as dressed dolls only. In the Transition catalogue they were sold both dressed and in a slip. The irises are no longer outlined, and a stocking groove has been added to each leg. This sweet pouting child has features placed low on her face. Some examples still have single-stroke eyebrows, but others, presumably slightly later ones, have feathered brows. Her cheeks are low and full. Her nose in profile is snub, and her upper lip thrusts out. Her chin line is firm with no double chin.

The hairstyles on these dolls are the same as those on the Graziano models which held the same numbers. 304 had braids which were held across the top of her head with bows. Doll 306 had a long curl wig parted in the middle.

Doll 307 appears to be the same smooth-eyed doll with a round face and slightly parted lips with teeth showing. It is hoped that someone will find an example of her to share with us.

 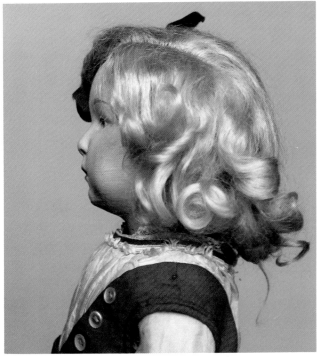

Illustration 110. 16¼in (41cm). The new Doll 16/300 was probably designed by Mr. Leslie. This early transition model has the thin pale paint, strong lip color and no leg grooves. The woodgrain shows through the paint. The modeling of her eyelids and chin dimple are clear and her blue eyes have strong intaglio carving. Her mouth has a fine straight darker red line running through the center. Her wig and silk dress are original. The incised mark is on her back. She dates to the end of 1911 or the beginning of 1912.

Illustration 111. In profile the new Model 16/300 shows a high round forehead, a much smaller nose and the softer chin line typical of a younger child. She has a round face as does the Graziano 16/300, but her eyes are rounder and her features are set lower in her face. Named Merilee by her original owner, her twin, Melvin, is shown in Illustrations 134 and 135.

OPPOSITE PAGE:
Illustration 114. 16in (41cm). This Doll 302 barely made it into the "Transition Period." She is much harder to find than the one based on K*R 114, and was not found in any of the early "Classic Period" advertising. She does appear in the transition folder, approximately November 1911. The only thing that allows her to be called "Transition" is the stocking groove cut in her leg. She also has a numeral "1" stamped into the back of her neck. This is the first wigged head shown in the earliest advertising.

Illustration 112. 16½ in (42cm). Even her tattered silk ribbon is original! Doll 16/301 is one of the new models that came out just six months after the company began doll production. She has a soft sweet face with strongly modeled eyelids. Her face, unlike the Graziano 301, is longer and more rectangular. Her nose is short and her lips are slightly parted with a dip cut into the lower lip. Until 1917 this doll had a short bob hairdo. Her button indicates that she is probably from the "Classic Period," as the earliest dolls do not have them in any of the company's literature. The dress appears to be factory original. If it is, it predates 1915. Even her union suit bow matches her hair ribbon. Her stockings and shoes are light pink. She has the leg groove and the incised mark.

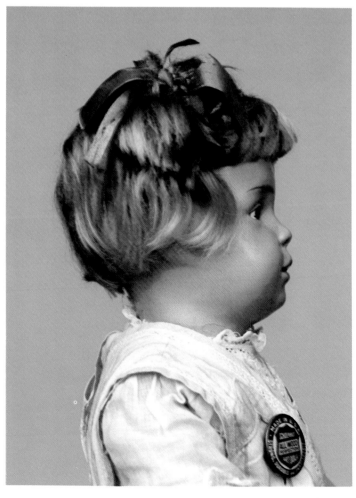

Illustration 113. The lower profile of Doll 16/301 seems to be the same as Dolls 102, 103 and 104 from the "Transition Period."

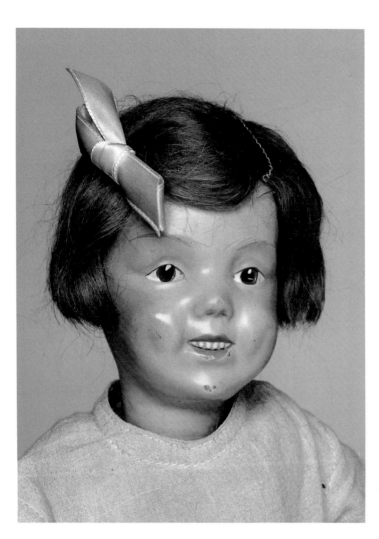

Illustration 115. 16½in (42cm). This doll came out in November 1911 as a Leslie redesign of the Graziano model. I have included her because even though her wig is not an original Schoenhut it is in the style that distinguishes Doll 303 from Doll 305. This doll has brown intaglio eyes with a deep brown lid line and a deep pink mouth with six strongly modeled teeth that have flesh color between them. She has good upper eyelid and cheek dimple molding and a slight lower eyelid. She has red eyebrows which just match her more recently acquired soft red mohair wig. She has the incised mark between her shoulders.

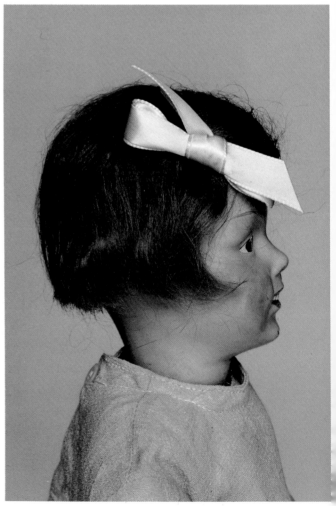

Illustration 116. Doll 303 in profile.

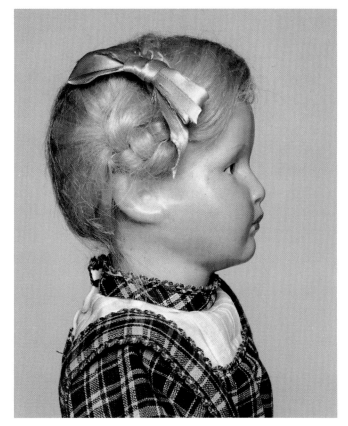

Illustration 118. The profile of Doll 16/304 is a little softer than that of the K*R model.

Illustration 117. 16½in (42cm). Doll 16/304 is an exact copy of 1911 Catalogue dress 705. It is her braids across the top of her head that makes her number 304. This child based on K*R's 114 appeared in the first Catalogue, but only in this dress. Her face had no number then. In November 1911 she took over number 304. This model continued to be made through the first half of 1912. She appears to be gone by the end of that year. She came as a blonde or a brunette. This one has blonde single-stroke eyebrows.

Illustration 119. A comparison of Kämmer and Reinhardt's 114 mold and Schoenhut's "Transition Model" 304 shows that Schoenhut based his 1911 model on the 1910 German doll that he brought back from Germany to his grandson Norman. The Kämmer and Reinhardt version which was modeled on the grandson of Franz Reinhardt has larger smooth eyes which achieve their depth by shading the grey blue irises on one side. The Schoenhut version has incised intaglio eyes with a raised white highlight dot. Both dolls had single-stroke eyebrows in the Graziano Period. When the Schoenhut dolls were revised in November of 1911, the painters began feathering the eyebrows. The Schoenhut doll still appeared in advertising in the Summer of 1912, but appears to have been dropped from the line before the end of 1912, as the new original designs became popular. The K*R doll appears taller because it is suspended up off the bottom of its base by the stand that was made for it. "Norman" K*R 114. 16½in (42cm). *Eleanor P. Swanson Collection.*

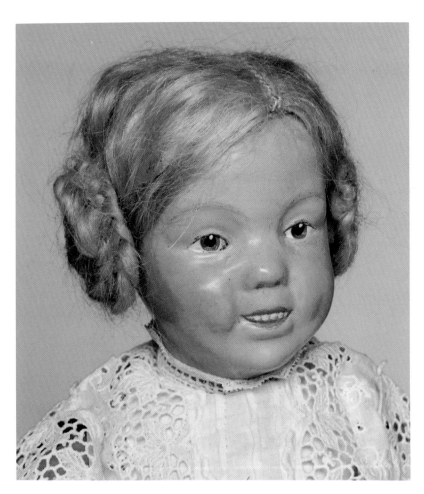

Illustration 120. 16in (41cm). This Doll 305 is again the Leslie version of the earlier smiling doll. Her rounder eyes and the placement of her feature makes her face that of a younger child. This makes her "prettier," and she sold well enough to stay on in the "Classic" line through 1916. Although her wig has been restored it is probably her original one styled in the "Transition" style of 305. Her brown intaglio eyes have both upper and lower eyelids molded. She has dark brown upper lid lashlines and blonde multi-stroke eyebrows. The brows are less sure in their painting than is usual and leads to the impression that her paint is not entirely original. Touch-up appears to be minor.

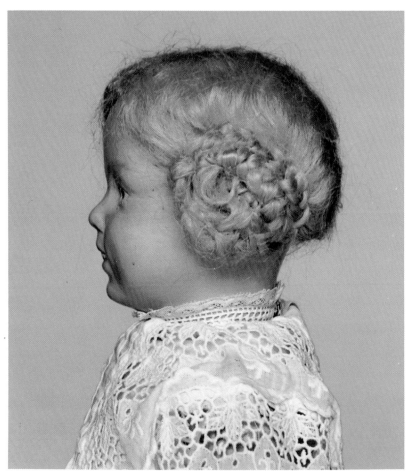

Illustration 121. The cheek dimple is strong enough to show even in this profile of Doll 305. Her six tiny teeth show but do not protrude.

Illustration 122. 16½in (42cm). The only difference between this 16/306 doll and Doll 16/304 is her hairstyle. Both dolls were offered as blondes or brunettes. This face became a part of the regular line of undressed dolls in November 1911. She continued in the line into the Summer of 1912.

Illustration 123. 16¼in (41cm). This example of Doll 16/306 has beautifully modeled eyelids accented with charcoal lid lines. Her intaglio eyes are very light blue. Her blonde coloring is carried through in her blonde single-stroke eyebrows. Her complexion is more florid than most early Schoenhuts. She has a gorgeous pale blonde original mohair wig. Her wonderful nurse's uniform is contemporary rather than original, but it fits her perfectly. She has the impressed mark. *Gail Hiatt Collection.*

400 Series — Wigged Boys

Doll 400 remains the little boy whose design was based on Kämmer and Reinhardt's 101. He now has a smoother finish and more natural coloring. He still has single-stroke eyebrows.

Doll 401 is changed entirely and is now the boy based on Kämmer and Reinhardt's 114. His description matches that of dolls 304 and 306. Examples have been found with single-stroke as well as feathered eyebrows. They also have the stocking groove. The iris of the eye is not outlined. His wig is a short, wavy bob, parted on the left side and brushed across his forehead in the same style as the earlier Graziano doll.

Doll 402 appears to be based on the original Graziano design, but he is considerably younger looking. His eyes are rounded and his features are set lower in his face. He smiles, but his mouth now has six "baby" teeth rather than four "second" teeth. He also has dimples in his cheeks. His smile is less gleeful, but it is also more innocent looking. His hair is parted on the left side, as was that of the earlier child with his number. Examples with this early hairstyle have single-stroke brows. Later in 1912 he was produced with a "Dutch bob" with no part in it. These dolls have feathered brows. He is the boy counterpart to Dolls 303 and 305. He did not remain in the line more than a year longer.

Doll 403 is now the round-faced boy with the dimple in his chin that remained in the line through 1924. The roundness of the face is similar to the Graziano model, but in all other ways he

is a new design; however, he still has the long curl wig with bangs in the "Fauntleroy" style. His dressed version is shown in the Fauntleroy royal blue velvet suit with a blouse trimmed with embroidery and ruffles. This doll is the boy counterpart to Doll 300 and apparently is also a wigged version of the new Doll 204. An example from this period has been found with early thin pale flesh paint and deeper rose mouth coloring. His original wig is styled in a wavy bob with a part on the left side and no bangs. This same hairstyle is found on the next model as well.

Doll 404 is a brand new doll. This doll is the boy version of the new 301 doll. As a boy, his short slightly wavy bob is parted on the left and brushed across his forehead with no bangs. He has a longer, more rectangular face than 403. His lips are fuller and appear ready to open. He has a soft round chin line in profile. He also is clearly related to the new models 102, 103 and 104. He stayed in the line, as a boy, through 1916.

In January of 1912 the company advertised that its new line of dolls would be ready for show on April 15, 1912, just eleven and a half months after the Schoenhut Doll first came on the market. The new line would be presented in four sizes. The "Transition" Period was therefore quite short with some of the models gone by April and others petering out later that summer. "Transition" models 100, 103, 104, 200, 201, 202, 302, 303, 306 and 400, are not shown in advertising after March 1912. Dolls 304 and 401 continued at least through that summer.

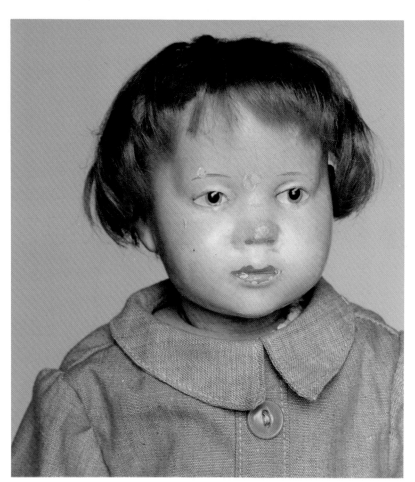

Illustration 124. 15½in (39cm). This is a particularly sweet example of Doll 16/400 from the early part of the "Transition Period." He has single-stroke eyebrows and brown lash line of the earliest dolls. His irises are not outlined and he has a stocking groove cut in his thighs. *Dot and Bud Hutton Collection.*

OPPOSITE PAGE:
Illustration 126. 16½in (42cm). What a collection of contrasts is shown in this all-original (except shoes) example. He has the pale pink flesh tone of the Graziano models with the deep red mouth and accent dots of the earliest "Transition Dolls." His iris is a single band of light blue, but his eyebrows are the single stroke of the earliest dolls. His blonde wig is thick and original, but very difficult to control. He has a distinct upper lid, folds under the eyes and a thrusting upper lip. He is clearly based on Kämmer and Reinhardt's Mold 114.

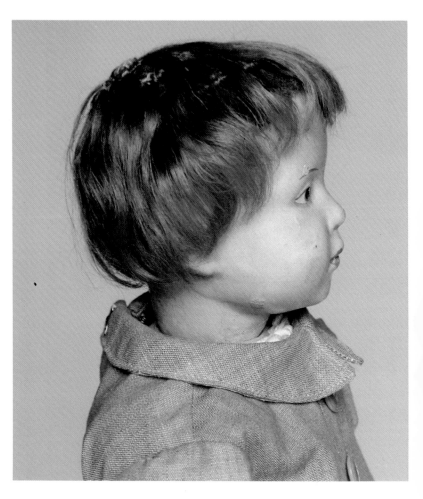

Illustration 125. This picture shows the heavy upper eyelid modeling, the short nose and small pointed chin of the 16/400 doll. *Dot and Bud Hutton Collection.*

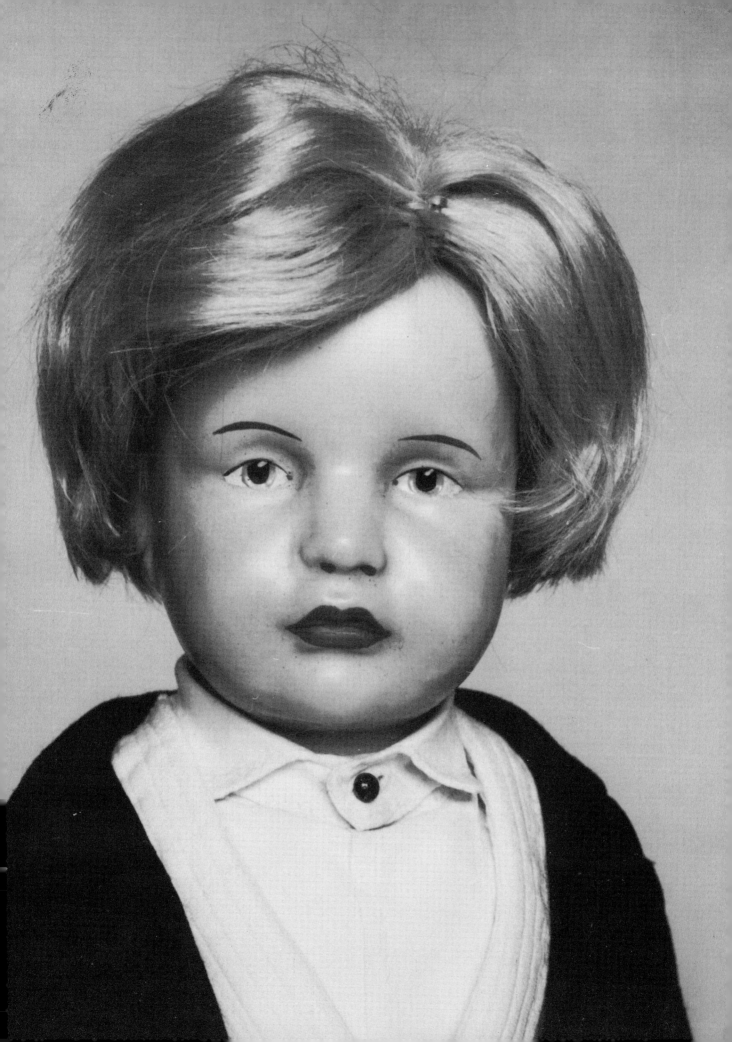

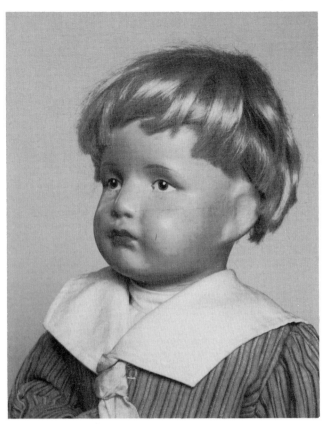

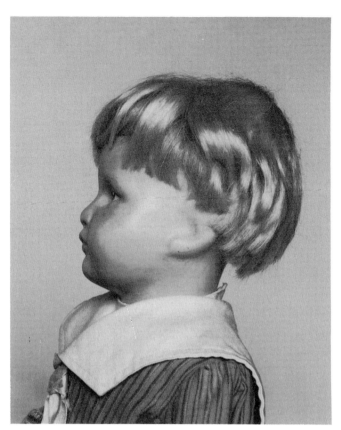

Illustration 127. 16½in (42cm). The replacement old mohair wig on this example had to be blonde. He has pale coloring, pink lips and accent marks with a fine red line running through his lips and light blue eyes. His blonde brows forced the decision. The modeling on this 16/401 is quite nice around the eyes and lips.

Illustration 128. The profile of Doll 16/401 shows that he has a determined chin.

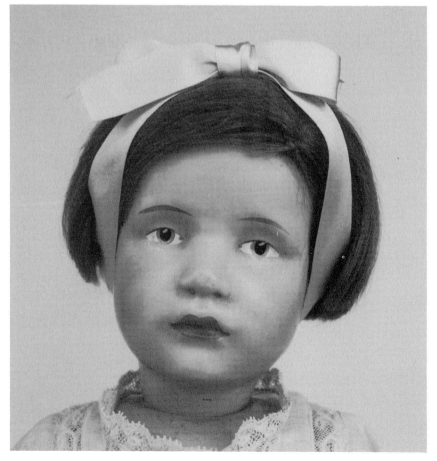

Illustration 129. This beautiful Doll 401 has been a girl ever since she was first purchased. The short immaculate bob as well as the boy's union suit give away the factory's intention, but the beautiful dress appears to be original and the stockings and boots were worn by girls as well as boys. Her coloring is with the natural tints that came in use at the beginning of 1912. The early single-stroke eyebrows are light brown. The bright blue intaglio eyes have dark brown upper lid lines. Her upper lids are lightly molded. *Photograph by Monty Moncrief. Becky Moncrief Collection.*

Illustration 130. 16in (41cm). This handsome brunette version of Doll 16/401 has very strong original lip color and the new oranger blush which began in the spring of 1912. He also has brown multi-stroke brows. His tosca mohair wig retains its original thickness and wave. His face captures the spirit of the Kämmer and Reinhardt 114 on which he appears to have been modeled. His intaglio eyes and feathered brows are Schoenhut variations. This model stayed in the line through the summer of 1912 and possibly beyond. *Roxanne LeMay Morison Collection.*

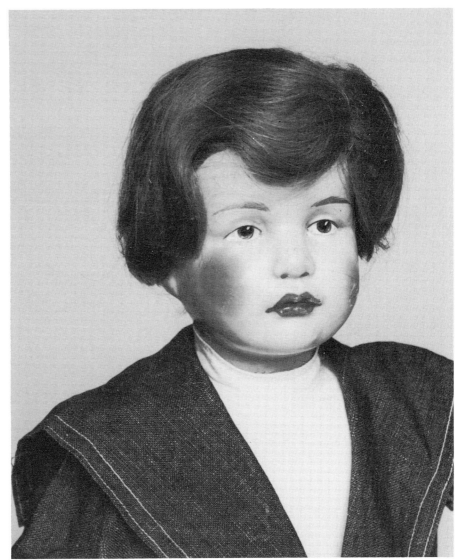

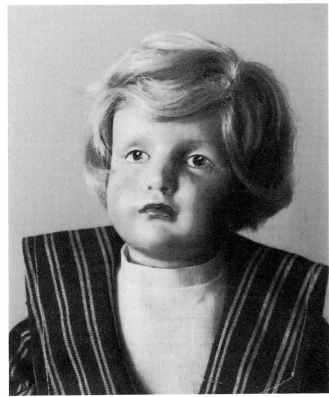

Illustration 131. 16in (41cm). The variation in color, as well as the sharpness of the modeling, really gives more variety to this particularly sweet model 16/401. The slight roughness around his left eye, the stronger lid temple modeling and his pale blonde eyebrows and hair all add to his appeal. His lips are strong and his blush is soft and even. *Diane C. Dustir Collection.*

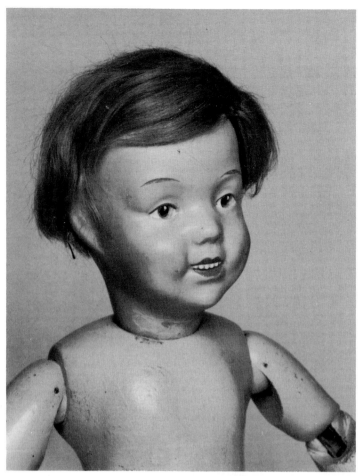

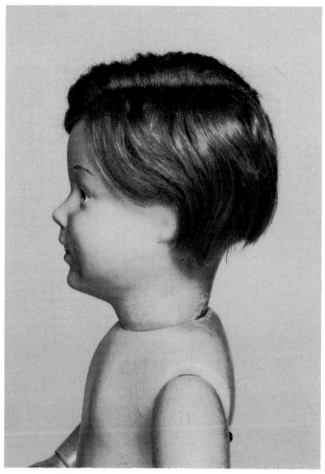

Illustration 132. 16in (41cm). This Leslie modification of the original Graziano Doll 16/402 is quite perky. He retains the single-stroke eyebrow of the earlier version and the strong pink lip color. His eyes are now round. His face is heart shaped and he has long dimples in both cheeks. His pupils are large and the light blue iris is very narrow. The temple modeling on this example is quite nice. The lightly modeled upper eyelids are lash-lined in black. He has a narrow red line under his sharply defined six teeth.

Illustration 133. The new profile, as seen on Doll 16/402, continues to have a strong chin line. The teeth show between the open lips, but do not protrude as did those of the earlier 402.

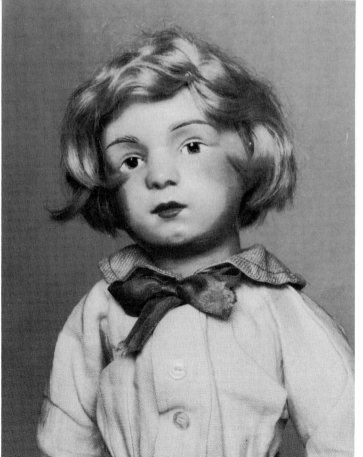

Illustration 134. 16¼in (41cm). This example of the new Doll 16/403 is a twin of Doll 16/300. (See Illustrations 110 and 111.) His pale pink skin is the same color as the Graziano models. The deep mouth color is typical of his period. The eyelid modeling, philtrum, lips and dimple are all clean and sharp. His wig with its side part is original. His suit, which is coordinated with his sister's dress is also original. He bears the incised mark and his legs have the new stocking groove.

Illustration 135. The profile of Doll 16/403 has a short nose and round chin line.

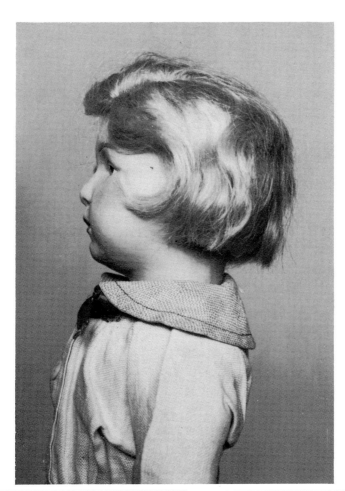

Illustration 136. 16in (41cm). This is the new Model 16/404 as shown in the "Transition" brochure. He is even factory-dressed and was produced with this face, wig style and costume as number 802. This is the boy version of the new 301 model and he also appears to have the same face and profile as Dolls 102, 103 and 104.

Illustration 137. The profile of new model 16/404 has the short uptilted nose, parted lips and slight double chin of this new and younger looking child.

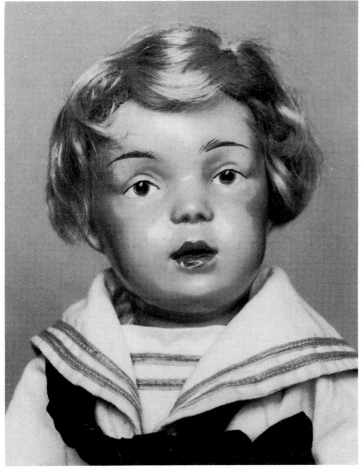

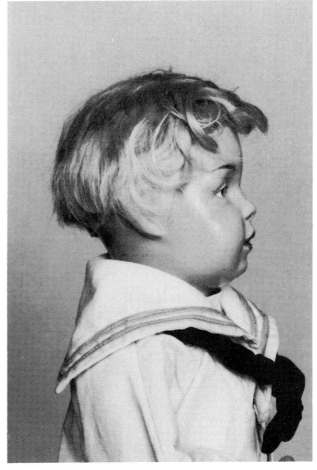

THE CLASSIC PERIOD
PART I
— APRIL 1912 to 1916

On February 3, 1912, Albert Schoenhut died suddenly in his sleep. The death was front page news in *The Evening Bulletin* that day and is found on page two of the first section in both *The North American* and the *Philadelphia Record* on the next day. The funeral took place on February 7, 1912, and was reported in a two-page obituary in the February issue of *Playthings* to have had several thousand people in attendance. He was not quite 63 years old, but he left a firm consisting of all six of his sons. He had already taken time away from the company to visit the Holy Land with his wife Emilie and daughter Caroline in mid 1911. He left his son Albert F. in charge during a period when his company was busily producing the most glorious special pieces, such as the band wagon for the Circus, as well as the "Teddy's Adventures in Africa," and the new Schoenhut Doll was rapidly changing its design.

Albert's sons were well trained to take over, and the fact that he already had let them to do it while he took an extended trip indicates that he had faith that they were ready and able.

The company appears to have gone on smoothly without the snags that trouble family enterprises that have been headed by a strong founder. According to grandson George Weber Schoenhut, son of Theodore, Albert gave exactly twice as many shares in the company to his eldest son Albert Frederick as he left to each of his other sons. Although this did not make him a majority shareholder, it was an indication that Albert F. was clearly expected to head the company, and at age 40 he assumed the presidency.

A booklet produced by the Schoenhut Company in 1912 listed the other sons in the following positions in the firm. Gustav Adolph, at 32, was the Treasurer. Theodore Carl, 30, was the Manager of the Mechanical Department. William George, 28, was the Manager of the Sales Department. Harry Edison, 22, became Manager of the Art Department and Otto Franklin, 20, was Assistant Manager of Sales.

The Schoenhut Company had made it a policy (according to an article in a 1908 issue of *Playthings*) to hire homeowners and family people to work for them. This was done because Albert believed that the work they produced would be more consistent in quality and the turnover of workers would be less. Until this time the toy industry had been a purely seasonal job with mass layoffs occurring after the new year and extending for six months until the factories got ready for the next big season, Christmas. Albert could not lay off workers of the quality he demanded and expect them to be waiting for him when the new season began. Therefore, the company made it a policy to have some work going on all the time. According to workers, the company also subcontracted itself during slack times to other companies outside the toy industry to keep its workers on payroll full time.

The company, which had reason to believe that it was the largest toy factory in the world, was in its prime, and the Schoenhut Doll entered its Classic Period when different faces were at their most prolific and greatest variety.

The January 1912 advertisement in *Playthings* announced, "Now watch our line grow...There will be four sizes —

14,16,19,21 inch Boys and Girls, more beautiful than ever." There were no pictures of the new line.

In March of 1912 there was another full-page ad in *Playthings*. The top half of the page was the picture seen in much of their advertising as well as on the doll box lids for the next 12 years. It has two dressed, wigged dolls holding up a shield with "SCHOENHUT ALL WOOD PERFECTION ART DOLL" written diagonally across it. (The dolls are models 301 and 403). Under the shield is an undressed "carved" hair doll (Model 205) in a reclining position.

The ad again states that there will be four sizes and that the "entirely New Catalogue of Schoenhut Dolls and Doll Dresses will be ready about April 15th." It also announced a new catalogue for the rest of the products due out at the same time. The picture at the bottom of the page gives a peek at the new line. It shows dolls of different sizes romping in a park scene. Some of the models are clearly recognizable as dolls 105 and 205. Others are less clearly identifiable.

By the time the June 1912 advertisement came out there were a number of dolls in the line that most people think of as true "Schoenhut dolls." There are no dolls from the original undressed Graziano models left. The only dolls left from the Graziano dressed dolls are those which took on the "Transition" Model numbers 304 and 401. The undressed girls are also shown in union suits for the first time.

During the "Classic" Period (a term invented for convenience to cover the most commonly known models) the number system used to identify doll models, hairstyle and even dress style had settled down into an easily understood pattern to aid the retailer and the company in making and filling orders. Up until then, although each face had its own model number, the dressed doll model meant a specific face, hair and costume. This meant that a dealer or even a customer who had no retailer nearby and wished to buy direct from the company, at retail price, had to send a long letter specifying any changes in combinations desired.

The new system allowed dolls to be ordered by size, face, wig style with a provision for wig color and, if desired, the dress style and color. The first number was the size desired (either 14in [36cm], 16in [41cm], 19in [48cm] or 21in [53cm]). The second number indicated which particular face and hair style was wanted (such as 102, the girl with "carved hair" in braids). The third number, if used, indicated the style of factory outfit desired if one wanted a dressed doll. The dolls were usually sent with a variety of hair and dress colors, but a customer could specify these colors as well. Thus a doll ordered as "14/313/530 Blonde" was easily identifiable as a 14in [36cm] girl with a long curl blonde wig and a "Peter Thompson" sailor style white linene dress with a blue collar and cuffs trimmed with narrow white braid.

Most of the boy's wigs had become one basic bob style with bangs and a center cowlick. One 16in (41cm) boy was still offered with a side-part bob with his long bangs brushed across his forehead, but this wig was not offered in the list of replacement parts in the catalogue. They were offered in blonde and "dark."

Illustration 138. 16in (41cm). This fine, all-original doll 16/101 has clear eyelid and brow molding. She has intaglio brown eyes with a brown upper lid line to suggest lashes. Her eyebrows and hair are dark blonde. There are a few strong comb marks, but on the whole her bobbed hair is quite smooth. She has the warm skin coloring of her period as well as the incised mark. *Sherryl Shirran Collection.*

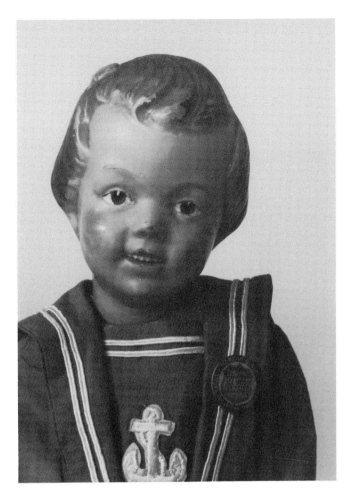

Illustration 139. The profile of Doll 16/101 shows some hand carving in her hair indicating that she is quite early. Her hair is also light brown. She has her original medium blue sailor dress, white stockings, union suit and white three-button boots as well as her pin.

Illustration 140. The comb marks in the 16/101's back view are lightly indicated in the tapered bob.

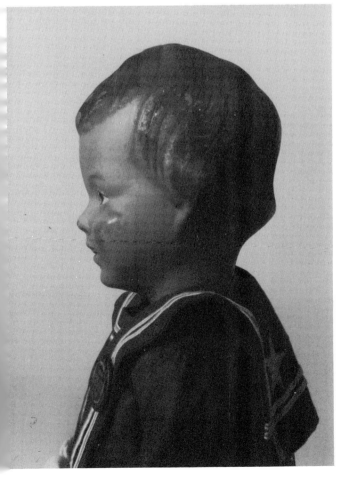

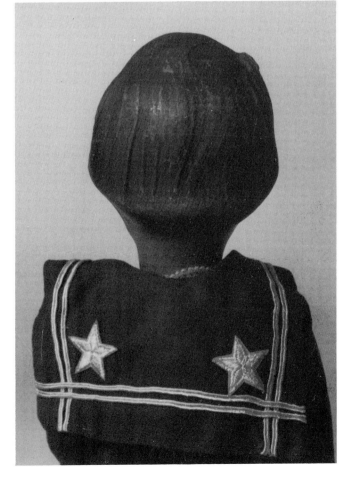

Most years "dark" simply meant tosca or a dull gold. In some years it seems to have meant a real brunette. The girl's wigs were still in a variety of styles on different faces. The replacement wigs were offered in three styles. One was a short bobbed style, with a left side-part and a silk bow holding the hair to the right, and bangs. The second wig had long curls, a side part with silk bow and no bangs. The third style was listed as "with plaits." These wigs were also offered in blonde and tosca. When a girl model was offered in more than one size, her hair style was usually the same in each size; however, a few of the dolls were offered in different hairstyles, depending on the size of the dolls. The variant hairstyle was simply indicated by an "X" after the model number. Even with the variety in wig styles offered, company catalogues stated that the use of tacks to fasten the wigs allowed the retailer to change the wigs easily in order to make a sale.

The "carved hair" doll numbers covered the hairstyle as well as the face. Examples found of carved hair dolls made in this period show both light and dark hair, as well as blue and brown eyes. There is, however, no provision in the wholesale catalogues for ordering light or dark hair on painted hair dolls. This, plus the scarcity of examples of variant hair color on any specific model, seems to indicate that these color changes were a result of paint availability or a special order rather than a regularly offered choice.

The designer of each character doll that survived the rapid period of model expansion that the company had gone through in the period from the end of 1911 to the beginning of 1914 is unknown. It is popularly believed that these dolls were designed by Mr. Leslie. However, Harry Schoenhut was 23 years old by the end of 1912 and was listed as Manager of the Art Department in company literature of that year. It thus seems more than likely that he participated in the design of at least some of these characters.

The series number pattern started with the first catalogue continued to be used. None of the original May 1911 models remained. Some of their model numbers were taken over by the new faces that had been designed by spring of 1912, and some model numbers were simply dropped.

The bodies of these dolls all had the groove cut into the thigh just above the knee, and the stockings were tied to the leg with a narrow silk ribbon. Dolls are still found with these ties intact. The torsos of these dolls appear to carry the incised, or impressed, mark on the back of the shoulders until about 1918. A few of the dolls have the oval sticker or decal mark. This indicates that the switch to the decal label occurred in about 1916 and that there may have been a period when these marks were used simultaneously.

The following models were offered:

The 100 Series — "Carved Hair" Girls

Doll 100 is gone from advertising by June 1912. Her number was not reassigned.

Doll 101 continues to be the young girl with molded short hair with a bow pulling her smooth hair to the right side. She generally has dark blonde painted hair with a pink or blue painted bow. During this period she came in the 14in (36cm) and 16in (41cm) sizes. Many examples from this period show clear eyelid modeling and detail in the hair molding. Gone, however, are signs of any additional hand carving to enhance the comb marks in the hair. Her eyes, which no longer have outlined irises, may be blue or brown. As with other "carved hair" girls with painted hair bows, the color of the bows has no set relationship to the color of the eyes. From 1917 to 1923 she was offered in the 14in (36cm) size only.

In that size she was part of the 1930 sale of "Kindergarten Dolls," all of which were "carved hair" previously discontinued models. These dolls were probably old stock freshened with new paint rather than a sign of new production. They are particularly smoothly finished with "suntanned" bodies. Dolls from this sale often have dark blonde hair even when the model was previously a brunette.

Doll 102 has survived from the "transition period" as the girl with heavy braids twisted behind her head and held with a sculpted and painted (pink or blue) bow. The nailed-on silk bows on the sides of her head are gone. Earliest examples have hand-carved details over the mold line. She appears in catalogues and in known examples with a rich dark reddish-brown hair paint or a "tobacco" shade of brunette and came with either blue or brown eyes. One example, with original paint, has been found with the dark caramel hair color. She appears to be from the 1930 sale of refurbished early "carved hair" dolls, but it is possible that she was a special order. This model must have been quite popular as she was made in all 4 sizes — (14in [36cm], 16in [41cm], 19in [48cm], 21in [51cm]). She is usually found in a worn state indicating that she was really played with and contributing to the feeling that she is "rare." In fact she became a company staple and was made in the two smaller sizes from 1912 right through 1923, giving her a longer production run than even *Miss Dolly*.

Doll 102 has the comfortable, stolid face found in photographs of little girls in small country schools taken in the years before World War I. Collectors seem to see her as a loyal friend who would stick by her more adventurous playmate. She is probably the model most desired by collectors. She is not a "pouty" or a "smiler." She simply is, and that is enough.

Doll models 103 and 104 which seem to have been hairstyle variants on 102 did not survive into this period. The similarity between their lower faces and that of 102 indicates that the company decided to test the market with all three models and retained the best seller.

Doll 105, was first shown in a *Playthings* advertisement in June 1912. Her short hair encircled by a thin ribbon band with a small neat bow in the back gives her a slightly more "well-kept" look. She appears to fit into either a small town or city setting. This doll is not a pouty, but she is also not comfortable looking. She appears to be really worried or at least concerned about what is going on around her. Her "sweet" face has full painted lips that often lose their paint on the upper edge as there is little sculpting detail to hold it. There is strong modeling where her lips meet, however, and this adds to her appeal. She also has strongly modeled eyelids and temples. She is usually found with brown painted hair. Her ribbon is either pink or blue and she was made with blue or brown eyes.

Doll 105 was produced in all 4 sizes through 1916 and in 14in (36cm) and 16in (41cm) sizes through 1923. She was also part of the 1930 sale.

Doll 106, the girl with the bonnet, also first appears in the June 1912 issue of *Playthings*. The designs on her cap and the colors used must have affected how she could be dressed. She has a very sweet face. It is less concerned looking than 105 but has sharper features than 102. There is a suggestion of a dimple in her right cheek which might deepen into a real one if she smiled. She also has a firm, slender lower face with a pointed chin. Her chin is slightly flattened on the point indicating the bone structure beneath, and larger examples appear to have a small chin dimple. Her profile, although still of a young child, is stronger than other carved hair girls. Her hair is modeled in short wavy wisps in front of her cap. It has been found with a dark blonde (caramel) colored paint or a fairly rich brown hair paint. Her eyes were either blue

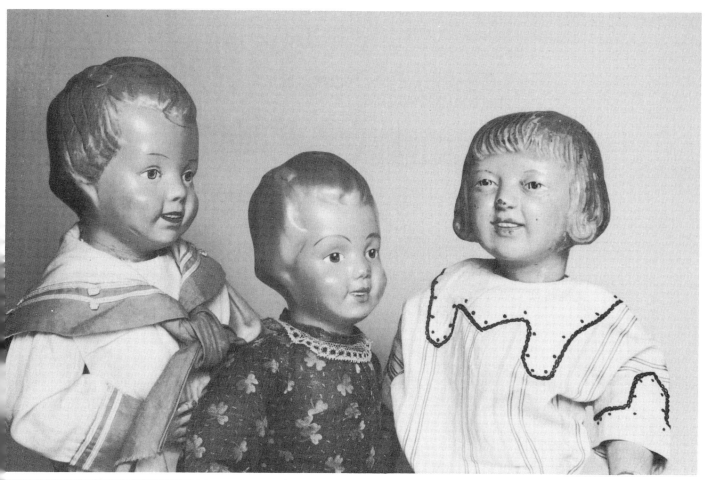

Illustration 141. Doll 101 fits all three of these dolls. They are examples done under the supervision of three different men. The doll on the right was designed by Graziano and was only produced from May to November of 1911. The doll on the left is the new version of 101 and appears to have been designed by Mr. Leslie. She was produced in this version from November 1911 to Spring 1912. The middle doll was the 101 that bears all the characteristics of Harry E. Schoenhut's work. Her surface is extremely smooth. There is much less hair, eyelid and philtrum modeling than that shown by the two earlier examples. The quality of the paint is excellent. All three dolls have the impressed mark.

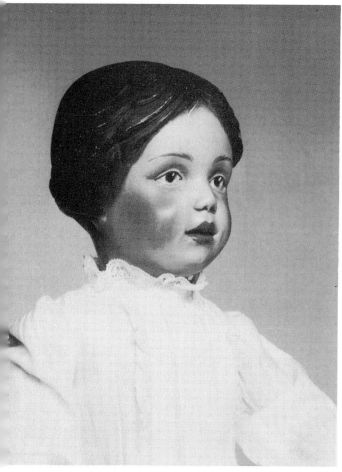

or brown. The upper and lower eyelid modeling appears to be strong on this child, and she is usually found with a deep intaglio iris and a sharply raised highlight dot. Her eyebrows are multi-stroke.

The decoration on her cream colored cap usually consists of red and yellow flowers, green leaves and gold trim. Other patterns and colors have been found which appear to be factory original. Doll 106 was the last of the "carved hair" girls. She was made through 1916 in 14in, 16in and 19in (36cm, 41cm and 48cm) sizes. Harry Schoenhut used the next number, 107, for his baby in 1913 indicating that the company knew they had already designed their last doll in this series. She was not part of the later sale of "Kindergarten Dolls."

Illustration 142. 19½in (50cm). This stunning Doll 19/102 is almost mint. Her upper lips are painted quite full just as they appear in the catalogue. She has her original union suit, shoes and stockings. Her dress is contemporary. She has light blue irises with large black pupils. In this large size tiny dimples show around her mouth and on her chin.

Illustration 143. 19¼in (49cm). This Doll 19/102 is old store stock recently found. Her upper eyelids are softly modeled, and she has a slight dimple to the right of her mouth. Her coloring is very even. The blush is on the outside of her cheeks. Her comb marks are quite clear. She has a union suit with a blue bow, and black Schoenhut shoes and stockings. *Gail Hiatt Collection.*

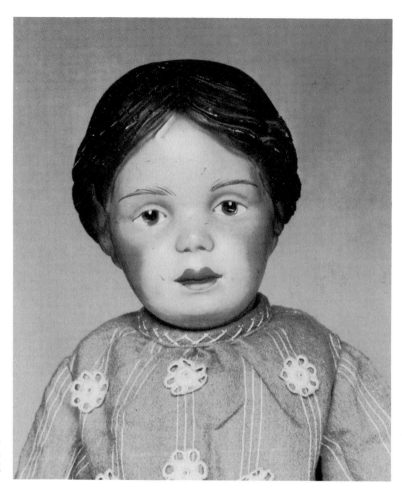

Illustration 145. The tobacco brown hair at the nape of the 19/102's head is completed with a blue bow.

Illustration 144. Doll 19/102 has fine comb marks throughout her hair. They show up particularly well with her lighter brown hair.

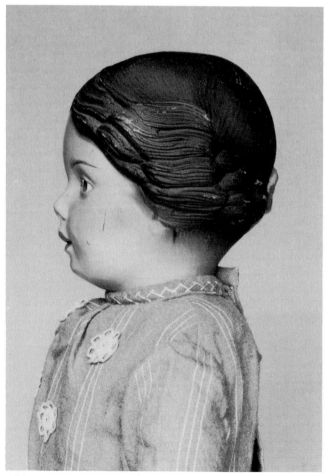

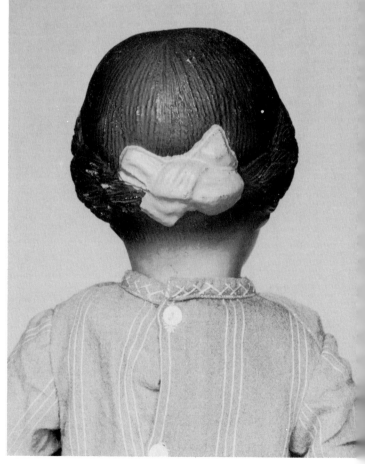

Illustration 146. This exquisite example of Doll 19/105 is nearly perfect in every way. Her deep brown intaglio eyes have both upper and lower lid modeling. She has black upper lid lash lines and feathered brown eyebrows. Her mouth has deep modeling between the lips. Her high upper lip is painted to fill its soft modeling. The blush is intact on her cheeks and above her eyes. *Photograph by Monty Moncrief. Becky Moncrief Collection*

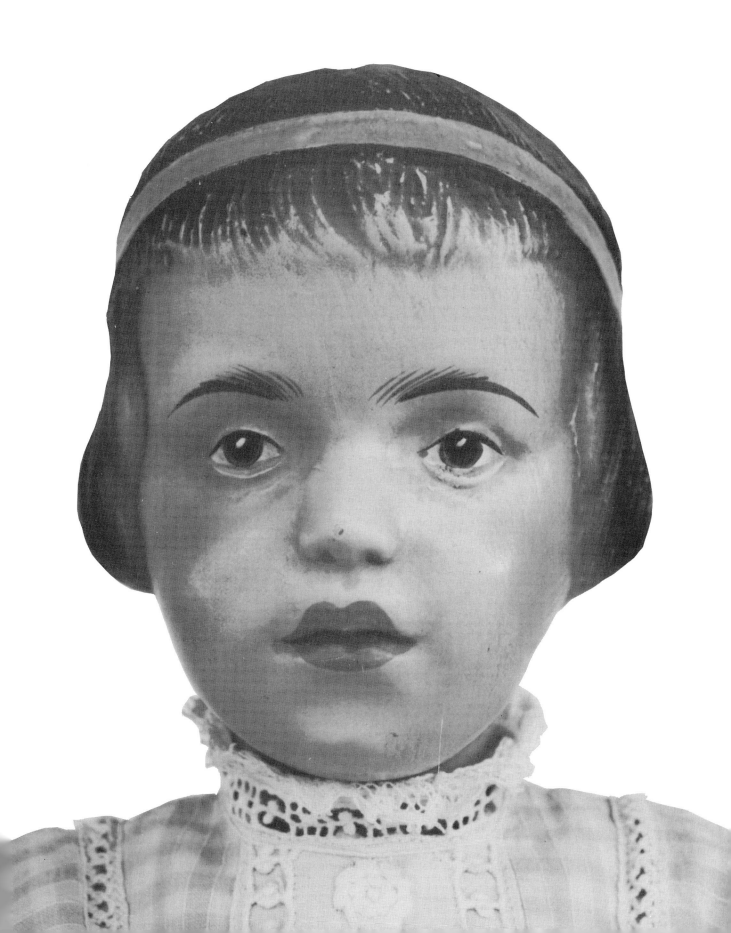

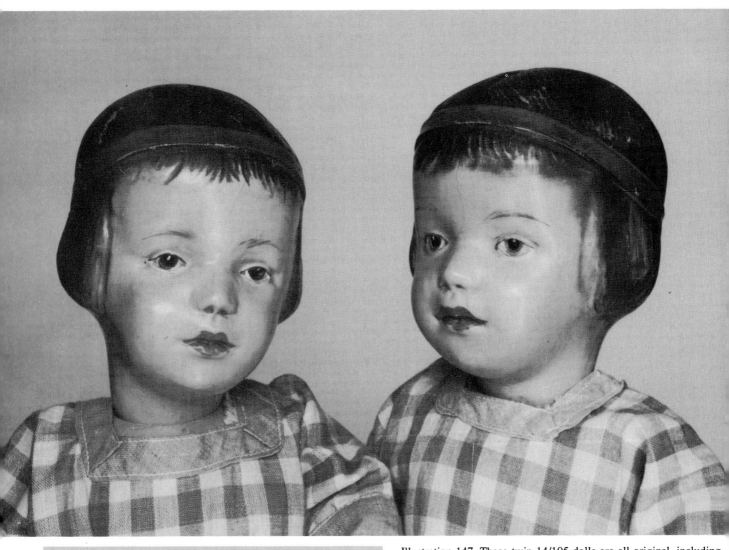

Illustration 147. These twin 14/105 dolls are all-original, including their stands. The blue eyed one has blue shoes. The brown eyed girl has brown stockings and brown slippers. Like most twins they have subtle differences. Even using the same molds the blue eyed doll seems to have a wider face and larger eyes and mouth.

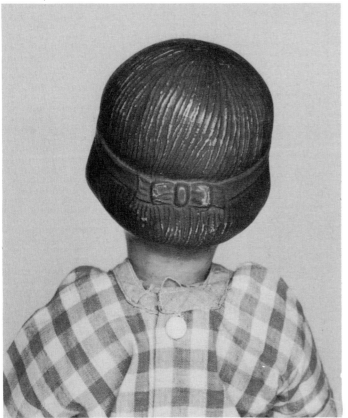

Illustration 148. As with most of the "carved hair" dolls finished in the hydraulic hot press there are fine comb marks in the back of the hair of the 14/105.

Illustration 149. 22in (56cm). This example of Doll 21/105 has both lower and upper eyelids modeled. She has a more peaceful look than many examples of her mold. She has pale skin with good blush on her cheeks and above her eyes which are medium brown intaglio with dark brown upper lid lines. Her mouth and accent dots are a medium pink. There is a red line between her lips which follows the modeling of her lips. Her eyebrows are fine and multi-stroke. They are straight and extend beyond her eyes. She has the decal mark.

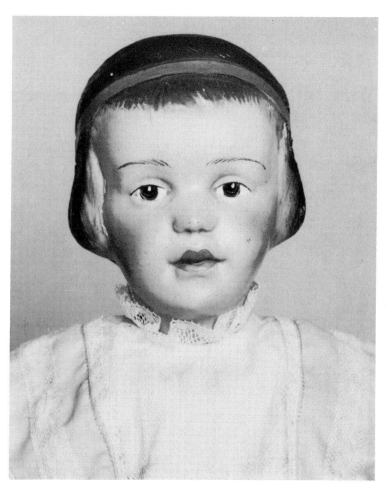

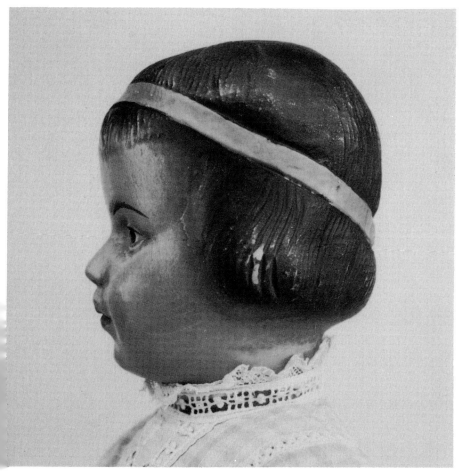

Illustration 150. The profile of Doll 19/105 shows that her hair is sprayed brown. The soft pink hair ribbon is hand painted. She appears to have some additional hand carving in her hair. Her profile is very similar to that of Doll 310 and the same child may have been the model for both dolls. *Photograph by Monty Moncrief. Becky Moncrief Collection.*

77

Illustration 151. 15in (38cm). Another blue eyed 14/105 dressed perhaps as a World War I "ally." Her dress is supposed to be Persian (Iranian). It is original and quite beautiful. Underneath it is her original union suit black stockings, with their original black ribbon ties and black leather slippers. Her coloring is soft and matte.

Illustration 152. 20in (51cm). This Doll 19/105 has strong blue intaglio eyes and well modeled upper and lower eyelids. She has dark brown very fine upper lid lines and then multi-stroke brown eyebrows. Wood grain and turning marks show through her very smooth shiny paint. She has strong pink mouth, nostrils and tear ducts with a light red line that follows her lip modeling curves. She has blush on her cheeks and a bit on her chin. Her iris paint extends beyond their intaglio modeling making her eyes appear larger. She has the decal label. *Regina A. Steele Collection.*

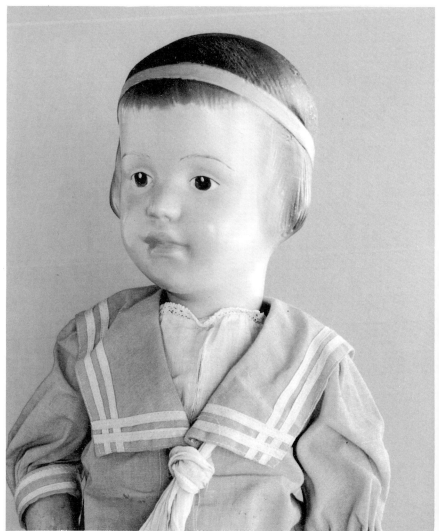

Illustration 153. 16½in (42cm). This stunning example of Doll 16/106 is almost perfect. She is a wonderful warm color with no wood grain showing. She has deep brown intaglio eyes with good upper and lower lid modeling. Her upper lid lines are dark brown as is her sprayed hair. Her eyebrows are feathered and slightly fly-away in the insides. She has a dimple in her right cheek and a slight one in her chin. There is blush on her cheeks, above her eyes and on her chin. The simplicity of her old white dress shows off her beauty. She has the decal mark. *Sara Kocher Collection.*

Illustration 154. 17in (43cm). This 16/106 has very strong modeling. Her comb marks, eyelids, dimples and philtrum are deeply indicated. She has light brown intaglio eyes with very dark brown upper lid lines. Her bonnet has the more frequently found yellow and red flower pattern with gilt trim. The tiny leaflets are lime green. *Regina A. Steele Collection.*

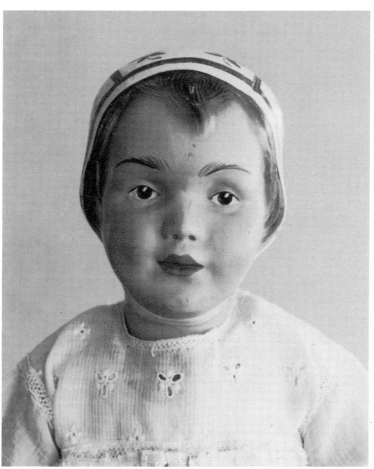

Illustration 155. 17in (43cm). This sweet example of Doll 16/106 has brown hair peeking out from her plain cream bonnet. She has feathered brown brows over her brown well modeled eyes, a strong pink color on her lips and accent dots and a deeper red line between her lips. All her paint is original, and her bonnet was never decorated. She has the oval sticker on the back of her shoulders. The profile is clear on this example with no wear on it.

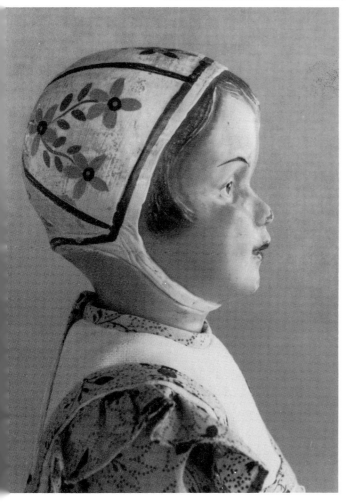

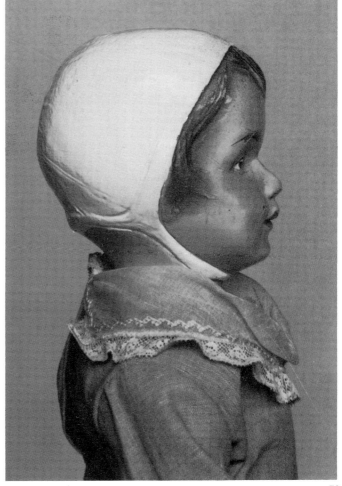

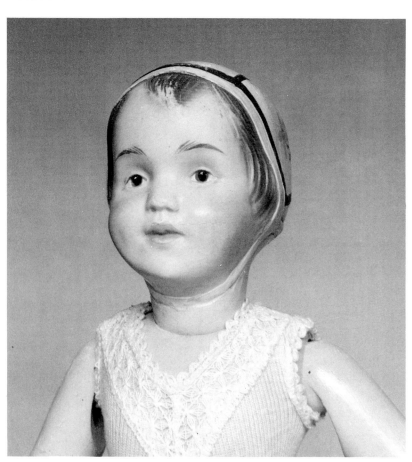

Illustration 156. 14½in (37cm). This smallest sized Doll 106 is a superb example. She has dark brown intaglio eyes with both upper and lower lids molded and accented with brown paint lines. The lower lid line is very thin and also translucent. She has a strongly raised highlight dot which sticks out beyond her upper lids and feathered dark brown eyebrows. Her paint is all-original and the blush and all details are strong. Her original union suit has a blue bow and she has white stockings and shoes. She has the impressed mark. *Nancy A. Smith Collection.*

BOTTOM LEFT:
Illustration 157. 16½in (42cm). This lovely example of Doll 16/106 has just enough wear to show all the comb marks in her hair. Her decoration is all there. She has deeply incised and very blue intaglio eyes. She has black upper lash lines and multi-stroke brown brows. Her lips and accent marks are a deep pink with a light red line between her lips. Her bonnet is the most usually found style — cream with red and yellow flowers, green leaves and gold trim. She has the oval decal on the back of her shoulders. *Photograph by C. Lee James. Virginia Schoenfeld Collection.*

BELOW:
Illustration 158. The bonnet of the 16/106 in the *Sara Kocher Collection* is the most frequently found version. It is cream with yellow flowers on the side panels and red flowers on the top panel. The painting is very sure and clean. The gold trim on this bonnet still has its shine.

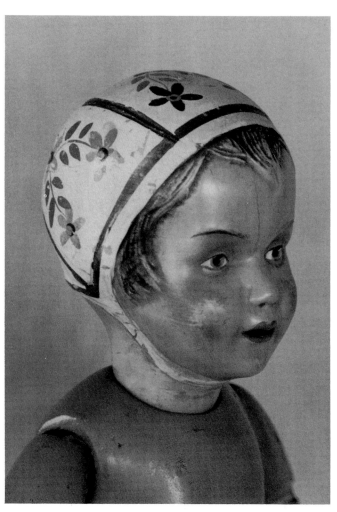

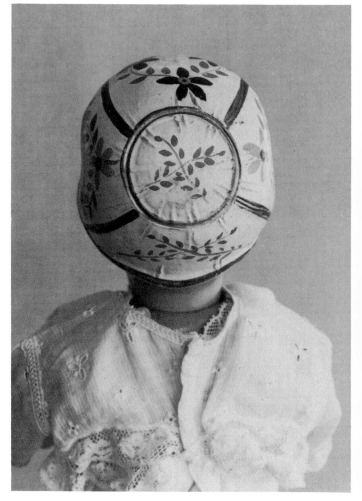

Illustration 159. 19½in (49.5cm). One is so used to thinking of this model as sweetly serious and sometimes even sad that coming across this 19/106 is a bit startling. She has such a broad, pleasant and comfortable face that her personality is quite different from her sisters. She has a slight smile, and her lips are wider and less sharply peaked than we are used to. She has brown hair with strong comb marks peeking out from her cream bonnet with red and yellow flowers, green leaves and gilt trim. Her light brown brows are feathered. She has lash lines and light blue intaglio eyes. Her dress is contemporary and appropriate even as it is as startlingly different as her facial decoration. Her mark is the decal placed upside down between her shoulders.

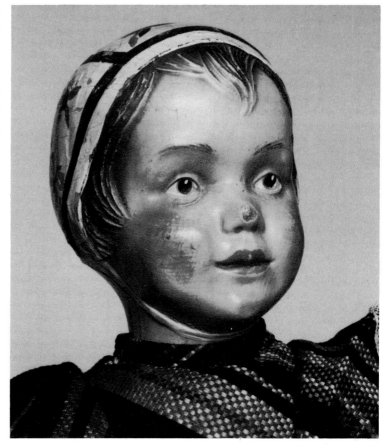

Series 200 — "Carved Hair" Boys

Doll 200, is gone from production.

Doll 201, the carved hair version of Kämmer and Reinhardt's 114 or "Hans" is also gone from advertising in 1912. He resurfaces briefly in a 1930 sale of "Kindergarten Dolls."

Doll 202 with his placid, older face was also gone. His model number, as well as those held by 200 and 201, was not reassigned to another face.

Doll 203, with his rounded eyes and younger face which had first appeared at the end of 1911, was a survivor. He now has strong comb marks in his wavy hair. Unlike some of the "carved-hair" boys of this period, these comb marks are in the front as well as the back of his hair and only a slight "blur" marks the sides of his hair where the mold seams meet. He has dimples clearly impressed in each cheek adding to his cheerful appearance. Although he is obviously modeled on the same face as that used in models 101, 303/305, and 402, his dimples are more clearly defined. The stronger teeth modeling in 203, as well as the slight space between them and his lower lip, add to the impression of a slightly more joyful smile. Whether this impression is due to a particularly strong example (much like bisque heads that are thought to have been poured in a fresh, new mold because the modeling details are so sharp) or a real difference in this model is impossible to say. There are not a lot of them around to compare. Perhaps more examples will surface, as interest in these dolls increases.

His strong profile has a sharp nose and a firm chin line. Although he has fat cheeks, he is not a chubby child or even one with "baby fat." His six small teeth indicate that he has not yet lost his baby teeth, but the rest of his features indicate that he is probably beyond kindergarten age.

Doll 204 which appeared in the first redesign at the end of 1911 continues into this period. This doll has many similarities to Doll 202 and is even difficult to distinguish from it in early catalogues. Studying the real dolls makes the differences quite obvious. Doll 204 is clearly a younger child. His features are set lower in his face, giving them the proportions of a very young boy. He has his short hair brushed forward with a swirl in his forelock. This forelock does not have the extra tiny curl at the end, as does that of model 202. 204's surface modeling is much smoother than that of 202, and there are no signs of hand-carved detail or the roughness of the modeling found in 202. His eyes are much rounder and have not yet been found with the two-tone iris.

Doll 204 is one of the models found with both light and dark painted hair, although there is nothing in the catalogues of this period to indicate these differences or that one could order them specifically. These different shades of hair in a "carved-hair" model are clearly shown in the photographs in the 1911 and 1912 catalogues, indicating that originally these differences were standard. Like the other models, 204's intaglio eyes came in either blue or brown. Doll 204 was made in the 16in (41cm) size only through 1916. He also appears in the 1930 catalogue sale of the "Kindergarten Dolls." In this catalogue his picture is shown in the 14in (36cm) size as well, but the number beneath that picture is 207.

Doll 205, shown in *Playthings* in June 1912, was a completely new design. He does not appear to be as young a child as 204. He shows less baby fat, and his features are more in the center of his face than the bottom half. He has an attractive face, although it seems blander than most of the characters. His eyes, which were painted either blue or brown, are intaglio, but the lids are less strongly modeled than those of some other Schoenhut characters. His longer hair which has been found in both blonde and brunette paint (although considerably more frequently in a rich reddish brown) is not very strongly modeled in the front. The side waves are raised, but softly modeled, and subject to early paint loss. In contrast to this softness in modeling the "comb

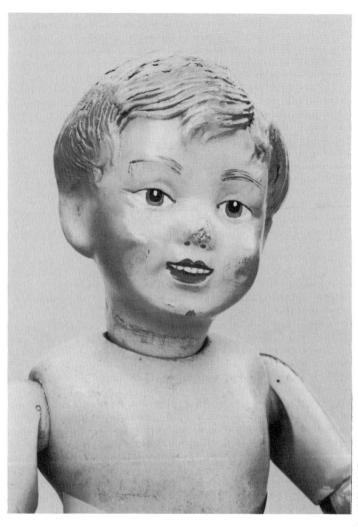

Illustration 160. 16in (41cm). This delightful 16/203 combines two different periods. He was made from November 1911 to 1916 only, but his paint details are from the years 1921-1924. The "stacked" brown eyebrows are clearly factory style from that period. His body also has the suntanned look and has been painted after assembling indicating that he was sent back to the factory for repainting as least five years after he was made and maybe as long as ten years. The company only offered repaint on a model for one or two years after its run was completed. Schoenhut had apparently survived its customer, but he is painted as dolls were then painted rather than copying an earlier example. His hair modeling has very uneven comb marks with some areas that are almost smooth. He has the incised mark. *Nancy Loisch Collection.*

marks" are strongly apparent in the back of his hair which turns under against the nape of his neck. His hair is brushed across his forehead in smooth, even bangs. It curls over the top of his ears, almost completely covering them.

This longer hair gave him a tremendous sales advantage over the other boys. If a dealer ran out of "carved-hair" girls and one was needed immediately (or at least before another could be ordered from the company), a simple costume change or the addition of a dress to an undressed doll could produce an instant "girl," and a sale was saved. This also worked if he were given to a boy who did not want him, or if he arrived in a house where dolls for little boys were not accepted, and he was transferred to a sister. Thus, although this doll may seem to have less character than others produced by the company, he was a marketing success and was the only "carved-hair" boy to survive past 1916 in any size. In fact, like models 101, 102, and 105 he enjoyed a longer production run than most of the wigged character girls and *Miss Dolly!*

Doll 205 was produced in all four sizes (the largest measuring 22in [56cm], although the catalogue stated it was 21in [53cm]) from April 1912 through 1916, and in the 14in (36cm) and 16in (41cm) sizes through 1923. He also reappeared in the two smaller sizes in the 1930 sellout.

Doll 206, a new design, has many similarities to doll 205. He has the long, softly waved hair that almost covers his ears. The hair is more strongly "carved" above his forehead. Even the side hair is a little more modeled than that of 205, although there is still a real "blur" line over and above the ears at the mold line. The back of his head has the cowlick and strong "comb marks" typical of the

other boys. His lips are thinner than those of 205 and are slightly parted to show two upper front teeth. He has an alert, curious look and gives a less bland impression than that of 205. So far his hair has only been found painted a dark brown. His eyes are slightly more strongly modeled than those of 205, but seem less strongly incised than those of the wigged girl model 309 who strongly resembles him.

Doll 206 was made only in the 19in (48cm) size through 1916. It is not clear, yet, when his production began. He is in the 1914 catalogue and may have been made as early as 1912.

Doll 207, another new design, is the last of the "carved hair" boys. He has a very sweet and young face. As with model 204, his facial features seem to be concentrated in the lower half of his face. He is not a chubby child, but he has the softer features of a younger child. He has a small round "pug" nose. His upper and lower eyelids are strongly modeled, and his eyes are intaglio. A flattened "M" shape is deeply cut between his upper and lower closed lips.

Doll 207's curly hair is brushed forward from his crown on the top. It has a short definite curl in the center of his forehead. Curls cover the tops of his ears. The strong comb marks in the back of his hair indicate waves ending in short curls at the nape of his neck. There is additional hand carving to complete the strong modeling of his hair.

Doll 207 was made only in the 14in (36cm.) size through 1916. He is difficult to distinguish from the earlier Doll 200 by looking at pictures alone. Comparisons of the actual dolls show that 207 has a wider lower face, and heavier cheeks. His features are placed lower in his face and in profile his chin is more pronounced. His eyebrow decoration is multi-stroke. Finally his hair (in the examples studied) has more "comb marks" in it. Doll 207 is shown in the 1914 catalogue and may date as early as the end of 1912. His number, but not his picture, is in the 1930 sale of "Kindergarten" dolls.

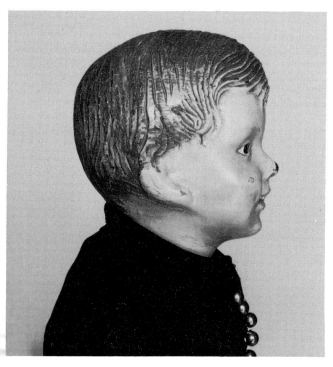

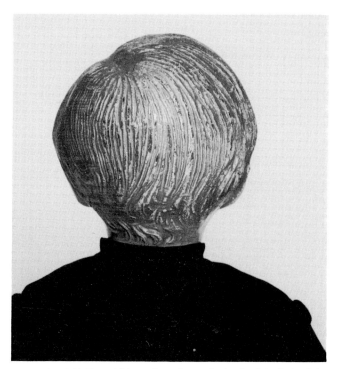

Illustration 161. 16in (41cm). This 16/203 boy is delightful in spite of his wear. He has excellent hair detail even over the mold line. His hair is brown and his eyes are blue. He has dimples in both cheeks. He has his original black stockings and shoes and a marvelous soldier uniform with navy blue wood tunic with brass buttons and a ribbon for valor. *Dolores Hoover Collection.*

Illustration 162. Beautiful comb marks on the back of the hair of the 16/203 soldier end in small curls at the nape of his neck.

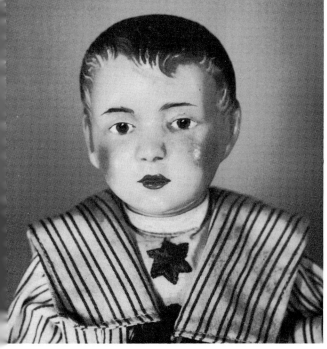

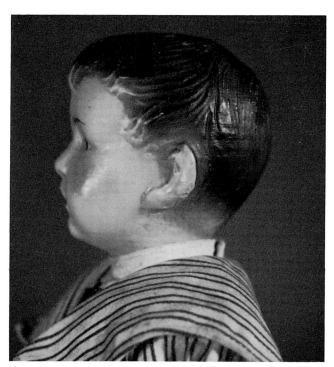

Illustration 163. 16in (41cm). This is a very special example of Doll 16/204. He has a pinkish complexion with an orange tone to the blush on his cheeks and above his eyes. His lips, nostril accents and tear ducts are coral with a slightly deeper tone filling in between his lips. His feathered eyebrows and hair are dark brown as is his upper lid line. His strongly modeled intaglio eyes are medium brown. His finger-nails are very pale pink. His modeling is sharp with upper lids and a slight chin dimple. He is completely original in suit 813 with original blue star and melting red silk ribbon tie. He has white stockings and oxfords. *Photograph by Quentin O'Sullivan. Diane C. Dustir Collection.*

Illustration 164. The features of Doll 16/204 are placed low on his face, as are those of a young child. He has the characteristic large Schoenhut ears. His hair is softly modeled in the front and sides with hand carving over the line where the mold front and back meet. The rear of the head has strong comb marks and curly tendrils on the back of the neck. *Photograph by Quentin O'Sullivan. Diane C. Dustir Collection.*

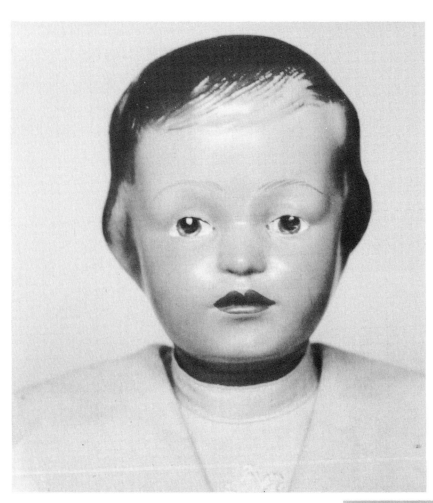

Illustration 165. 16¾in (43cm). This 16/205 is in remarkably good shape. His incised mark dates him in the first half of this model's production (1912 to 1923 in this size; this example 1912-1917 or 1918). The only wear is on his hair in spots where there are no comb marks to hold the paint.

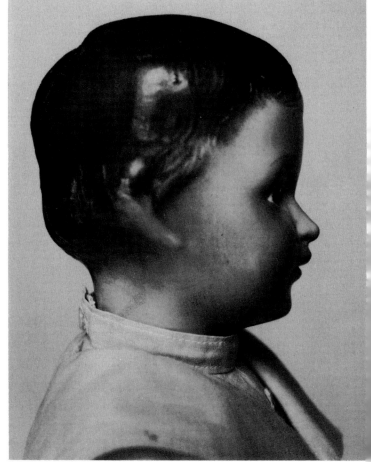

Illustration 166. As this profile view of Doll 16/205 shows, there are no comb marks to cover the band created where the two halves of the heated, hydraulic press molds met. His profile is very distinct with a prominent upper lip and chin and a high forehead.

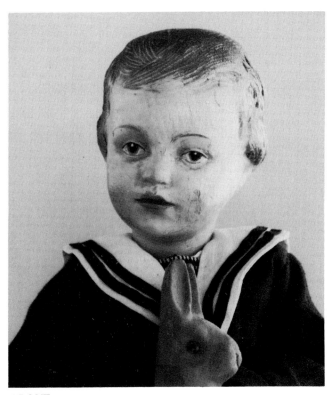 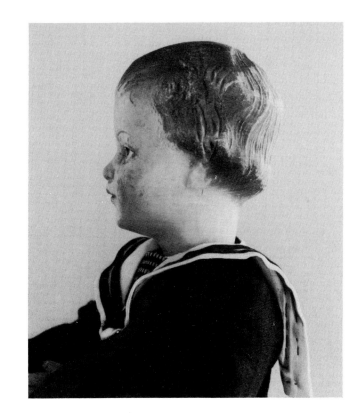

ABOVE:
Illustration 167. 16½in (42cm). There is diagonal wood grain showing through the thin paint on this early 16/205. He has upper and lower lid modeling and a nice philtrum groove. His light blue intaglio eyes have very large pupils and charcoal upper lid lines. His brown brows are lightly feathered. His mouth and tear ducts are pink. He has no nostril dots. A slight blush remains on his cheeks. The molded brown comb marks are strong in the front. He has the impressed mark. This doll is far from mint shape, but he is very appealing. *Regina A. Steele Collection.*

ABOVE RIGHT:
Illustration 168. There are hand carved comb marks over the seam line on the sides and top of the head of the early 16/205 boy.

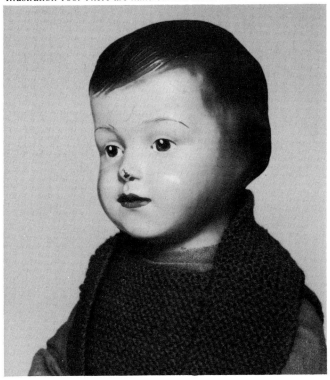 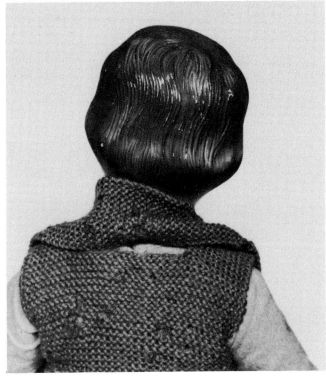

ABOVE:
Illustration 169. 22in (56cm). This superb example of Doll 21/205 is in his original World War I Army uniform. On top of that he has a hand knit vest, scarf and even a ski helmet to protect him from the cold on the Western Front. His modeling is quite good for a doll this large. The biggest Schoenhuts tend to be less crisp in their detail. This one has deep blue intaglio eyes, dark brown hair and eyebrows which are still intact and nice philtrum, temple and eyelid detail. *Louise H. Christoffers Collection.*

ABOVE RIGHT:
Illustration 170. As is usual with the "carved hair" dolls the comb marks on the back of the hair of the 21/205 doll are strongly indicated.

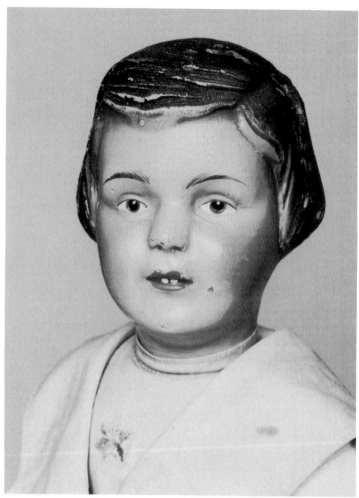

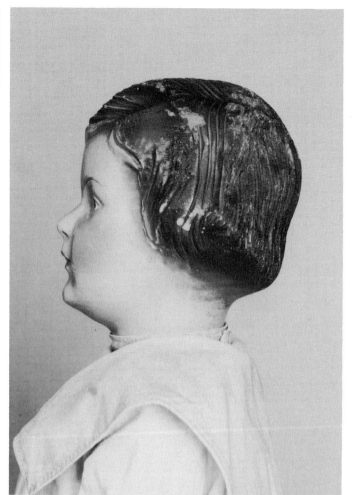

Illustration 171. 19¼in (49cm). This boy is properly called Doll 19/206/ 812 blue for he is completely factory original (although the blue on his suit is quite faded). He appears to be an older child with a very direct gaze. His smaller blue intaglio eyes have strong upper and lower lid modeling. His upper lids are lined with dark brown. He has brown feathered brows. He has blush on his cheeks, above his eyes and on his chin. His mouth, nostrils and tear ducts (which are very tiny) are pink. He has a light red line between his lips and two teeth show. He has the impressed mark.

Illustration 172. The profile of the 19¼in (49cm) boy is as strong and direct as the front of his face. The features are not crowded into the lower half of his face which adds to the feeling that he represents an older child. His longish bob is very similar to that of Doll 205 and appears to have some additional hand carving in the deep grooves over the mold line.

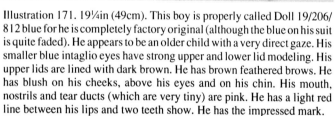

Illustration 173. Back view of Doll 19/206, showing how the hair is brushed back and to the right side and hangs straight down on the side. The deep grooves appear to be hand carved. He has the impressed mark. Like many of the "carved" hair Schoenhuts this model has strong comb marks in the back of his hair. *Ella and Larry Corn Collection.*

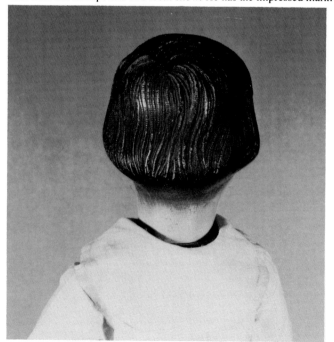

OPPOSITE PAGE:
Illustration 174. 14¼in (38cm). This slightly sad little boy 14/207 has beautifully incised eyelids above and below his tiny blue intaglio eyes. His upper lids are lined with fine translucent charcoal lines. He has short feathered brown brows. He has a broad short nose. His mouth, nostrils and tiny tear ducts are a bright pink. He has a light red line between his lips. His orangy blush is intact on his cheeks and above his eyes. He has his original union suit under his very well made sailor suit which is not old, but is made from old fabrics complete with bone buttons on his bell bottom pants. He has the impressed mark. His dark brown hair is strongly molded on front, sides and back.

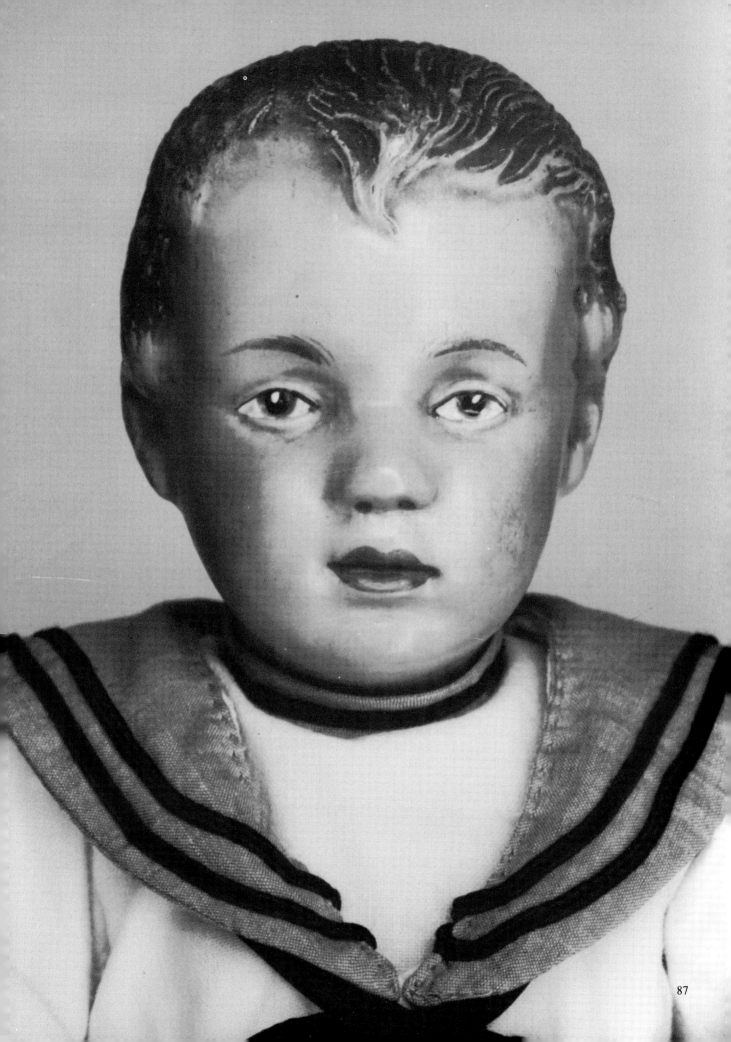

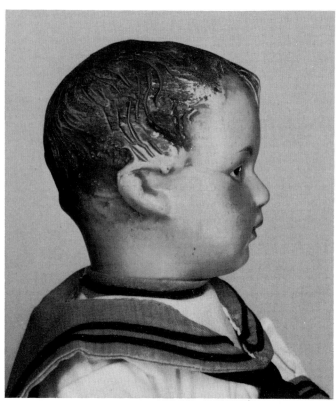

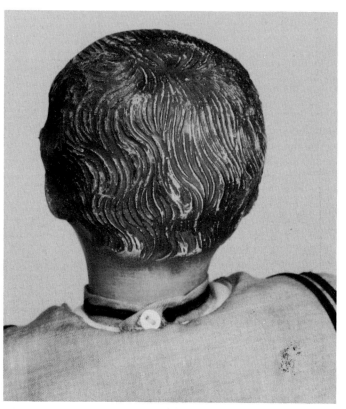

Illustration 175. The snub nose of Doll 14/207 is fairly straight. He has the soft low features of a young child. Even in profile his eyelid modeling is quite distinct. He has grooves cut into the blur line caused where the mold pieces meet, but his ear is not quite as clearly defined as that of the next example. He has impressed mark.

Illustration 176. The comb marks on the back of Doll 14/207's head show wavy hair swirling out of a central cowlick. His hair is brushed forward on the top and sides. It might even be curly if it were longer.

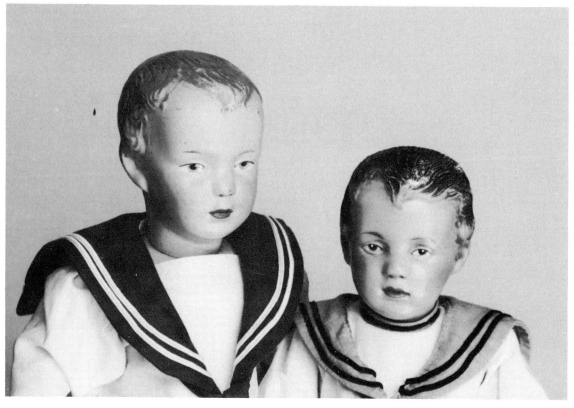

Illustration 177. Dolls 16/200 and 14/207 look identical in old catalogues. The similarities are rather like those between Dolls 16/202 and 16/204. The later doll looks like a younger brother to the earlier doll in both cases. Doll 200 has lightly modeled eyelids, a distinct double chin and a narrower nose. He also has single-stroke eyebrows and his curls have the early shiny finish. Doll 207 has much more strongly modeled eyelids, a fuller mouth, smaller eyes and a heavy lower face. Both dolls have similar modeled curls with strong comb marks.

Illustration 178. 14½in (37cm). This example of Doll 14/207 is much softer in his modeling. His light brown intaglio eyes are pulled down onto his lower lids giving him larger and rounder eyes and a very sweet expression. He has long narrow multi-stroke brows. His coloring is warm, but not "suntanned" as the later dolls were. Best of all his face paint is mint and original. His hair curls are modeled but there are few comb marks. He has the impressed mark.

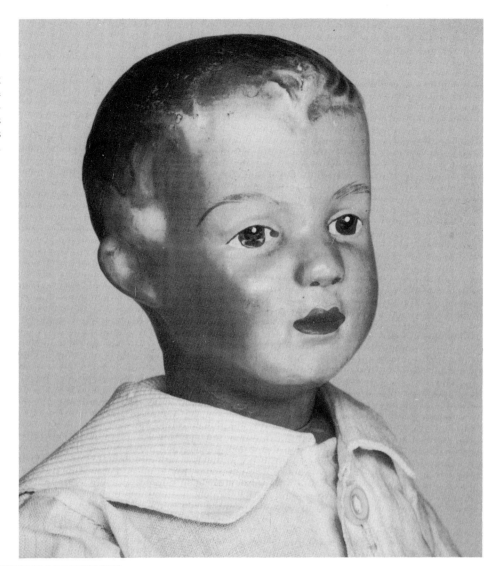

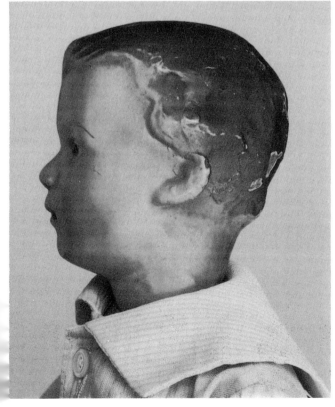

Illustration 179. A Doll 14/207 has a completely defined ear which is smaller than most of the boys. His features are low on his face. He has a snub nose and out-thrust upper lip. Looking beyond the paint loss in spots on the back of his head one notes that he has almost no comb marks which is very unusual for a "carved hair" Schoenhut. He has traces of the numeral "2" on the back of his neck.

Series 300 — The Wigged Girls

Model 300 with her round face and narrower eyes is first shown in the "Transition Period" at the end of 1911. Her most distinctive feature is the dimple in her chin. There seems to be a lot of variety in this model depending on whether the artist rounded the eye decoration within the rather narrow molding. In some examples the upper lids are incised, while in others they are not. Also, the lip painting gives her expressions that range from sweet to fairly downcast. Occasionally one of these models is found without the distinctive dimple. The round face and other features, including the profile remain the same. These examples without the dimple seem to have the decal mark and are probably from the final years of production when the molds were not replaced as they wore out.

Doll 300 came with either blue or brown eyes. She could be ordered as a blonde or with brown hair. Through 1916 her model automatically came with a long curl wig. From 1917 until the end of her production in 1923, she could be purchased either as 300 B with a bobbed hair wig or as 300 C with the original long curl style.

Doll 300 was made in the 16in (41cm) size only. Her boy counterpart was model 403.

Doll 301 also appeared first in the "Transition Period." She has round eyes and a longer, more rectangular face than 300. Her lips are not as tightly closed as those of 300, and she has a "softer" look as a result. She is particularly sweet and slightly anxious looking because of this, as well as her wide open eyes. She has a soft, round chin line and a slightly square jaw.

Doll 301 came with brown or blue eyes and a short blonde or tosca bobbed hair style with bangs through 1916. After 1916 she was sold as 301 B, with bobbed hair or as 301 C with a long curl wig. The post 1916 dark wigs are sometimes a rich, reddish-brown rather than the lighter and golder tosca color.

Doll 301 was made in the 16in (41cm) size only and was one of a few character models to survive to the end of Schoenhut doll production in 1924. Her male counterpart was model 404. She also bears a strong resemblance to doll 102.

Doll 302, which appears to have been modeled on Kämmer and Reinhardt's 101, *Marie*, is gone from the line. She was the most heavily photographed model in the early 1911 advertising, but she does not show in any of the spring 1912 advertisements in *Playthings* and apparently was in production for only about 11 months.

Doll 303 was the surviving number of the merging of models 303 and 305. She is the revised rounder and younger face of the smiling child in the original 1911 catalogue. She now has five baby teeth, with a hint of a sixth, clearly showing in her open/ closed mouth. As in Doll 203, she now appears more cheerful than gleeful. Her eyes are rounder and though her temples and eyelids are nicely modeled her smile does not seem to extend through her eyes. Her profile is sharp with an uptilted nose, well defined mouth area and strong chin line.

Doll 303's wig style now had a center part and braids which crossed the top of her head and were fastened with silk ribbons on the opposite side, above her ears.

This model was made in the 16in (41cm) size only from the end of 1911 through 1916. She did not survive the drastic streamlining of the line that occurred in 1917.

Dolls 304 and 306 which had been redesigned at the end of 1911 on Kämmer and Reinhardt's 114 *Gretchen* were apparently still in production in June 1912, but were dropped from the line by the end of that year. The company's early dependence on certain German designs was at an end, and their own original designs were completely in place.

Doll 307, the first of the "smooth eye" character dolls, survived with a change in hairstyle. This doll appears to have a rather square face with heavy cheeks and a small, slightly open/ closed mouth with four teeth. She is not smiling, as are models 303 and 305. Her smooth round eyes are detailed with stippled paint on the iris to give them depth. This would have been an easier modeling job, but it took an extra painting step to make the eyes look real.

Why have I never come across this model before? Is it because she is similar enough to the early *Miss Dolly* that I have simply passed her by without "seeing" her? Her face appears to be squarer than *Miss Dolly's* and her mouth seems smaller. At first, friends who searched with me thought that 307 had strongly carved teeth, while *Miss Dolly's* were only dabbed on; however, further searches disproved this theory. In any case there is, as yet, no photograph of the real doll to share. If you find her, please share her with all of us.

Doll 307 was produced in the 16in (41cm) size only. She was now sold with a long curl blonde or tosca wig. Her eye color is unknown, but as the other "smooth eye" models of the period have been found with both blue and brown eyes, it seems safe to assume that she was made with both eye colors as well. She was made only through 1916. She appears to have had no boy counterpart.

Doll 308 may be the most popular of the many Schoenhut faces. She has an alert, intelligent and sensitive face. She is the most easily found of the character dolls, especially in the 19in (48cm) size which was produced for about a dozen years. If one could only have one Schoenhut, this is probably the one to go for. It is easy to see why her production run was so long by Schoenhut standards. Her temples are well modeled, as are her eyelids and her deeply incised intaglio eyes. Her lips are clearly defined. Her full lower lip has a deep dip in the center. Her upper lip, which is thinner, has two peaks and a central dip. The incised space between the lips is curved and fairly deep. It sometimes is accented in the decoration with a darker pink line. The painting of the lips often curls up at the corners giving her a pleasant serenity. The painting of her eyes varies considerably among different examples. Sometimes they are very round adding to an impression of innocence as well as curiosity. Painting more narrowly confined to the eyelid modeling gives her a very different, although still attractive appearance.

Doll 308 was produced in the 14in (36cm) and 19in (48cm) sizes at this time. She is clearly shown in advertising as early as July 1913, and since she holds the next number up from one of the original Graziano dolls, it is likely that she was actually in production when the new line appeared in the spring of 1912.

In the 14in (36cm) size her wig was parted in the center and braided in two long braids that were fastened around her crown with two silk bows over the ears. In this style she was produced through 1916. Because her male counterpart (405) was produced in this size through 1924, it was easy to switch wigs and sell "her" with either a short bob or long curls after 1916. Occasionally a late model shows up, in original dress, with a boy's bob. It may even have a girl's union suit indicating that she was not a quick clothing switch as has sometimes been found on model 205. These examples have a very smooth finish and a tanner skin tone. They also seem to have less eye modeling and a narrower eye decoration as well as the decal mark. They seem to be from the early 1920s. The quality of the painting is excellent.

The 19in (48cm) size of 308 was produced until the end of the character line with the close of the 1924 season. At first she

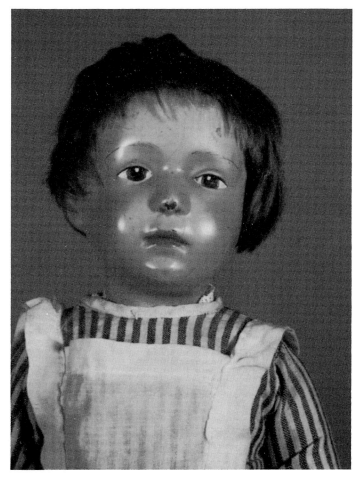

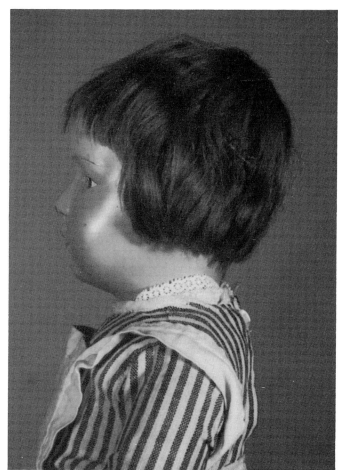

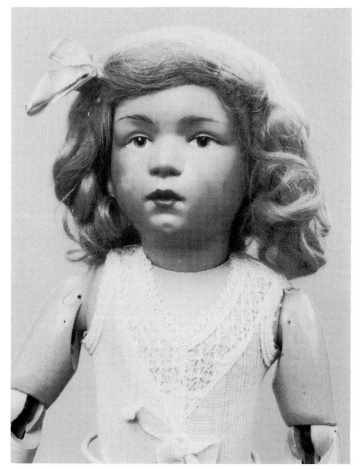

Illustration 180. 16¼in (43cm). This charming model 16/300 is in her original homemade nurse's dress. The modeling of her temples, lids and dimple are quite sharp. Her original underwear is missing and her plain bob may mean that she was manufactured as a boy, but she has clearly been a girl since 1915. She has the impressed mark. Her black upper lash line accentuates the deep intaglio carving of her eyes. Her brows have short multi-stroke brown "hairs." Her name is "Ursula Unrah" and she came to her original child for Christmas 1915.

Illustration 181. The roundness of the face of Model 16/300 is carried out in her profile. The cheeks are heavy and evenly round. The nose is short and straight. The lips are slightly parted and the small chin is definite and well formed.

Illustration 182. 16in (41cm). This Doll 16/300 is quite pretty and she was found in her original, though heavily damaged box with "16/300" printed on it and "BLONDE" in pen and "blue" in pencil written on it. Her ribbons, stockings, stocking ties and slippers appear to have once been blue but have faded to white, or dull cream. Her blonde mohair curls are quite dusty. Her crisp modeling of eyelids, temples, mouth and dimples indicate that she is quite early. Her model number has no B or C after it. Until 1917 this model was only offered with a long curl wig. Her brows are feathered and light brown. Her eyes a strong blue. She even has her original stand, but no pin, which may mean that she pre-dates the pin.

91

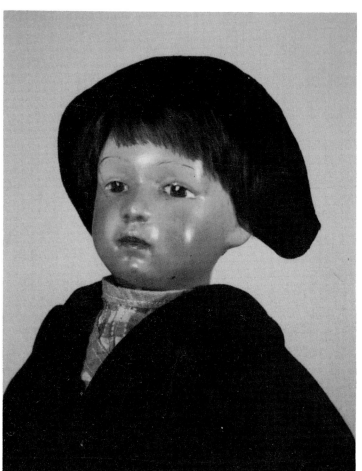

Illustration 184. 17in (43cm). This superb example of Doll 16/301 is the Flower Girl from The Wedding Party shown in the Chapter on Special Orders. She is entirely factory-original and in mint (although somewhat dusty) condition. Her deeply-incised blue intaglio eyes have distinct, slightly droopy upper lids and some lower lid modeling. She has lightly feathered dark blonde eye brows. Doll 301 has a soft rectangular face with a round jaw line. Her color is intense with deep pink mouth and accent dots and good blush. Her lips have a deeper red between them to accent their open/closed appearance. Her softly arched brows give her a sweeter, less anxious look than many other examples of her model number. She has the impressed mark. *Becky and Jay Lowe Collection.*

Illustration 183. 16½in (42cm). This Doll 16/300 has a homemade Schoenhut style blue and white checked two-piece cotton dress and her original drop-waist black coat and velvet hat. Her eyes are painted narrower than most examples of this doll. Her upper eyelids are incised but in general she has softer modeling. Her wig (which has been given a "trim") appears to be original although it is of very fine dark brown human hair. Schoenhut family members say that the company made human hair wigs on special order, usually from hair saved from a family member of the person placing the order. She has the impressed mark.

Illustration 185. Doll 16/301's profile shows a short uptilted nose and a protruding upper lip as well as a small firm chin with a round "second" chin behind it. Note the modeling below her eye. *Becky and Jay Lowe Collection.*

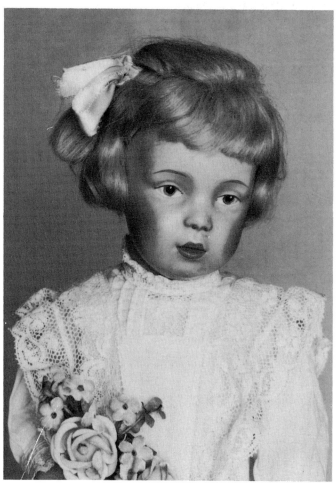

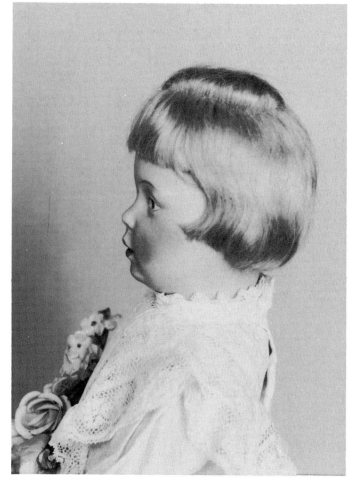

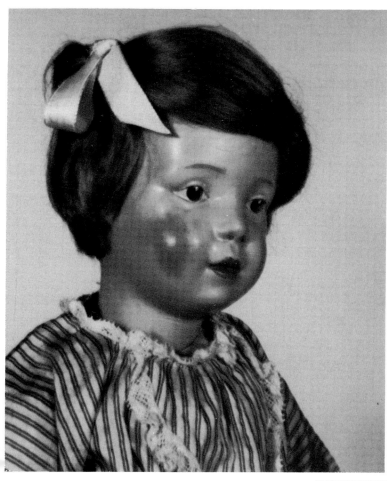

Illustration 186. 16in (41cm). This is how the doll, sold to me as Doll 301, looked when I first saw "her." The dealer, who is quite knowledgeable about a wide variety of dolls, said "I can't understand why her hair is so different. The wig seems original." It is, but "she" is really a "he." This happens with all kinds of dolls and one never knows the difference. Because Schoenhut's wigs and union suits were set for each model, it is more obvious when the switch occurs (provided the original wig is retained). He makes a great girl, but he is rarer as a boy. (See Illustrations 231 and 232 for "her" description.) The nice thing about this wig is that the very distinct profile of this model (which as a girl is 16/301) shows off so well.

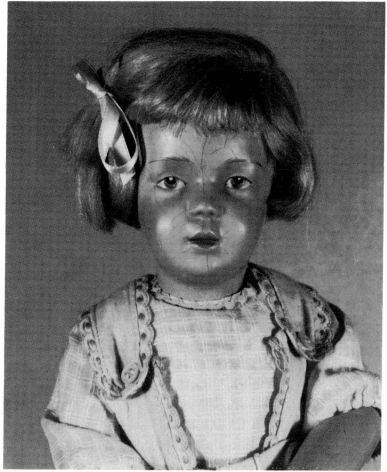

Illustration 187. 16½in (42cm). This sweet example of Doll 16/301 has bright blue intaglio eyes. She has slightly molded eyelids and a brown upper lid line. Her light brown feathered brows are slightly arched and she is a more peaceful looking child than most of this model. Her face is a rectangle with a rounded chin line. She has a long philtrum. Her mouth is small and her lip decoration does not fill the molded lines. She has the impressed mark. *Ella and Larry Corn Collection.*

was listed as 19/308X. The "X" stood for the bobbed hair that was standard on this size 308 through 1916. In this size she survived the line cut of 1917. From 1917 through 1924 she was offered as 19/308 B with her usual bob or as 19/308 C with a long curl wig.

1917 brought a new size 308. Listed as 21/308 B and 21/308 C she actually measures 22in (56cm). This doll has a huge head which makes her difficult to balance safely on her stand as she is quite top-heavy. Further, although she remains quite a pretty doll, her features lose a lot of the molding detail in this size. This size was made through 1924.

Doll 309 has a very distinct face. Her lips are slightly parted to show two upper front teeth. She has a slight smile giving her a very pleasant look. The modeling around her eyes and temples is deep. Her nose in profile is sharp and she has a very strong chin line. This doll seems less innocent than 308, but she is perhaps a little more curious and alert.

Doll 309 was offered as 19/309 X with a long curl hair style and as 21/309 with a short bob with bangs. She was made only through 1916.

Examples of Doll 309 have been found as a boy. Boy and girl examples have also been found in the 16in (41cm) size. The boy may be the result of a convenient wig switch; however, it is becoming apparent that during the years 1912 and 1913 a tremendous amount of experimenting was going on with a rapidly growing line of character faces. It seems likely that the 16in examples of this model were made during this period. Perhaps a boy was offered then as well. There certainly was a "carved hair" boy with this face (206).

Doll 310 has such a sweet, sad face that one wants to console her. Her most distinctive feature is her upper lip which is quite full and has two real peaks. In profile this upper lip sticks out as far as her nose and has a squared off front edge. Her lower lip is not as full as 308's. It does not have the dip incised in it. The philtrum above her upper lip is long and deeply modeled. Her eyes are not as deep as 308's and 309's but the lids show.

Doll 310 came in all four sizes with a long curl wig. She was produced from 1913, and possibly earlier, through 1916. Her male counterpart was Doll 407. She also may have been designed on the same child as Doll 105. She appears to be a wigged version of that doll.

Doll 311 has a small heart-shaped face with distinct eyelid molding and a slightly pursed mouth. The slight dimple, or flattened spot in her right cheek, her pointed chin and her profile reveal that she is actually the wigged version of 106, the "bonnet head" doll.

This doll was offered in the 14in (36cm) and 16in (41cm) sizes during this period. Both sizes were sold with a short bob. The hair was swept straight across her forehead in an "unfussy" style, which shows off the small distinctive features of her face. She was only produced through 1916.

Three examples of 19in (48cm) 311 Dolls have been found, indicating several of the dolls may have been made in all four sizes during the 1912 and 1913 experimental (or perhaps more accurately labeled "explosion") period. Her "carved hair" equivalent also dates from spring 1912. The 19in (48cm) size of this doll is not shown in any advertising or catalogues after 1913.

Model 312 is a number given to a 14in (36cm) softly rounded face doll with a short bobbed hairstyle. This doll has a younger face with a tiny pug nose, a straight mouth and a distinctly straight shadow between her lower lip and her chin. This doll has a determined look and reminds one of Ramona Quimby of the books by Beverly Cleary. She has a lot of character, even though she is clearly modeled on a younger child than many of the other

dolls. Her eyes are oval and small. Her chin line is round and shows some "baby fat" although none of these characters could be described as "chubby."

Doll 312 has only been found in the 14in (36cm) size only. She probably began production in the 1912 to 1913 period. (She is shown in a July 1913 advertisement in *Playthings*.) She survived the line cut in 1917 and was from that date through 1924 offered as 312 B with her usual bobbed hairstyle or as 312 C with the long curl wig.

Doll 312 has also been found, in original factory dress and wig, as a boy. It is possible that, as such, he should have a missing 400 series number such as 406 or 408, but because he has not yet been found in a catalogue, we cannot arbitrarily assign him a number so his pictures are included here.

Doll 313 is the second of the "smooth eye" characters. This doll has a rounded jaw and a receding chin. Her convex eyeball has a blue or brown iris which is accentuated with a darker color stippled around its outside edge. Her mouth is small and in the small sizes she has the look of a younger child.

Doll 313 was made in all four sizes with a long curl wig. This wig as it "relaxes" with age can absolutely overwhelm the dolls with smaller features. Because of her receding chin she seems particularly modeled on a real, but not very pretty child. She appears in a *Playthings* ad as early as July 1913. She went out of production at the end of 1916.

Doll 314 is the last of the "smooth eye" characters. She has a broader face than 313 and a round but firmer chin which is not receding. Her mouth is wider, but her lips are thinner and pressed firmly together. Despite her broad, open looking face she appears to represent a more determined looking child. Her eyes were apparently made in blue or brown and are decorated in the same manner as the other "smooth eye" dolls.

Doll 314 was offered in the 19in (48cm) size in the 1914 to 1916 catalogues and may have been produced earlier. A charming example is on display at the Mary Merritt Museum in Douglasville, Pennsylvania. She is actually 17in (43cm) tall, but her head seems the right size for a 19in (48cm) doll. She has been placed on the chubbier 17in (43cm) toddler body designed by Harry Schoenhut rather than the 16in (41cm) child body. The combination of this body and her round determined face is particularly delightful. Her clothing appears to be completely original, and she may have been produced this way as a special order. This model came with a long curl wig that was fastened with its part higher up on its head than 313's. She went out of production at the end of 1916.

Doll 315 was the last of the long line of character faces offered by the company. Finding an example of her in her original box, verifying her identity, was a great thrill! She has a distinct open/closed triangular shaped mouth with the peak at the top and the long side at the bottom. She has four carved teeth. She also has a dimple in the middle of her chin.

Doll 315 was apparently made in the 21in (53cm) size only. Although she appears in the 1914 to 1916 catalogues in a long curl wig, the example found in her original box has a short, straight, blonde bob with bangs. Another example has been found with an apparently original wig which is a short wavy bob without bangs such as that found on Doll 311. Doll 315 is shown in a doll booklet produced by the company in approximately 1914. Although the booklet is undated, the clothing numbers date it before 1915 and the pictures of Harry Schoenhut's infant place it at or after June 1913. She may have been produced even earlier. She went out of production at the end of 1916.

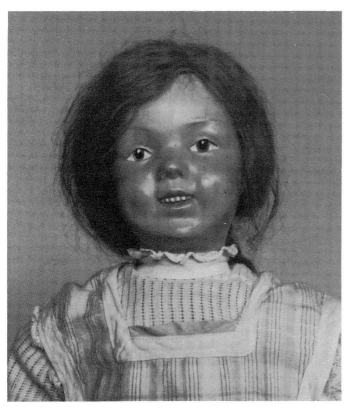
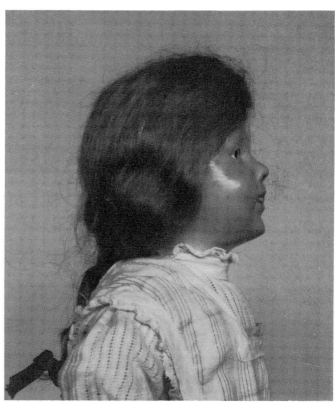

Illustration 188. 16in (41cm). Doll 303. Her blue intaglio eyes are combined with her original tosca mohair wig on this fine example. Her pink and blue plaid "jumper" with attached guimpe is not shown in catalogues but is probably original. *Dorothy Dixon Collection.*

Illustration 189. Doll 303 has a strong sharp chin, a slight dimple in her cheek and an uptilted nose. *Dorothy Dixon Collection.*

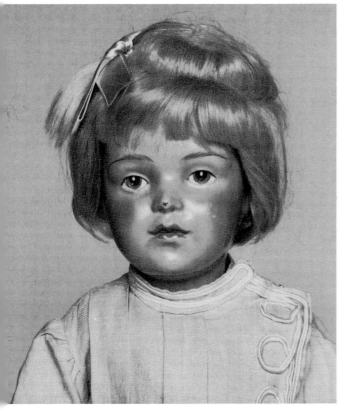
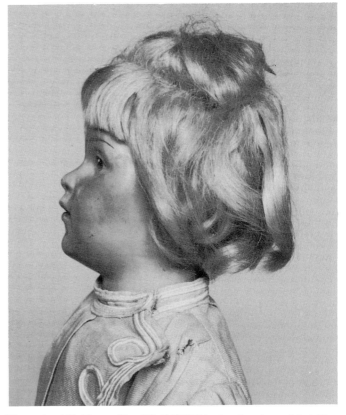

Illustration 190. 19½in (50cm). This 19/308 has deeply modeled intaglio eyes and eyelids. Their color is an intense blue with an extra large pupil and iris which gives her eyes a very round eyes. She has dark brown lash lines on her upper lids. Her brows are brown and feathered. The blush above her eyelids, on her ears and her cheeks is intact.

Illustration 191. The profile of Doll 19/308 is also sharply modeled. She is an early example with the incised mark on the back of her shoulders.

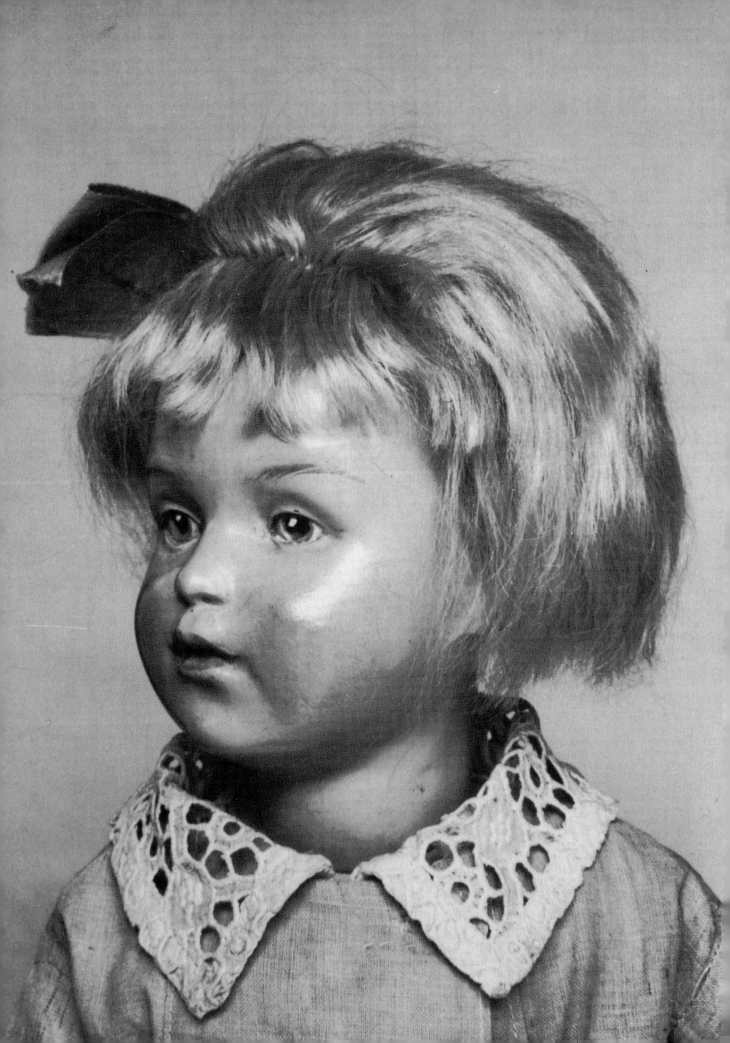

Illustration 192. 19½in (50cm). This blue eyed blonde version of Doll 19/308 has deeply-incised intaglio eyes with her well modeled upper eyelids lined in black. She wears a light blue linen coat dress with an eyelet collar and her original union suit which has a white bow on it. She has the incised or impressed mark.

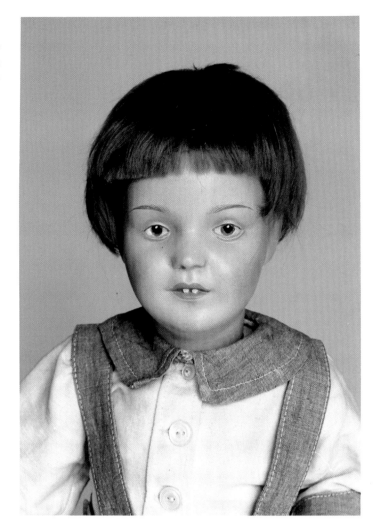

Illustration 193. 16¼in (41cm). This 16/309 arrived in a dress with a heavy black human hair wig glued on. When the dress was removed, he had a boy's union suit as well as original black stockings and black button boots, so it seemed best to make him a boy with an old, Schoenhut tosca mohair bob. Since we have not found the 16in (41cm) size of this doll in a catalogue yet, it is assumed that he dates to 1912-1913 and that this particular doll was originally a boy. As a boy we do not know his number. Perhaps he is the missing 406. He has cleanly modeled upper and lower eyelids, blue intaglio eyes, a black upper lid line and feathered brown brows.

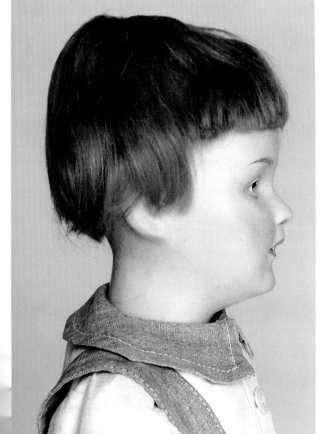

Illustration 194. The 16¼in (41cm) boy's profile is as sharply defined as are those of the 21in (53cm) size examples.

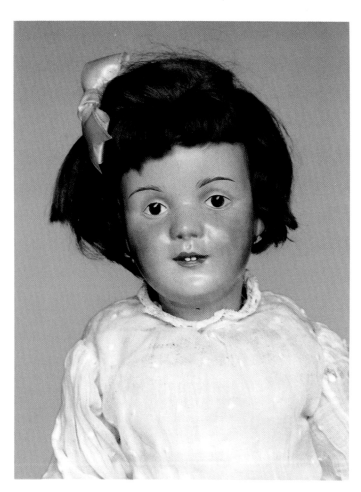

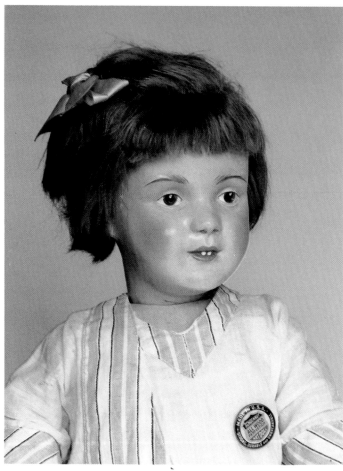

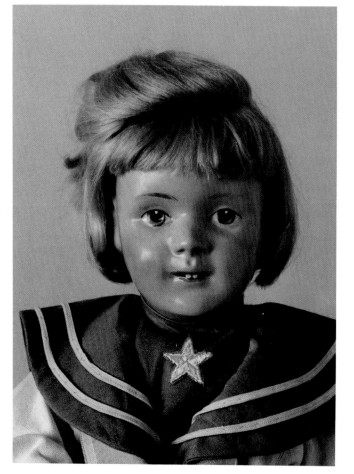

Illustration 195. 21½in (55cm). Another delightful curious 309 which has deep modeling, feathered brown brows, dark brown intaglio eyes, and a darker brown upper lid line. Her union suit and slip are factory original with white bows on both. Her white dotted Swiss dress is contemporary. She has the impressed mark.

Illustration 196. 21½in (55cm). This super example of Doll 21/309 has beautiful coloring. Her orangy blush is intact on her cheeks, above her eyes and on her chin. She has beautifully modeled upper and lower eyelids, medium brown deeply incised intaglio eyes, a dark brown upper lid line and feathered (slightly fly-away) brown eyebrows. Her mouth, nostrils and eye dots are a bright orange pink. There is a light red line on the inside bottom of her upper lip. Her teeth are clearly molded and the white paint just fits the modeling. She has a tosca mohair bob. Her mark is impressed.

Illustration 197. 21in (54cm). The eyes of this unusual Doll 21/309 are not deeply intaglio and her lids are barely modeled, but her blue iris is outlined with a fine black rim. Her lash line is also black. She has feathered light brown eyebrows and a soft pink mouth with a red center. Her paint is "mint." *Diane C. Dustir Collection.*

Illustration 198. 16½in (42cm). This 16/310's powder blue intaglio eyes accented with brown upper lash lines and feathered eyebrows are outstanding. She is beautifully modeled and her color is rich. She has a very expressive face. Her blonde mohair wig has long curls and a huge silk ribbon. This doll is all-original and definitely not typically dressed. *Becky and Jay Lowe Collection.*

Illustration 199. This doll was found as a head and may be an artist's model for doll 310. She is just a bit more of everything than the usual. Her intaglio eyes are a little deeper, her modeling a little crisper, her lips a little fuller. She even has a suggestion of a dimple in her chin. She has been carefully retouched in the center of her face and her left ear has been rebuilt by her owner. It has been done in such a minimal way that her original paint has been retained. She is marked with a raised "5" on the back or her head. *Frank Mahood Collection.*

Illustration 200. Profile view of Illustration 199. *Frank Mahood Collection.*

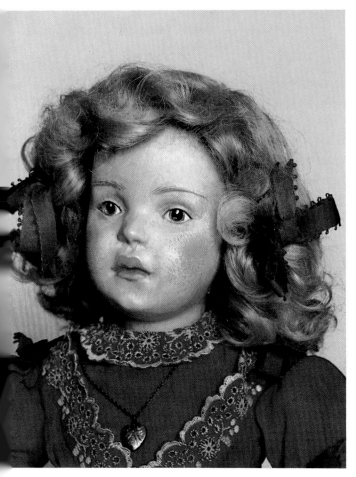

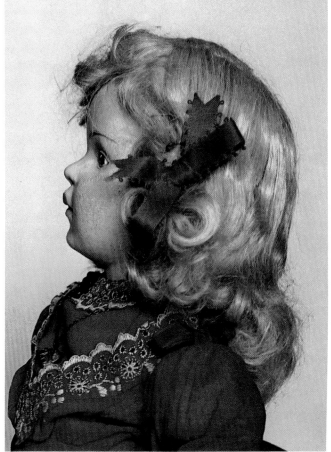

RIGHT:

Illustration 201. 17in (43cm). This beautiful 16/310 has everything going for her. Her paint is so bright and glossy that it would be easy to believe that she has been repainted but she has not. She has brown feathered brows over her brown intaglio eyes and a black upper lid line. She has good blush above her eyes, on her cheeks and her chin. She has a deep pink mouth and accent dots. The deeper pink line through her mouth follows the curves between her lips. Her long curl tosca mohair wig has relaxed to a heavy wave. She has her original union suit (with a pink bow) and what appears to be original homemade clothing.

BOTTOM LEFT:

Illustration 202. 15in (38cm). This size, 14/311, is particularly dear. Her heart shaped face and pointed chin are particularly obvious. Although the dimple in her right cheek is only a suggestion in this size, the modeling around her mouth is very strong. Her eyes are deep brown intaglio with well modeled lids and feathered brown brows. Her original brown mohair wig retains its original set. She has a deep pink mouth with a red line between her lips and pink tear ducts and nostril dots. Her blush is good on both her cheeks and above her eyes. She is the train bearer from the Wedding Party in the Special Order chapter and is factory original. She has the impressed mark. *Becky and Jay Lowe Collection.*

BOTTOM RIGHT:

Illustration 203. 19in (48cm). The coloring on this 19/311 is particularly beautiful. Her modeling is also a little finer and deeper than that usually found. She has strong modeling of her philtrum and the space between her lips as well as the dip in her lower lip. She has deep pink accent dots and mouth. The red line between her lips carefully follows the shape of her lips. She has slight dimples in both cheeks — lower in the left cheek — and the flattened end of her sharp chin has a hint of another dimple. She has the impressed mark. *Mostly Dolls and Toys.*

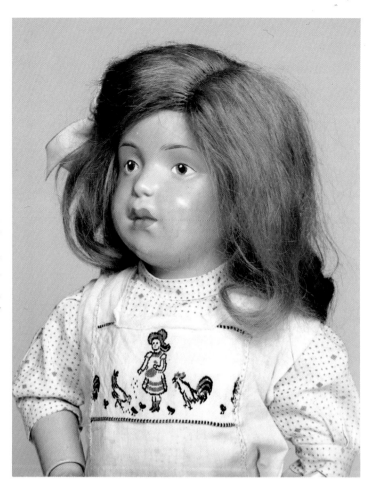

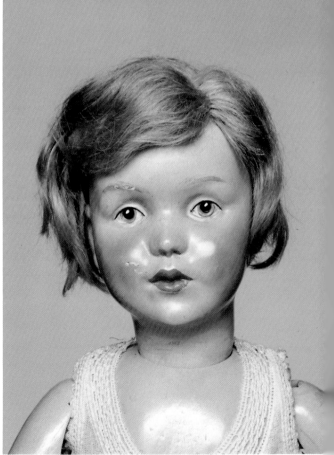

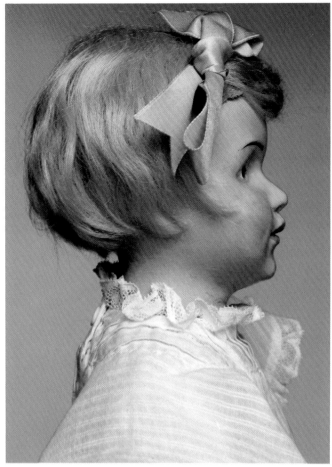

Illustration 204. 19½in (49cm). This 19/311 must date from the 1912-1913 years when the company was experimenting with different models in different sizes. She is not shown in any catalogues from 1914 on in this size, but her carved haired version, the bonnet headed doll 106, is.

Illustration 205. The 19/311's profile is quite strong. She has a good sized nose, a protruding upper lip and a firm chin line which has a flattened point at the tip and a suggestion of a dimple in it.

Illustration 206. 16¼in (42cm). This is a particularly early example of Doll 16/311 as her factory-original outfit is shown in early 1912 advertising. She is a sweet example with a heart shaped face, strongly modeled eyes, lids and temples, a slight dimple in the right cheek and full lips. The intaglio modeling is quite deep in her eyes and both the upper and lower eyelids are indicated in the molding. She has the impressed mark.

Illustration 207. Comparison of 16/106 (16in [41cm]) with 16/311 shows these dolls have the same face. They were both made from 1912-1916 only, and have a great deal of charm.

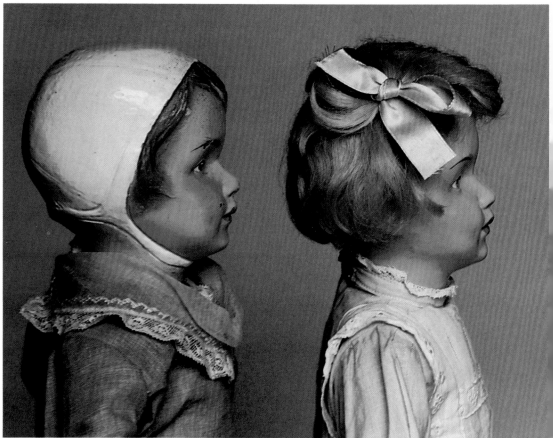

Illustration 208. Profile view of the dolls in Illustration 207.

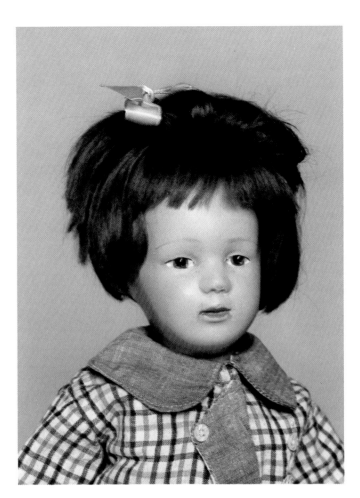

LEFT:
Illustration 209. 15in (38cm). This Doll 14/312 has small rich brown intaglio eyes and dark brown upper lid lines. She has light upper and lower eyelid modeling and her multi-stroke brows are thin, light brown. Her mouth, nostrils and tear ducts are medium pink. Her slight blush is quite orange in tone. Her wig is a combination of brunette mohair upper layer thatched over a bottom row of slightly greenish tosca on its original factory base which is still nailed on with the original tacks. It is likely that the upper thatch was added later to replace a moth eaten earlier layer. She has the impressed mark.

BOTTOM LEFT:
Illustration 210. 15in (38cm). The paint on this boy is very thin light pink. The wood turning marks and some grain show through it. His blush and deep pink accent dots are intact. The blush on his cheeks and above his eyes is pink rather than orange in color. He has good eyelid modeling with a thin charcoal upper lid line. He has light blue intaglio eyes and light brown feathered brows. There is a light red shading line on the bottom inside of his upper lip. His scrappy blonde mohair wig and his union suit are original. As a girl, his number is 312. This example has clearly been a boy all his life, but we have not found him in available catalogues. He may date from 1912-1913 when a lot of experimenting was going on. He has the impressed mark.

BOTTOM RIGHT:
Illustration 211. Note the turning marks and wood grain showing throughout the sides of the boy's face. There is not a lot of gesso or filling under the paint and he is probably quite early.

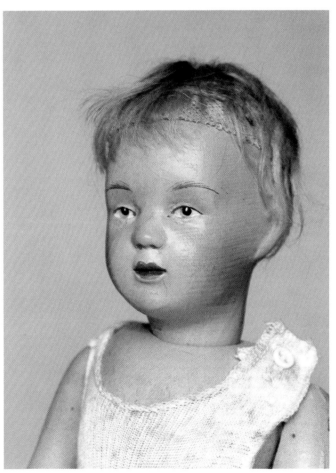

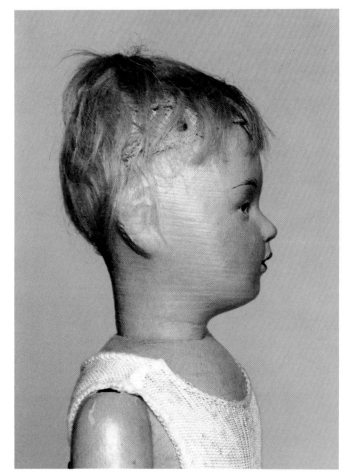

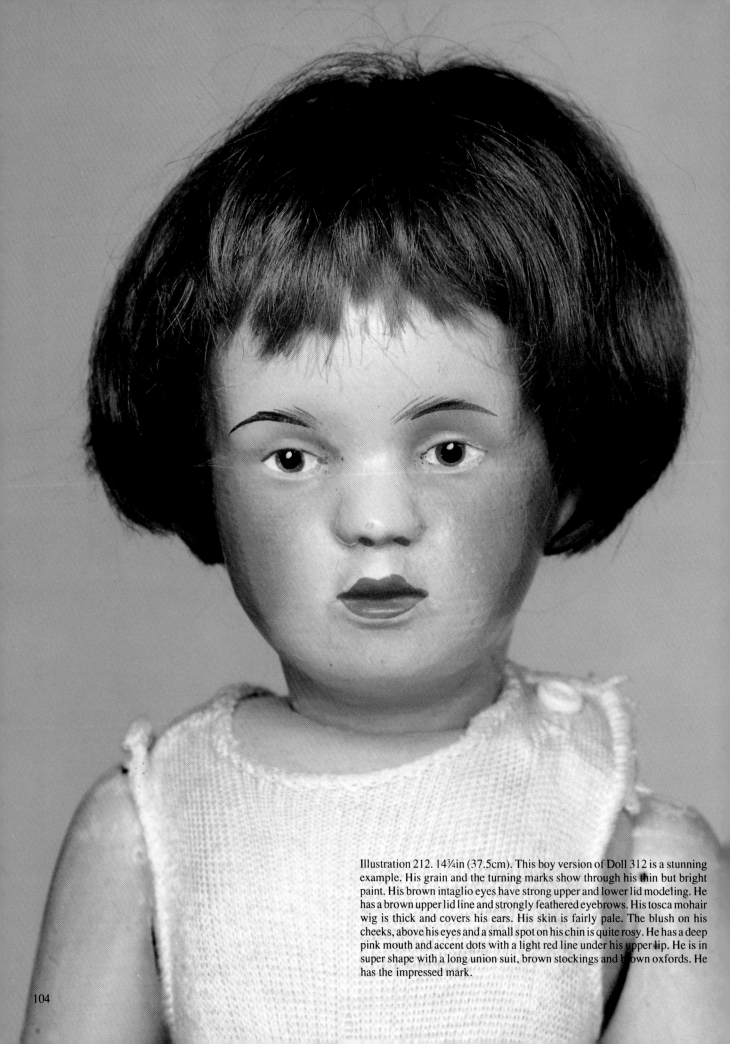

Illustration 212. 14¾in (37.5cm). This boy version of Doll 312 is a stunning example. His grain and the turning marks show through his thin but bright paint. His brown intaglio eyes have strong upper and lower lid modeling. He has a brown upper lid line and strongly feathered eyebrows. His tosca mohair wig is thick and covers his ears. His skin is fairly pale. The blush on his cheeks, above his eyes and a small spot on his chin is quite rosy. He has a deep pink mouth and accent dots with a light red line under his upper lip. He is in super shape with a long union suit, brown stockings and brown oxfords. He has the impressed mark.

Illustration 213. 15in (38cm). This example of 14/312/516/1 has small intaglio eyes of a rich brown. She has black upper lid lines and faded brown multi-stroke brows. She has the pug nose and small face of a young child. She also has a very clear impressed mark.

Illustration 214. 15in (38cm). This doll is complete in the catalogue as 14/313/530 blonde. The last number (530) stands for her Peter Thompson suit with its original slip and drawers, all of which is worn over a union suit indicating that she came undressed and her original owners purchased the dress and underwear separately. Her blonde mohair wig is very full and as the curls have relaxed it overwhelms her small face. She has lightly modeled upper lid, black lash lines over her stippled blue eyes and blonde feathered brows.

Illustration 215. The profile of the blonde girl is very much that of a real child.

Illustration 216. 14½in (37cm). This exquisite example of Doll 14/313 is just beautiful. She has large gray-blue-green stippled eyes and very straight light brown multi-stroke eyebrows. Her pink lips are fuller than usual and she has good modeling through the eyes, philtrum and mouth. The deep pink line running through her mouth follows the lip lines. Her wig is quite full, but not overwhelming. She has the impressed mark. *Diane C. Dustir Collection.*

Illustration 217. 14½in (37cm). This brown eyed, tosca haired example of Doll 14/313 is particularly sweet. Her long curl wig is full enough to be pleasing but does not overwhelm her face. She has been played with as her worn eyebrows and lack of cheek blush clearly show. The painting of her eyes is particularly nice as she has a clear direct gaze. Her soft pink lips are full and emphasized with a bright red line between the lips. She has the impressed mark, an original dress which might be factory and her original factory pin which dates her to around 1915-1916. *Photograph by Monty Moncrief. Siger Davey Collection.*

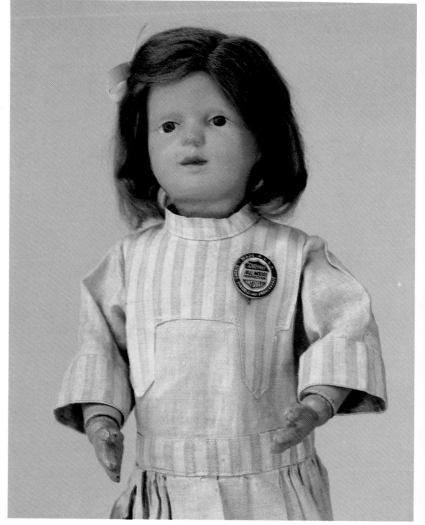

LEFT:
llustration 218. 19¼in (49cm). This example of Doll 19/314 has brown stippled eyes and a very direct gaze. She has brown multi-stroke eyebrows with some feathering. Her tosca mohair wig is original. It has been extremely difficult to find this model in such an original state. Her coloring is very soft. She has a good deal of charm. *Betty O'Sullivan Collection.*

BELOW LEFT:
Illustration 219. 19½in (50cm). This doll 19/314 with the broad face and snubby nose of a very young child always tickles me. At 19in (48cm) she is so tall for the youth of her face. Her head is the correct size for her body, but one cannot help but feel that she ought to be a toddler. Her eyes are smoothly modeled convex with dark brown over and around the lighter brown iris center. Her lid line and lightly feathered brows are a red-brown. Her wig is an old strawberry blonde mohair replacement which goes well with her face, but is not a Schoenhut style.

BELOW RIGHT:
llustration 220. The 19½in (50cm) girl's profile is that of a very young child with round low cheeks that do not obscure her snub now, tightly closed mouth and firm small chin with a roll of flesh behind it. This is another doll that gives one the feeling that it is a portrait of a particular child.

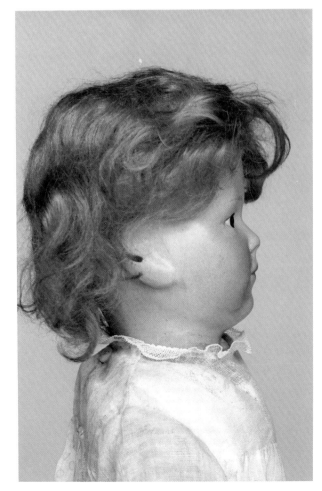

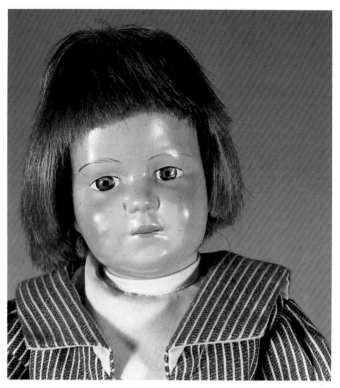

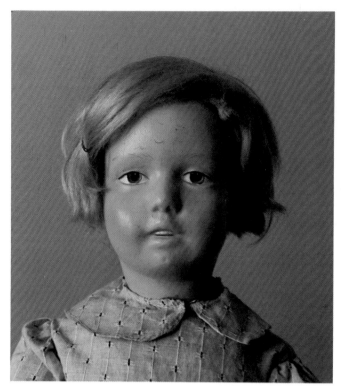

Illustration 221. 19in (48cm). This superb example of Doll 19/314 has been made up as a boy with an auburn human hair wig. His eyes are very blue with both light and dark blue paint stippled together. He has his broad face emphasized with flesh folds under his eyes and a distinct double chin. His brows are thin, brown and feathered. He has dark brown lid lines. He has a light pink mouth and accent dots with a bright red line through the center of his mouth and excellent cheek blush. This head was only produced from 1912-1916, but it is on an unmarked Schoenhut body from the mid to late 1920s and he is elastic strung. Probably the head and body are original to each other and the head was simply taken from stock. *Ella and Larry Corn Collection.*

Illustration 222. 21in (54cm). This version of Doll 21/315 combines clear modeling and very soft decorating. She has upper and lower eyelid modeling, real indications of her mouth and cheek muscles and a strong tiny chin dimple. The medium blue of her irises completely fills the space between her eyelids making her eyes appear larger than those of the only other example we have found. Her lip paint is just a little darker than that of her skin and more nearly matches her cheek blush. She has a stronger red line under her four molded teeth. She has no mark. *Charles and Barbara Buysse Collection.*

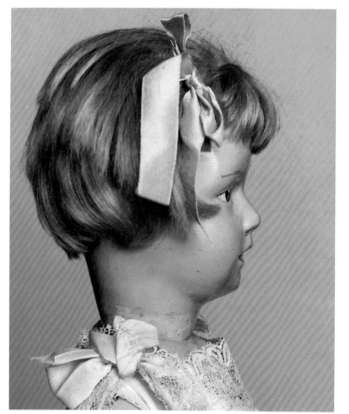

OPPOSITE PAGE:
Illustration 223. 21½in (54.5cm). This example of Doll 21/315 came with parts of her original box, including the end panel with its label and her model number on it. She has medium brown intaglio eyes with both upper and lower lids modeled. The intaglio incising is fairly deep and the iris paint spills a little over its molded edge. She has dark brown upper lid lines and very straight multi-stroke light brown eyebrows. Her open/closed mouth has an upper tooth ridge with four dab-painted teeth. The teeth are not separately modeled. A straight red line beneath the tooth ridge emphasizes the open look of her mouth. She has pink lips, eye dots and nostrils and a small round dimple in her chin. She also has her original blonde mohair bob although this doll was shown in the catalogue with a long curl wig. She has the impressed mark.

Illustration 224. The profile of Doll 21/315 shows her straight nose, open/closed mouth and receding chin.

Doll 400, which was designed on Kämmer and Reinhardt's 101 (*Peter*), was out of production. His number was not reassigned to another model.

Doll 401, which had been redesigned at the end of 1911 on Kämmer and Reinhardt's 114 (*Hans*), was shown in June 1912 advertising but was dropped from production soon after. His model number was not reassigned.

Doll 402, with his smiling face, which had been revised at the end of 1911 to have rounder eyes and a younger face is found in an ad in *Playthings* dated June 1912 in a bobbed wig with bangs. He does not appear in subsequent advertisements but is shown in the company produced booklet, *Forty Years of Toy Making*, also dated 1912. Apparently he was out of production around the end of that year. His number was not reassigned.

Doll 403 came out in its final form during the first stage of design revisions at the end of 1911. His round face with narrow eyes and distinctive chin dimple was the matching face to 300. The only change in 1912 was in his wig. The Fauntleroy shoulder length curls were cut, and he now had a neat bob with bangs that just covered his ears.

Doll 403 was made only in the 16in (41cm) size. He was produced, as were all the other characters, with either blue or brown eyes and a blonde or tosca wig. He was in production through 1924, giving him a longer production run than any other wigged boy.

Doll 404, which came out at the end of 1911, continued through this period. He retained his left side-part bob with long bangs brushed across his forehead and swirled into the rest of his hair. His face is the same as 301's. He is much more difficult to find, than she, as he went out of production at the end of 1916. He was made in the 16in (41cm) size only.

Doll 405 was the male counterpart of 308 and was made in the same two sizes — 14in and 19in (36cm and 48cm). He makes a handsome youngster. He had the standard boy's bob, brushed from a cowlick at the center back of the top of his head. He was made in both sizes from at least 1913 through 1924, but unlike 308 he was not produced in the 21in (53cm) size.

Doll 406 is a missing number. Since the numbers on either side of it were assigned to models, it is assumed that a face once had this number. Both 309 and 312 have shown up in original boy's wig, union suit, shoes and socks. Perhaps one of them held this number in the 1912 to 1913 period. Time, and a lucky find of company doll catalogs from this period, will probably tell.

Doll 407 was the male counterpart of 310 and has the same large upper lip and anxious face. His hairstyle is the usual boy's bob with bangs. Unlike 310, he appears to have been produced in the 19in (48cm) and 21in (53cm) sizes only; however, like 310 he was last made in 1916.

Doll 407 appears to have been the last of the wigged character boys, all of which apparently had equivalent girl models.

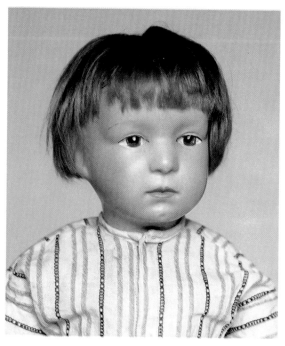

Illustration 225. 16½in (42cm). Another sweet boy 403 dressed as a girl. He has a tosca bob and brown eyes with well modeled upper lids. His mouth has been painted with a particularly determined look. *Barbara Pio Collection.*

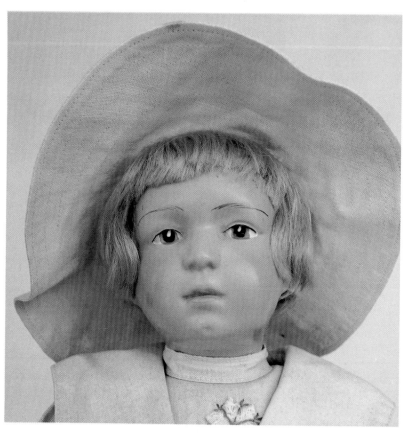

Illustration 226. This is a blue eyed blonde version of this doll. Because he is factory-original his full number is 16/403/812. His upper eyelid modeling is softer. The blue paint of his intaglio eyes has been pulled down onto his lower lid giving him a rounder eyed look than other 403s. *Photograph by Monty Moncrief. Becky Moncrief Collection.*

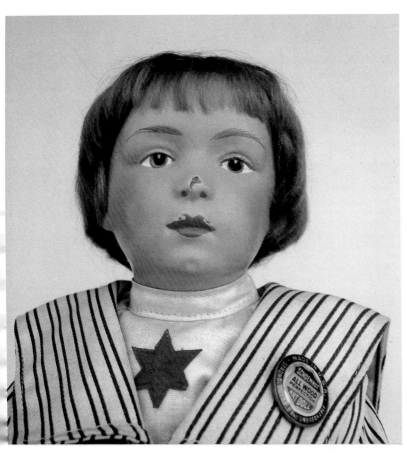

Illustration 227. This brown eyed brunette whose full number is 16/403/813 is completely factory-original. He has deeply incised light brown intaglio eyes with detailed eyelid and temple modeling. He has feathered brown eyebrows and dark brown upper lid lines. His particularly full mouth is the deep rose color which was used for a short period of time early in the "Classic Period." The dimple accents his firm chin. *Photograph by Monty Moncrief. Becky Moncrief Collection.*

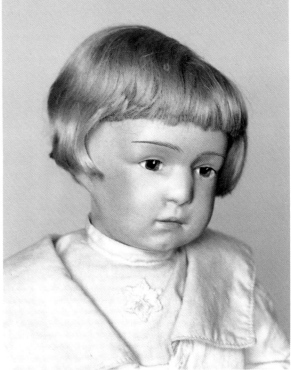

Illustration 229. This factory-original example of Doll 16/403/812 Pink even retains his original hair style set. He is the ring bearer from the Wedding Party. He has good eyelid modeling above his deep blue intaglio eyes. He has dark blonde multi-stroke brows. His color is softer than the other children in the wedding party, but it is in the original paint colors. He has no wear on his paint. The iris paint extends beyond the intaglio carving making his eyes appear larger. *Becky and Jay Lowe Collection.*

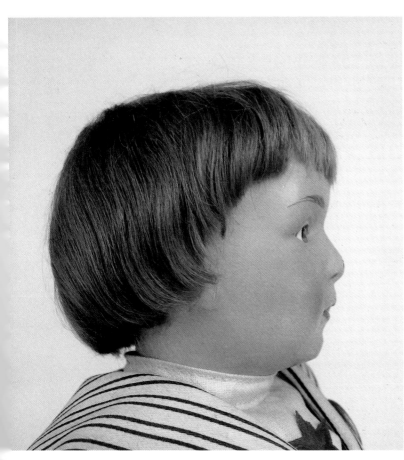

Illustration 228. Profile of boy in Illustration 227. *Photograph by Monty Moncrief. Becky Moncrief Collection.*

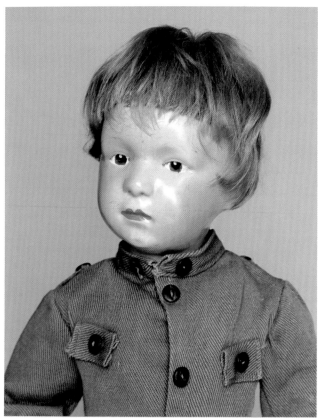

Illustration 230. 16½in (42cm). Doll 16/403 dressed as a World War I soldier. He might be from as early as 1915 when the war was raging in Europe. He may also be from 1917 when America became officially involved. His eyes are dark blue intaglio. His upper lids are lightly incised and he has faded, thin, light brown multi-stroke brows. His paint is medium in color with a deep pink mouth with a light red line between the lips. The dimple is definitely there in his chin, but it is not very deep. His mark is clearly impressed.

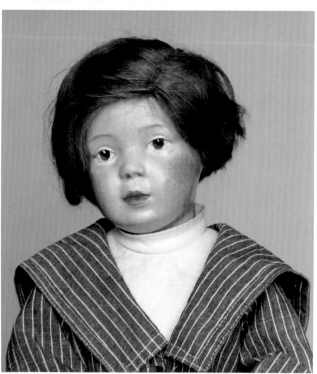

Illustration 231. 16in (41cm). This brown eyed brunette version of 404 has rich coloring and detail. As a boy, he was only made through 1916 and is not often found. He has strong upper and lower lid modeling with fine brown upper lid lines. His brows are soft and light in color. They are multi-stroke, but give the impression of a smeared single stroke. His flesh color is light. He has a beautiful orange blush, pink orange mouth, nostril and tiny tear ducts.

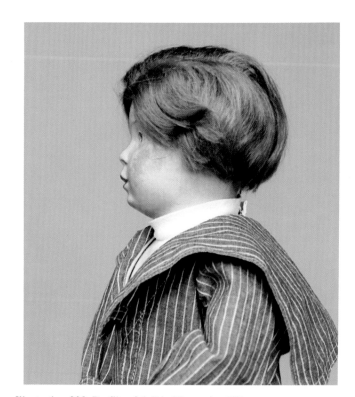

Illustration 232. Profile of doll in Illustration 231.

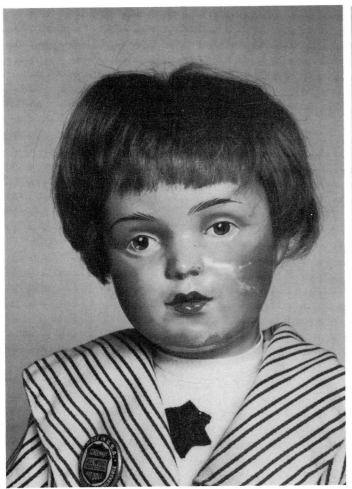

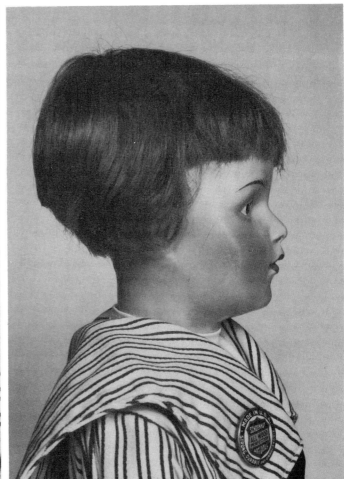

Illustration 233. 19½in (49cm). His full number is 19/405/813, as his "Russian Suit" is factory original. This size 405 was made from 1912-1924, but his suit is pre-1920, and he probably dates from 1912-1916. Dark brown feathered brows are above deeply incised brown intaglio eyes. His irises do not quite fill the space modeled for them. He has the impressed mark.

Illustration 234. The boy in the "Russian Suit" has a straight smallish nose and his lips are full. He has a firm chin. His nose is a little smaller, his lips are thinner and his chin a little stronger than those of Doll 407.

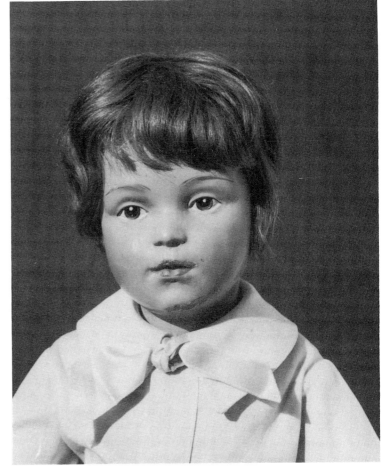

Illustration 235. 19½in (49cm). Doll 19/405. He has strong modeling including both upper and lower eyelids, temples and the groove in his lower lip. His paint is soft and natural looking. He retains the blush on his cheeks, chin and above his eyes. His white shirt, black stockings and oxfords are factory made. He was the childhood doll of Dorothy Schoenhut and is named Alexander. *Ruth Zimmerman Collection.*

Illustration 236. 15in (38cm). The way this boy is decorated, he has a sadder look than most 405 dolls. His arched, thin light brown multi-stroke eyebrows seem raised in question. His eyes are very dark blue intaglio and are rounder than usual with the paint extending beyond the molded part of the iris. His deep pink lips are quite full, particularly at the edges where it often curls up slightly in this model. There is soft blush on his cheeks and a thin red line between his lips. His original blonde mohair wig is a bit brassy and not very thick. He has his original union suit, brown stockings and brown oxfords with kaki tape ties. He also has the impressed mark.

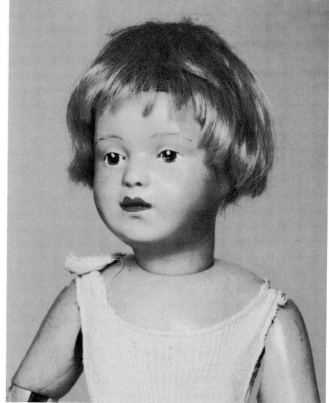

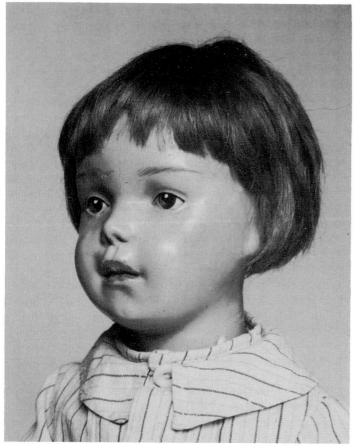

Illustration 237. 19½in (49.5cm). This 19/407 has the high upper lip peak and straight horizontal brows typical of this model. His eyelids are clearly modeled and he has deep intaglio brown eyes. He was found dressed as a girl but his tosca mohair bob makes him a boy and the same mold as girl 310 who had a long curl wig. He now has an old Buster Brown style suit from another Schoenhut. This angle shows his pointed uptilted nose, strong philtrum modeling and deep line incised between his lips. He has the impressed mark.

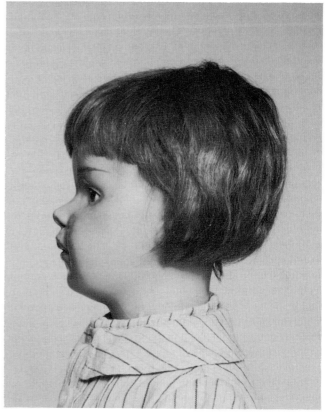

Illustration 238. The out-thrust and flattened upper lip as well as his upturned nose helps identify the 19/407 boy in profile and clarifies his difference from 405.

Illustration 239. 21½in (55cm). This example of Doll 21/407 is particularly fine. His eyelids, philtrum, and mouth modeling are typical of this model. He has pale flesh and good cheek and lip color as well as a little blush above the eyes and a strong red line through the center of the mouth. He has the impressed mark.

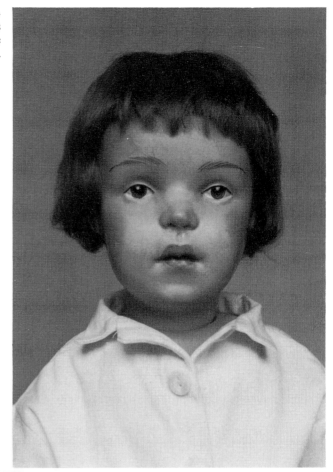

To sum up this chapter there were a great many different faces in the character dolls produced by the A. Schoenhut Company before America's entry into World War I. Although during the years 1912 through 1916 there were more wigged girls offered than "carved hair" girls in each size, there were as many or more "carved hair" boys offered in each size as wigged boys. All "carved hair" dolls in the 19in (48cm) and 21in (53cm) sizes ended with the 1916 season. These dolls were advertised for younger children as they stayed neat. The larger sizes would have been uncomfortable for smaller children to carry about. (The *Cabbage Patch Kids*™ are 16in [41cm] tall for the same reason.) Most of the wigged characters did not survive the line cut of 1917 and some of them are rarer than some of the "carved hair" models. In any case the well-loved "carved hair" dolls are not necessarily older than the wigged dolls. Lastly, intaglio eyes date from the same period as convex "smooth eye" dolls. The remarkable Schoenhut Company produced everything at once!

In 1917 Harry Schoenhut entered the American Army, and the Schoenhut Doll line went through another dramatic change.

Cabbage Patch Kids™ is a trademark of Original Appalachian Artworks, Inc., Cleveland, Georgia, U.S.A. All Rights Reserved.

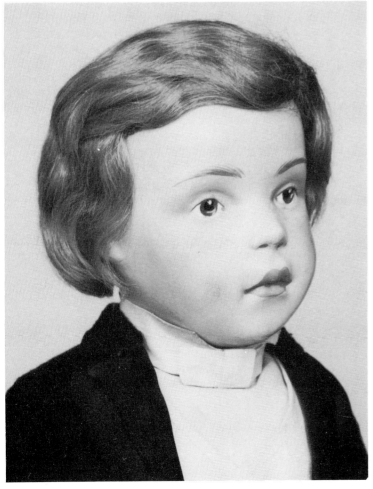

Illustration 240. 21½in (55cm). This example of Doll 21/407 has a wig style that was shown in catalogue pictures dated 1912. It makes him look older than other 407s which works well because he is the groom in the Wedding Party. His modeling is softer than that of the other examples we have seen. His brown eyes are intaglio. He has light brown feathered brows which are slightly arched. His mark cannot be checked under his sewn-on clothes. He has been specially dressed for the wedding at the time he was made. *Becky and Jay Lowe Collection.*

MISS DOLLY

At the end of 1914 Schoenhut announced the arrival of a new star for the 1915 season in advertising which stated: "*An Invitation to Meet Miss Dolly Schoenhut* Who Can Do Almost Everything But Talk. No, Miss Dolly is not a real girl, but you can hardly tell the difference." She was called *Miss Dolly* by the company, but she also had a model number just as the rest of the line. Her number was 316.

There were several reasons for the company, which had repeatedly announced that its dolls were designed on real children and did not have the usual "doll face," to add an item that clearly was modeled on the idea, if not the actual head, of a typical German "dolly" face doll. This German doll was still very popular with the American public. American composition dolls were being manufactured, but had not yet taken over the American heart or pocketbook. Trade embargoes against foreign goods and particularly German goods were in effect even as America was still trying to stay out of the European war. This meant that the supply of German dolls could not be replenished, and as stocks dwindled, the demand did not. The Schoenhut Company was quick to see the advantage of filling the void created by the loss of German dolls.

Another reason was the fact that little girls who had set their hearts on a "pretty" doll with lots of lace, ruffles and ribbons were not to be satisfied with a character face doll. Many children truly loved their Schoenhut dolls, as their well played with appearance attests. Some children, however, had one desire and that could only be met by a real "dolly." Schoenhut dolls were very appealing to adults because of their sturdiness and the ingenuity of their jointing. One woman told me that her father showed her Schoenhut jointed toddler to every visitor who came to the house because he was so entranced with the construction. She found the doll ugly, but she never told him as she did not want to disappoint him. For these children *Miss Dolly* was ideal.

She was either designed on an actual German doll, as had been some of the early Grazianos, or she was based on the idea of the "dolly." In different sizes and with the artwork of different decorators, one can guess which bisque dolls inspired her, but this search is only a game. What she has are the characteristics of a popular "dolly." Her face has heavy round and rather low cheeks. In profile her cheeks obscure most of her upper and all of her lower lip. Her chin has a soft, round, second one behind it. Her ears are also quite small, unlike other Schoenhut dolls. Her nose is short and upturned. She also has the open-mouth look of her bisque cousins. Her mouth is not actually open, but was carefully modeled to appear as if it is. Her parted lips show four upper teeth. The early models have a deeply incised space between the teeth and the lower lip which is sometimes accented with black paint. Her skin is often fairly pale, and her rosy cheek blush is a peach tone. She also has blush above her eyes and sometimes on her ear tips and chin.

Miss Dolly is a smooth-eyed doll with brown or blue painted eyes. Her iris was given depth with a stippling of darker color around the edge. After she was decorated her eyes were varnished to give her a glass-eyed look like the German bisque dolls she imitated. Her upper lid line is dark brown or black and she has both upper and lower lashes just like a real "dolly."

As originally presented in her fancy decorated display box, *Miss Dolly* had a luxurious long curl, mohair wig in either blonde or tosca tied with a silk ribbon bow. The ribbons appear to have been white, pink or light blue, and their color was indicated on the box label in pencil. Frequently the hair ribbon and that on the union suit matched, and sometimes the shoes and stockings also matched the ribbons. Doll 316 was offered in all four sizes both dressed and "undressed" (with union suit, shoes and stockings as well as stand). The two larger undressed *Miss Dolly* sizes also had a "fancy slip." The "Dolly" in her presentation box on the cover of *The Schoenhut Doll Catalogue* for 1915 is shown with the famous Schoenhut doll pin. It is the first time this pin is shown in company literature. In succeeding years new photographs of character dolls and babies also display this pin, which may have come into general use in 1915. The company used its old pictures over the years until a design change occurred and then it only replaced the necessary pictures. Thus character doll 19/308 continued to be shown with the bobbed hair wig without the pin for the rest of her production, but the new pictures taken of 19/308 C for the 1917 and later catalogues show the pin. This economical use of old pictures in both catalogues and advertisements has made it more difficult for toy historians to date changes in Schoenhut products. It does, however, make excellent business sense.

Miss Dolly's price in 1915 and 1916 was the same as a character girl of the same size with a long curl wig. The bobbed hair character girls were always less expensive.

Starting in 1917 *Miss Dolly* as a part of the consolidated line was offered with either a short, straight, bobbed hairstyle with bangs or with her original long curl hairstyle. Her prices rose a little faster than those of the other dolls, and it then cost as much for a bobbed hair 316 as for a comparably sized character girl with a long curl wig. The models and their boxes were now marked as 316 B or 316 C to indicate the hairstyle.

In 1920 *Miss Dolly's* eyes began to be decorated with a decal rather than paint. The decal was much more detailed than any paint decorating could have been. It had "threaded" lines through the iris and a dark rim around the edge. Another decal design achieved its appearance of depth by using tiny dots of darker color concentrated toward the outside of the iris rim. The use of the decal on the smooth convex modeled eye involved less labor, which was rapidly becoming much more expensive. *Miss Dolly* must have been a good seller as she is found more frequently than any other Schoenhut doll except the "Copyright" baby. For ten years she was offered as an alternative alongside the character dolls. 1924 not only marks the end of the character doll line; it was also the last year that the original *Miss Dolly* (316) was produced.

Illustration 241. The real *Miss Dolly*, in this case Doll 16/316, still tied in her original display box.

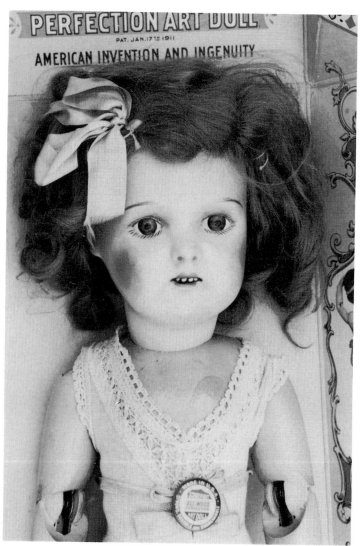

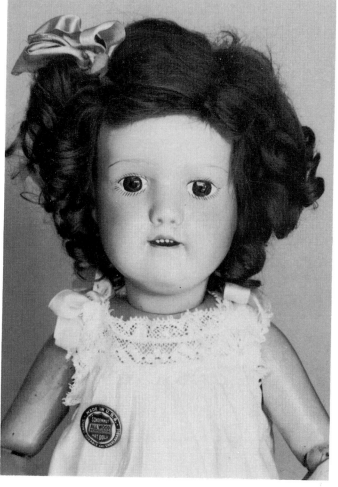

ABOVE:
Illustration 242. 17in (43cm). Still in her box, this Doll 16/316 is an early example. Her face paint is matte and pink-like bisque of her period. Her brown stippled eyes are shiny. There is blush above her eyes and even in her well-formed small ears, which in her case have a suggestion of the ear canal. Her brown brows are lightly feathered and widely spaced. Her upper lid line is brown, and she has many fine black lashes both above and below her deep-set eyes. Her mouth and accent dots are pink. Her teeth and inside of her mouth are deeply modeled. Each tooth is separately incised. All of this is accented with original black paint over red.

ABOVE RIGHT:
Illustration 243. *Miss Dolly's* hair still has its original curls. Her heavy round cheeks dominate her profile. Her nose, upper lip and chin are not completely obscured. Her eyes are quite deeply set, and the eyeball is very round increasing the similarity to a German bisque.

Illustration 244. 19½in (50cm). This is a very alert looking Doll 19/316. Her wig color is the richer brown that appears to have been made from about 1917 on. She is old store stock so even her hair ribbon is original, and matches the ribbons on her slip, her stockings and her shoes. Her skin color is pale and matte-finished, like bisque, with a soft, light peach blush. Her lips and accent dots are light pink. Her painted brown eyes are stippled and varnished over to give them a glass-like finish. Her upper lid line is brown. Her eyelashes are charcoal. Her multi-stroke brown brows are long, thin and slightly feathered. She has the impressed mark.

118

Illustration 245. 19½in (50cm). This blue-eyed blonde *Miss Dolly* 19/316C has threaded blue decal eyes. Her blonde multi-stroke brows are glossy. She is later than the Brunette 19/316, and her teeth have less modeling. Her bright upper lip has higher peaks. She has the decal mark. *Dot and Bud Hutton Collection.*

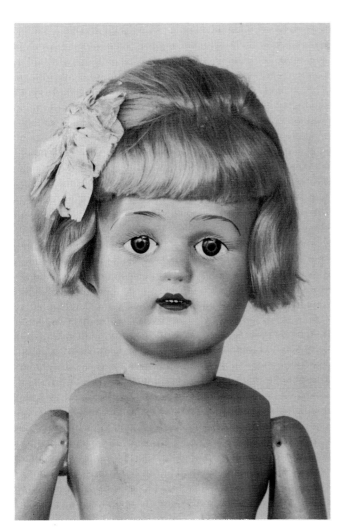

Illustration 246. 22in (56cm). A wonderful Doll 21/316B with her original set still in her blonde mohair bob. Even her fragile pink silk hair ribbon is original. Her blue decal eyes have the threaded pattern. Her lid lines and painted upper and lower lashes are black. She has dark blonde feathered brows. Her blush is peachy. Her mouth and accent dots are a light pink red, and the inside of her mouth, below her well modeled teeth, is a darker red. She has the decal mark and dates from 1920-1924. *Photograph by C. Lee James. Virginia Shoenfeld Collection.*

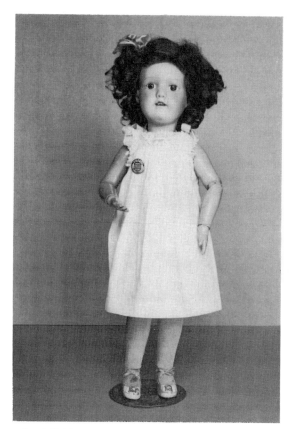

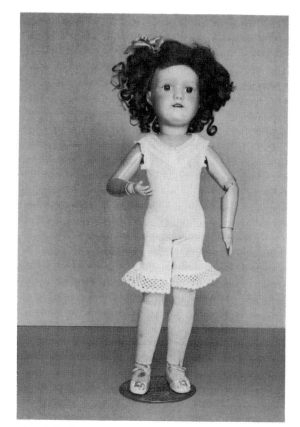

Illustration 247. The two larger sizes of *Miss Dolly* were presented with a "fancy slip" over their union suits. Beginning in 1917 all the 19in and 21in (48cm and 53cm) undressed girl dolls are pictured in the catalogues with this same slip. Note that her hair ribbon, slip ribbons, stockings and shoes are light blue. The Schoenhut pin is first shown on a *Miss Dolly* in the box in the 1915 catalogue. By 1917 all the new dolls photographed for the "condensed" line are shown with it.

Illustration 248. Under the slip of this 19in (48cm) *Miss Dolly* is a particularly nice union suit. Although it has no ribbon, the crochet lace around the legs is deep and covers her stocking tops easily.

Miss Dolly with Moving Eyes — Doll 317

Harry Schoenhut applied for two patents on his inventions of sleeping eyes and their placement in a hollowed out wooden head on March 22, 1920 and March 26, 1920. These inventions required the previously patented design for an eye printed on decalcomania film. Ultimately only the patent applied for on March 22 was used by the company, but copies of both patents, which were granted in the summer and fall of 1921, may be found in the appendixes in the back of the book. The eyes and their placement in the head are discussed in the chapter on Infants. The new dolls were shown in advertising in *Playthings* in January of 1921. Now *Miss Dolly* was even more like the bisque dolls that she emulated. This new model, which had molding changes that allowed her eyes to move smoothly, and therefore is not the same in appearance to 316 but is similar to her, was given a new model number — 317.

As a result of the space needed for her eye movement, Doll 317 has a remarkably flat face in profile. Her nose is snub and barely extends beyond her lips and small round chin. She also has a rounder, shorter chin line without the second chin.

Doll 317 was never actually called *Miss Dolly* by the company, but she was obviously designed to compete with the same type of doll that had been so popular before the war and was soon to slip into the American market for one last fling. She was offered in all four sizes with either a long curl wig or a short bobbed one. All the dolls, including the characters, were slightly larger than they had been although they all retained their original

size indications for ordering. Thus 14/316 and 14/317 as well as the smallest characters were now 15in (38cm); 16/316 was 17in (43cm); 19/316 was 19½in (50cm); and 21/316 was actually 22in (56cm) in height.

In 1924 Doll 317 was offered with elastic stringing as well as with the traditional metal springs. These dolls came in the same four sizes as the spring-jointed dolls and were numbered 140/317 B or C, 170/317 B or C, 190/317 B or C and 210/317 B or C. The elastic strung version had the traditional Schoenhut body without the spring joints. The elastic simply passed through the places where the springs normally were placed. Thus the same pieces were used for both bodies although the groove at the ball part of the joints is not cut as deeply, allowing a tighter fit for the joints. The elastic strung, or "Basswood Elastic" dolls as they were called by the company, did not have holes in their feet, shoes or stockings as a stand was not used with them. The "Basswood Elastic" dolls were obviously less expensive to produce and could be placed on the market at a much cheaper price. This was of great importance to the Schoenhut Company as trade with Germany as well as Japan was becoming freer again in the United States, and the competition of cheaper toys from abroad was affecting the market for the expensively produced Schoenhut dolls and pushing them into the "Luxury" doll category.

The Schoenhut Company kept the spring-jointed doll upon which it had built its reputation along with the new "Basswood Elastic" doll through 1928 and possibly 1929. Doll 317, which continued after 316 was dropped from production with the end of the 1924 season, was not made in any form by 1930.

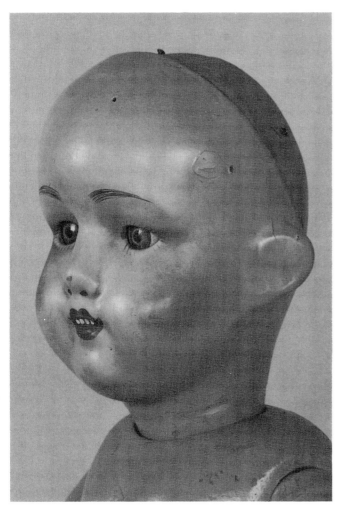

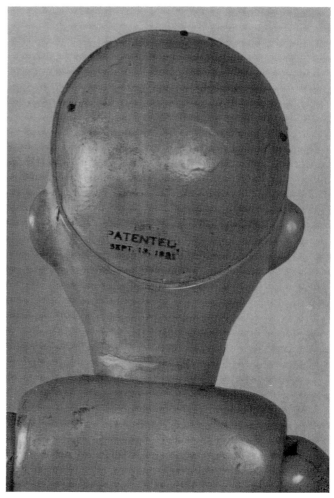

Illustration 249. With her wig removed we can see the small ears which are typical of all the "Dollys" but not of Schoenhut characters. This example is interesting because of her different decorating details. Her lips are a good deal fuller than those of most other 317s, and there is a definite curl at the corner of the mouth which is painted medium red with a large deeper red center. Her eyebrows are stacked and shorter than those of some her size. *Photograph by C. Lee James. Virginia Schoenfield Collection.*

Illustration 250. This Doll 19/317 has had her original light brown mohair wig removed so that we can see her wooden pate, the three nails that hold it in place and the patent mark for her sleep eye mechanism. She has no mark on her body. *Photograph by C. Lee James. Virginia Schoenfield Collection.*

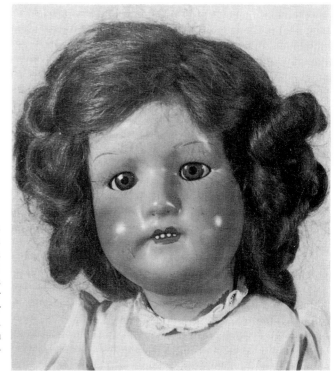

Illustration 251. 19¾in (50cm). This beautiful example of Doll 19/317 is the childhood doll of Phyllis Schoenhut O'Hare, youngest of Albert's grandchildren. Her original rich reddish-brown mohair long-curl wig is in excellent shape. She has the warm color and very smooth finish typical of the later Schoenhut dolls. Her eyes are a bright blue with tiny dark dots which become quite closely placed near the iris rim. She has both upper and lower very fine black lashes painted around her eye sockets. Her mouth and accent dots are medium pink. The inside of her mouth is red. There are four white teeth dabbed on to complete the open-mouth "German Dolly look." She has widely spaced, lightly feathered eyebrows. She is unmarked. *Phyllis Schoenhut O'Hare Collection.*

Illustration 252. 17in (43cm). Her brown decal eyes have threading indicated with black. She has been given a haircut by her first owner, but she retains a lot of charm. Her red brown hair is the post 1916 brunette color. Her eyebrows are well washed but still "stacked." This example of 16/317 has particularly well modeled teeth. *Roxanne LeMay Morison Collection.*

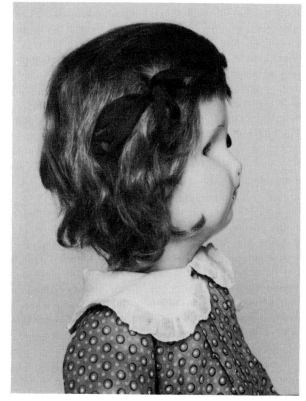

Illustration 253. The profile of Doll 16/317 shows a remarkably flat face with a very tiny nose and large, low cheeks. *Roxanne LeMay Morison Collection.*

THE SCHOENHUT MANIKIN
1914 to 1918

The "Schoenhut Manikin" appeared in The "Schoenhut Doll" Catalogue for 1914. He was not advertised as "new" in that catalogue, and it is possible that he was manufactured even earlier than that date, but complete doll catalogues from 1913 have not yet been found. He was clearly presented as a Manikin for "Students of Fine Art, or as Dressed Figures for Window Displays" rather than as a play doll. He appears to have been designed by Harry E. Schoenhut and came out earlier than Miss Dolly.

The Manikin came in the 19in (48cm) size only. Some variations on him were made in different sizes (or heads) and are covered in the chapter on Special Orders. The Manikin posed on a large sized Schoenhut stand and was constructed with the same spring joints as the play doll. His unique feature was a ball joint at the top of his hips. The chest section of his torso fit over the rounded top (or built-in ball) on his lower torso allowing him great flexibility to bend, lean or rotate at the waist. His other joints are the same as those of the play doll.

The Manikin came with one head style. He was a young man with short "carved" hair, well defined eyelids, intaglio eyes, a rather large nose and typically (for Schoenhut) large ears. His lips are thin and his jaw line firm. His features are modeled in a way that allows a good deal of difference in his appearance depending on how he is decorated. Individual models can appear to change as the light hits them from different angles. He is quite slim.

The Manikin was presented in five models or dress variations. As with the play dolls, the first number indicates the size in inches. The "Manikin not dressed. For Art Students" was given the number 19/175. At $42.00 a dozen he was about 50¢ a doll more expensive than the 19in (48cm) "carved hair" undressed play doll of 1915. This is taking into account that prices given in the Schoenhut catalogues appear to have been suggested retail prices and that dealers got a discount of up to 50% depending on the retail worth of their order.

The "undressed Manikin" was truly undressed, having no union suit, shoes or socks. The sophisticated construction, particularly of the waist joint, would have made him more expensive to produce. The rest of the dress variations were clearly labeled "For Window Display" although they must have had appeal as a play doll and some may have been sold for that purpose.

There were three sports figures. Model 19/175/1 was a "Basket Ball Player, with Ball." He has a dark sleeveless shirt (more like a "T" shirt than today's "tank top"), lighter shorts, dark ribbed socks and a pair of ankle-high thin leather sport shoes that look like short lace-up boots. He carries a round, apparently leather, ball. Model 19/175/2 is a "Foot Ball Player" in full uniform (with none of the heavy padding that we are accustomed to seeing today.) He has a brown leather helmet with a nose guard as well as a laced-up leather football. An excellent example is shown (Plate C1) in The Collector's Encyclopedia of Dolls by Dorothy S., Elizabeth A. and Evelyn J. Coleman, published by Crown Publishers, Inc. in 1968. It is in the collection of the Smithsonian Institution. His tan cotton lace-up oversuit with small leather shoulder and elbow "pads" are contrasted by his colorful striped jersey and socks. He also has light brown leather shin guards and boots. His nose guard is separate from his helmet and hangs from a cord around his neck. Both the Foot Ball [sic] and Basket Ball [sic] players sold for $72.00 a dozen. The last sports figure 19/175/3 was dressed as a "Base Ball Player, with Ball" [sic] and is positioned to pitch the ball. His outfit is quite simple. He has a shirt with elbow-length sleeves and knickers with a belt. His socks are white with a dark band at the top, and he wears the same ankle-high boots as the other two figures. He was offered at $66.00 a dozen.

The last figure 19/175/4 is dressed as a farmer in an "Over-all Suit and Straw Hat." He also has the boots worn by the other dressed Manikins. His long sleeved cotton shirt has a small print on it and seems to be the same material used for the shirts of some of the Circus personnel (the Farmer and the Negro Dude). His outfit is finished with a bow tie. He was also listed to sell at $66.00 a dozen.

The Manikin has usually been found unmarked, as are other figures used in art classes. He has been found with the incised Schoenhut Doll mark placed in a vertical position on the upper torso from the waist to the arm pit. This mark runs up the side of the body and is usually hidden by the arm. He has been found with the impressed mark running vertically up the back of his thigh, but when this occurs, the back of the thighs are flattened and not fully modeled. The figure has also been found with the oval decal mark on the back of his shoulders. It is possible that the changeover to the decal mark, which is thought to be later than the incised mark, occurred during this five year period; however, as with many mass produced products, this changeover may not have occurred at one time, as early heads have been found with decal marked bodies indicating that both marks may have been used simultaneously for some time.

The same five figures were offered at the same prices at least through 1918. As the prices of the play dolls rose dramatically over these years, it seems likely that these figures never had great demand and could not have taken a price rise. Stores often wanted their own special figures, of various sizes, for their windows and many of the special orders may have come from this time. In any case, with his extra flexibility and interesting face modeling, the manikin is a real treat to see and not often found.

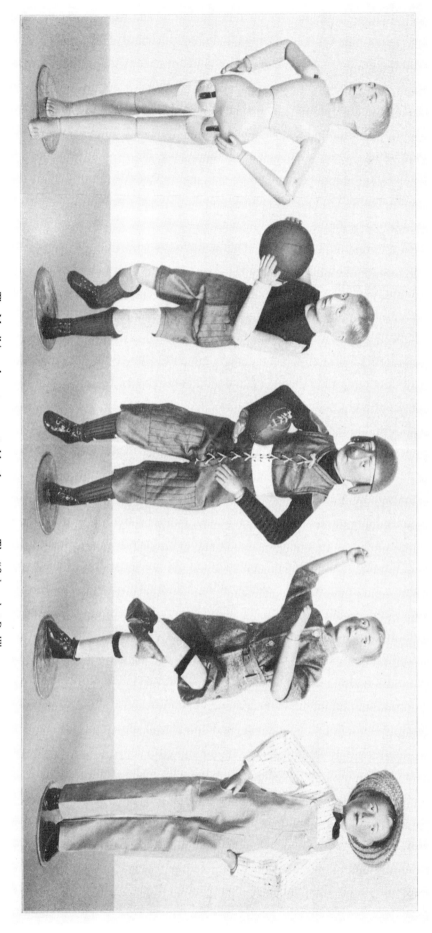

The Manikin as he was presented by the company. The "Schoenhut Doll" Catalog All Wood Perfection Art Doll 1914.

124

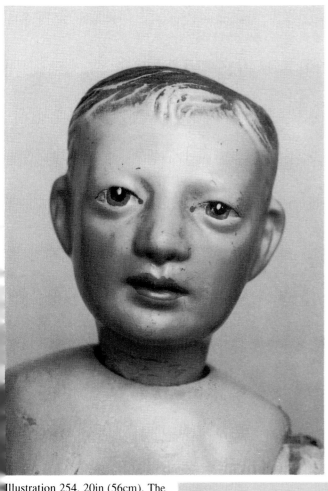

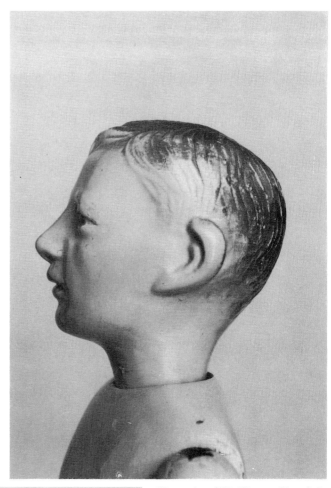

Illustration 254. 20in (56cm). The *Manikin* has strong features. Harry Schoenhut modeled his figures in plasticene and then had molds made. Apparently there was a step involving a plaster of Paris model on which the completed detail work before the mold was made.

Illustration 255. The profile of the *Manikin* shows the large nose and ear which appears in much of Harry Schoenhut's work. This profile view depicts the cheek muscles and lower lid clearly. This example is unmarked.

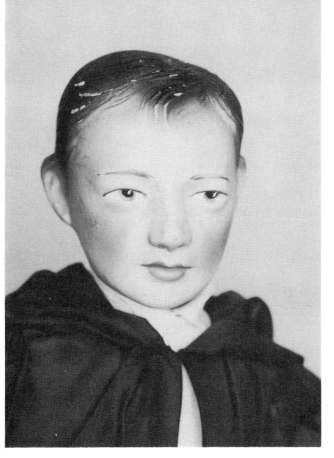

Illustration 256. 20n (51cm). This example of the Schoenhut *Manikin* has a very different look. His face has a very matte finish. The skin is quite light. His eyes are light blue. His dark brown upper lid lines are painted on the inside of the modeling which narrows the appearance of his eyes. His medium brown multi-stroke brows are quite straight. His blush is strong and "mint." His full lips are peachy pink with a darker line on the inside bottom of his upper lip. His sprayed hair is dark brown. He is the priest in the Wedding Party. *Becky and Jay Lowe Collection.*

125

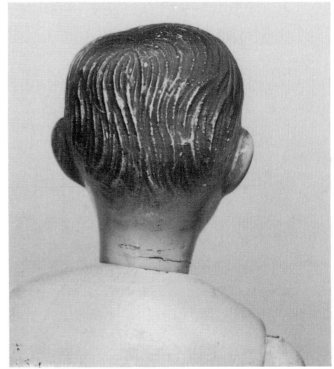

Illustration 258. The back of the *Manikin's* head is asymmetrical as are those of real people. He has the usual strong comb marks. *Manikins* came with the incised mark, the sticker or often with no mark at all as this one did.

Illustration 257. 19in (48cm). This example of the *Manikin* was especially dressed by the factory as the *Ring Master* from the Circus. He is in this chapter because his paint has not been specially modified, as has that of the *Lion Tamer* which appears in the chapter on Special Orders. His intaglio eyes are blue with brown upper lid lines. He has feathered brown brows. He has deep pink lips and accent dots and a soft orange blush. His white shirt and pants combination seems to be the same fabric as that used for the company's regular Ring Master. *Donna and Keith Kaonis Collection.*

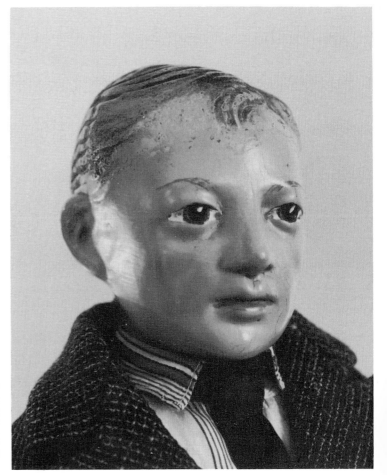

Illustration 259. 20in (51cm). This handsome *Manikin* is all-original in his tweed suit, striped silk shirt and fine silk tie. He even has perfect miniature black men's oxfords. His brown intaglio eyes are quite large with big pupils and black upper lid lines. He has well-modeled eye lids and even an indication of cheek muscles. He has additional carving to augment his molded comb marks on the sides and top of his head. *Dot and Bud Hutton Collection.*

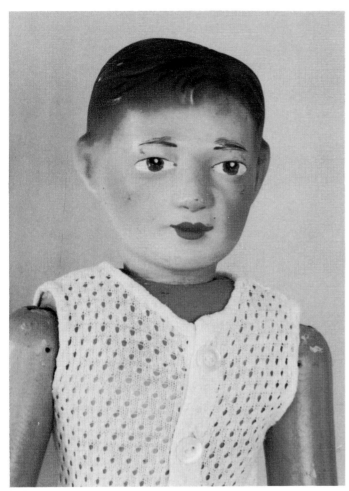

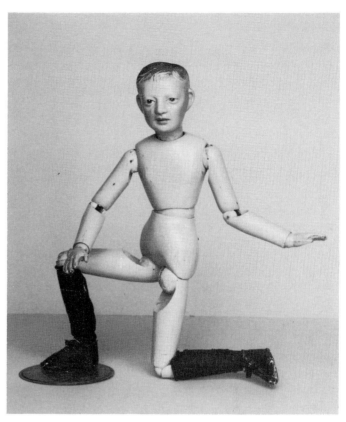

Illustration 261. The flexibility of the *Manikin* made him a better lay figure for art classes as well as for store window displays.

Illustration 260. 19½in (50cm). This handsome example of the *Manikin* is one of several found with post World War I decorating. His modeling is not as sharp as some. His paint is matte with very good color. He has blue intaglio eyes which are quite large and have brown upper lid lines. His brown brows are stacked with a number of shorter strokes indicating that he was probably painted around 1920. His mouth and accent dots are a strong orange pink, and he has a broad red line in between his lips. His dark brown hair is spray painted. He is marked with the oval decal on the back of his shoulders. *Photograph by C. Lee James. Virginia Schoenfeld Collection.*

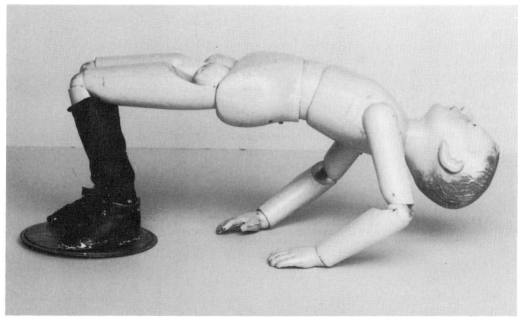

Illustration 262. The added ball joint at the waist gives the *Manikin* figure more flexibility for positioning.

THE CLASSIC PERIOD
PART II
1917 TO 1924

By the time America entered World War I the toy industry was already affected. Restrictions against German products had been in place for several years, and as a result, American toy makers expanded their products and manufacturing output dramatically. Even during Albert Schoenhut's lifetime company advertising had made much of the fact that its fine quality toys were American toys made for American children, appealing to their customers' love of durability, quality and patriotism.

At the same time that protection from foreign competition aided the growth of the American toy market, the cost of materials and labor rose sharply. Many of the products sold by Schoenhut had remained constant in price from 1906 through 1914. The basic Circus Clown sold for $4.00 a dozen in 1906 and still was priced at $4.00 a dozen in 1914. The dolls had even dropped in price as more of the molded details could be done by machine. A 16in (41cm) "carved hair" child which had come on the market for $3.00 retail in 1911 cost approximately $2.35 in 1915.

Suddenly prices began to rise rapidly. These changes occurred each year from 1915 through 1918. By 1918 the basic clown's price had risen by 50% and the 16in (41cm) "carved hair" child was now about $4.20.

At this point the company could hold its prices by streamlining the entire line and limiting variety. This meant fewer faces to learn how to paint, particularly if the faces were often the same ones presented in different sizes and with two hairstyles for each wigged girl.

During this time changes had occurred in the Schoenhut family structure. Five of the six Schoenhut sons, and one daughter, were now married and had children of their own. Harry Edison, who had headed the art department for the five years since the death of his father, was not married and he entered the American army in 1917 and served in France for 18 months.

With Harry in France and pressure to keep prices at a reasonable level for the consumer, the doll line was cut considerably with the selection of the surviving models made from among the best sellers and the least expensive ones to produce.

All 19in (48cm) and 21in (53cm) "carved hair" models were eliminated after 1916. The best selling 14in (36cm) and 16in (41cm) "carved hair" children remained. Among the girls these were Doll 101, in the 14in (36cm) size only and Dolls 102 and 105, in both 14in (36cm) and 16in (38cm) sizes. Doll 205 (which was always a boy according to the company but could double as a girl in an emergency) was made in both smaller sizes.

The line of wigged character girls was cut drastically. In the 14in (36cm) size only Doll 312 remained. In the 16in (41cm) size Dolls 300 and 301 remained. In the 19in (48cm) size the survivor was Doll 308 and in the 21in (56cm in reality) size a new Doll 308 was created. All other models were eliminated.

The boys were cut to one doll each in the three smaller sizes. Doll 405 (whose face was the same as 308's) was retained in the 14in (36cm) and 19in (48cm) sizes. Doll 403 (whose face was the same as 300's) was made in the 16in (41cm) size.

Thus four basic face designs were all that was left of what had been a line of 12 different faces (of wigged characters) the year before.

The company expanded that variety, at no extra cost to themselves, by offering each wigged girl in two wig styles. One was the long curl wig and the other was a short bob with bangs. This immediately appeared to double the number of wigged girls to be had. By keeping different faces for the 14in (36cm) boy and girl models, dealers could switch wigs to provide their customers with even more choice.

Miss Dolly (316) was offered in all four sizes and, for the first time, in a short bobbed wig as well as her heavy long-curl one.

The babies appeared to remain unaffected by the changes, and their line (which is taken up in detail in the next chapter) remained the same from 1914 until 1919 when the Schoenhut "Walkable Doll" was introduced.

After a period of terrific expansion, 1912-1914, the line stayed stable just through 1916. After 1916 the majority of wigged characters and some of the "carved" hair faces (plus all of their large size versions) were discontinued. They disappeared completely, explaining the rarity of many of the different faces as well as the tendency of collectors to refer to all the child dolls as either "the dolly face" or "the character face." The doll line also lost its separate catalogue and was incorporated into the general toy catalogue. Only the Schoenhut boats retained a separate catalogue for a little longer.

No further changes were made to the line until the "Walkable Doll" of 1919 and the introduction of the dolls with sleeping eyes in 1921.

Harry Schoenhut returned safely from World War I as a lieutenant. He resumed his position in the company and married Olga F. Dorfner on October 18, 1919. In the meantime Albert Schoenhut's third son, Theodore Carl, had died of tuberculosis on March 19, 1918, leaving his wife and son, George Weber Schoenhut (who as a child appeared in several company catalogues and as an adult was a part of the founding of O. Schoenhut Incorporated after A. Schoenhut ceased in 1935).

The character dolls that are left in this second or late "Classic Period" show subtle changes in their appearance, particularly in the early 1920s.

The molds used to finish the dolls have less sharply defined detail. The "carved hair" dolls have fewer comb marks in their hair. The dolls all have less eyelid and temple modeling and in general they have a softer appearance. Dolls 300 and 403 may be found without their characteristic chin dimple. They are also without the upper lid modeling and their eyes are usually quite narrow. There were no smooth-eyed characters left. Slowly, from 1917 through 1924, the intaglio eyes lost their depth. It seems that as the molds became worn in the early 1920s, they were not replaced with fresh ones. The eyes in the late character dolls were not really intaglio, but rather concave in their appearance.

This does not mean that these last characters were inferior to those made before 1920. The paint is particularly

beautiful on these dolls. The flesh is a rich warm color, and the blush and decorating is vibrant without being garish. The surface is very smooth, and there is no wood grain showing. The eyebrows are multi-stroke and have a "stacked" look from 1921 through 1923. The eyes continue to be offered in blue or brown. The top quality mohair wigs are offered in a new rich, true brunette, instead of the tosca color used earlier, as well as a blonde which sometimes has a "brassy" tone. The bodies no longer had an extra coat of varnish over the paint and have a "suntanned" appearance. All the dolls from about 1918 on have the decal mark. This mark seems to have appeared as early as 1916, but was apparently used along with the impressed mark for about two years.

Dolls 101, 102, 105, and 205 were made through 1923 when all production of "carved" hair characters stopped. These same dolls, along with Doll 16/201 which had not been offered since 1912, all reappeared briefly in the 1930 catalogue where they were advertised as "The only Educational Doll for Kindergarten Work."

The Schoenhut company produced a separate school supply catalogue in which such wonders as the Patty Hill blocks were offered. These products particularly appealed to schools that were a part of the Progressive movement in education, and they are not offered in the regular company catalogues. It is possible, though it does not appear to be likely, that the "carved hair" dolls continued to be offered to schools only throughout the late 1920s. The school catalogues that I have been able to find seem to have the same production schedule as the standard catalogues. Thus the 1918 school catalogue sells the same doll line as that offered in the general toy catalogue.

A few "carved hair" children have been found which are painted in quite a different style. They have very rosy cheeks and light pink mouths and accent dots. They also have honey-blonde painted hair. These same colors are found on the composition child designed by Harry Schoenhut which appears in the 1930 catalogue. These seem likely examples of the dolls advertised in that catalogue as "...for Kindergarten..."

The wigged characters lasted only one year longer. Doll 16/300 was made through 1923. Dolls 14/312, 16/301, 19/308, 21/308 as well as 14/405, 19/405 and 16/403 were produced through 1924. They do not reappear in any sales advertisements or catalogues after that date.

Illustration 264. This is Doll 16/301, her dog and her little girl. The doll has lost her stockings and shoes. Her hair is mussed, but she appears to be much loved. Her little girl's clothes appear to date to about 1920. *Courtesy Vicky Candido.*

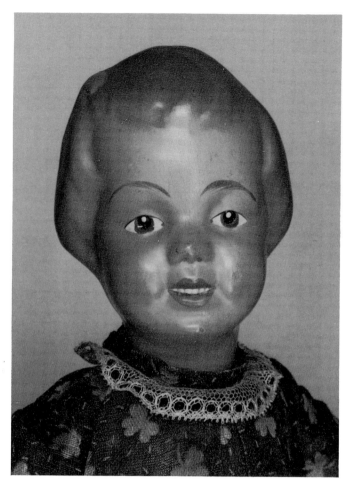

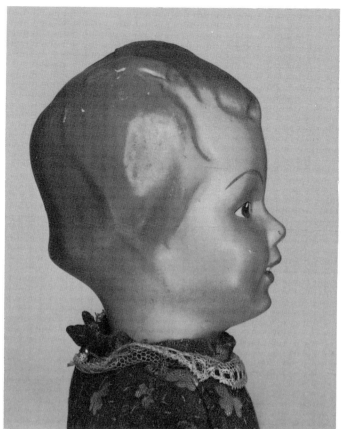

Illustration 266. There is still a sharp, clear profile showing on Doll 14/101, but there is no additional hand carving. The mold line shows on this doll.

Illustration 265. 14¾in (38cm). This example of Doll 14/101 is almost mint. She has many indications of being late. Her modeling is very soft with only a suggestion of eyelids, and her paint is very smooth with an almost glass-like quality. However, she cannot be very late as she does not have a "suntan." Her brows are arched and she has the impressed mark.

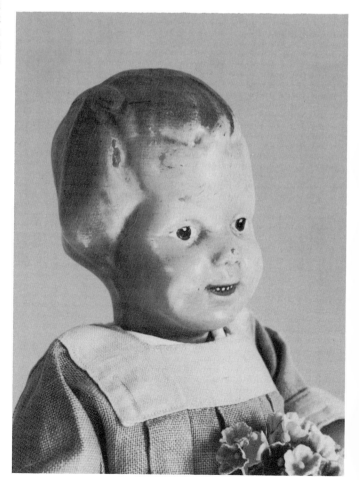

Illustration 267. The face modeling on this late Doll 14/101 is quite clear. She has both upper and lower lids, a strong philtrum and a broad smile with clearly separated teeth. Her paint is thin because she has been cleaned and washed, but her round brown intaglio eyes are quite nice. The inside of her mouth is clear and there is a soft indication of her outer mouth in a pale pink. There are traces of her original light brown eyebrows. She has the decal mark. *Dot and Bud Hutton Collection.*

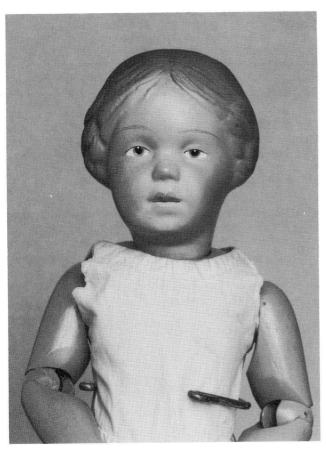

Illustration 268. 14¼in (36cm). This is a late example of Doll 14/102 and probably dates to the 1930 reissue of "carved hair" dolls. Her "sun tanned" coloring, pink blush and very soft honey colored hair are all similar to the composition child of that year. She has a translucent light pink mouth, nostril accents and tear ducts. Her upper lip has fine outlining and she has a dark pink-red center line which goes straight between the lips, ignoring the modeling. Her light blue eyes are mildly intaglio. Her upper lids are lined with translucent charcoal grey. Her eyebrows are made with fine, pencil thin strokes. Her hair is very lightly modeled when compared to earlier examples. Her sun-tanned body has been "freshened up" (factory repainted to match the color of the later head). She has the oval sticker mark. *Becky and Jay Lowe Collection.*

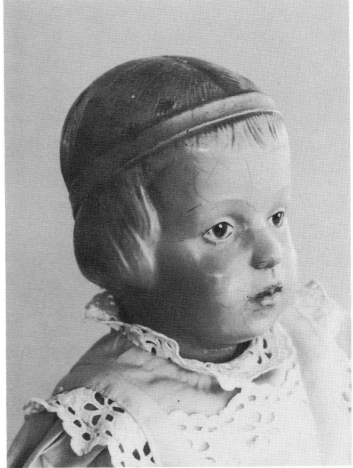

Illustration 270. 16½in (42cm). This sweet 16/105 has dark blonde hair which is a real contrast to the usual brunette versions of this doll. She still has good eyelid, eyebrow and philtrum modeling. Her dark brown eyes are deeply intaglio. Her upper lid lines are also dark brown. Her body has the "suntanned" appearance and has the decal mark. The comb marks on the back of her hair are also clear, but they are almost gone from the top and sides of her hair. *Sara T. Kocher Collection.*

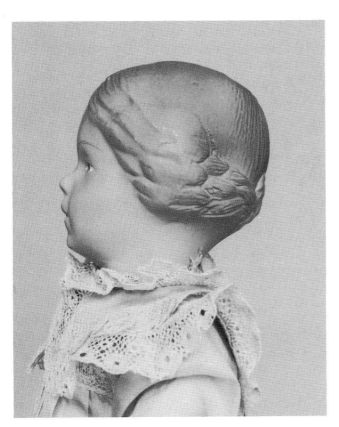

Illustration 269. Profile view of the 1930 reissue of the "carved" hair, 14/102, doll. *Becky and Jay Lowe Collection.*

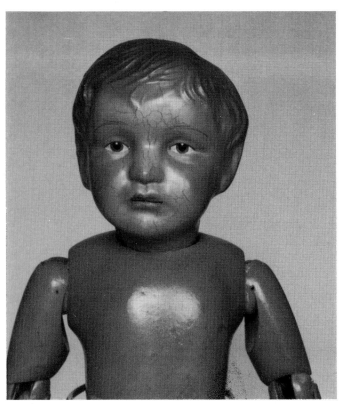

Illustration 271. 16in (41cm). This 16/201 may be an example of one of the 1930 sale of earlier "carved hair" models. His skin is "suntanned" looking. His blush, lips and hair are similar in color to that of the composition child of that year. He has brown intaglio eyes and fine long blonde eyebrows. His entire face is covered with a web of fine crazing, but the paint has held firmly this way for years. This crazing is common in these late dolls. Possibly it was caused by the fact that there are several coats of factory paint on these dolls, and they may not be totally compatible with each other.

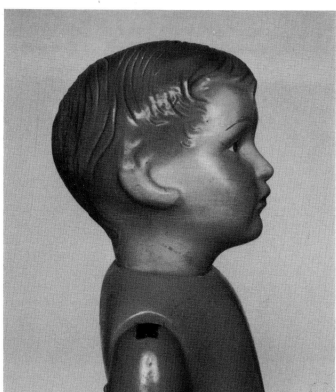

Illustration 272. Profile view of the 16/201 boy.

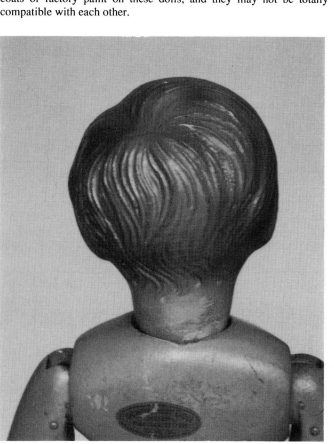

Illustration 273. The strength of the comb marks and lid modeling of the 1930 "carved hair" dolls indicate that these examples were refurbishing of earlier molded stock rather than entirely newly modeled dolls. There is even evidence of hand carving over the "blur" caused where the molds meet.

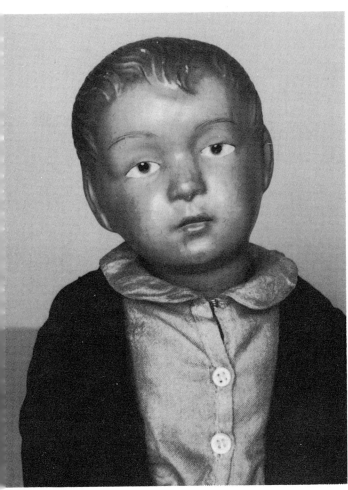

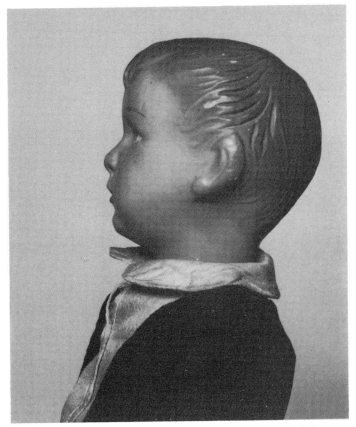

Illustration 275. As this profile view of Doll 16/204 shows, there is heavy carving on the side of his head indicating that he was molded at an early date and painted later.

Illustration 274. The paint on this Doll 16/204 looks factory-original but quite late. He is a real blonde with multi-stroke blonde brows. His eyes are light blue intaglio. The whites are quite large. His color is soft with pale pink lips and a red line through his mouth. This doll has walkable body which appears original to him.

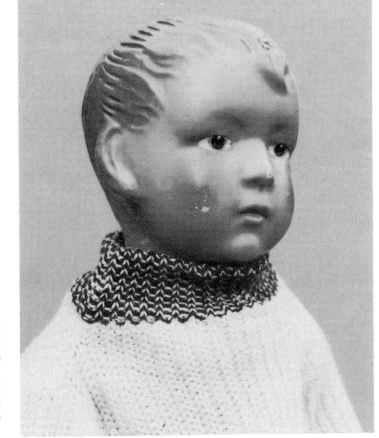

Illustration 276. 16¼in (41cm). This example of 16/204 was bought at auction as a repainted Schoenhut. His purchaser took him home and scrubbed him with an abrasive powder to remove some repaint. As he cleaned, his buyer began to suspect that he was a factory repaint. His color is very similar to that of the composition child. He has a dark suntanned body with decal mark, blonde hair like the composition child and appears to be one of the "Kindergarten Dolls" offered by the company in 1930. They were refurbished examples of earlier carved-hair models. His modeling is very soft. His eyes are large as the paint goes beyond where the lid line would be if he had them. The mouth is barely tinted. There is a darker line running through the center. He still has grooves cut in the side of his hair to cover the blur of the mold edges. He has the oval decal mark.

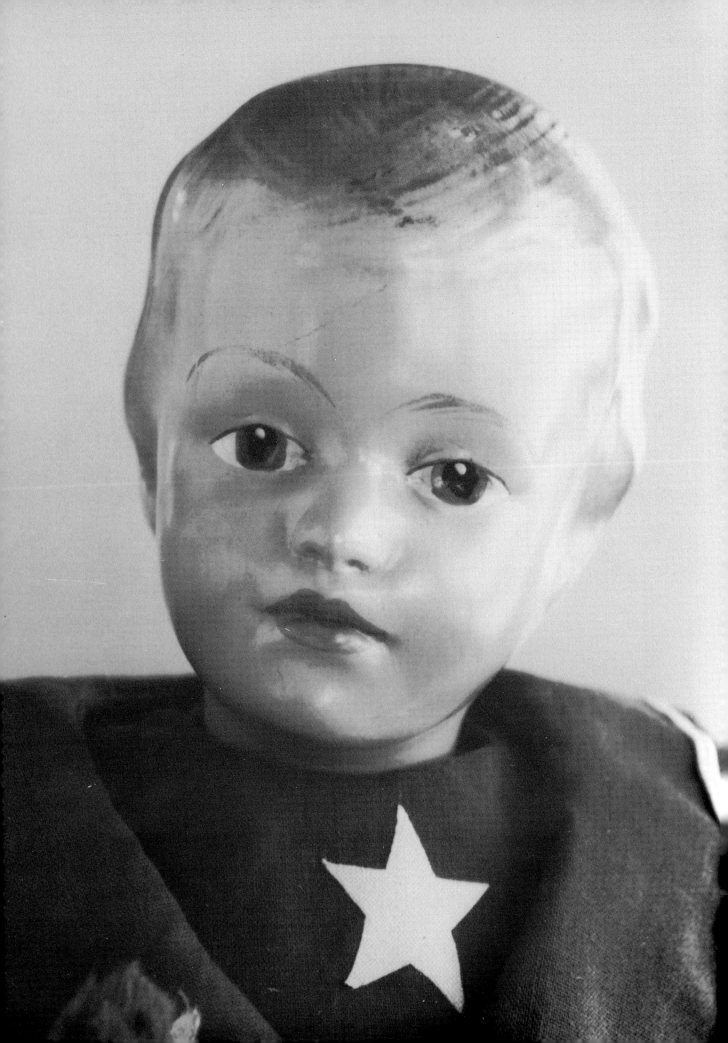

OPPOSITE PAGE:
Illustration 277. 14½in (37cm). This mint example of Doll 14/205 has such smooth paint that it is difficult to photograph him. He has light brown intaglio eyes with well-modeled upper and lower eye lids. He has dark brown upper lid lines and thin, multi-stroke, long brown eyebrows. His blush is a soft peach. He has a pink mouth, nostrils and tear ducts. There is a light red line between his lips. He has the decal mark. *Regina A. Steele Collection.*

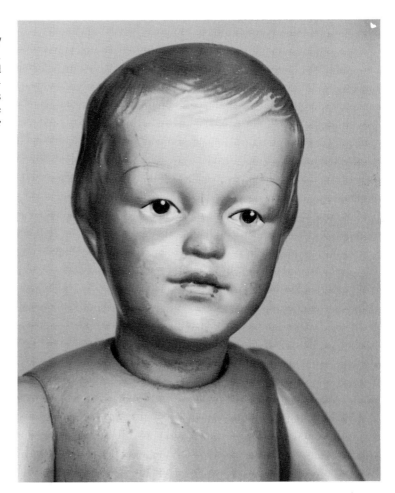

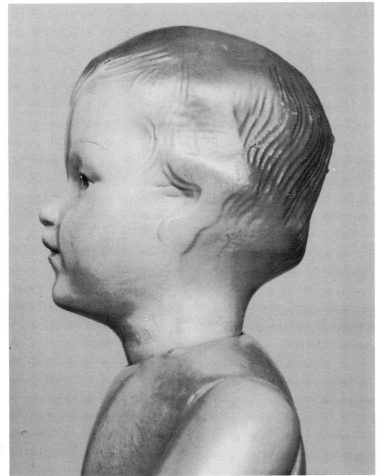

Illustration 278. This beautiful blonde 14/205 head is on a "Walkable" body which appears to be original to it. As a factory original blonde, he is unusual. His skin is pale. His cheek blush is pink. The bright blue paint of his irises are extended beyond their modeling particularly on the bottom. He has black upper lid linings and widely spaced thin blonde brows. His body has the "Walkable" decal label.

Illustration 279. In profile the 14/205's blonde hair and ear show very little modeling as his mold has become quite worn at this late date. His eyedot is still raised enough to show in profile, and the modeling of his features is quite fine. The company no longer did any hand carving to cover the space where the mold front and back meet.

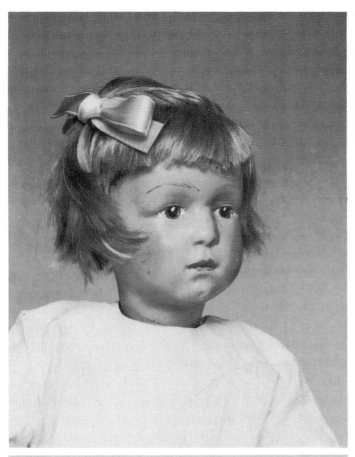

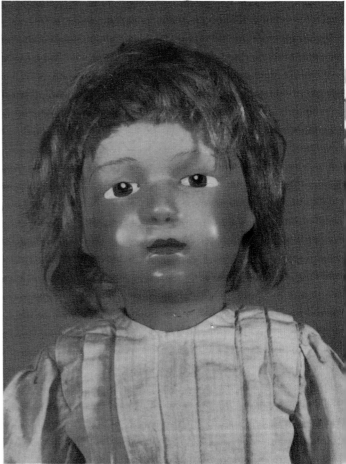

TOP LEFT:
Illustration 280. 16in (41cm). This fine 16/300B is only identifiable as a World War I example by her bobbed hairstyle which became a choice for this face when the entire line was revamped in 1917. Her blue eyes are deeply intaglio, and her eyelids, temples, dimple and philtrum are distinctly modeled. She has a gentle blush on her cheeks, above her eyes and just a touch on her chin. Her mouth and accent dots are orangy pink, and there is a thin light red line running between her lips. She has the impressed mark on the back of her shoulders. Her original owner named her Janie Brenner.

TOP RIGHT:
Illustration 281. 16½in (42cm). This late 16/300B is typical of her period. Her modeling is much less detailed. She has lost the upper lid modeling, her philtrum groove and the dimple is a flattened spot on her chin. Her eyes are more concave than intaglio although the white dots are still raised. Her paint is beautiful. Her wig is mohair but appears large and is not a usual style. It is probably not original. Her mark is the oval decal. She dates about 1920.

LEFT:
Illustration 282. 16½in (42cm). This is a sweet example of Doll 16/300C. She has light lid crease modeling and a soft dimple in her chin so she probably dates before 1920. Her intaglio eyes are light brown with medium brown upper lid lines and multi-stroke brown brows. She has a soft light skin color and a peach blush on her cheeks only. Her mouth, nostrils and tear ducts are pink. Her original Schoenhut mohair wig is dark blonde or very light tosca. She has the decal mark. *Regina A. Steele Collection.*

Illustration 283. 16in (41cm). This is about as perfect an example of model 16/301B as one could hope to find. Her tosca mohair wig still retains its original "set." Even her pink silk bow is original and is in splendid condition. Her less strongly modeled eyes, fine eyebrows and decal mark indicate that she belongs to the period 1917-1924. Her clear matte paint makes her very natural looking. As her eyes are still (although softly) intaglio, she probably dates about 1920. *Photograph by Monty Moncrief. Siger Davey Collection.*

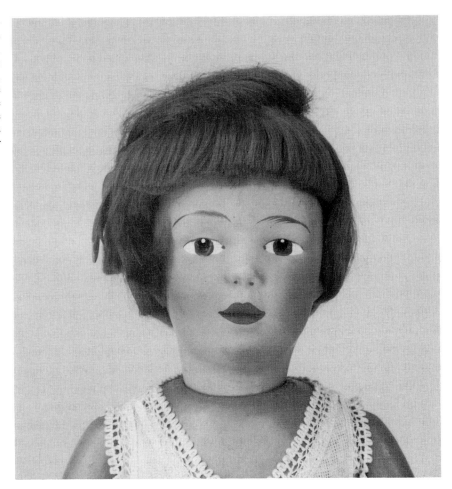

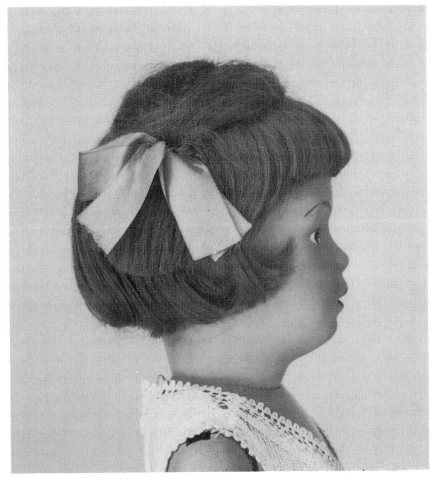

Illustration 284. Model 16/301 B's profile is even softer than that of the earliest examples. Her hair is the slightly reddish shade of brown that came out in 1917. She has her original union suit (pink bow of course), black stockings and shoes and the Schoenhut pin. *Photograph by Monty Moncrief. Siger Davey Collection.*

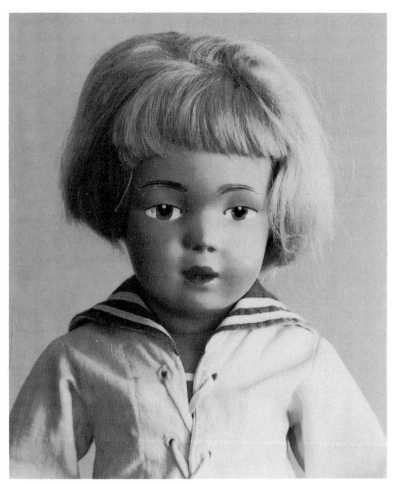

Illustration 285. 16½in (42cm). This is a charming example of Doll 301B from the early 1920s. The top knot has been released, and its bow is gone as it has been dressed as a boy for many years. The structure of the wig is clearly a girl's bob. She has beautiful coloring with a "suntanned" look and a healthly peach blush. Her mouth and accent dots are deep pink. Her eyes are a strong medium blue concave with brown lid lines. Her eye dots are raised in the molding. Her mohair bob is pale blonde. She has the decal mark. *Sara T. Kocher Collection.*

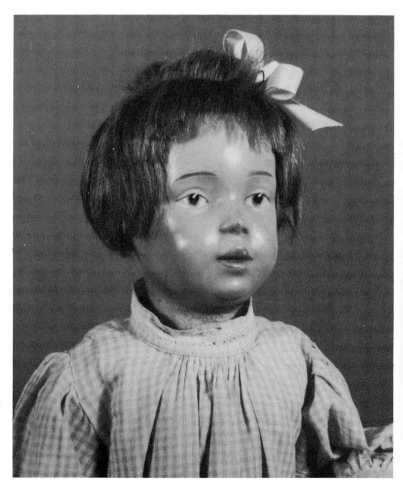

Illustration 286. 16½in (42cm). This example of Doll 16/301B is an early example from the World War I period. She has good eyelid modeling and true intaglio eyes. Her brown brows are slightly feathered. Her mouth and accent marks are pink, and she has a deeper line between her lips. She has a nice old pink and white homemade dress, factory original union suit with a white bow and factory brown two button boots. She has the impressed mark. *Dot and Bud Hutton Collection.*

Illustration 287. 15in (38cm). This 14/308B model has rust brown intaglio eyes with dark brown upper lid lash lines. She has well-modeled upper lids and lightly molded lower lids. Her paint is pale with light pink mouth, tear ducts and nostrils. There is a deeper pink line which follows the modeling between her lips. She has thin multi-stroke brown brows. She also has the decal mark.

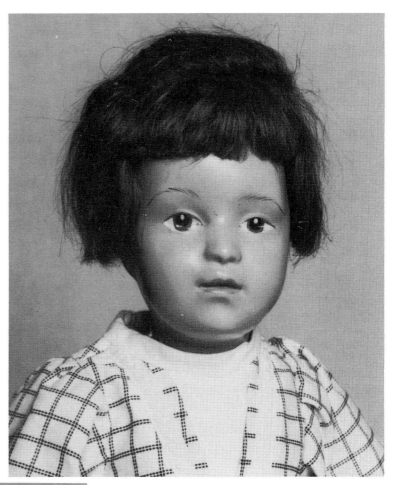

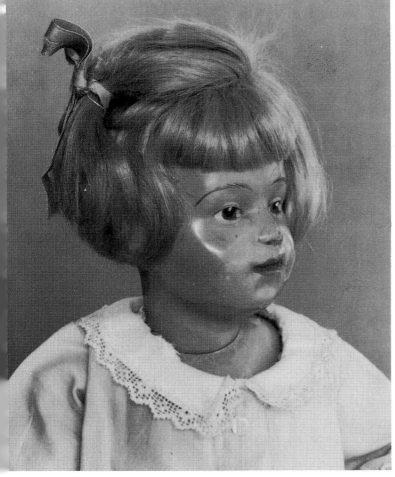

Illustration 288. 15¼in (39cm). Even though Doll 14/308 is not shown in catalogues after 1916, there are many examples from the later period. This was easy as this head was used for the 14/405 boy through 1924. The pre-1917 version of 308 came with long braids wound around her crown. After 1916 the wigs available for girls were bobbed with bangs or a long curl with a side part. This example is 14/308B is shown for her hairstyle. She probably dates about 1918. She still has clear eyelid modeling, clear light skin with the orange blush on her cheeks. Her lips, nostrils and tear ducts are pink. She has the decal mark. *Sara T. Kocher Collection.*

Illustration 289. A fine example of a later Doll 19/308. Her eyelids and lips are less strongly modeled. Her paint is very smooth and natural in color. Her multi-stroke brows are long and arched. Her eyes are large and the irises are light brown. Her mouth and accent dots are deep orange pink. There is a red line between her lips. She is completely factory-original and mint with pink hair bow, slip bows, stockings and shoes. *Photograph by Monty Moncrief. Becky Moncrief Collection.*

Illustration 291. 15in (38cm). The loss of eyelid modeling as the aging molds were not replaced gave the artists more leeway in making the size of the eyes different. The result in this example of Doll 14/308C is that she has particularly large dark blue, slightly intaglio eyes. Except for a few tiny bumps the paint is smooth and nicely colored. The blush is usually on the cheeks only in these later examples. Her light brown eyebrows are multi-stroke. Her lash line is also light brown. She has a light red line between her pink lips. Her long-curl blonde wig was cut years ago by some child who probably expected it to grow out again. *Dot and Bud Hutton Collection.*

Illustration 290. The profile of Doll 19/308 is both softly and clearly molded. Her brown mohair wig is unusual in the perfection of its condition. *Photograph by Monty Moncrief. Becky Moncrief Collection.*

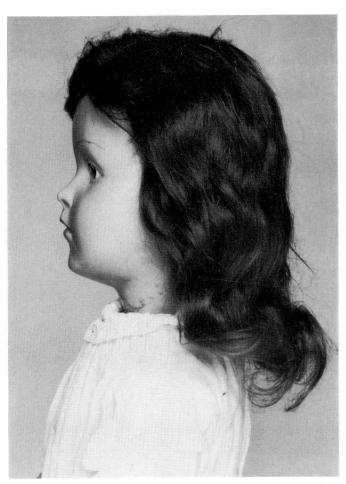

Illustration 292. 22½in (57cm). This example is sadder than the 308 usually looks. Her head is massive and seems out of scale with her body. It also causes her to be even taller than most 21in (53cm) dolls are. Her dress is original to her and may be factory-original circa 1919.

Illustration 293. This model is 21/308C for her long curl wig which is a rich red brown — a new color in 1917. Her eyes are rust-brown, and the lid molding is not as deep as in the 19in (48cm) versions of this mold. She has fine thin multi-stroke brows and black upper lid lash lines. She has the impressed mark.

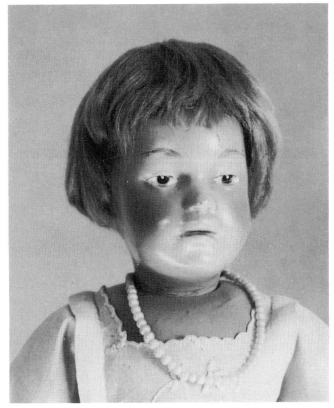

Illustration 294. 14½in (37cm). Technically this doll is a 405 due to her boy's bob, but she is wearing an apparently original girl's union suit under her homemade pink linen dress with white hand-embroidered trim. Her suntanned paint, high cheek color and stacked eyebrows date her to 1921-1924. She is in excellent condition all over. The artist who painted her made her light blue eyes quite tiny. She has the decal label. *Dot and Bud Hutton Collection.*

Illustration 295. 15in (38cm). This beautiful example of Doll 14/308C comes from the period when this face was officially released as a boy only, but she is clearly original with her long-curl mohair wig and her girl's union suit, brown stockings and slippers. She even has her original button which indicates that the dolls still had these pins in the 1918-1920 period. Her blue eyes are slightly intaglio with brown lid lines and dark blonde multi-stroke eyebrows. Her paint is quite smooth and vibrant, but it does not have the suntanned look of the dolls of the 1920s. The shreds of her original ribbon and the bow on her union suit are both white. Her red dotted swiss dress with tatted trim appears original to her. She has the decal mark. *Dot and Bud Hutton Collection.*

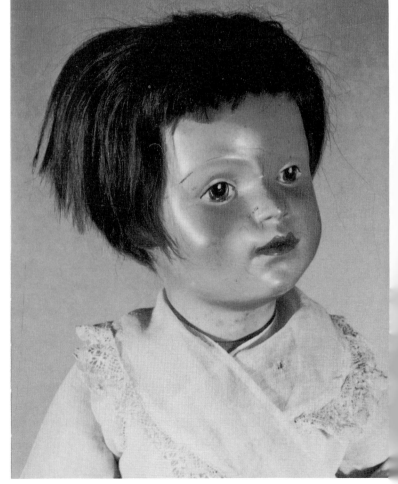

Illustration 296. 19¼in (49cm). A brown-eyed brunette version of Doll 19/308. Her light brown intaglio eyes have black lid lines. She has strong pink coloring in the mouth, nostrils and tear ducts. There is a deeper pink line through the middle of her mouth and shading on her upper lip. Her fine multi-stroke brows are faded but still there. The thinness of them is typical of dolls made in about 1917. She has the impressed mark. *Ella and Larry Corn Collection.*

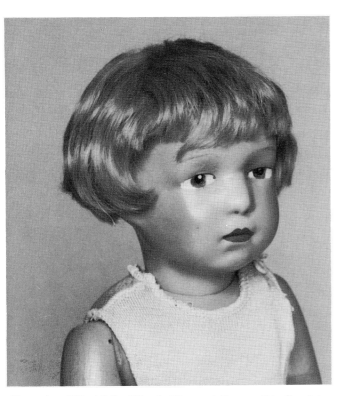

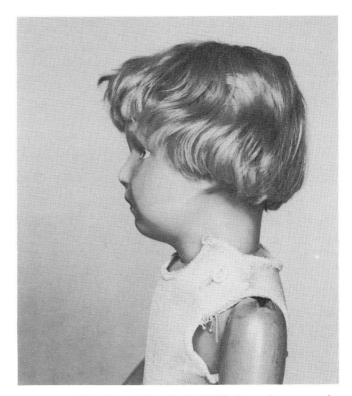

Illustration 297. 16½in (42cm). The modeling on this fine late example of Doll 16/403 is very soft. There is no real dimple, but you can tell where it should be. The eyes are wide ovals with no clear lid modeling. They are more concave than intaglio. The iris is a fairly dark blue. His paint is very smooth and a warm natural color. His mouth and accent dots are a deep orangy-pink. There is a thin red line through the center of his mouth. He has thin light brown multi-stroke eyebrows and darker brown upper lid lines. His thick blonde mohair wig shows his ear lobes. He has the decal mark.

Illustration 298. The profile of Doll 16/403 shows the same snub-nosed, round-featured look as the earlier models.

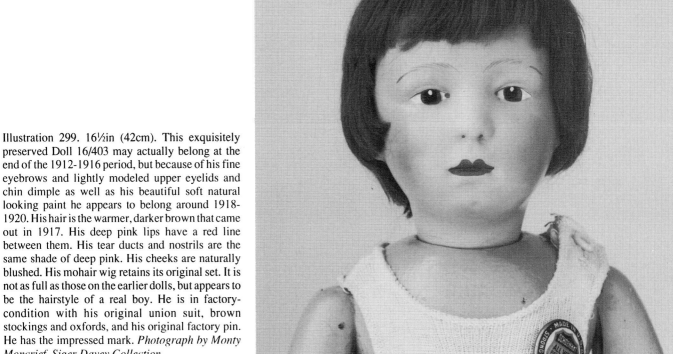

Illustration 299. 16½in (42cm). This exquisitely preserved Doll 16/403 may actually belong at the end of the 1912-1916 period, but because of his fine eyebrows and lightly modeled upper eyelids and chin dimple as well as his beautiful soft natural looking paint he appears to belong around 1918-1920. His hair is the warmer, darker brown that came out in 1917. His deep pink lips have a red line between them. His tear ducts and nostrils are the same shade of deep pink. His cheeks are naturally blushed. His mohair wig retains its original set. It is not as full as those on the earlier dolls, but appears to be the hairstyle of a real boy. He is in factory-condition with his original union suit, brown stockings and oxfords, and his original factory pin. He has the impressed mark. *Photograph by Monty Moncrief. Siger Davey Collection. .*

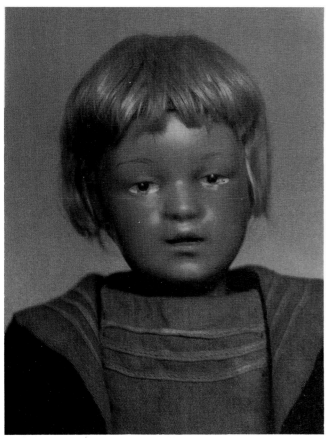

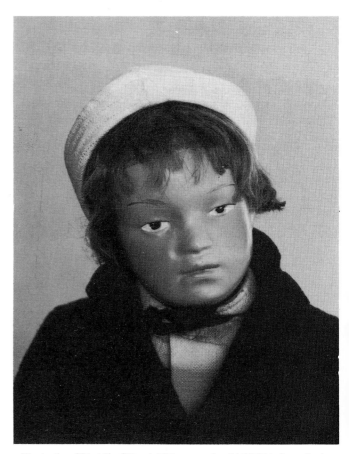

Illustration 300. This post-World War I example of Doll 14/405 has the smooth, less detailed modeling of the later examples. The paint and decoration are of excellent quality, rather suntanned (as dolls then became) and very smooth with no hint of wood grain. This serious child is an example of one of the boys who has been a girl for years. All real little girls of this period did not wear giant bows in their bobbed hair. Their fine hair could not support them.

Illustration 301. 15in (38cm). This example of 14/405 is from the late "Classic Period," circa 1919. His lower eyelid is still molded, and his philtrum is lightly indicated. He has the smooth shiny surface of this period. His blush and lips are a soft pink. There is a fine red line on the bottom of his upper lip. His multi-stroke brown eyebrows are slightly stacked. He has light blue, slightly intaglio eyes and charcoal upper lid lines. He has the decal mark. *Sara T. Kocher Collection.*

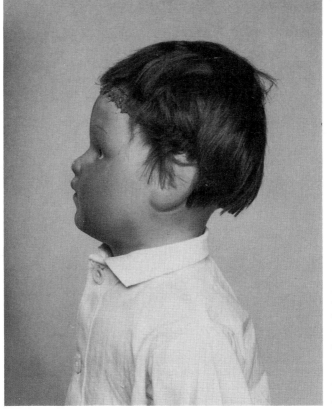

Illustration 303. In profile, it can observed that like the rest of his modeling, this boy is very soft compared to earlier 405s, and his identification is therefore questionable. His rich brown mohair wig is worn but original, and the color used in the later period. He has a decal oval mark on the back of his shoulders. *Roxanne LeMay Morison Collection.*

Illustration 302. 19½in (49.5cm). This 19/405 is an excellent example of the quality of paint and decoration of the later (1917-1924) characters. He has an even, deep and glossy flesh color. The blush on his cheeks, chin and above his eyes is widespread. He has deep pink lips, nostrils and tear ducts with a red line straight through his mouth. He has light brown intaglio eyes and a narrow dark brown upper lash line. The eyelid modeling is very soft, indicating a worn mold that was not replaced. His eye whites extend considerably onto his cheeks. He has light brown short multi-stroke eyebrows. His hat, short knee length pants, stockings and shoes are all white and factory-original. He is missing only his red jacket with the brass buttons from outfit 818. *Roxanne LeMay Morison Collection.*

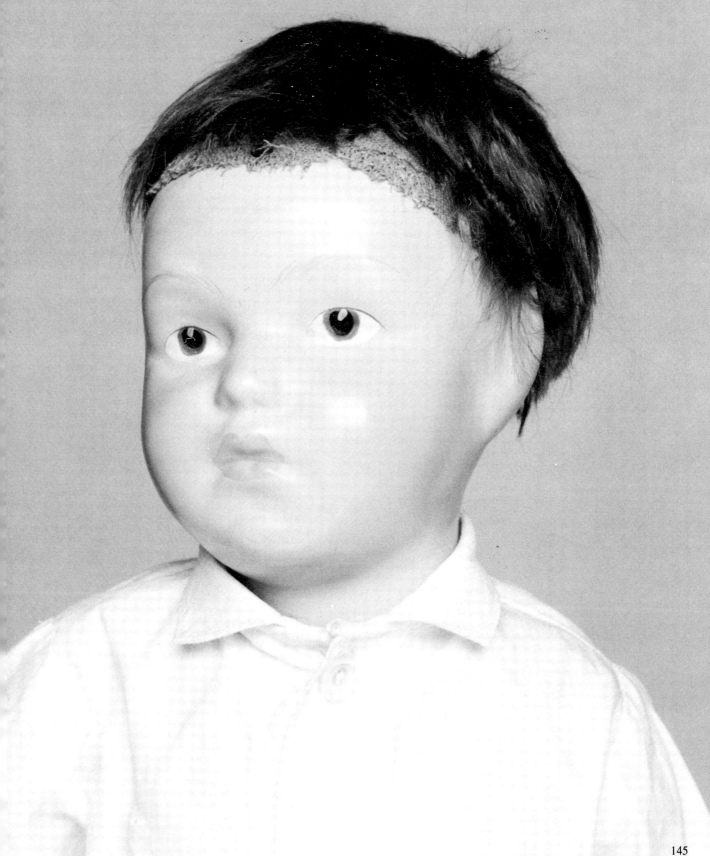

THE SCHOENHUT INFANT DOLLS

The Schoenhut Infant dolls divide into two design styles. The first style is represented by the 1911 "babies" named by the company *Tootsie Wootsie* and *Schnickel-Fritz*. These dolls appear in the first Schoenhut doll catalogue in 1911 and were produced through 1912. The second style includes dolls bearing a copyright mark assigned to Harry E. Schoenhut on December 31, 1913. In addition to the "copyright babies" are several other designs, and adaptations of the designs of others, produced by Harry E. Schoenhut until he left the company in 1930.

The original two "Infants," as the company called them, are not really babies. They were produced on fully-jointed child bodies and have the look of active toddlers. Their more mature faces have the strong character look found on the earliest Schoenhut dolls. The designs of these early Schoenhut faces have been attributed to M. (Adolph?) Graziano. I have been unable to find a designer's name listed in the early catalogues. George Schoenhut, who worked at the original company, has reaffirmed his belief in a letter dated April 13, 1988, to his cousin Phyllis that this was the name of the original doll designer. He further stated that he believed this information is written in a company brochure.

The remainder of the infant designs are attributed to Harry Edison Schoenhut, the next-to-youngest son of Albert Schoenhut. Harry Schoenhut's dolls are characterized by a much younger appearance with larger eyes and a rounder, softer lower face.

The Graziano Infants

As with the character dolls produced in the "Graziano Year" (May to November 1911) and the "Transition Period" (November 1911 to April 1912 or, in the case of the infants,

through the 1912 Christmas season), there are differences visible in different examples of the actual dolls.

The earliest examples appear to have a good deal of hand carving in their facial features as well as in their hair. Their eyes have the irises outlined in a darker color, and there is no stocking groove cut into the thigh.

"Transition Period" decorating detail changes include the change from a thin coat of pale pink paint, with no gesso coat below it, to a smoother warm flesh tone over a gesso coat which hid the wood grain beneath it. The blush also changed from pink to an orange tone, and the irises lost their outlines.

Tootsie Wootsie was registered in the U.S. Patent Office by Albert Schoenhut on June 6, 1911. This doll was described, in the 1911 catalogue, as a 15in (38cm) fully-jointed infant with "imitation hair carved on the solid wooden head, painted in natural colors." The doll was given the numbers 15/50 (for undressed doll in slip, boots and stockings with stand), 15/51 (dressed in plaid rompers) and 15/52, in an elaborately lace and tuck trimmed white lawn "short" dress which was ankle length.

The actual *Tootsie Wootsie* doll has a rectangular shaped face. It is the younger looking of the two infants with low, fat cheeks and wide open eyes that resemble semi-circles set on the flat edge. There are molded upper and lower eyelids, temples and cheek muscles. The nose is tiny, uptilted and snubbed. The philtrum has a circle shape rather than the typical groove and the upper lip extends beyond the nose. The mouth is deeply open/closed with a molded tongue and up under the upper lip two teeth are painted on a slightly molded gum-line. There are no bottom teeth showing. In profile the nose, lips, tongue and chin extend well beyond the heavy cheeks. The forehead is high. The hair is only slightly molded, giving the impression that it has been

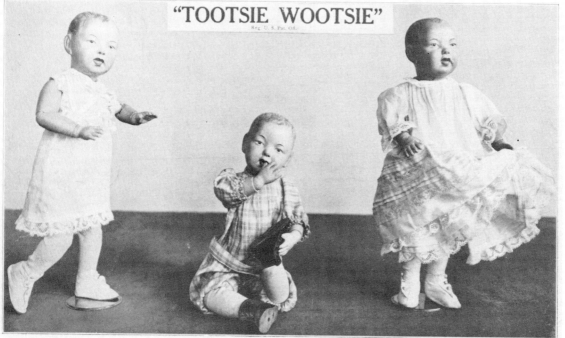

15/50   15/51   15/52

Illustration 304. This cut from...*Illustrated Catalogue...Dolls The A. Schoenhut Company*, dated 1911, shows the three ways that *Tootsie Wootsie* could be purchased. Retail prices ranged from $3.00 each "with slip, stockings, shoes and metal stand" to $6.50 dressed in "infants first short dress...of white lawn, with lace and embroidery trimmings...white lawn Drawers and Petticoat with Bodice, trimmed with lace."

Illustration 305. 15in (38cm). This is a wonderful example of *Tootsie Wootsie*. The light blue slightly intaglio eyes have dark brown upper lid lines. There is good modeling around the temples and mouth. The blonde eyebrows are single-stroke. The hair modeling is light on all *Tootsie Wootsies*, but this is one of the strongest examples. The pale skin paint is original. The lips and accent dots are deep pink. The tongue is light pink. The orange cheek blush is faded but still shows. This is the light dull paint of the earlier models although it does not have outlined irises. The blonde translucent wash on the hair is also the sign of an older doll. With its upper lip thrust forward and the short round philtrum, it is a great doll. It has the incised mark. *Dot and Bud Hutton Collection.*

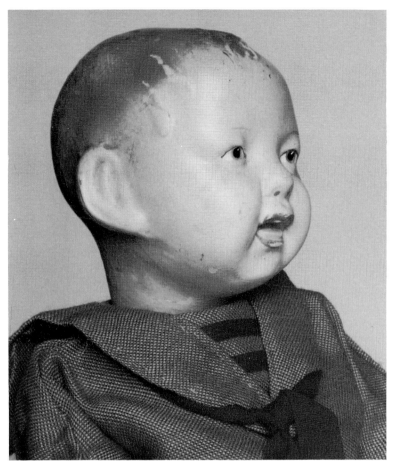

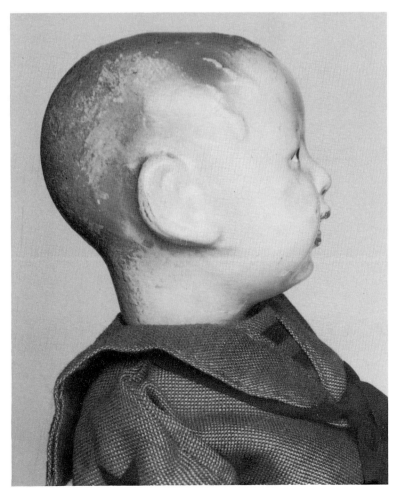

Illustration 306. This profile of *Tootsie Wootsie* illustrates the impression that the hair of the doll is "drizzled on." The large ears stick out slightly. The snub nose looks perpetually stuffy. *Dot and Bud Hutton Collection.*

147

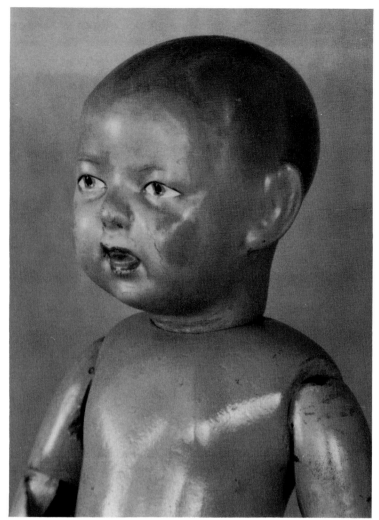

Illustration 307. 14½in (37cm). This *Tootsie Wootsie* is in super shape. The doll appears to have a perpetual stuffy nose and is obviously a "mouth breather." It is a blonde with slightly modeled hair and blonde single-stroke brows. The blue eyes are well-modeled with clear lower lids and slight pouches below those lids. The nose is very "pug" with an extended upper lip with a small round circle instead of a groove in the philtrum. The mouth and accent dots are medium pink with a light pink tongue which rests on the lower lip. The blush is an orange tone. The upper lid lines are black. The mark is impressed. *Photographs by C. Lee James. Virginia Schoenfeld Collection.*

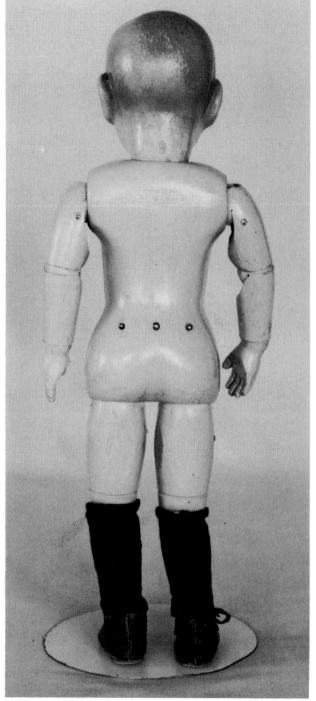

Illustration 308. The back full view of *Tootsie Wootsie* shows the "9" mark found on the necks of these dolls. Is it a "9" or a copyright symbol? *Photograph by C. Lee James. Virginia Schoenfeld Collection.*

148

"SCHNICKEL-FRITZ"

Reg. U. S. Pat. Off.

15/77   15/75   15/76

Illustration 309. The first presentation of *Schnickel-Fritz* in the initial *...Illustrated Catalogue...Dolls The A. Schoenhut Company* shows the three ways that he could be purchased. They ranged $3.00 each undressed to $5.35 with the "infant's first short dress."

drizzled onto the head. The ears are unusually large. The doll is delightfully ugly with a strong character face that appears to be a portrait of a real child. This doll that seems to be the inspiration or a cliché, "a face that only a mother could love," may not have appealed to a great many people. The doll's gender is never given in the catalogue, but the name and the elaborateness of the dress would support an argument that it was meant to be a girl. There is nothing traditionally "feminine" about the doll's head. The examples studied have an oval mark impressed in the back of the neck. Although some collectors see it as a numeral "9," it appears to be a copyright sign.

Schnickel-Fritz was also registered in the U.S. Patent Office on June 6, 1911. He was the only other doll given a name in the company catalogues. His description in the original catalogue is the same as that of *Tootsie Wootsie*; however, this doll appears to represent a child that is a little older and has a thoroughly mischievous look on his face. (This one just can not be seen as a girl.) As with *Tootsie Wootsie, Schnickel-Fritz* came on a fully-jointed body. The numbers assigned to the doll were 15/75, (in slip, boots and stockings — "undressed"), 15/76 (in plaid gingham rompers), and 15/77 (in an "infant's first short dress"). The last is considerably less elaborately trimmed than the *Tootsie Wootsie* dress. There is a lace trimmed yoke and cuffs but no rows of tucking, bands of insertion, or lace at the hem, as has *Tootsie Wootsie's* dress. The lower retail price reflected these differences.

Schnickel-Fritz's head design appeared on a movable head *Rolly Dolly* in five different sizes ranging from a little over 6in (15cm) to 14in (36cm) tall. It also appears as the "Grotesque Baby" on the Circus show wagon which came out in 1910. These are two of several links that can be found between the designs of the earliest Schoenhut dolls and the company's toys.

The doll's face is that of a grinning child. His tiny eyes are crinkled with glee. He has both upper and lower eyelids molded. Even the facial muscles around his cheeks, nose and chin are involved in his smile. He has an open/closed mouth with two upper and two lower teeth. They are lightly molded as well as painted. Depending on his individual decoration he can look quite calculatingly mischievous or more innocently cheerful.

Although his hair is short, it shows strong molding detail including comb marks and a cowlick swirl. In profile his nose is "snub;" his cheeks are high and not full enough to hide his upper and lower lips. He has a firm round chin. His ears are large.

By the end of 1911, or the beginning of 1912, the names *Tootsie Wootsie* and *Schnickel-Fritz* were dropped, and only their numbers remained through the rest of their production. It is probable that their production ended when the company introduced Harry Schoenhut's infants in the spring of 1913.

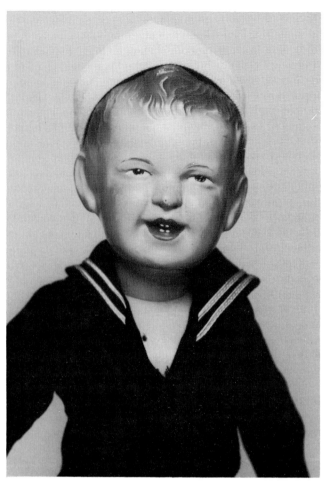

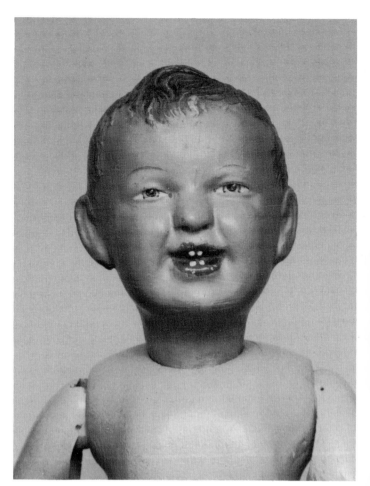

Illustration 310. 15in (38cm). This doll, named Tim, has laughing brown eyes which are very narrow, a brown upper lid line and slightly feathered eyebrows. There is very clear, crisp modeling all over his laughing face and hair. The hair comb marks are accented with additional hand carving. He has two original sailor suits. This one is fine navy blue wool and appears to be very well made but probably not a factory one. His white "linene" sailor suit looks just like one in 1912 advertising. His shoes and stockings are black and Schoenhut originals with the proper holes, but the surprise is that he is elastic strung. He has the impressed mark. *Margaret Dowling Collection.*

Illustration 311. 15in (38cm). This is one of the earliest *Schnickel-Fritzs*. He has many signs of hand carving particularly in his hair. His light blue intaglio eyes with their characteristic darker blue ring are wider open than most *Fritzs*. He has clear modeling of both upper and lower eyelids. His lips and accent dots are a bright pink-red with a darker red filling the entire inside of his mouth. His hair and single-stroke eyebrows are light brown. He has the impressed mark. *Charles and Barbara Buysse Collection.*

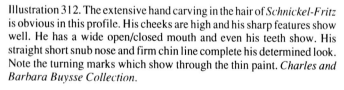

Illustration 312. The extensive hand carving in the hair of *Schnickel-Fritz* is obvious in this profile. His cheeks are high and his sharp features show well. He has a wide open/closed mouth and even his teeth show. His straight short snub nose and firm chin line complete his determined look. Note the turning marks which show through the thin paint. *Charles and Barbara Buysse Collection.*

OPPOSITE PAGE:
Illustration 313. 15in (38cm). This beautiful *Fritz* has the smooth finish and pale skin coloring of the "Transition Period." He is probably from 1912. He has laughing light blue eyes with brown upper lid lines and nicely feathered brown brows. He appears to be mold-finished with no additional hand carving. He has deep pink lips and accent dots. His orange blush extends around the outside of his eyes and onto the upper lids. His hair is true brunette. The black paint inside of his mouth is factory-original and was probably an experiment to make him look truly open-mouthed.

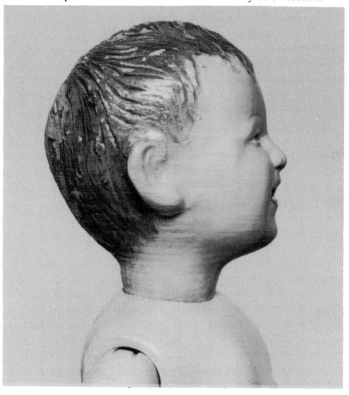

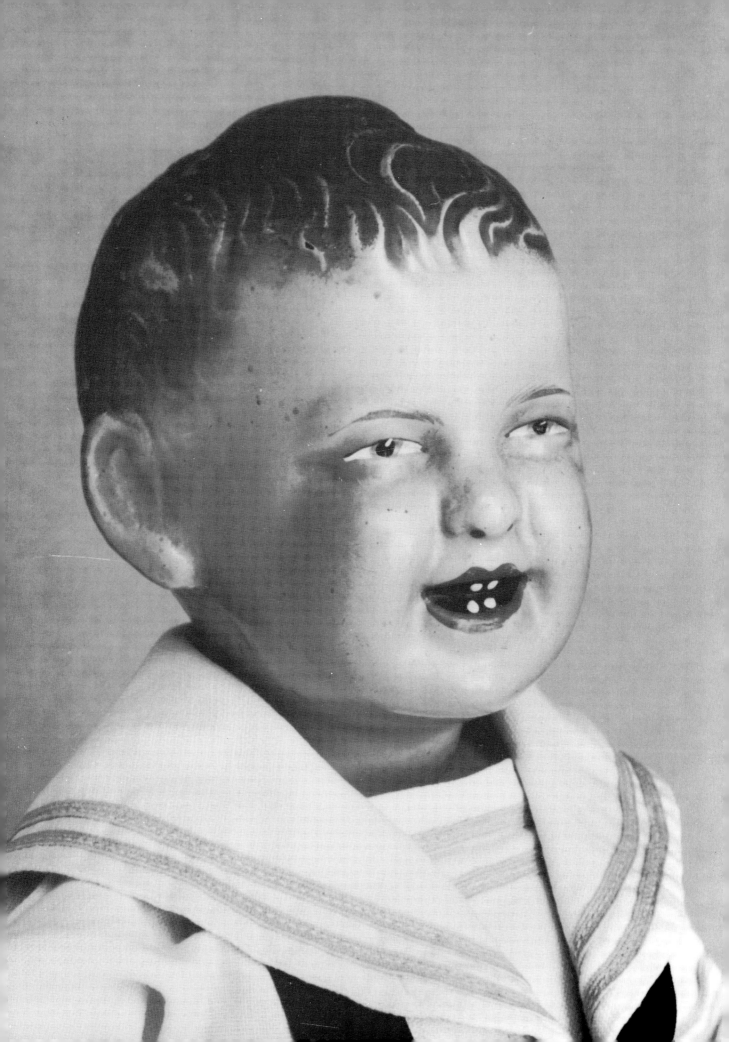

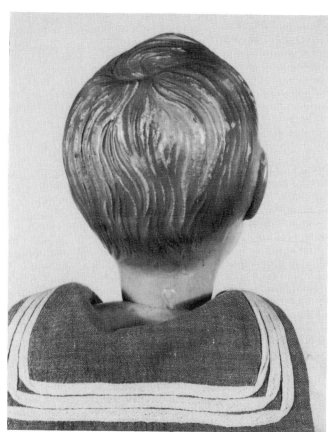

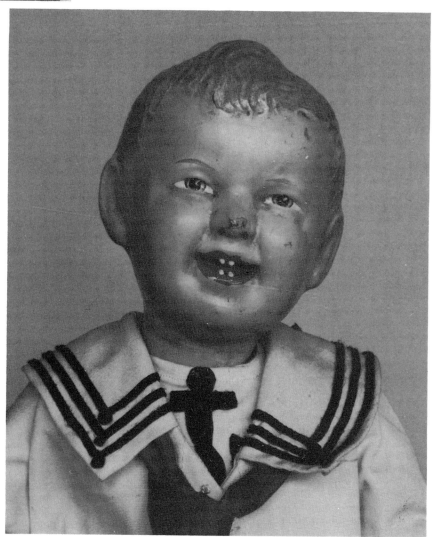

Illustration 314. The back of *Schnickel-Fritz's* hair is very clearly molded with his swirling cowlick and the wavy short hair coming from it. *Margaret Dowling Collection.*

Illustration 315. 15¾in (40cm). An earliest *Schnickel-Fritz* has wonderful larger, blue outlined irises. His blonde glossy hair is deeply modeled with a lot of hand carving. His blonde single-stroke eyebrows are also glossy. His light skin is quite matte in its finish. The lips are bright, and the inside of his mouth is accented with dark red. He has the impressed mark. *Dorothy Dixon Collection.*

Harry Schoenhut's Babies

Although Phyllis Schoenhut O'Hare, Harry's daughter and the youngest of the Schoenhut grandchildren, says that her father always wanted to be a doctor, his obvious design skill would be hard to ignore for a father trying to build a family business. Harry studied at the Pennsylvania Museum School of Industrial Art and the Pennsylvania Academy of Fine Arts. He studied sculpture under Charles Grafly. He was listed in company publications as Manager of the Art Department before the end of 1912.

Harry's designs appear to have been Infants 107, 108, 109W, and 110W; *Miss Dolly* 316; her sleep-eyed counterpart, 317; the non-commercially distributed Schoenhut version of Grace Storey Putnam's *Bye-Lo*, a splendid character infant; and the composition child doll.

Dolls 107 and 108 have a copyright design granted to Harry Schoenhut on December 31, 1913. Both first appeared with painted hair in a full-page ad in *Playthings* in June 1913. They seem to be the same design in different sizes. Differences in the chin molding and eye painting appear among examples of both mold numbers.

Doll 107 is a painted hair doll with no distinct hair modeling. It was produced on a fully-jointed body that is slightly chunkier than the child body and with no stocking groove or thigh nail to hold its stockings up. This doll was 14in (36cm) high so that it appeared in scale with the 16in (41cm) and 19in (48cm) child dolls being produced at that time. It was sold undressed (in a chemise with no shoes or stockings but with a stand) or dressed in checked rompers with shoes, stockings and stand. It was also sold dressed in a "short" (ankle-length) white lawn, yoked dress with shoes, stockings and stand.

This doll head was also produced on a bent-limb baby body, described in the catalogue as having "Nature Arms and Legs." The wooden body was quite naturally modeled with a chubby baby torso. It was spring-jointed at the shoulders and hips as well as the neck. Each arm and leg was made in three pieces which allowed for more modeling detail. The pieces (foot, calf and thigh or hand, lower arm and upper arm) were doweled and firmly glued before they were painted giving them a smooth one-piece look. Occasionally, one finds an infant whose limbs show separation lines at these points or has even lost part of a limb, but on the whole this method provided a very sturdy and rather heavy doll. The seated 107 measures 9in (23cm) from the floor to the top of its head. Its catalogue number was 13/107, as stretched out it measures 13in (33cm) from top of head to toe tip. In 1917 an 11in (28cm) fully-jointed 107 toddler was put on the market. This smallest size was not released on a baby body.

A wigged version of model 107 (designated 107W) is shown in 1914 company advertising as well as in the Marshall Field catalogue of the same year. It may have been produced within a few months of the painted hair version. The wig was a typical baby bob of the period. It came in "blonde" or "tosca" mohair according to catalogues.

Depending on the strength of the final molding process, Doll 107's chin can appear almost non-existent with a line seeming to fall from the mouth into the neck socket giving a profile not unlike an ice-cream cone. Other examples have a tiny, receding but distinct chin. Differences in the decoration on this doll presents a sweet, somber or fretful baby.

William F. Schoenhut, thirteenth grandchild of Albert Schoenhut and the last to be born during his lifetime, told the Schoenhut Collector's Club Convention in October 1986 that he was the original model for the infant doll designed by his uncle and

godfather Harry E. Schoenhut. Harry lived with Bill's parents while Albert, his wife Emilie and their daughter Caroline travelled to the Holy Land in 1911. At that time Bill's mother was pregnant with him. Harry modeled the baby on Bill when he was approximately nine months old. Bill showed us the original plaster model of the bust submitted with the copyright application. It bears a remarkable likeness to him even 75 years later, although Bill told us that at the time his mother complained that her son did not have all those "bumps on his head."

Doll 108 is apparently a larger, and therefore more detailed, version of the 107 model. This doll was also released on a fully-jointed toddler body in a 17in (40cm) size as well as on a seated Nature Limb body (measuring 11in [28cm] from rump to top of head, but called 15/108 to reflect its measurement from top of head to toe tip). After the first few months of production, number 108 was also sold with a short mohair bob (108W).

The 108 Dolls were also sold in the same three dress categories (undressed, in rompers or in a dress) as 107. In both body models undressed dolls came without shoes and stockings. The seated babies came either undressed or in an elaborate, long Christening-type gown with a lace-trimmed bonnet, flannel petticoat and diaper. Both infants were sold through 1926.

Two of the 108W Dolls pictured belong to Phyllis Schoenhut O'Hare who says that her father brought her dolls from the factory, "before they were even marked." One of the dolls shown is a toddler with "walker arms" and fully-jointed legs. This combination in a Schoenhut family doll, straight from the factory, makes some of the other "mixtures" occasionally found in Schoenhut dolls seem more legitimate.

On December 30, 1919, William G. Schoenhut, who was listed in 1912 as the Manager of the Sales Department, was granted a patent for a "Joint for Dolls." This was for the "Schoenhut Walkable Doll" which came out in 1919. A copy of the patent may be found in the Appendixes in the back of this book. The doll was produced in the three infant toddler sizes (11in [28cm], 14in [36cm] and 17in [43cm]) using the "patent" heads (107, 107W, 108 and 108W). The doll was jointed at the neck, shoulder and hips, "so that it can be sat down" (catalogue description).

The arms are constructed in pieces which are joined in the same manner as the "Nature Arm." They are slightly curved so that the doll can be led by the child. The hip joint appears to be a tongue and groove construction. There is a small wire piece which protrudes from the back of the joint if it still functions as a "walker." When a child walks the doll, the drag on the doll's foot allows the doll's leg to straighten or hyper-extend. When the child shifts the doll's weight to its other foot, the non-weight bearing leg pops forward and the doll appears to take a step. Special shoes with a slight wedge built into the sole made this process easier (but not very easy) to accomplish. As with all Schoenhut toys, the playing child does the "work," increasing its dexterity, imagination and ability to persevere. The company recognized this in its advertising by stating that the doll was "Not Mechanical."

Although these dolls were described as "sitable," it takes a lot of gentle but firm pressure to accomplish this position. It can be done, at least with some of the dolls.

The Walkable dolls had the regular infant numbers with the 0 removed from the number. Thus 11/107 as a walker became 1117 (no /).

The Walkable doll was sold "undressed" only. This meant that it came in a "slip," special shoes and stockings that were nailed onto the one-piece legs. The white lawn infant dress could be "special ordered." The doll did not have holes in its feet, shoes or socks as it did not use a stand. After its initial release in the infant chemise type slip, the undressed doll was sold in a

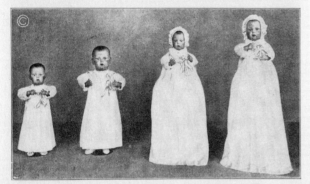

Illustration 316. Initial advertisement for the new "Schoenhut Infant Doll" in *Playthings*, June 1913. A similar advertisement in a Circus booklet put out by the Schoenhut Company at about the same time states "not made with Mohair Wigs," but advertising had the choice of wigged with a "w" after the number by early 1914 at the latest. The smaller size of each infant had the 107 head; the larger was 108. The rompers were numbered 554 and 555, the lawn walking dresses were models 550 and 551, and the long white lawn dress, flannel petticoat and diaper with lawn "cap" were numbered 552 and 553. The prices ranged from $2.50 to $5.00 each.

"combination slip." This appears to have been the Schoenhut slip standard on the larger girl dolls with legs instead of a slip with a loose hem.

This body is sometimes found with heads 109W, 110W or even carved haired character heads on it. It seems likely that the company complied with requests for a different head on their new "Walkable Doll" which was produced through 1924.

In 1924 the Schoenhut Company began producing an elastic-strung version of Dolls 107 and 108 as well as the sleep-eyed *Miss Dolly*, (317). This less expensive doll had no holes in the feet, shoes or socks and therefore no stand. The bodies were the standard Schoenhut wooden bodies in the child, toddler or baby styles, with less groove cut in the ball part of the joint to allow more tension and less floppiness in the stringing. These models were sold at the same time as the final years of the spring-jointed bodies and were not later substitutes for those dolls. It is important to note that, while the company was apparently struggling to make a cheaper product, the quality of the finish on these dolls is just as fine as on the earlier examples of the same models. The numbers given to these dolls by the company had a zero at the end of the size portion of the number to indicate the elastic stringing. Thus 11/107W (11in [28cm] Model 107 with a wig) became 110/107W (11in [28cm] Model 107 with a wig, and elastic stringing).

In this same year (when the reduced size circus also came onto the market) the "Schoenhut Stuffed Dolls with mamma voices" were brought out. These dolls took advantage of the growing popularity of the chubby soft bodied dolls of the day. They came in two sizes, 14in (36cm) with head 107W and 16in (41cm) with head 108W. Their catalogue numbers had the size digit numbers reversed to distinguish them from the jointed toddlers. Thus they were designated 41/107W and 61/108W. The hollowed-out wooden socket heads were mounted on a composition or wooden shoulder plate which was attached to the soft body. The heads could turn, which was an appealing detail. The cloth

arms on these dolls extended to the wrist and were finished with a wooden hand. Both dolls came wigged only, as they had their heads hollowed out to make the total weight appealing to younger children and easier to manage with the lighter body, and therefore had a pate to cover. The only way they were sold was fully-dressed in a romper, shoes and socks (no underwear). This doll was not an effort to produce a cheaper doll. In the years it was offered along with the spring-jointed, elastic-strung and "Walkable Dolls," it was more expensive than similar sized undressed fully-jointed infants whether elastic or spring-strung and less expensive than the more elaborately dressed jointed infant dolls, with the larger one being sold for $5.50 retail. It is the only form of infant left by the 1927 catalogue but was not shown by 1930.

On March 22, 1920, Harry Schoenhut applied for a patent on his invention for sleeping eyes and their placement in "a substantially solid head." The patent application shows detailed drawings of cuts made inside the head to receive the eyes and the rocker as well as the eyeball decoration and the notched disk which keeps the eyeballs in their sockets without restricting their movement. The patent was granted on September 13, 1921, and that date is frequently found stamped on the pates of the sleep-eyed dolls. The sleep-eyed dolls were listed as "NEW" and "LATEST" in the 1921 doll and toy catalogue. Model 317 was produced along with the standard *Miss Dolly* through 1924. By 1925 only the movable eye version of this doll was produced.

The infant with the movable eyes also appeared in 1921. Unlike the *Miss Dolly* it did not survive the painted eye infant. It was produced only through 1923. These dolls, with their removable pates, all had short, bobbed mohair wigs. The eyeballs are wooden with an eye printed on "decalomania" (the quote is from the patent application), and lids painted on the balls above the decal. The eyes themselves have pale blue or brown irises with black "threading" through the outer portion. The irises are also rimmed in black and a fairly large pupil completes the detail.

154

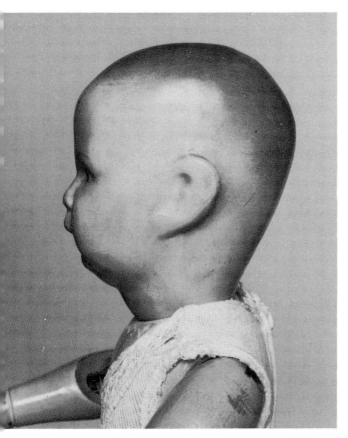

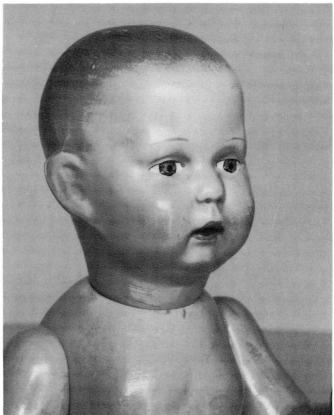

Illustration 317. 14in (35cm). This sharply modeled Doll 14/107 is an early example with the impressed mark on both his head and back. He has medium blue eyes with a dark stippled outline on the irises. His one-stroke brows and painted hair are caramel colored. His mouth and accent dots are pink, and, typical of many of the copyright babies seen. One upper lip peak is much higher than the other. There is a deeper pink oval in the center of his mouth. He has a trunk of hand-sewn original clothes. His profile shows much clearer modeling of the ear and chin line, with a tiny double chin, than is apparent in most 107 heads. *Roxanne LeMay Morison Collection.*

Illustration 318. This is an early example of Doll 13/107 in excellent original condition. The upper eyelids are molded. It has the impressed mark on the back of its neck.

There is an eye white and also a black lid line on the decal. The movable-eye doll also has upper and lower eyelashes painted around the socket opening. The lower face is both bigger and more strongly modeled than are the painted eyed babies. There is a more pronounced lower jaw and chin. The mouth is open with two metal teeth behind the upper lip. There is no visible tongue, but a flashlight shown through the opening reveals red on the inside of the cardboard backing plate. Both models came on fully-jointed and "Nature" limb baby bodies. They have also been found on the "Walkable Doll" body.

Doll 109W, as the smaller doll was labeled in catalogues, has a perky and slightly surprised look on her face. She has a small oval opening in her mouth and when looked at "face on" appears to be smaller than the painted one on the same size 107. The great difference between these two models is apparent in their profiles. 109W's cheeks are lower and rounder. The mouth profile shows a deep opening. The chin is pronounced, and there is a soft but definite second or double-chin affect. The upper lip, or philtrum, is shorter in Doll 109W. The eyes are rounder and the temple modeling less pronounced than that found on Dolls 107/107W. I have referred to this doll as a she because literature put out by the Schoenhut Company promoted the infants as baby sisters for the older dolls.

By the time the sleep eyed babies appeared all the fully-jointed infants were sold either undressed ("slip, no shoes or socks") or dressed in a short white lawn dress with ribbon and lace trimming. The dresses were knee-length and high-waisted little girl dresses of the period. No rompers were offered. Of course many people dressed these dolls as boys and they are quite appropriate this way. Doll 109W never came in the tiniest 11in (28cm) size.

Doll 110W is similar to 109W but has some easily observable differences. From the front it has a wider mouth opening and a smile which is indicated in the temple modeling as well as in the mouth shape and decoration. The upper lip is longer and slightly more prominent. In profile the nose is less snub and the upper lip extends further and appears more relaxed. The doll appears alert and cheerful. She has the double chin line and rounded features of a young child. There is a strong round chin. The eyebrow decoration, as in Doll 109W, tends to be short, stacked and arched high above the eye socket increasing the look of intelligent curiosity. The fully-jointed toddler model of this doll is listed as being 17in (43cm) tall, as is the comparable 108/108W doll.

Occasionally the 110W head is found on a 19in (48cm) child doll body. There are several explanations for this. The first is that the company, in its catalogues and advertising literature, continually stressed the flexibility achieved by changing the wigs and clothes to suit the customer. Special dolls, such as the Chinese babies shown in the Coleman's *Collector's Encyclopedia of Dolls, Volume 2*, and later in this book, The Wedding Party, owned by Becky and Jay Lowe, and the Japanese young men in the collections of the Philadelphia Civic Center Museum and the

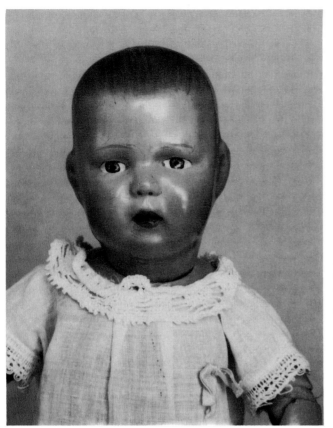

Mary Merritt Doll Museum, were an important part of the way that the Schoenhut Company operated. Americans were famous for assuming that "bigger is better," and it seems likely that some people wanted the biggest doll possible and specially ordered the doll that way. Another plausible explanation in the case of 19in (48cm) 110W is that these dolls were assembled by doll hospitals from parts bought at the auction held when the company went out of business. If this is true, the dolls are just as legitimate as the Schoenhut *Bye-Los* which are found on the typical *Bye-Lo* bodies with celluloid hands. In both cases the head is on its original body. Either explanation is only made more possible by the company's willingness to repair its dolls and the fact that it sold simple tools which enabled doll hospitals to assemble and disassemble their dolls. It further distributed patterns for these tools so that handy people could make their own.

Illustration 319. 14in (36cm). This almost mint example of Doll 14/107 was found with the original factory chemise under a homemade dress. The paint is factory-original. The body appears to be factory-repainted in the mid 1920s either to "freshen the doll up" for its original owner or a younger sibling. This was a tradition at Christmas time in my family in the 1940s and seems to have been true in many Philadelphia families for years. The doll has light brown painted hair with straight darker brush accents running from the forehead back to just above the nape of the neck. It has blonde single-stroke brows and blue-gray stippled eyes with a narrow brown upper lid line. The mouth and accent dots are a medium pink with a larger than usual rose oval inside the mouth. The finish is very smooth and glossy. Both the head and torso have the decal mark.

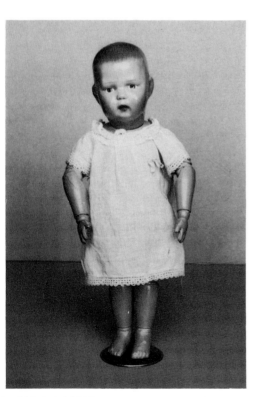

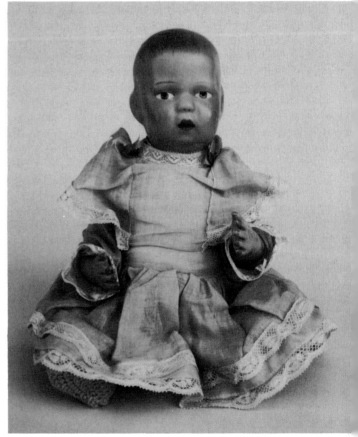

Illustration 320. Doll 14/107, just as it came from the factory, in a chemise with a narrow blue bow on the left chest, no shoes or stockings.

Illustration 321. This baby measures 9in (24cm) from its rump to the top of the head or 13in (33cm) from toe tip to top of head. This example of Doll 13/107 has the fine, smooth finish developed under Harry E. Schoenhut's direction. This one really looks like a girl. Her single-stroke eyebrows are quite long. Her mouth is unusually full, and she has a sweeter, less fretful face than many other examples. Her stippled concave eyes are blue with brown upper lid lines. Her paint is perfect. *Photograph by Monty Moncrief. Becky Moncrief Collection.*

Illustration 322. 9½in (24cm) measuring from rump to top of head and 13in (33cm) from toe to top of head, this sweet Doll 13/107W shows off its small size "Natural Limb" body. Note the abdomen with the suggestion of a navel and the fat creases in the well-shaped arms and legs. The arms are individually sculptured so they are not identical. *Roxanne LeMay Morison Collection.*

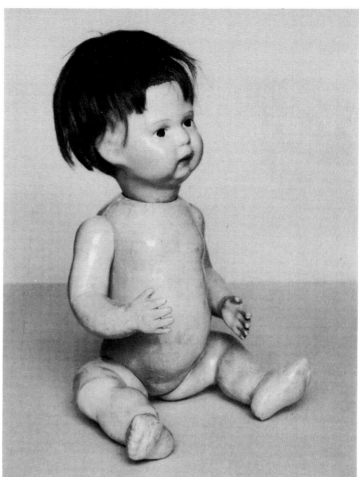

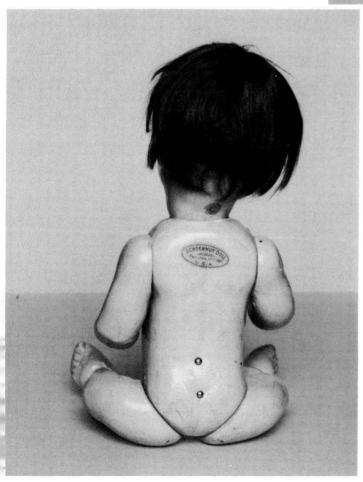

Illustration 323. The back view of Doll 13/107W shows two small dimples at the base of the spine and a slight buttocks molding. The two pins hold the spring joints in place. The oval decal mark is easier to place on the curved body shape. *Roxanne LeMay Morison Collection.*

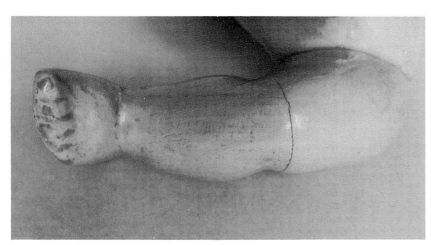

Illustration 324. This photograph of the 13/107W baby shows fine lines where the doweled parts of the leg are glued together, allowing the wood to be molded with a more natural appearance. *Roxanne LeMay Morison Collection.*

Illustration 325. The arm of 13/107W shows only the slightest indication of the lines at the elbow and wrist where the three pieces are joined with dowels. *Roxanne LeMay Morison Collection.*

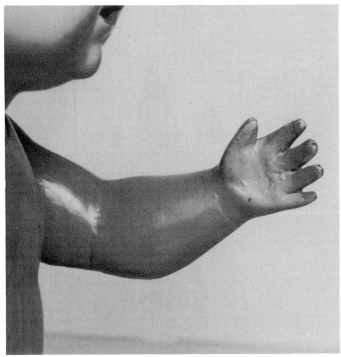

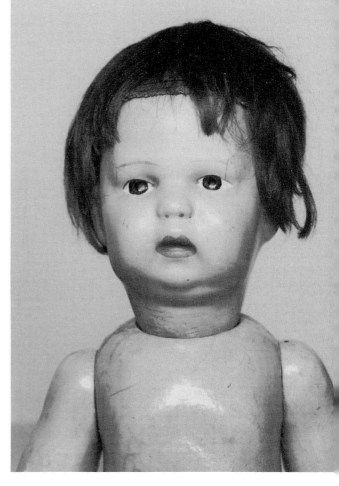

Illustration 326. At 13in (33cm), measured from toe to top of head, this 13/107W on the "Nature Limb" body is the same size head as that used on the 14in (36cm) toddler doll. This example has unusually dark eyes which appear to be brown at first glance but are really an indigo blue with even darker stippled outline. There are light brown upper eyelid lines and caramel single-stroke eyebrows. The lips and accent dots are pink with a deep pink oval in the center of the mouth. The cheek blush is a soft orange. This doll has a clear double chin. It has the round cream sticker or decal with blue writing on the head and the oval decal mark on the back of the torso. *Roxanne LeMay Morison Collection.*

Illustration 327. 11½in (29cm). This is the smallest of all the Schoenhut dolls and was only produced on the fully-jointed toddler body. Her eyes are very dark gray (almost charcoal) with dark brown upper lid lines. She has light brown single-stroke eyebrows and her original thick brunette mohair wig. Her deep pink mouth is quite evenly painted. There is a deeper pink oval painted in the center of her mouth. Her short lawn dress with lace and ribbon trim appears to be original. She has the round sticker on her head and the oval decal on the back of her shoulders.

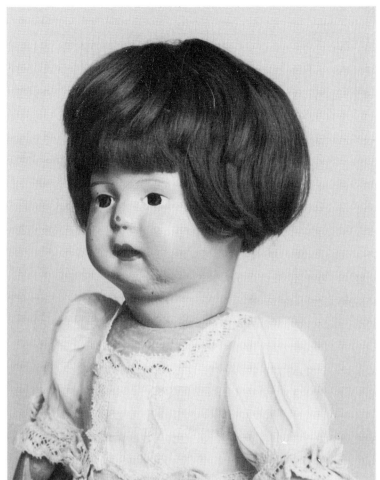

Illustration 328. William F. Schoenhut showing the plaster bust that was designed on his baby likeness by his uncle Harry Edison Schoenhut in 1912. Mr. Schoenhut showed this plaster original in October 1986 at the First Schoenhut Collector's Club Convention. *Photograph by Betty O'Sullivan.*

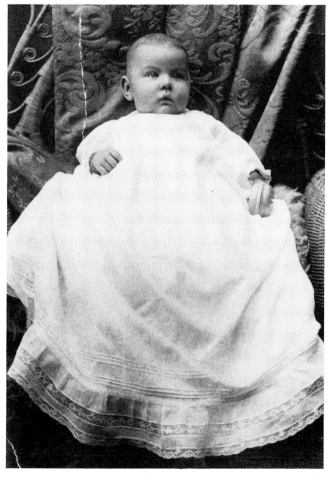

Illustration 329. Inscribed on the back of this original photograph is "William F. Schoenhut, born Oct. 29th 1911, age 3 months." This photograph of the infant Bill Schoenhut, taken in early 1912, shows the prominent upper lip, ears and heavy cheek characteristics of the infant Schoenhut doll. Bill's mother complained that her son did not have as many "bumps" on his head as the doll has. *Photograph Courtesy William F. Schoenhut.*

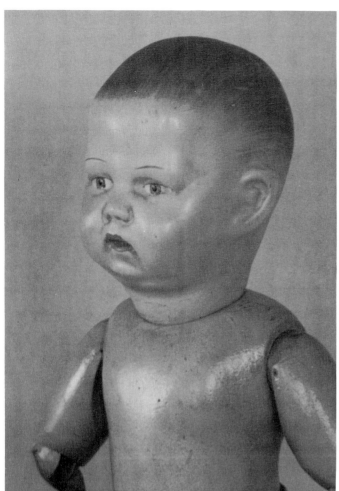

Illustration 330. 16½in (42cm). This is a particularly nice example of Doll 17/108 with the fully-jointed toddler body. His light reddish-brown hair is still in excellent condition. The smooth eyes are a bright blue with darker stippling. The paint on the iris is glossy, causing natural reflecting points. There is blush on the cheeks and above the eyes. The short single-stroke eyebrows are light brown and the upper lid lines are a darker shade. The lips and accent dots are pink with a light red oval in the center to give an open/closed look to the mouth. There is a copyright decal on the back of the neck and an impressed mark between the shoulders. *Photograph by C. Lee James. Virginia Schoenfeld Collection.*

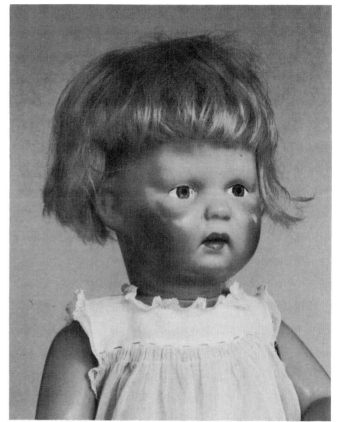

Illustration 331. 17in (43cm). "Dorothy", a childhood doll of Phyllis Schoenhut O'Hare, daughter of Harry E. Schoenhut, was named after an older cousin. Her color is particularly attractive. Her skin is light. Her eyes are a lighter gray-blue with brown upper lid lines. Her cheek color is a warm rosy blush. Both "Dorothy" and her companion "Doris" have pink lips and accent dots. Neither doll has the darker center oval in the mouth that is usual in doll 108. "Dorothy" has a spring-strung toddler body with fully-jointed legs and "Walkable" one piece arms. She is unmarked. *Phyllis Schoenhut O'Hare Collection.*

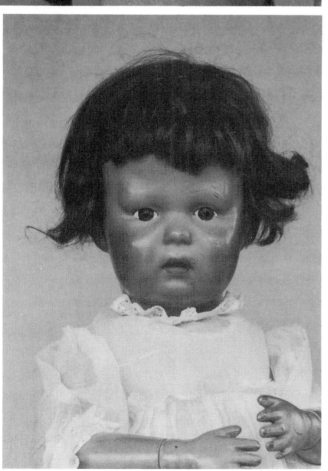

Illustration 332. 17½in (44cm). "Doris," a 17/108W has blue-gray painted eyes, with stippling, and brown lid lines. Her modeling around the temples, mouth and chin is particularly strong. Her eyebrow color is gone, but they are clearly indicated by shine. Her skin tone is darker than that of "Dorothy" and is beautiful with her thick wavy brunette mohair wig. Her head is marked with the impressed copyright circle. Her fully-jointed, spring-strung toddler body is painted in the suntanned 1920s style and is unmarked. Her clothes are factory original. *Phyllis Schoenhut O'Hare Collection.*

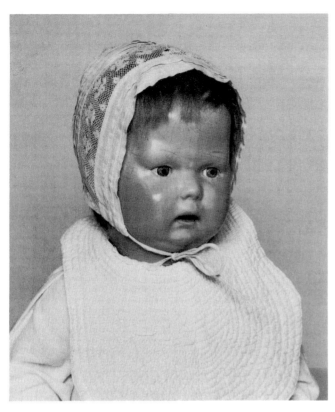

Illustration 333. 15in (37cm) when measured from toe tip to top of head; 11½in (29cm) from seated rump to top of head. This example of Doll 15/108W appears to be an earlier one. The eyes are a light gray-blue with stippled outline. There are black lid lines at the edge of slightly molded lids and caramel single-stroke brows. The mouth, nostrils and tear ducts are soft light pink. The oval in the center of the mouth is red. The original mohair wig is dark blonde. The mark is impressed in the head. There is no mark on the "Nature Limb" body. *Roxanne LeMay Morison Collection.*

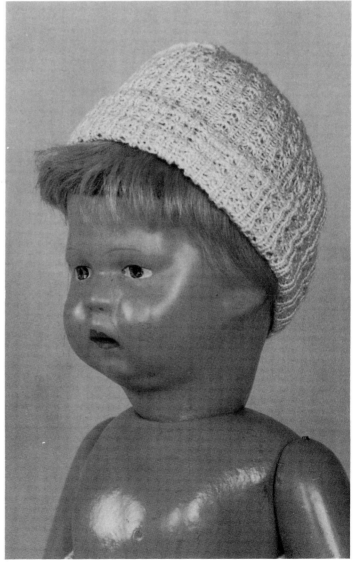

Illustration 334. 14in (36cm). This is Doll 1417W (head 107W on the 14in [36cm] "Walkable Doll" body). Her eyes are a dark sea-blue stippled with brown upper lid lines. Her brows are straight blonde single-stroke. She has pink mouth and accent dots and a red oval in the center of her mouth. There is a soft orange blush on her cheeks. She has a blonde mohair bob and the earliest oval decal mark on the back of her shoulders as well as the round copyright sticker on her neck. *Photograph by C. Lee James. Virginia Schoenfeld Collection.*

161

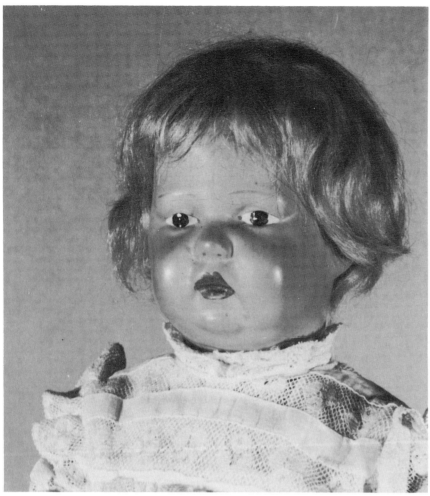

Illustration 335. 18in (44cm). This 1718W (head 108W on the "Walkable" body) is in very good condition. Her sea-blue eyes have blonde brows. She has medium pink mouth and accent dots with a deeper pink in the center of her mouth. *Ella and Larry Corn Collection.*

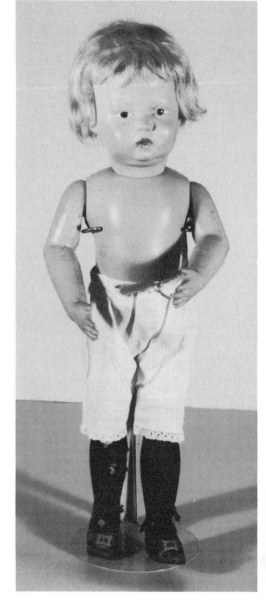

Illustration 336. The 1718W has the small circular copyright sticker on the back of her neck. Her "Walkable" body has its original black stockings and wedged shoes. *Ella and Larry Corn Collection.*

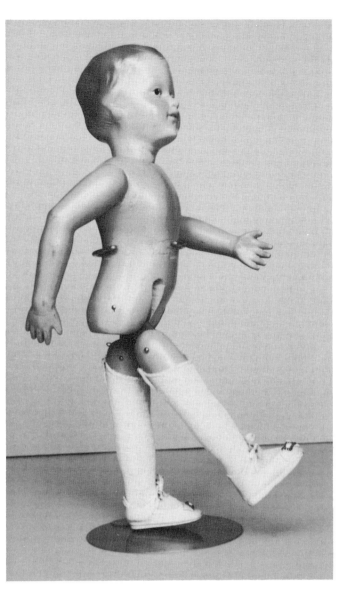

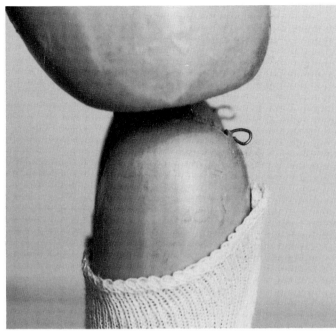

Illustration 337. The "Walkable" body shown in profile. Pressure has just been placed on the doll's left leg holding it in a vertical position. The pressure has just been released from the doll's right leg and the spring in the back of the top of the leg forces the leg to kick forward. The wedges on the "Walkable" doll's shoe sole help the action. The head is a 14/205 which was still being made in 1923. This combination may have been a special order. The slots in the front of the doll's torso allow for plenty of leg movement. They also allow doll to sit.

Illustration 338. The two simple wire springs put the "Walkable" legs in tension when they are extended by holding the doll so that the leg is either straight below the body or slightly hyper-extended behind the body. When the weight of the doll and the child's force is released, the leg kicks forward, appearing to take a step.

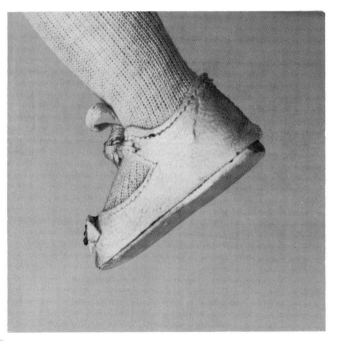

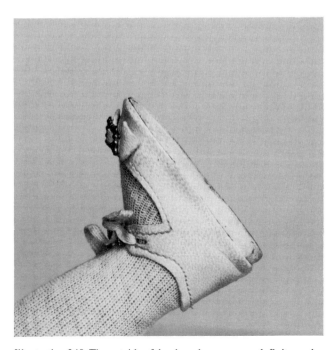

Illustration 339. The inside of the "Walkable" doll's shoe shows only a slight indication of a wedge in the sole.

Illustration 340. The outside of the shoe shows a more definite wedge. The sole resists slipping on the walking surface.

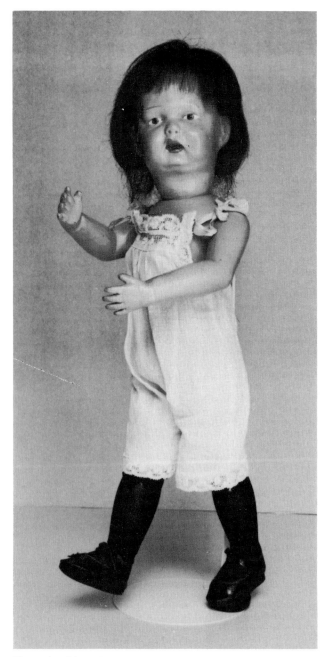

Illustration 341. After the first year the "Walkable" doll was sold in a "combination slip" made from the Schoenhut doll slip with legs sewn into it. The stockings are tacked to the back of the doll's thigh. In this photograph the doll's left leg is held in the extended position with a film canister cap, which makes the shoe sole look thicker than it actually is.

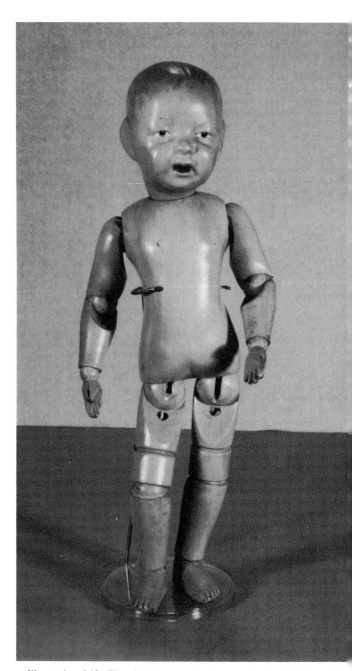

Illustration 342. The elastic-strung body was the basic Schoenhut body with a modification in the groove cut in the ball part of the thigh and elbow. The elastic actually passes through a small hole in the bottom of the ball and then enters the lower part of the arm. In the thigh the incomplete groove keeps the elastic from having too much play. The elastic is held in the feet and hands by small nails just like the circus animals. *Ella and Larry Corn Collection.*

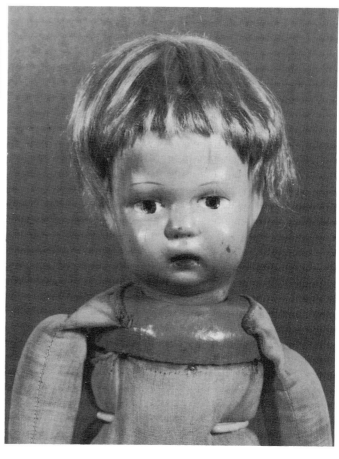

Illustration 343. The basic body of Doll 41/107W is the same design as that of the larger Doll 61/108W and similar to the Schoenhut *Bye-Lo*. The differences are the shoulder plate which is wood and the tube shaped arms which are tacked to the shoulder plate instead of being sewn to the cloth body. *Dot and Bud Hutton Collection.*

Illustration 344. 14in (36cm). This example of Doll 41/107W has hazel eyes with brown flecks. The upper lid lines are brown and the single-stroke eyebrows are blonde to go with the blonde mohair bob. This smaller size has less temple modeling and a rounder mouth painted on giving it quite a pleasant face. This doll has the small round sticker on the back of the head. *Dot and Bud Hutton Collection.*

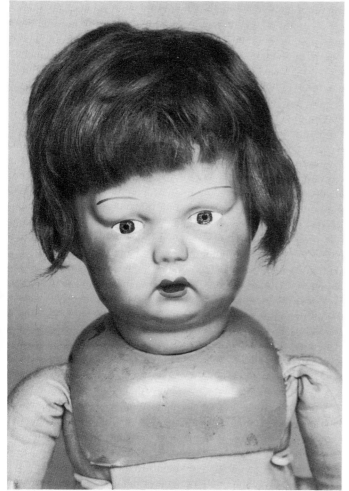

Illustration 345. 17½in (45cm). This exceptionally clean example of "Schoenhut's Stuffed Dolls with Mamma Voices" is larger than the catalogue description of 16in (41cm). Its head is "made as hollow as possible to give it extreme lightweight." This one weighs 1¼ pounds, which makes it fairly easy to carry around. He has blue stippled eyes with brown lid lines and single-stroke brows. His mouth and accent dots are pink. There is a red center oval in the mouth. This is one of the "sulkier" 108 heads. This doll is unmarked. The shoulder plate on this example is light composition-type material and fits over the arm attachments.

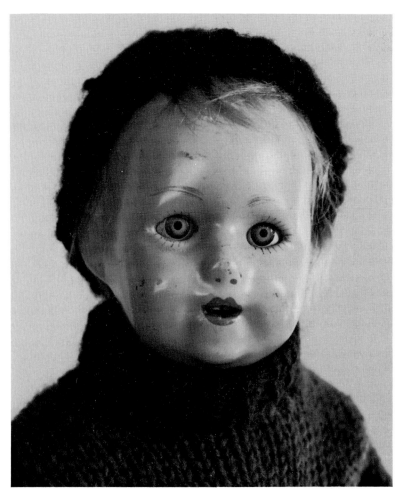

Illustration 346. This alert-looking example of Doll 14/109W seems to have a rounder eyecut than most, accenting his brilliant blue decal eyes. (For details on decal eyes see Appendix). The widely spaced spikey eyelashes are brown as are the stacked eyebrows. His lips and accent dots are deep pink. His sparse original chestnut mohair wig is mostly covered by his well-made hand-knit sweater and cap set. *Dot and Bud Hutton Collection.*

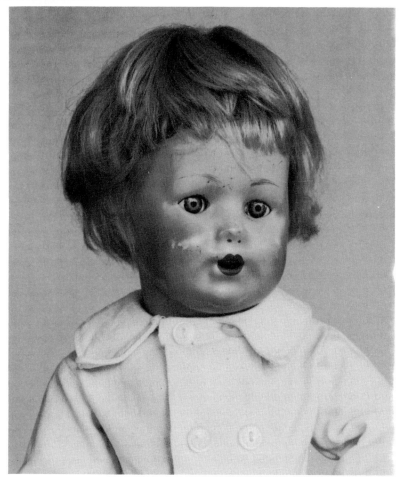

Illustration 347. 14½in (37cm). This sweet Doll 14/109W has been dressed as a little boy rather than as an infant or toddler. He has bright blue sleep eyes. His dark blonde brows are stacked, and he has a blonde mohair bob. His skin is a peach tone with an orange blush and light red mouth nostrils and tear ducts. His outfit is factory-original and appears in the chapter on Original Clothes. His fully-jointed spring strung body has the oval decal mark. *Phyllis Schoenhut O'Hare Collection.*

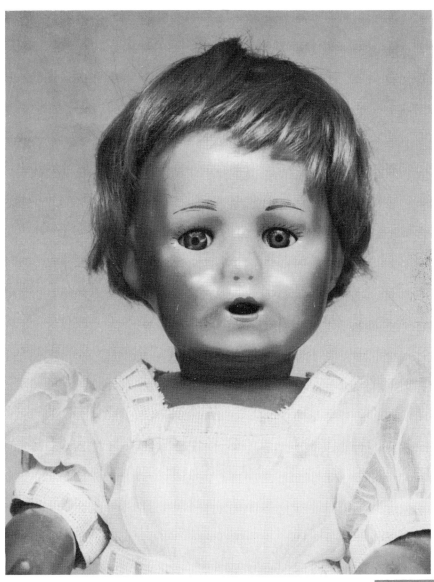

Illustration 348. 14in (36cm). Following the company numbering pattern this doll would have been numbered 1419W if she had been a standard product. She is the 14in (36cm) "Walkable doll" with the 109W head. Her round mouth and high-arched stacked eyebrows give her a perpetually surprised look. The mouth on the 109W head is small, and the two tiny teeth often do not show in photographs, but they are there. This example has fairly light skin with orange blush on cheeks, chin and a tiny bit around the eyes. Her lips and nostril dots are light peach. Her decal on wood sleep eyes are bright blue with the usual shading around the iris rim. She has the "Walkable" Doll decal mark on the back of her shoulders.

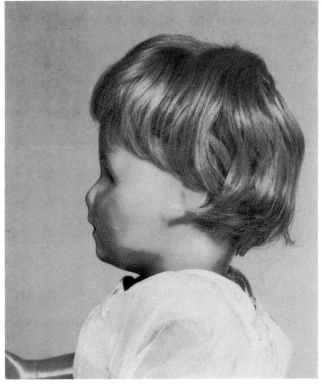

Illustration 349. The profile of the 109W shows the high forehead of a very young child. The features, which are placed in the lower half of the face, are small but distinct. The cheeks are fat, but do not overwhelm the lips, tiny nose and chin. All the sleep eye dolls have wigs to cover the removable pate which is needed to get at the tunnel which holds the mechanism. This tunnel is just big enough to hold the teeth and the eye movement.

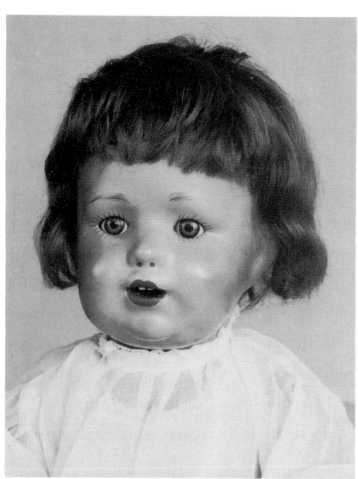

LEFT:

Illustration 350. Measuring 15in (38cm) from toe to head top, this is a delightful example of Doll 15/110W. She has bright blue sleep eyes with a black lid line at the top of the decal on the wooden eyeball. There are tiny black upper and lower lashes painted around the eye socket. She has warm, peachy skin paint with an orange cheek blush. Her stacked brows are brown. Her lips, nostrils and tear ducts are all a bright, light red. She has two even metal upper teeth in her open mouth. Her wig is a beautiful reddish-brown mohair. She has the patent stamp on the bottom of her pate. Her body is unmarked. *Phyllis Schoenhut O'Hare Collection.*

BOTTOM LEFT:

Illustration 351. 19¼in (49cm). This delightful doll is properly labeled 19/110W because her 17/110W head is on a 19in (48cm) child body. The head and body appear to be original to each other. Perhaps she was a special order or maybe she was assembled by a doll hospital when the parts were bought at the auction when the company closed. She has wonderful brown decal sleep eyes which fit extremely well into the eye sockets. Her mouth and accent dots are deep pink. She has dark blonde stacked eyebrows. Her lashes are black. Her blonde mohair wig has been washed and the wig cap is frail. The result is very childlike fine hair. She has the decal on the back of her shoulders and "PATENTED//SEPT. 13, 1921" stamped in blue on her crown. Her teeth are metal, painted white and set in her mouth unevenly.

BELOW:

Illustration 352. The profile of the 110W is much stronger then other Schoenhut designs. It resembles a young child rather than a real infant. Dolls with strong character faces are easier to make with painted eyes. She must have been quite expensive to make.

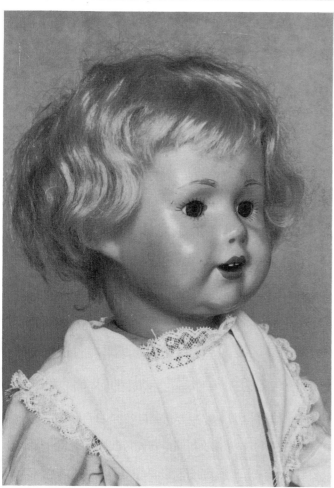

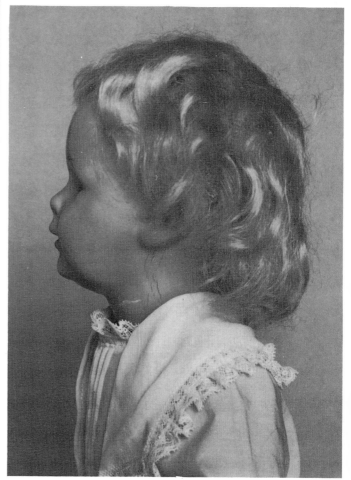

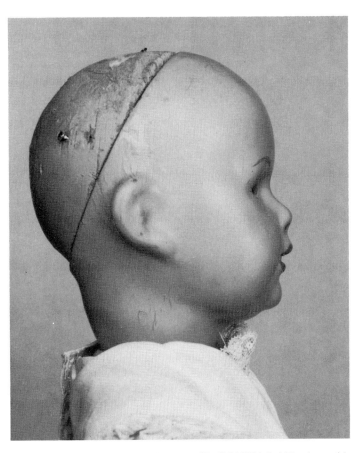

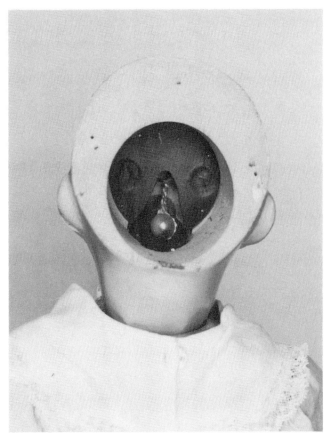

Illustration 353. The thick wooden pate of Doll 110W is held in place with several long nails. Without her wig the modeling of the back of her neck and her stick out ears show well.

Illustration 354. The pate of Doll 110W is removed to show the tunnel cut into the wooden head to hold the eyes and their rocker. The wood is quite thin in the front of the face to allow the teeth to be placed right against the upper lip and the eyes to fit the socket without leaving a space. The eyes are held in place with a round heavy cardboard plate which has a notch cut in it to allow the lead mechanism to have weight-free movement.

Harry Schoenhut's Bye-Los

In 1925 Harry Schoenhut designed an exact replica, in wood, of the Grace Storey Putnam *Bye-Lo* baby. There have been several theories about the history of this doll. The one that is supported by primary source material, rather than just repeating second-hand stories, is that proposed by Ruth and Robert Zimmerman in the February/March 1983 *Doll Reader*® and in a follow up in the June/July 1985 issue of the same magazine. The reader is referred to these articles for a probable history of the doll. The purpose of this section is to describe the two dolls known to have been completed in the Schoenhut factory.

These special dolls still belong to their original owner, Phyllis Schoenhut O'Hare. They are both in almost "mint" condition, although Phyllis reports that they were really played with as they were her favorite dolls because their soft bodies made them huggable. The heads were made in two pieces, front and back. Unlike the other sleep-eyed dolls produced by the company the heads are completely hollow.

Tool marks evident on the inside of another *Bye-Lo* head owned by Ruth Zimmerman indicate that the head may have been hollowed out after the front and back were glued together. It is clear that the tool marks overlap onto both sides of the head. The eyes of all these dolls are glass and they sleep.

The two dolls presented have a 13⅛in (34cm) head circumference. They are on cloth bodies similar in construction to the "Mamma" doll. The torso is rectangular and contains a crier (inoperative). The legs are seamed down the middle to allow a foot shape. They were made separate from the body and attached to the bottom of the torso allowing the dolls to sit easily. The arms are simple, slightly shaped cloth tubes with a typical carved wood Schoenhut hand at one end and a tab ending at the top to attach the arm to the shoulder. The necks of the doll heads are flanged and are slid into a casing at the top of the body rather than using the socket head and wooden shoulder plate of the "Mamma" doll. The casing on both dolls is held tightly around the neck with dark red heavy cotton crochet-type cord. The only difference in the finishing of the two bodies is that one (the boy) is complete as described while the girl has lace at the neck joint as well as the dark red cord. Both dolls are 17in (43cm) long on their original factory bodies.

One particularly interesting feature of the four heads studied (including the Zimmerman and one owned by Winnie Langley) is that the color of the skin shades and hair are not identical. All the heads were in very good to original condition so the differences are in the initial decorating. This may be because the dolls never entered full production and some experimenting with affect was being tried. While paint is subject to fading in time, the condition of the heads and the variety of shading suggest that fading is not a sufficient reason for the observable differences in coloring. In the case of the "twins" belonging to Phyllis Schoenhut O'Hare, these differences are accented by the neck joint finishing and the difference in eye coloring.

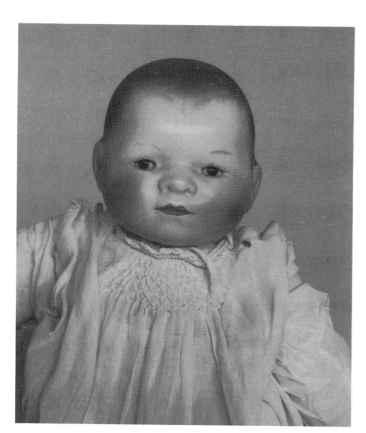

LEFT:
Illustration 355. 12¾in (32cm) head circumference. This Schoenhut *Bye-Lo* can actually be placed next to a bisque one and will pass unnoticed except for its beauty. The color glows with the light and clarity of the bisque ones. Her eyes are blue glass and sleep. She has soft brown eyebrows and hair. She is mounted on a *Bye-Lo*-type (frog shaped) body which has celluloid hands. She is unmarked. *Winnie Langley Collection.*

BOTTOM LEFT:
Illustration 356. 17in (43cm). Head circumference 13⅛in (34cm). This *Bye-Lo*, named "Freddy Carl" after a cousin, has a soft, matte, pink skin with a deep rose blush which extends around the outside of his brown glass sleep eyes. His mouth and nostrils are a pink orange. He has fine black lashes with soft "smudge" eyebrows. His medium brown painted hair is lightly modeled. *Phyllis Schoenhut O'Hare Collection.*

BELOW:
Illustration 357. "Freddy Carl's" profile shows well-modeled folds at the back of his neck and the typical *Bye-Lo* flat face. *Phyllis Schoenhut O'Hare Collection.*

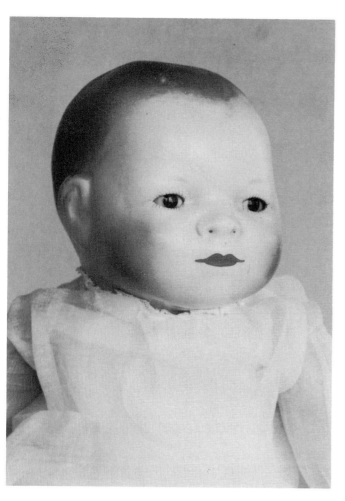

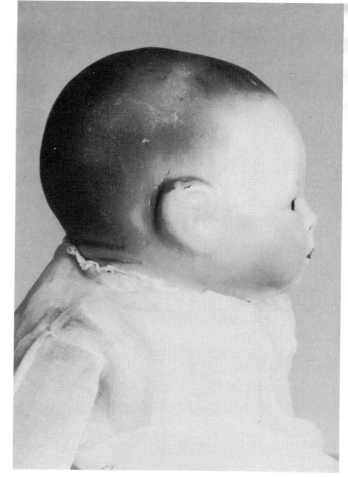

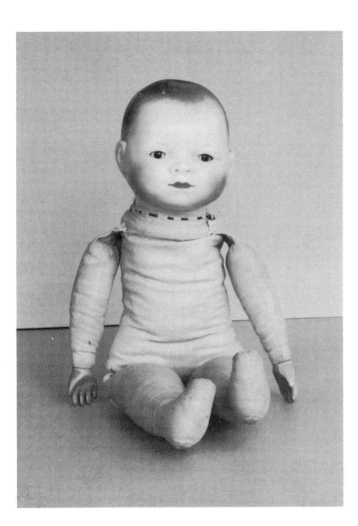

Illustration 358. "Freddy Carl" shows off his trapezoid-shaped pink cotton body with the same dark red cotton cord holding his head in place as that used of the Schoenhut Circus figure clothes. Note the flat unstuffed top of his tube-shaped arms, which acts as a hinge joint. The cloth at the bottom of the arms is tied onto a groove in the wrist of the wooden hands before the arm is turned right side out. There is a vertical seam running down the front and back of the legs and the length of the foot sole. He also has a voice box. *Phyllis Schoenhut O'Hare Collection.*

Illustration 359. Examining "Freddy Carl" and "Mary Loy" together shows the differences in their coloring and decorating details. The doll on the left has a matte finish; the doll at the right has a paler base and a gloss shine. On the left doll, the hair is lighter. His eyelashes are finer and longer, and he has light "smudge" eyebrows. The upper lip of the doll on the right has higher and sharper peaks. Both dolls are in excellent condition. *Phyllis Schoenhut O'Hare Collection.*

"Frieda," A Family Portrait

It is tempting to call "Frieda" the "crown jewel" of Phyllis O'Hare's remarkable collection of the dolls made by her father. This is so even when one knows that the cuddly *Bye-Lo* twins would be the outstanding favorites of the child who loved them. "Frieda" appeals to the collector not just because of her rarity (although it does not seem that she could be any rarer), but because of her strong character face. Here is an original portrait showing Harry Schoenhut's remarkable artistic talent at its best.

"Frieda's" head has a broad face with deep-set eyes. She has modeling above and below the large eyes that indicate the muscles below the skin used in smiling or frowning. Her nose is sharper than the same sized 108W. The philtrum above her upper lip is strongly defined. Her mouth is wider than the Copyright

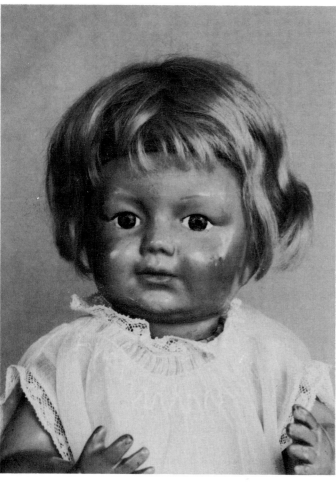

Illustration 360. 15in (38cm) from toe tip to top of head. 12¼in (31cm) head circumference. This doll's head is a real portrait of Phyllis Schoenhut O'Hare. Her lips and accent marks are a very soft pink. She has a peach blush. Her dark blue-gray eyes are stippled to give them depth. She has translucent black upper lid lines and pale blonde single-stroke eyebrows. Her wig is a thick blonde mohair bob which is long enough to cover her ears. She has a square chin, a distinct long oval philtrum and a slight long dimple in her chin as well as soft fold in the flesh under her eyes. She is unmarked. *Phyllis Schoenhut O'Hare Collection.*

Baby, and the upper lip has two sculpted peaks. Her chin, viewed from the front, is prominent and has a slight cleft or long dimple in it. In profile "Frieda" is a delight. She has the chubby cheeks apparent in all the Harry Schoenhut babies, but her nose, lips and chin stand out rather than being overwhelmed by them. There are even slight folds in the flesh between the eye sockets and the cheeks.

"Frieda's" decorating is fairly soft. Her mouth is a peach color defined far more by the modeling than the color. Unlike the Copyright Infants, she has no strong colored oval in the center of her mouth. Her eyes are a deep gray-blue with a black pupil and stippling around the edge of the iris to give them depth. "Frieda's" eyebrows are softly arched single-stroke and match her thick, short blonde mohair bob. "Frieda's" head is mounted on the larger sized wooden "Nature" limb baby body used in the manufactured 108(W) model.

A recent close inspection, made by Charles Buysse, revealed that her head is actually made of cardboard molded between positive and negative molds under very high pressure and possibly while the cardboard was wet. The cardboard (about the thickness of the back of a note pad) has excellent, crisp modeling, and no wrinkles have been created under this procedure which may also have used considerable heat. The pieces were stapled together, and a white gesso was applied to seal the surface and fill in any pits (as well as to hide the staples) before the oil paint base and decoration coats were added.

"Frieda" is clearly a portrait of a real child. Phyllis O'Hare named her after another cousin whom she felt, as a child, resembled the doll. Frieda Schoenhut was born in 1907 and became a "favorite aunt" to her much younger cousins. Comparisons of the doll with a photograph of Phyllis taken when she was a few years older than the model for the doll show that she had the same square chin with a slight cleft, the long defined philtrum, nose shape and softly arched brows as the doll. Her face is longer and slimmer than the doll's, but her photograph is clearly of an older child. This could be a family resemblance. In any case Phyllis's age seems more in line with the probable time that the doll was made, especially considering the fact that the head is cardboard. It seems unlikely that we will know, for sure, who was the original model for this splendid doll. The family traits appear strong in her. Phyllis and her cousin George both mention that there were plans to model a doll on her that were not carried out.

Phyllis also says that her father was a great photographer and modeled dolls from photographs taken at every angle. He used this technique when he modeled a head of her. This head was done at an older age than the doll model. Phyllis says that she could never have sat still long enough for her father, but his use of photography was a great help. It must be noted that the profile of the plasticine model of Phyllis and the doll "Frieda" are almost identical.

It is not known why this doll was never put into production. Perhaps she was designed as the company was scaling down infant production. A single example of a commercial version of this portrait was found by a doll dealer in a Philadelphia house. Although the modeling and head size are identical to "Frieda," her decoration is remarkably different. The paint is matte and the flesh is the same healthy sun tanned look of the later Schoenhut characters and "Dollys" with sleep eyes. Her cheeks, the outside of the fold of flesh above her eyes and her ear tips are blushed with a soft, natural rosy orange. Her mouth paint is a strong pink-orange. It is not as broad as the original "Frieda" and does not stretch the length of the modeling. In addition her lips are much fuller from the upper lip peaks to the bottom of the lower lip. Her eyes are rounder as the paint has been pulled down over the clearly

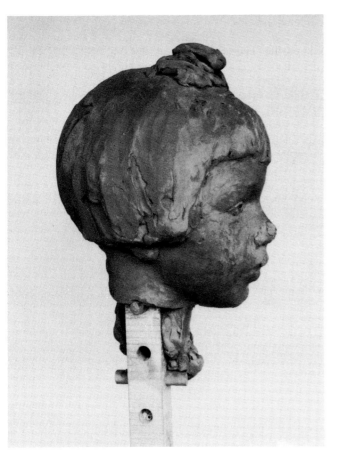

modeled lower lid line. The color is a light gray stippled with a darker blue gray around the iris margin. Her upper lid line is charcoal gray and her single-stroke eyebrows are dark blonde and widely spaced. The whole affect makes her eyes more "staring" than those of the original "Frieda." She is, however, a delightful and more commercial version of a truly fine portrait. The commercial version of "Frieda" (which may be a prototype) is on a fully-jointed spring-strung toddler body. The head is attached with elastic which exerts less pressure than a spring and has kept the light head from splitting. Her body has factory repaint so that it matches the head exactly in color. She has Schoenhut stockings which are nailed to the back of her thighs as were those of the "Walkable" Doll. She wears lace-up white boots and a typical Schoenhut baby "slip" (chemise). Although the doll has holes in her feet, neither her stockings nor her boots have holes in them. They are like those used for the elastic strung toddlers.

The portrait, "Frieda," may have been passed over for general production by the company because she is clearly a portrait of a specific child and not a typical doll design. As such, she is a special tribute to the artistic level of her maker.

LEFT:
Illustration 361. Head of Phyllis Schoenhut O'Hare sculpted by her father Harry E. Schoenhut. *Phyllis Schoenhut O'Hare Collection.*

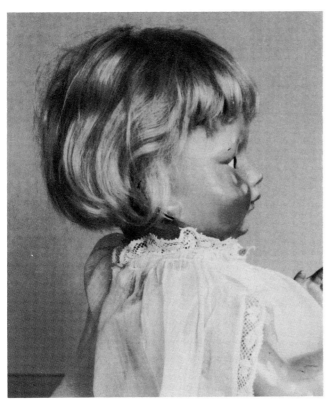

Illustration 362. The doll's profile, compared with that of the sculpted head of Phyllis Schoenhut O'Hare as a young girl shows a striking similarity between the two figures. The slightly uptilted nose tip, prominent upper lip and distinct chin are the same.

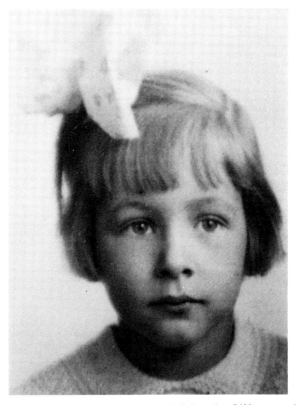

Illustration 363. This photograph of Phyllis Schoenhut O'Hare, as a child, shows the same light hair, soft brows, triangular nose, long oval philtrum, lips and square chin with a slight dimple or cleft that show in the portrait doll. Phyllis is a few years older in this picture than the doll appears to be and has the slimmer face of a young girl who in no longer a baby. *Phyllis Schoenhut O'Hare Collection.*

173

Illustration 364. 17½in (45cm). After the softness of the decoration on the portrait doll, this apparent prototype for a commercial version of the doll is quite a shock. She has the exact same modeling details — the triangular nose, long oval philtrum, distinct chin with a slight long dimple, and the fold of flesh under the eyes; however, the painting causes the difference. This example has the white of the eye pulled down over the molded lower lid line. The eyes are a light gray-hazel, which is achieved by a blue base paint stippled with yellow. She has brown upper lid lines and single-stroke caramel colored eyebrows. There is a red line in the center of her salmon-pink cupid bow mouth and slight shading on the top and bottom of her lips. The lip painting extends above and below the modeling. Her head is mounted on the spring-strung toddler body. She has the factory chemise of the undressed babies, but she also has factory stockings and white lace-up boots. Her body is marked with the oval decal.

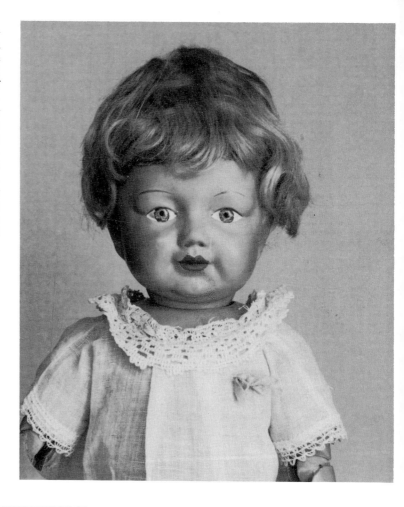

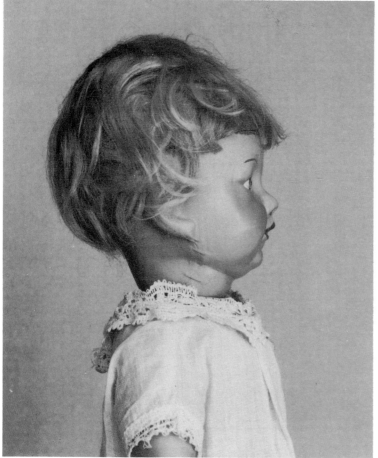

LEFT:
Illustration 365. The profile of the commercial version of the portrait doll shows the same uptilted nose, out-thrust upper lip and firm chin line. It also shows the staples that hold the front and the back of the doll's head together.

OPPOSITE PAGE:
Illustration 366. 15½in (39cm). This example of the Composition Child owes her unusual height to the fact that her head has been mounted (with elastic) to a spring-strung fully-jointed body. Several examples of this combination have been found. It seems likely that they were put together by doll hospitals after the auction of Schoenhut parts in early 1936. Her modeling is crisp. Her dark blue eyes are really intaglio. She even has a small round philtrum which shows better on the actual doll than it photographs. Her upper lid lines are black. Her characteristic blonde eyebrows are sharply arched. She has the strawberry blonde hair usually found on the composition child. Her cheek blush is faded but it is still visible. Her mouth and nostrils are a soft orange-pink. There is no darker color between her lips, and she has no tear ducts indicated. The body has the decal mark.

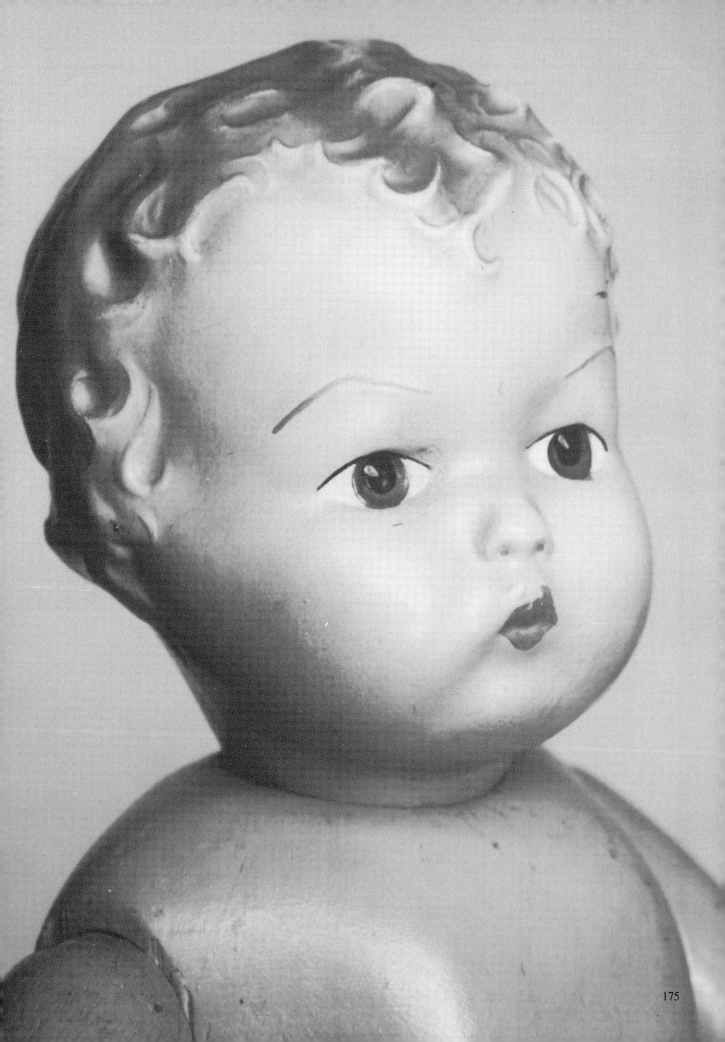

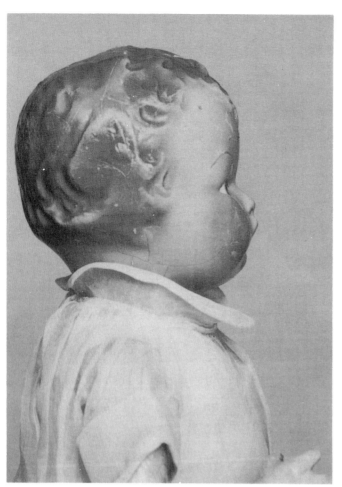

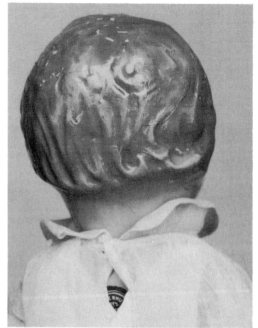

Illustration 367. 13in (33cm). This example is clearly factory original and appears as model number 13/26 in the 1930 catalogue. Her eyes are concave rather than intaglio. The profile of the composition child shows a high forehead, tiny pug nose, out-thrust upper lip, and distinct chin line. The blur in the hair modeling, where the molds meet on the composition child, appears even on the crisply modeled examples. The neck hole on these dolls is so tiny that one cannot see into the head to check the nature of the "composition."

Illustration 368. The rear view of Doll 13/26 shows that her curls are quite short and brushed to her right. Her mark which was standard on many of the toys in the 1930s appears in the Appendix, and her clothes are in the chapter on Original Clothing.

The Composition Child

Harry Schoenhut designed his last doll shortly before he left the company in 1930. Although she is a child doll, she is included here because she represents a very young child. She was designed under Harry Schoenhut's time as "Manager Art Department," and there is no better place to study her. In the 1930 catalogue she is listed as "New! Schoenhut's Fine Composition Doll." She is described as made of wood-flour composition, elegantly painted and handsomely dressed. She (occasionally one is found in original clothes dressed as a boy) is 13in (33cm) tall, jointed at the neck, shoulders and hips. Her "*Patsy*-type" body has a bent right arm and a straight left one. Her second and third fingers are molded together on each hand. The composition used for the body is so hard that a nail can be driven through it without chipping or cracking it. She is strung just like the circus animals. An elastic cord is attached to the top of one leg with a nail driven crosswise through the leg and elastic. The elastic passes up through the torso catching the head which is hooked on, and then goes down into the other leg and is held in place by another nail. The arms are attached to each other in the same way with a single elastic passing through the torso between them. Although the only hook is on the head usually producing a nightmare during necessary restringing, it is fairly easy to work the nails out from the inside and restring these dolls. This sturdy little doll stands firmly, without help, on her own two feet.

The head of the doll, which appears to be a lighter plaster composition, has crisply molded short curly hair which is a reddish-blonde color on most of the examples that I have studied. The eyes are the same bright blue as the intaglio eyed characters, although they are more accurately described as concave on many examples of the composition child. Her brows are a single-stroke tan arch that extends completely over her eye. She has a button nose and a pink "rosebud" mouth. Her fat cheeks are blushed (as are her well-modeled knees). The whole affect is of a cute, slightly grumpy toddler. The mark, when it is present on the back of the torso, is a circular red, white and blue sticker with "Schoenhut Toys Made in U.S.A." printed on it.

The composition child was always sold dressed. The 1930 catalogue shows seven different dress styles and one sunsuit with hat. The dresses are cotton or organdy, fairly simple but nicely trimmed. Each doll had cloth slippers with a tiny nickel buckle and white socks with a colored band at the top to match the dress. All models cost the same. The model numbers are consecutive from 13/21 through 13/28.

Although the paint is susceptible to peeling, as are most of the American compositions of that period, this doll appears to be stronger than most of her contemporaries. The quality of her construction, decorating and dress are good. She is not, a Schoenhut "all-wood Perfection Art Doll," but she is among the best of her type.

The only other dolls to be shown by the company that year were three girls and three boys from the old "carved haired" character series (one 16in [41cm] pouty boy had not been offered since before 1915). They were listed as "the only educational doll for Kindergarten work." They were probably old stock being offered rather than new production. There are no dolls of any kind by 1931. In any case, Harry Schoenhut had already left the company and gone into the manufacture of hosiery. He has left the collector and the historian with a fine group of dolls that are the epitome of everything for which American dolls were known-sturdiness, good design and quality.

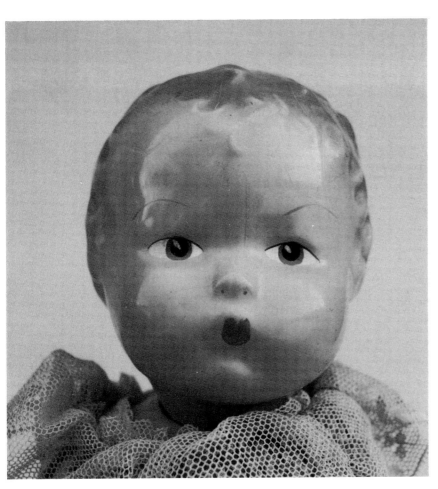

LEFT:
Illustration 369. 13in (33cm). This is one of the more softly modeled examples with less-detailed curls and concave eyes. Her bright blue eyes have charcoal lid lines. She has red-gold hair and arched single-stroke eyebrows. Her mouth and nostril dots are rose and her cheeks are gently blushed. *Photograph by Monty Moncrief. Becky Moncrief Collection.*

BOTTOM LEFT:
Illustration 370. 13in (33cm). This example of the composition child is in excellent condition. Her molded red-blonde curls are clear. Her thin, light-tan eyebrows have the sharp peaks characteristic of this doll. Her bright blue eyes are slightly intaglio with black upper lash lines. Her original dress does not appear in the 1930 catalogue but the fabric used is found in the clothes of other factory dressed dolls and Circus personnel. *Ruth Zimmerman Collection.*

BELOW:
Illustration 371. 13in (33cm). This is an interesting example of the composition child for at least two reasons: She has very sharp modeling. Her blue eyes are really intaglio rather than the concave of most examples. Her curls are very clear and crisp, and her nose and philtrum are quite detailed. At present she has no cheek blush, lip color or accent marks and they may have faded with time, but her eyebrows are very clear and they are brown. Her hair is brown also. She is unmarked. Perhaps she is an early experimental model. *Phyllis Schoenhut O'Hare Collection.*

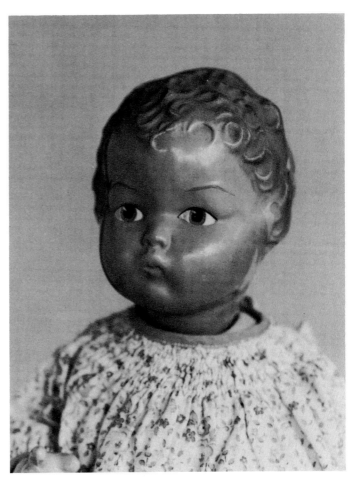

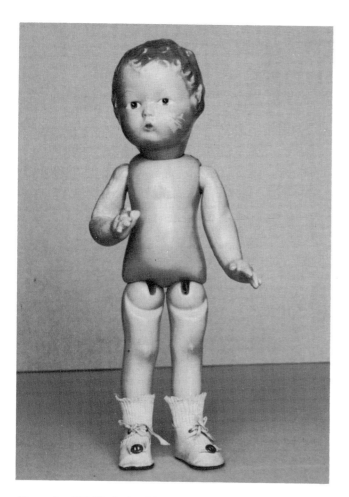

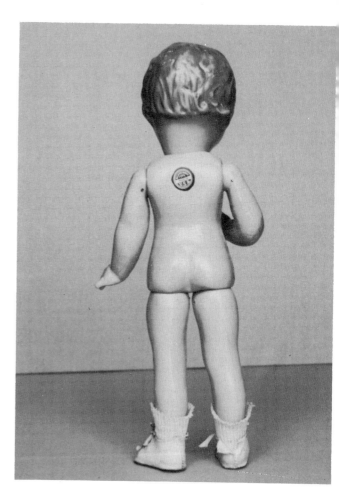

Illustration 372. The body of the composition child is a very heavy wood composition and before it was painted, it was dark brown, the color of chipboard. It has nails driven into the limbs to hold the elastic cord just like the Schoenhut circus animals. It is a sturdy construction and very well balanced, as she can stand easily alone. The body is a *Patsy* style with the right arm bent and the left arm almost straight. Her knees are well blushed. The fingers are separately molded except the second and third, which are molded together. Her feet are clearly different, having toes and even toenails modeled.

Illustration 373. The rear view of the composition child shows that the buttocks are indicated. The nails holding the elastic show at the top of her arms. She is marked. Many are not and have gone unrecognized as Schoenhut products.

Illustration 374. Picture of unknown child holding Doll 14/107. *Courtesy of Becky Lowe.*

178

SPECIAL ORDERS

The "Special Order" dolls are a group of dolls from various times in the company's history that are clearly Schoenhut products but appear to have been made for particular occasions or customers. They do not appear in the regular doll catalogues although several of them utilize heads and bodies of regular models. These dolls present a treasure hunt as most of them have no known history. Instead we rely on stories that have been passed down about them, whether they are true or not. Research on each one will take years; the pursuit is most of the fun. The reader may judge both the stories and the hunt, and perhaps in time, more prime source evidence will be found to add to their identification.

"Gallagher and Shean," or "Mr. Common People"

These remarkable dolls with their hand carved heads have long been thought to represent the vaudeville team and Broadway actors Ed Gallagher and Al Shean. They first performed together in 1912 in an operetta called *The Rose Maid.* They disbanded in 1914 and did not speak to each other for six years. In 1920 Al Shean's sister, Minnie Palmer, mother of the Marx Brothers, brought them back together. They were not famous until they performed a number *Oh! Mr. Gallagher and Mr. Shean,* which they published and wrote themselves. It was a hit in the 1922 Ziegfeld Follies. Apparently it was originally written by vaudevillian Eddie Foy's son Bryan. Foy is said to have written a new verse for each town they performed in, and vaudeville lore sets the number of verses at 1000. They worked into the 1923 season when a contract dispute with the theater managers and producers, the Shuberts, forced them off the stage in the middle of a performance in Philadelphia on November 7, 1923. The dispute was settled in 1924, and Gallagher and Shean appeared together on tour in The Greenwich Village Follies. They argued in the middle of a tour in 1925 and split up for the last time.

Ed Gallagher formed a new team with actress Fifi D'Orsay. He later had a breakdown and was committed to a sanitarium in 1927. He died there at the age of 56 on May 28, 1929. Al Shean continued to play major parts on Broadway into the late 1930s and supporting parts in films through 1946. He died on August 12, 1949 at the age of 81.

The dolls, themselves, present a puzzle. They appear to be quite early. Not only are their heads hand carved, but their bodies appear to be early 16in (41cm) child bodies. Albert Schoenhut was not a woodcarver. Harry E. Schoenhut worked in modeling clay and cast and refined his work in plaster of Paris and hot press molds were made from the model. Lastly the dolls do not look like any pictures of Gallagher and Shean taken during different periods of their lives. Most notably, neither Gallagher nor Shean, in the pictures of them found in the Theatre Department of The Free Library of Philadelphia, wore the facial hair of the dolls.

The solution to the puzzle may be in an article found in *The North American,* dated December 10, 1911, an original of which is in the collection of Harry McKeon. *The North American* was a Philadelphia newspaper that listed itself as a direct descendent of the *Pennsylvania Packet* and therefore claimed to be the oldest daily newspaper in America. The article is about two dolls made by Albert Schoenhut and modeled after cartoon characters created by Herbert Johnson. "Mr. Common People" before his election is described as "sour-visaged and determined." The second figure represented "Mr. Common People" after his election, and he is described as "decidedly changed in expression, his chin lengthened to show an accession of self-confidence, and a cigar in his mouth to give him a sort of 'don't care' appearance."

The three pictures at the top of the article show close-ups of the faces of both dolls as well as a small full-length shot of one of the dolls. One appears to be identical to the "Gallagher" doll in modeling. The second doll is remarkably similar to the "Shean" doll, but not quite identical. The clothes appear to be somewhat different and neither doll is shown in profile which would make positive identification (or its rejection) much easier.

Illustration 375. Both dolls are 16in (41cm) tall. Mr. Common People Before the Election, or Mr. Gallagher, is indignant from his toes to the hairs on the top of his head. His partner, on the right, is the self assured Mr. Common People After The Election or Mr. Shean. *Billie Nelson Tyrrell Collection.*

Visits to the newspaper archives of the Philadelphia Free Library and their helpful librarians turned out to have all the satisfaction of searching for a treasure. It revealed a series of political cartoons by Herbert Johnson that appeared, regularly, on Page One of *The North American* and in a completely different tone from newspapers that we read today. This newspaper had a point of view that was clearly stated in every article and lead to a hunt for the story behind "Mr. Common People" who appeared over and over in these cartoons. "He" was angry and frustrated for a great length of time and then delighted by the election of the reformist Keystone party's Rudolph Blankenburg as mayor of Philadelphia in the fall of 1911. (Edwin Wolf's *Philadelphia: Portrait of an American City* states about Blankenburg that "even his enemies admitted that he was a man of integrity," and that the new mayor had promised a businessman's administration and was able to keep that promise by negotiating graft free contracts which saved the city hundreds of thousands of dollars. Four years later the Republican "machine," which had split over the primary choice in 1911, reunited and ousted the reformers.)

The cartoon "Mr. Common People" was really several people with common features. All were middle-aged white males who were balding. All had mustaches which usually, but not always, extended into their sideburns with clean shaven chins, and all looked remarkably similar to the two dolls in question.

The North American article says that Albert "evolved" the dolls when he disappeared from the factory for a day. However, it does not say that he carved the heads himself. Even his sons were reported not to know where he went. If these are indeed the "Common People" dolls, who made them?

According to family history, Albert's oldest brother Wilhelm Friederick (born in Goeppingen on April 15, 1840) was a wood carver of great skill. He sailed to Philadelphia with his second wife and their four daughters in 1894. Although he is known to his great nephews and nieces as a fine detail carver of decorated furniture, he is believed to have worked with Albert on numerous occasions. He may be the carver of these special heads. Several of the earliest child dolls have felt rings to seat their individually-produced heads into their mass-produced torsos.

Illustration 376. Pictures of Gallagher and Shean as they appeared around 1922. Both men had strong chins. (From sheet music published in 1922 by Jack Mill, Inc. Copyright by Ed Gallagher and Al Shean.)

Illustration 377. Original clipping from the December 10, 1911, copy of *The North American* sent to Albert Schoenhut with a letter from the newspaper. *Harry R. McKeon Collection.*

BEFORE ELECTION

AFTER ELECTION

THIS IS HOW IT HAPPENED.

"MR. COMMON PEOPLE"

Albert Scroenhut, the famous toy maker, has devised an interesting wooden doll, which is a clever presentation of a figure in North American cartoons.

TOYMAKER EVOLVES 'MR. COMMON PEOPLE'

Figures Modeled After Those in Herbert Johnson's Cartoons in the N. A.

BEFORE AND AFTER NOV. 7

Albert Schoenhut, the Kensington toy manufacturer, has been celebrating the result of the election in an entirely original way. According to one of Mr. Schoenhut's sons, who are many in number and are also toymakers, the father disappeared from business a few days ago and during his absence of a day kept his whereabouts a mystery. All that the sons know about it is that when he came back he brought two figures carved and modeled to represent "Mr. Common People," the well-known figure in Herbert Johnson's cartoons in The North American.

The face of one of the dolls was made to represent "Mr. Common People" as he felt previous to the election. He is shown to be sour-visaged and determined. The metamorphosis which was brought about by the result of the election is shown in the face of the second figure, which portrays "Mr. Common People" decidedly changed in expression, his chin lengthened to show an accession of self-confidence, and a cigar in his mouth to give him a sort of "don't care" appearance.

Both of the "Mr. Common People" dolls are wonderfully jointed, so that they may be posed in any position possible, this being a feature of the toys which Mr. Schoenhut manufactures.

Mr. Schoenhut sent the dolls to The North American to keep the editors and cartoonists company, and they have been photographed, their pictures appearing herewith.

THE NORTH AMERICAN

Pennsylvania Packet, 1771: Daily Adverti
United States Gazette, 1789: The olde
Newspaper in America   *Philade*

December the eleventh,
1911.

Mr. Albert Schoenhut,
Adams & Sepviva St.,
Philadelphia, Pa.

Dear Sir:

    We believe you will be interested in the attached clipping which appeared in our issue of December 10th.

    Please accept same with our compliments.

        Very truly yours,

        THE NORTH AMERICAN

        E. D. Edmondson
        Advertising Manager

Illustration 378. The letter accompanying the clipping about Mr. Common People Dolls. *Harry R. McKeon Collection.*

CAUGHT BETWEEN BASES

Illustration 379. This Herbert Johnson cartoon shows "Mr. Independent Voter" (one of the many different names given his Mr. Common People hero) anticipating with delight the running down of Republican machine candidate George H. Earle, Jr., who is between William Penn and Rudolph Blankenburg, the latter being the independent Keystone Party's candidate. The baseball setting was a tribute to Connie Mack and his "A's," who won the World Championship for the second consecutive year ten days later. *Free Library of Philadelphia.*

These two dolls have similar felt rings to enable their necks to fit the torsos smoothly.

"Gallagher" or "Mr. Common People: Before the Election" is 16in (41cm) tall. His head has great detail in the carving of frown creases, the wrinkles around his eyes and the hair. His bushy eyebrows have individual hairs. His mustache extends into his sideburns and is carved to a fine, sharp edge. His receding chin is covered with "stubble." His nose is wrinkled and bumpy. His light brown intaglio eyes have deep lid creases which are edged in a black upper lash line. He appears to be outraged. His ears are well detailed.

The carved details are enhanced by the painting. His creases and wrinkles are accented with a darker shade of flesh color. His hair is a mixed salt-and-pepper gray with the brush strokes again accenting the comb marks. His hair grows around the crown of his head, leaving a large bald area on the top and back of his head. He is the doll that most resembles the cartoon in the newspaper article. Even the details of his frown creases are the same.

The doll's clothes appear to be contemporary, and possibly original, to the doll. His white shirt has a wing collar. He is wearing a striped silk cravat and a beige linen vest. (The doll in the newspaper is wearing a floppy plaid silk bow tie. The picture is not clear enough to see if he was wearing a vest). The doll wears an original union suit, gray pants and a black tail coat. His outfit is completed with black shoes, which are not Schoenhut-made, white spats and a handkerchief tucked in his breast pocket. He does not wear the glasses that are shown on "Mr. Common People" or in pictures of Ed Gallagher.

"Shean" or "Mr. Common People: After The Election" is also 16in (41cm) tall. He is similar in many ways to the first doll, being a man of upper middle age with bushy gray eyebrows and straight gray hair brushed back from his face and brow. He also

has a mustache and extensions to his sideburns. These two areas of facial hair are not joined together as they are on the previous doll, and as they seem to be in the newspaper picture. There are no signs that this area of hair was removed from the doll after it was made. He has a lower brow than the "Gallagher" doll. His head has a similar bald area in the back of the crown. In profile he is an utter delight. His nose is sharp and straight with no bumps. His chin is thrust out, as described in the article, and a tightly rolled paper cigarette or small cigar juts out of the corner of his mouth. His eyes are intaglio and deeply carved. The irises are black, as is the upper lid line. His wrinkles and creases (due this time to his satisfied feelings) are also accented in a deeper flesh tone paint.

This second doll is also dressed in what appears to be contemporary, if not original, clothing. His trousers appear to be the same check as shown in the newspaper article. He wears a white linen dickey with a collar. His jacket is green and does not have the tails shown in the article. He is wearing black stockings and white slip-on shoes (not Schoenhut) and a union suit under everything else. He also does not have the wire rim glasses that are shown in *The North American* article. Both dolls have original Schoenhut stands and "Shean" has a Schoenhut pin. The pin may have been added over the years as there is no indication that the earliest dolls ever had pins.

It is possible that Albert made a few different "Mr. Common Man" dolls (perhaps one for himself?) which might explain why the first doll appears exactly like "Mr. Common People: Before the Election," and the second doll is similar, but not exactly like the one in the article. Whatever the origin of these dolls, they are excellent examples of one-of-a-kind work. The carving is remarkable in its capturing of the personalities as well as the form of these characters. It is a great treat to spend the morning with them. Both are from the collection of Billie Nelson Tyrrell.

Illustration 380. This cartoon by Herbert Johnson, published in *The North American* on November 10, 1911, shows several Mr. Common people sending the political machine packing right after the election of Rudolph Blankenburg as mayor of Philadelphia. *Free Library of Philadelphia.*

BLANKENBURG BEGINS HIS
TASK OF RECLAIMING CITY;
THEN GOES AWAY TO REST

"BACK TO THE TENDERLOIN!"

THE NORTH AMERICAN

SENATOR PENROSE RETURNED TO TOWN YESTERDAY

Illustration 381. The streets of Philadelphia are full of Mr. Common People who have taken over the city with great confidence in this cartoon dated November 14, 1911, one week after the election. *Free Library of Philadelphia.*

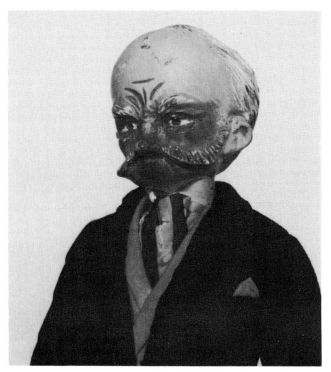

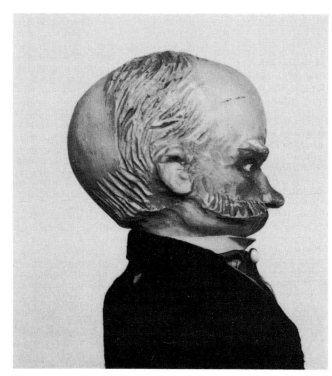

Illustration 382. 16in (41cm). "Mr. Common People Before The Election" (or Mr. Gallagher) is a fantastic character with a hand carved head. His narrow eyes are light brown intaglio with black upper lid lines. His frown is accented by scowl lines in his forehead and wrinkles and pouches around his eyes. He is flushed with anger from his sucked-in chin to above his eyes. His heavy eyebrows are low and tilted toward the bridge of his extraordinary nose. His lips are pursed and barely visible. His nostrils and tear ducts are accented with red. His well-carved hair is iron gray. *Billie Nelson Tyrrell Collection.*

Illustration 383. The profile of Mr. Common People before the election, or Mr. Gallagher, is every inch indignant! He has a long bumpy nose, a powerful mustache and a large upper skull (which undoubtedly is because he is a thinker). His ears are unusually small for a Schoenhut. The back of his head shows that he has become mostly bald. *Billie Nelson Tyrrell Collection.*

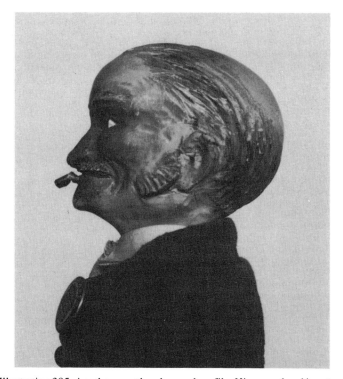

Illustration 384. 16in (41cm). "Mr. Common People After the Election" (or Mr. Shean) is just as tickled as his friend was angry. His wide open eyes are deep intaglio and completely black with raised white reflection dots and black upper lid lines. He is also flushed, but this time with success. His small chin is thrust forward in cockiness, and his smile lines are deeply carved and accented with paint. *Billie Nelson Tyrrell Collection.*

Illustration 385. Another great hand carved profile. His upper head is not as large as the previous doll, but he is a successful middle-class and middle-aged man.

GRAND ATTRACTION FOR THE HOLIDAYS

STORE AND WINDOW DECORATION

Good Old "Santa Claus" with his Sleigh and Reindeers

Furnished complete as shown in illustration **except** the small Toys in the Sleigh. These small toys or other novelties, can be filled in by the purchaser to suit his own taste.

The Reindeers are carved from wood, nicely painted and equipped with gay harness. The Sleigh is made from wood, painted and decorated with bright colors. Santa Claus is a fully Jointed All-Wood-Doll with a very characteristic face.

These goods are not carried in stock, and are made to order only. All orders are made up Oct. 1st. Place your order before Oct. 1st.

No. 000/0 (*Santa*) Total length over all 5 feet; Total weight packed for shipment, 50 lbs..$30.00

Illustration 386. This Santa Claus, sleigh and four reindeer were featured in *The Illustrated Catalogue and Price List for 1914*. His face is similar to that seen in German papier-mâché candy containers of that era. The set in the Margaret Woodbury Strong Museum may have been mounted on its platform by the company for the convenience of the store setting it up as the individual pieces shown here require some cleverness to mount it, preserving the reins and harnesses.

"Good Old Santa Claus with His Sleigh and Reindeer"

A superb Santa Claus was featured in the 1914 *...Illustrated Catalogue ... And Price List for 1914 The A. Schoenhut Company*. He has all of Page Two and is listed as a "grand attraction for the holidays" for store and window decoration. Santa came with a sleigh and four carved wood reindeer. The total length of the set-up was five feet. The catalogue further stated that this was not a stock item and was made to order only. The orders were to be made up on October first. The catalogue number was No. 000/0. It was listed at $30.00 which may have been a retail price as there are several references to a 40% and even a 50% discount on catalogue prices over the history of the company.

Over the years the company made many Santa Claus figures. There was a four foot mechanical clockwork Santa (with a four hour action) and a Santa mechanical picture in the 1890s, and a 36in (91cm) Santa assembled like a circus figure (with joints at elbows and knees as well as shoulders, hips and neck) was shown in the 1907 catalogue. There were Santa Rolly-Dolly toys from 1908 to 1933. The company's weather vane was Santa in his sleigh. As Christmas was the most important season for toy manufacturers and seasonal toys for spring and summer were not yet an important part of the manufacturing and selling picture,

Santa Claus was of even greater importance before the 1930s than he is in 1990s society. Albert Schoenhut himself aged into a Santa Claus-like figure and he was described as such in local newspaper accounts and was even said to have given small toys to curious youngsters who were daring enough to sneak into "Santa's" factory.

This wonderful display item was a natural for the company to make. The only thing surprising is that apparently very few were made, probably due to the unusually high price. There are only two of these set-ups known at present, and they are quite different in their details. The one appearing here is so like the one shown in the 1914 catalogue that it may be the prototype used in the catalogue. The reindeer are carved and painted wood. They are mounted on green and red painted pedestals in running position. Their harnesses are trimmed in dark blue felt with red and gold edging and brass bells. The sleigh is dark blue with bright red orange runners, all trimmed with gold lines. The sleigh was advertised as coming without toys so that the purchaser could load it with his own products. In the catalogue it is naturally loaded with a variety of small Schoenhut items.

Santa, himself is described as a "fully Jointed All-Wood - Doll with a very characteristic face," just as he is shown in the catalogue. He is 16in (41cm) tall on a fully spring-jointed body.

185

Illustration 387. The complete set up of Santa and his sleigh in the *Rosalie Whyel Collection* is well preserved. The reins no longer travel from the bridles to Santa's hands, but most of the original harness remains. The sleigh is blue with beautifully detailed red-orange runners. The reindeer, which are removable from the mounting posts, continue to hold their galloping positions after almost eighty years. *Photograph by Charles Backus. Rosalie Whyel Museum of Doll Art.*

Illustration 388. 16in (41cm). Santa Claus himself is an individually carved character head on the standard spring-jointed body used for the 16in (41cm) Schoenhut doll. The metal hooks embedded in the hardwood hands allow Santa to manage the multiple reins with the expertise expected of him. The wonderful character face of this Schoenhut Santa is in beautiful, original condition. His face is more ruddy than his body. He has detailed carving of plump cheeks and a large nose. His smiling eyes are bright blue with black upper lid lines. He has well-modeled upper and lower eyelids with laugh wrinkles on the bridge of his nose as well as at the corners of his eyes. The crease lines in his forehead support his expressively mobile, carved bushy eyebrows. All his skin creases, as well as his lower lid line, are accented with translucent tan paint. The hairs in his bushy white brows are accented in gray. *Photograph by Charles Backus. Rosalie Whyel Museum of Doll Art.*

His hands have metal hooks in the palms to allow him to handle the reins. His head is a hand carved portrait and not based on any of the standard Schoenhut character dolls. He has strongly carved bushy eyebrows accented with gray and white paint. Like others of the hand carved "Special Order" dolls, he has wrinkles carved into his forehead and nose and laugh lines at his temples as well as heavily carved upper and lower eyelid pouches. All these lines are accented with translucent light brown paint. His eyes are bright blue and are smooth rather than the more usual intaglio. The highlight dots are painted off-center, as were those of the Graziano designed dolls. He has black upper lid lines as well as brown translucent lower lid lines. Both his cheeks and his round nose are blushed. His mouth is broad with thin lips. A hole in the right side allows him to hold a bright yellow pipe. He has his original white mohair beard and mustache, and a replaced wig has been carefully made to match them. Underneath all his hair he has the characteristic Schoenhut large ears. His body has the impressed mark.

Santa is dressed in blue cotton trousers, Schoenhut black button boots and white stockings. He has black oilcloth spats, like the Circus ringmaster and lion tamer, to finish the impression of high black boots. His outfit is completed with a long hooded red woolen jacket trimmed in white wool and closed with a black oil cloth belt. This jacket is the only difference visible between this Santa and the catalogue picture in which the jacket and cap appear to be separate pieces. Differences in detail between catalogue pictures and actual Schoenhut pieces are so frequent that the more one searches through original catalogues, the more one realizes that a piece's "authenticity" can not be fairly judged by these comparisons. Apparently, the company photographed many of its initial design or prototype models, some of which were "enhanced" in the actual modeling, so that the photographs would reproduce clearly, and did not change these pictures as they modified designs in the production.

This is the only known example of the 1914 Santa with a hand carved portrait face. There is another Santa and sleigh set up in the Margaret Woodbury Strong Museum in Rochester, New York. Although the colors used to decorate the sleigh are different and the whole set up is mounted on a base, the sleigh itself is clearly marked Schoenhut, and it appears to be factory produced and modified, possibly to make it easier to set up. The doll is based on a standard character child doll which has been specially painted and wigged for the model. The eyebrows are white mohair and not carved. This may have been done to considerably reduce the price, as it was much easier to modify a hot press-finished standard model than to hand carve a special head.

The special example shown here embodies many things dear to collectors. It is Christmas, Santa Claus and American Folk Art combined. Santa Claus, his sleigh and four reindeer are in the Rosalie Whyel Museum of Doll Art. The photographs were taken by Charles Backus.

The Stetson Hat Man

John B. Stetson first made hats in 1865. His name became synonymous with a style he originated. He established the Stetson Hat Company located at Fourth and Montgomery in Philadelphia from 1886 to the 1960s. The company regularly employed five thousand workers and maintained a small community with its own hospital and school for the families of its employees. The company and its all-important name were sold by the family in the 1960s. Hats with the Stetson name are still manufactured but not in Philadelphia. The Stetson and Schoenhut families were friends, according to family sources, and this doll was made especially for John B. Stetson, who is said to have used

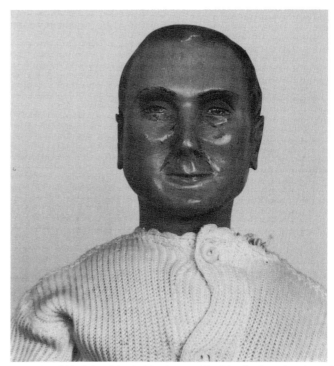

Illustration 389. 21in (54cm). *The Stetson Hat Man* looks quite pleased to represent such an American institution as the Stetson Hat Company. His hand-carved head is asymmetrical and not at all doll-like. His light brown irises are outlined and have a distinct sparkle. He has slightly bushy eyebrows and wrinkles carved around his eyes. Younger than the "Gallagher and Shean" dolls, his features are smoother, but he still has a decidedly character appearance. He has the sticker mark. *Billie Nelson Tyrrell Collection.*

it as a display piece and in his company advertising. He is larger than the Manikin produced by Schoenhut and was designed to specifically appeal to other clothing retailers as a figure to show off their latest lines.

His hand carved head has great character. He is a younger man than "Gallagher and Shean" and has a less comic appearance, but his exaggerated chin and upturned lips give him the appearance of a man with a strong sense of humor (and probably an easier temper) than the previous dolls. Although his features are generally strong, he has a much smoother appearance than the old men as well as less detail in the skin and hair carving. The decorating follows the carving but does not enhance it. The carving also appears less technically skilled than that of the earlier dolls. It is, however, a delightful portrait of a specific person and not at all doll-like in its appearance.

The Stetson Hat Man is 21in (54cm). His head is placed on the largest child body produced by the company. The back of the torso is marked with the oval sticker used from about 1916 on. His face is slightly asymmetrical (as are those of real people). He has deeply set eyes which are painted light brown and outlined in a darker brown-black as are his eye-lids. He has strong dark brows (not heavily carved), a large pointed nose and chin, thin lips under a long philtrum, and large ears carved close to his head. His hair appears to be spray painted as is the hair of other "carved hair" dolls produced by the factory. He may have been designed by Harry Schoenhut as he appears to date from the period just before World War I when Harry headed the Art Department. His smooth, less-detailed finish, as well as his mark, support this dating.

Whether he was made for pleasure (as was Connie Mack), as a gift or by special order, he is clearly a "one-of-a-kind." He is in the collection of Billie Nelson Tyrrell.

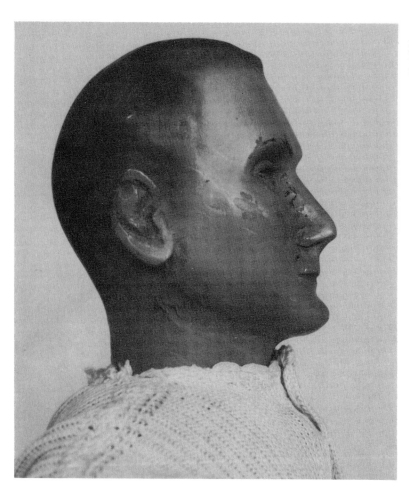

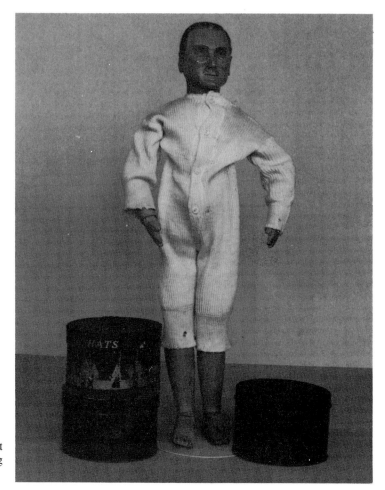

Illustration 390. In profile *The Stetson Hat Man* shows a thick neck, strong jaw line, and characteristic for Schoenhuts, a large nose and ears. The back of his head is quite smooth with no comb marks.

Illustration 391. Posing with his original miniature Stetson hat boxes *The Stetson Hat Man* is dressed as he has been for years in long knit underwear.

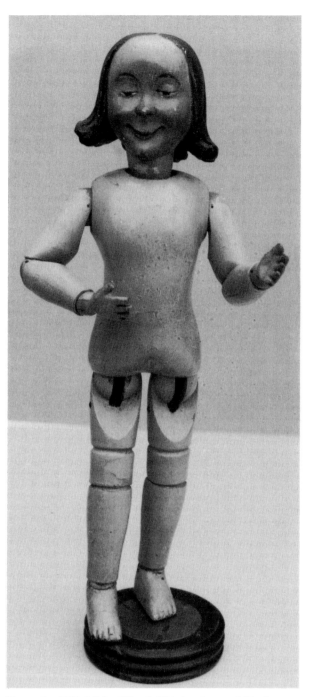

Illustration 392. 14½in (37cm). This hand carved *Moritz* captures the essence of the famous Wilhelm Busch character who originated in Germany but came into many American nurseries when the popular book was translated. He and his friend Max were truly horrific in their pranks and got their "just deserts" in the end when they were ground up to be goose feed. *Photograph by Quentin O'Sullivan. Mary and Carl Hansen Collection.*

Illustration 393. *Moritz* has a long oval shaped head with a pointed chin. He appears inordinately pleased with himself. His single-stroke black eyebrows are arched. His entire eyeball is modeled with the upper lid over most of it. His eyes are brown and both his upper and lower lid lines are brown. His smile is emphasized by the length of his philtrum. *Photograph by Quentin O'Sullivan. Mary and Carl Hansen Collection.*

Moritz

Moritz is apparently a one-of-a-kind doll based on the well-loved comic character which had already been made by Schoenhut in a 7½in (19cm) size with *Max*, his partner in outrageous mischief, to fit the Humpty Dumpty Circus. He measures 14½in (37cm) tall. His body is the standard body for the 14in (36cm) character child. His head is apparently hand carved wood. His hair has the long bob with flipped out ends typical to *Moritz*, but does not have the expected curl sticking up on top of his head and it is painted black rather than golden.

His features are delightful. He has a long oval face with a high round forehead, ski jump nose, pointed chin and pronounced cheek bones. Both his upper and lower eyelids are completely carved, rather than just indicated, and his eyes just peak through them. His philtrum is long and tear-drop shaped over his smiling thin lips which have a curl at each end. His upper lip

is thrust a little in front of the bottom lip, and his chin juts out. His profile shape is reminiscent of *The Stetson Hat Man*, and he may have been carved by the same person.

Moritz' face has naturally-colored flesh that matches his body paint. His cheeks are blushed with an orange pink. His mouth is described by his owner as "strawberry pink." He has pink nostril dots and tear ducts. His tiny eyes are very dark brown with black pupils. He does not have highlight dots. Both the upper and lower eyelids are lined with brown. His eyebrows are single-stroke crescents painted just above the bony arch which is modeled. His body bears the impressed mark between its shoulders. One feels that somewhere there must be a *Max* to go with him, but he has not become public yet. Because of his materials, hand carving and mark, he probably dates to the 1912 to 1916 period. He is in the collection of Carl and Mary Hansen and all of his photographs were taken by Quentin O'Sullivan.

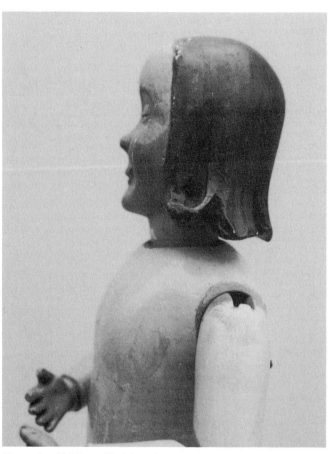

Illustration 394. In profile *Moritz* has a small "ski jump" nose and a strong pointed chin. His forehead is quite round. He has some of the feel of *The Stetson Hat Man* and may have been carved by the same person. *Photograph by Quentin O'Sullivan. Mary and Carl Hansen Collection.*

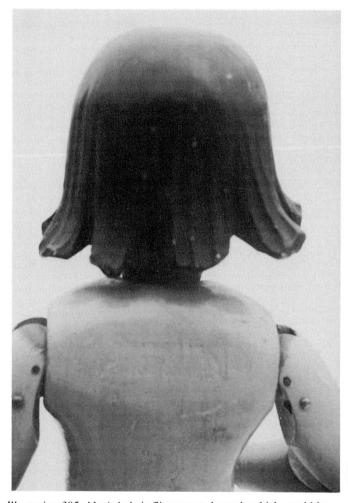

Illustration 395. *Moritz's* hair flips out at the ends which would have made it impossible to reproduce with steam press molding. He seems to have been owned by only three people over the years. *Photograph by Quentin O'Sullivan. Mary and Carl Hansen Collection*

The Lion Tamer

This 19½in (50cm) *Lion Tamer* is in this section because he is more than a "*Manikin*" dressed as a lion tamer. His right hand is individually carved to hold a whip. His feet are carved to represent boots. They have one hole in each foot so that he can stand in various positions for display, but he is not designed to stand on tiptoe. Lastly, his facial decoration is exactly the same as that of the *Lion Tamer* in the famous Schoenhut Circus. He was probably made for a window display or to place high above the section of the toy department in which the Circus was sold. Examples of the elephant, donkey and clown, as well as some of the props, have been found in this scale. They must have made an impressive display when placed in an active scene.

The *Lion Tamer* has a "*Manikin*" head with brown intaglio eyes. His hair is spray painted a medium brown, and he has a darker brown, neatly trimmed, mustache and goatee painted on his face. His body, with the exception of the right hand and feet,

seems to have the standard *Manikin* form. His individually carved right hand holds a whip much like the Circus prop but without the red and white decoration. His costume is identical in appearance and fabric to the corresponding Circus figure. He has black leggings to simulate boot tops. Ivory cotton with a chintz-like finish was used to make his pants and shirt. He has a separate stand-up collar. His jacket is a medium blue pure wool felt, trimmed with a mustard gold felt "braid" trim, which is also identical to the Style Three Circus Lion Tamer. (See Ackerman and Keller's *Schoenhut's Humpty Dumpty Circus From A to Z* for an in-depth study and explanation of styles.)

The *Lion Tamer* was made during the period that Harry Schoenhut headed the Art Department and was probably individually modified under his direction. He appears to date from the 1914 to 1918 period. His mark, if he has one, could not be checked without causing damage to his clothing. This character is from the collection of Billie Nelson Tyrrell.

Illustration 396. 19¾in (50cm). *The Lion Tamer* fits perfectly with the large display sized Circus figures and was probably designed as a special item for shops to attract customers to the toy department. His outfit is identical to that of his Circus counterpart. His head has been specially decorated to match the circus figure and his right hand is specially carved to hold his whip. The fabric used for his costume is identical to that used for the Circus Lion Tamer. His jacket is blue felt trimmed with golden yellow felt. He has a stiff collar and white polished cotton pants and shirt combination. He even has the separate fabric boot tops. Instead of *Manikin* feet he has boot-shaped feet with a well-shaped heel and a single hole in the bottom of each foot to accept a stand. *Billie Nelson Tyrrell Collection.*

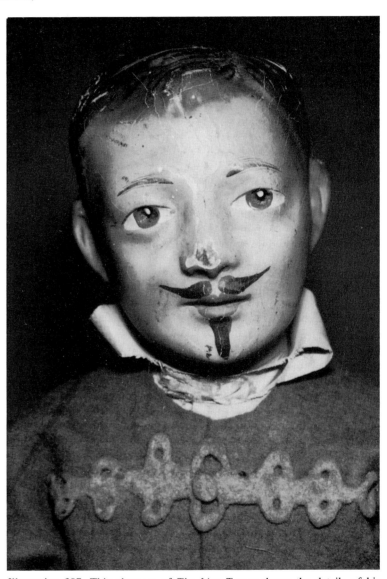

Illustration 397. This close up of *The Lion Tamer* shows the details of his decoration. His intaglio eyes are medium brown. He has a dark brown, neatly trimmed, mustache and goatee. His mouth and accent dots are pink. His eyebrows are well-feathered. His color and blush are very good. *Photograph by Dorothy McGonagle. Billie Nelson Tyrrell Collection.*

Illustration 398. The family resemblance between the groom (21/407) and the little trainbearer (14/311) is striking. Both have brown eyes with well-modeled lids, feathered brown brows, tosca mohair wigs with the same styling, and full lips. Her chin is pointed, and she has a suggestion of a dimple in her right cheek, but both share a long face shape. *Becky and Jay Lowe Collection.*

The Wedding Party

This Wedding Party is completely original with each member having not only their factory original clothing, shoes and stockings but their silk hair ribbons as well. Three of them have their original stands. They appear to have always been together. Most of the dolls are standard factory models. The children's clothes are the top of the factory line. They were, however, carefully chosen to go together. One can easily imagine a family resemblance to each other in some of the dolls. The adult characters are specially dressed, and the bride was probably specifically painted and wigged for this set. It seems likely that they were to commemorate a specific wedding.

The bride is the most unique figure. She is 19in (48cm) tall. Her head is Graziano's Dolls 16/300 and 301 painted in the colors and style of the classic period. Her intaglio eyes are a vivid blue with no iris outline. Her skin tone is the peachier color of the post-1911 dolls with the oranger cheek blush. She has the single-stroke eyebrows characteristic of the earliest dolls. Her hair is a thick fine tosca mohair parted in the middle and pulled down and back into a smooth chignon with a braid around it. It is probably made from a regular heavy long-curl wig which was not curled and was therefore long enough to arrange in her adult style. By mounting her older-looking Graziano head on the "Manikin" body, she has the proportions and appearance of a young woman rather than a child.

Her fine silk dress is "melting," but it retains its simple lines. The bodice is high necked and has vertical pleats. Her long full sleeves are gathered at both the tops and the wrists. She has a long full skirt gathered directly onto the bodice. The dress also has a long full train which makes it more formal than it might have been. She is carrying a bouquet of wax orange blossoms.

Her groom is Doll 21/407 with brown intaglio eyes, feathered brown eyebrows, and a brown mohair wig with a side part. He is on the standard child body which makes him 21in (54cm) tall. He is dressed in a black wool felt tuxedo, with silk-lined lapels and covered buttons. He has a white shirt, tie and vest. He has Schoenhut black leather oxfords and stockings.

The priest is a regular "Manikin" with brown hair and large intaglio blue eyes. Because he has not been played with his color is still quite vibrant.

He is dressed in a long black cossack. Under his robe he has a shirt front with a padded cloth wrapped around and tacked to his torso. He also has black felt trousers which are tacked to his body at the waist. He has black stockings and lace-up Schoenhut boots.

The flower girl is Doll 16/301 with a light blonde, bobbed mohair wig, blue intaglio eyes and exquisite coloring. Her dress is white batiste elaborately trimmed with lace. It is a "top-of-the-line" factory dress, Model 538, which is found in *The "SCHOENHUT DOLL" Catalogue* for 1914. It has an added lace-trimmed over panel, as does the catalogue example. She has white stockings and slippers. She is carrying a small pink bouquet. She is 16in (41cm) tall.

The ring bearer is Doll 16/403 with blonde hair and blue eyes. He is wearing factory outfit 812 with pink shield, collar and belt. His oxfords and stockings are white. He carries a small pink pillow. He is also 16in (41cm) tall.

While the first two children with their blue eyes, short, wide faces and blonde hair seem to be related to the blue-eyed, round-faced bride, the little 14½in (36cm) train bearer with her slender face, pointed chin, brown eyes and dark smooth mohair bob seems clearly to belong to the family of the groom. Her sharp profile and firm chin make a perfect little sister for him. She is Doll 14/311. Her white batiste dress with its vertically tucked, long-waisted bodice is trimmed with both eyelet and lace. It is factory dress 539 also shown in the 1914 catalogue. The dress was made to have a wide silk sash. Neither of the girls have the advertised pink or blue silk ribbon trim on their dresses, and as they have matched edge-trimmed white hair bows, the colored ribbons may have been excluded from the beginning. She is also wearing factory-original stockings and slippers which are missing their buckle trim from the toes. (These were originally light blue, but have faded to "white.")

Again we do not know for whom, or what occasion, this spectacular group was produced. Because the bride's head is quite early and the heads for the groom and train bearer were not made after 1916, it seems likely that the party was produced before 1917. The groom's hairstyle is that given to Doll 407 in 1912 and 1913. The use of the "Manikin" makes a pre-1914 date improbable. The children's clothing is found in the 1914 catalogue. Although the ring bearer's pink shield, collar and belt were not offered as a standard color choice until 1915, it might have been an earlier special order. The girls' dress models were not shown after 1914. Thus we can reasonably date this entire group to 1913 or 1914. The group is from the collection of Becky and Jay Lowe.

Illustration 399. *The Wedding Party.* From left to right: 19in (49cm), 16in (41cm), 21in (53cm), 19½in (50cm), 14½in (37cm), 16in (41cm). *Photograph by Virginia Caputo. Becky and Jay Lowe Collection.*

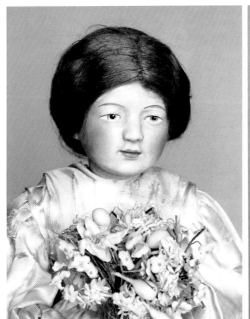

FAR LEFT:
Illustration 400. 19½in (50cm). This lovely bride from *The Wedding Party* uses the Graziano head design 300. Although her golden eyebrows are single-stroke just like the 1911 children, her coloring is the warm natural tone of the 1912-1916 dolls. Her face is quite round, and its shape is emphasized by her heavy light tosca mohair wig which is beautifully styled. She has both upper and lower eyelid modeling, light blue intaglio eyes with dark brown upper lid lines. Her skin is a light peach. Her lips, nostrils and tear ducts are medium pink. Her lips are shaded in the center with a deeper pink. *Becky and Jay Lowe Collection.*

LEFT:
Illustration 401. The bride's profile shows the detail of her hairstyle. Her center-parted wig is brushed down and back into a chignon which has a braid made from part of her hair wrapped around it. *Becky and Jay Lowe Collection.*

193

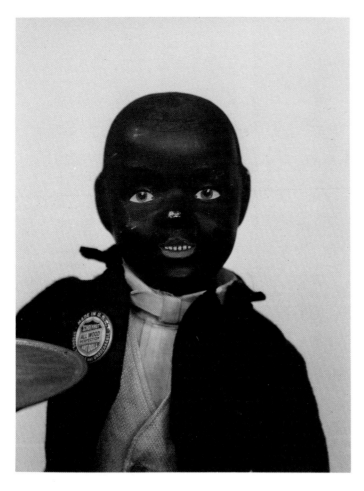

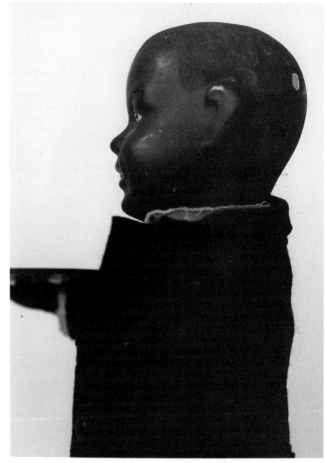

ABOVE:
Illustration 402. 16in (41cm). This doll, *The Black Waiter*, was undoubtedly made by special request. William F. Schoenhut, who worked at the original A. Schoenhut Company, says that the firm frequently filled special requests and would make almost anything desired by a customer. This doll is based on Dolls 16/303, 305 and 402, all of which were the same smiling head with different wigs. He is very black and his brown eyes stand out as a result. He has black upper lid lines and feathered multistroke eyebrows. The black decoration shows because it is shinier than the skin paint. His lips and accent dots are red. His hair is textured possibly using sawdust or fine sand and glue with even blacker paint on top. Where his nose has a rub and where his clothes cover his body, the body paint is the usual pink. There are fine black lines separating his teeth. *Billie Nelson Tyrrell Collection.*

TOP RIGHT:
Illustration 403. The *Black Waiter's* profile is strong. It is a child's profile but not that of a baby or toddler. *Billie Nelson Tyrrell Collection.*

RIGHT:
Illustration 404. The *Waiter's* tray is the largest size Schoenhut doll stand inverted and fastened to his right hand with a small screw. He appears to have been dressed by the factory. The heavy black wool felt coat is made from the same material as that used to dress early Circus personnel. The shoes and stockings are factory accessories. He has a complete white shirt with a pleated front and a well-finished vest. His short silk trousers have dissolved over the years. *Billie Nelson Tyrrell Collection.*

The Black Waiter

The Black Waiter is an example of a standard child doll modified as a special order. He is thus what collectors call a "colored white doll." This is a doll not modeled on a black person, but simply a white doll painted black. He would be child Doll 16/305 or 402 without his wig. Instead he has a very short hairstyle which appears to be applied to his head with a mixture of paint and sawdust or sand. This gives it the texture and finish of hair clipped very close to the skull. His face, lower arms and hands are painted black, against which his brown intaglio eyes appear light in color. The parts of his body which were covered with clothing are painted the standard Caucasian skin color used on the regular doll line. He has six teeth, and a fairly strong pink-red color is used to accent his eyes and nostrils, as well as his lips which are in a slight smile. An even darker, shinier black is used on the multi-stroke eyebrows, the upper lid lash line, and to accent the inside of his mouth.

He is beautifully, if meltingly, dressed in his original clothing which consists of a white shirt with pleated front, finely finished vest with a geometric pattern woven in the cloth and metal buttons, cream silk knee-length trousers (badly melting and exposing his "white" thighs), and a black wool felt coat with tails. He also has factory-original white stockings and leather oxfords as well as his original stand. His "tray" is made from the largest size doll stand without a post. It is fastened to the palm of his right hand with a small screw.

Although we do not know why he was ordered, it is clear from his decoration and clothing that he was produced in the Schoenhut Factory probably during the 1912 to 1916 period. He is from the collection of Billie Nelson Tyrrell.

The Chinese Babies

The Chinese Babies use the smaller version of the Copyright Baby with "Nature Limbs" designed by Harry Schoenhut in 1913. What makes them special is their decorating and their wonderful elaborate costumes. It is likely that they were made for a special exhibit, but we have not found their origin. They measure 9in (23cm) from rump to top of the head. Their heads and forearms are a pleasant golden shade. Flesh that is covered by their elaborate costumes appears to be standard factory pink, like that of *The Waiter*. Their eyes are smooth and painted black with no pupils. There are black upper lid lines, and there is a curl at the end of the lash line that gives a suggestion of an Oriental eyelid fold. The eyebrows are dark brown single-stroke and very slightly slanted. The babies have a healthy cheek blush. They have red lips with a narrow line left unpainted between them. The dolls are completed with smooth black paint for hair with an added black floss, waist-length braid. The painting is not exaggerated in its portrayal of Oriental features, and the dolls have a good deal of gentle dignity.

The costumes are as fine as any found on the German bisque Chinese babies produced by J.D. Kestner in, and after, 1914. They appear to have been made of Chinese silk and have elaborate silk embroidered panels with beads, "jewels" and coin trim. The pair studied are clearly meant to be a boy and a girl and are dressed accordingly.

The girl has a rose silk tunic with wide, gold silk lower sleeves and gold silk trousers. The tunic has a black, stand-up "Mandarin" collar with gold braid trim. The wide sleeves have fine embroidered edges, finished with tiny round pearls. The trousers, from the knees down are also elaborately embroidery-trimmed. Over all this is a tan silk vest which is bound around the edges with turquoise silk and rows of braid. The front and back panels are finely embroidered with flowers, a dragon and curling "wisps." Fastened to the over-vest are round "silver" coin-like pieces. Her cap is pale gray blue silk trimmed all around with embroidery, fuchsia silk piping and macramé pink net with fringe hanging down over two-thirds of her face and hair. There are large rose pompons surmounted with gold embroidered shapes on either side of her head. Braided silk cords ending with three beads and a long tassel as well as two cream and gold embroidered panels hang from the sides of her cap onto the front vest panel.

The boy is also magnificent in his style. His basic tunic color is gold silk with turquoise panels embroidered on top with pearls and beads and at the bottom of the panels as well as the lower legs with white, six-petal flowers. His tunic has a Mandarin-style collar similar to that of the girl. The sleeves have braid trim and are bound in turquoise silk, trimmed with "pearls." His cap's base is gold silk, trimmed with rows of braid, two smaller green pompons on each side, as well as cords with two blue beads and a gold metal decoration above the long tassels. He does not have the macramé veil. Their slippers have a black silk base with finely embroidered uppers.

We cannot check the dolls for possible marks without endangering their glorious and fragile clothing. Because they are dressed almost identically to the finest of the Kestner Oriental babies, they may date to as early as 1914. They may also date later as they could have been part of the Sesquicentennial Celebration in Philadelphia (1926). In the end the date is a mere curiosity as their special charm speaks for itself. They are from the collection of Keith and Donna Kaonis.

Illustration 405. The *Chinese Babies* are special because of their decorating and their elaborate costumes.

Illustration 406. At 13in (33cm) from toe tip to top of head when lying down, this *Chinese Baby* boy is based on Harry E. Schoenhut's Doll 13/107, the baby with "Nature Limbs." His color is a warm gold with deep cheek blush and an even deeper pink red lip and accent dots. His elaborate costume is described in the text.

Illustration 407. This baby is 13in (33cm) from toe tip to top of head when lying down. The doll appears to be a girl, perhaps because of the pink fringe "veil." Her costume is also described in the text.

Illustration 408. 15¾in (40cm). The *Japanese Man*.

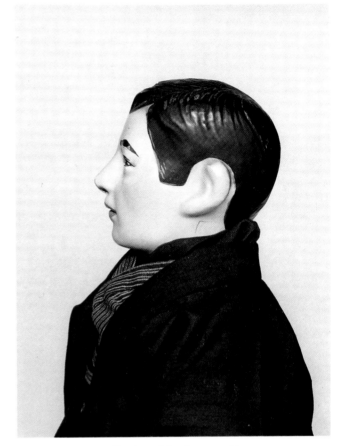

Illustration 409. Profile view of the *Japanese Man*.

The Japanese Man

The Japanese man is not a one-of-a-kind, but he was a special order. There are five examples of him, two of which are completely dressed, in the Civic Center Museum, which was called the Commercial Museum and used to display Philadelphia's many fine manufactured products. This may provide a clue to why, and when, they were made. Another example may be seen at the Mary Merritt Museum in Douglasville, Pennsylvania. Other examples are found in at least three private doll collections. All the examples are identical in decoration and dress. One is presented here.

He has the *Manikin* head mounted on the 16in (41cm) child doll body which makes him 15¾in (40cm) tall. His head shows signs of having been originally painted as a standard Manikin and then carefully painted over to give him "Oriental" features. His head has a golden tan flesh color with a soft orange pink blush on his cheeks and ears. His lips are rose, shaded with black paint. His nostrils are also painted with rose first, and then overdone with black so that the deep pink color shows through. He has no painted tear ducts. He has black intaglio eyes with black upper and lower lid lines painted to a half-moon shape. There is a second, thinner black line on the inside half of the upper eyelids to indicate eyelid folds, and shading to emphasize the eye sockets. Above his eyes he has wavy, but not slanted, eyebrows. They appear to be single stroke, but have brush hair marks giving the impression of multi-stroke brows. He had brown spray painted hair which has black hair painted on top with straight, side brushed bangs and square-cut sideburns in front of his ears. The black hair is painted below the comb marks onto his neck in the center back

of his head. There are fine silver accents in his hair which seems to have been done to emphasize the straightness and shine of Oriental hair.

His body has the "sun tanned" color that seems to have been used on the dolls in the mid and late 1920s. Unlike the *Chinese Babies* and the *Black Waiter* the lower arms are not specially colored to match the head. The head on this size body makes him look proportionately like a youth, perhaps a rather serious student, rather than a full grown man. He does not have the light-colored obi of a small boy, nor would his features fit this identification. When asked what he thought was the reason for the choice of the 16in (41cm) body with the *Manikin* head, Bill Schoenhut said that he thought it was probably because "we thought all Japanese people were short."

His costume is multi-layered, well made and carefully finished. The predominate color is black. There are striped patterns using brown, caramel tan, and white in different combinations and with minor variations among the different dolls seen. This example's outfit has a fine black layer around the neck which may actually be an "under" shirt. Over this is a short, finely striped kimono which extends just below the knees and has wide legs in it. Over this is a divided, ankle length pleated skirt of black, brown, tan, and very fine white stripes with a self-belt which wraps twice around his body and ties in the back. The pleats are tacked-in across the front with tan thread, probably temporarily to keep them sharp. Over all of this is a short black natural silk jacket with wide short sleeves. The top half of this jacket and the sleeves are lined with a shiny gray silk. He has knee-high black socks which do not have holes in the soles. They are tied just below the knee

Illustration 410. 25½in (65cm). This unique lady doll uses the largest size 317 head. She has brown decal over wooden sleep eyes with long fine lashes both above and below them. Her brown brows are feathered. Her lips and nostrils are pink, and there is red accents around her teeth. There are no tear ducts. Her long brunette human hair wig is piled up on top of her head. It appears to be original. Virginia Schoenfeld has dressed her in Edwardian style using old white cotton voile with rows of lace insertion and tucking. The doll has her original black stockings and shoes. *Photographs by C. Lee James. Virginia Schoenfeld Collection.*

Illustration 411. The body of the *Lady Doll* really is wood and has the Schoenhut spring joints. The feet also have the two holes in each sole. Her hands look like German composition hands, but Virginia Schoenfeld says they are wood and are also spring strung. Her body, which is also long enough to give her adult proportions, has been shaped to resemble the German lady dolls that became popular, briefly, around 1910. *Photograph by C. Lee James. Virgina Schoenfeld Collection.*

Illustration 412. This shows the spring joints in the *Lady Doll's* knees, as well as the two pins at the top of her buttocks which anchor the leg springs. The body is unmarked. The doll may have the patent mark stamped on the pate under her wig. *Photograph by C. Lee James. Virginia Schoenfeld Collection.*

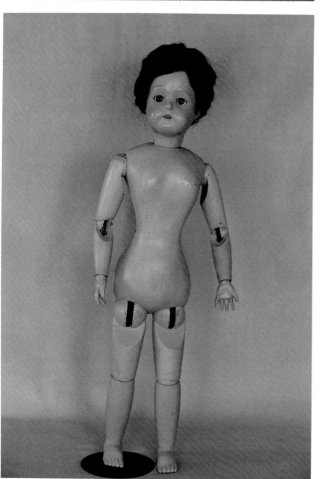

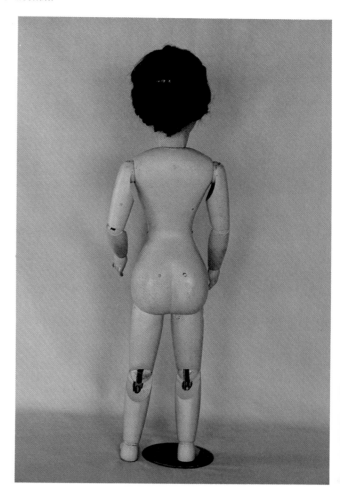

joint with black thread. Other examples of this doll also have these socks. Apparently he was not made to use a Schoenhut stand. Perhaps he was made to kneel in a display. We did not disturb his clothing to see if he is marked.

People at the Civic Center Museum told me that there was a major special display of Schoenhut items at the old Commercial Museum, perhaps connected with the 1926 Sesquicentennial exhibit. It is possible that the *Chinese Babies* and the *Japanese Man* are connected to, what Philadelphia hoped would be, a major international fair. Although we do not have more than a theory about why and when these dolls were made, they are beautifully-produced special factory examples.

The Lady Doll

When I first saw pictures of the Lady Doll in Marlowe Cooper's *Dimples and Sawdust, Volume No. 2*, (copyright 1968), she appeared to be a Schoenhut 317 head on a German lady doll body from about 1910. In fact she looked like Simon and Halbig's mold 1159. Virginia Schoenfeld, the doll's owner, is a determined collector who really knows how to share with other collectors. She approached me when she heard I was studying Schoenhuts saying, "Of course you will want to use my Lady Doll." I explained I could not travel to Colorado for one doll picture. She could not bring the doll to a Convention — besides she had others I should see. I needed extremely clear photographs using the new 25 ASA film. She got her nephew C. Lee James to photograph her dolls exactly as I specified. The result of his work is found throughout the book. The result of Virginia's sharing is that this doll has found her way to these pages, and I have learned a lot.

The doll is 25½in (65cm) tall. She does have the 21/317 head with brown sleep eyes. She has long, fine widely-spaced eyelashes above and below her eyes. She has the usual black eyelid line at the top of the decal on the wooden eyeball and a painted eyelid above that. She has brown feathered, but not stacked, eyebrows. Her color is an even, peach tone with a soft cheek blush. Her mouth and nostrils are pink. There is a red accent inside her mouth and around her four teeth. Her brunette wig is quite long and made of human hair. It is parted on the left, like the usual long curl wigs the company produced, and piled up on top of her head. The fact that it is human hair does not mean that it is not a factory product. Several Schoenhut family members have told me that the factory made human hair wigs by special request, sometimes from the hair of a family member of the customer.

Her body had been my main question. Virginia had extra pictures taken of the doll showing the holes in her feet. The pictures included here show all the details of Schoenhut work. The body is wooden. The spring joints show clearly. The pins that hold the spring system together are all there and located as they are in known Schoenhut dolls. The arms and legs are the same used for the 21in (53cm) model, which by then actually measured 22in (56cm). Her hands are beautifully detailed and were probably specially made for her. Her 10½in (27cm) torso is unique. It is enough longer than that of the largest child doll to give her the extra 3½in (9cm) of height. It is wood and shaped with a proper, but not exaggerated, bust and hips as well as a slender waist. As a result of its length, the arms do not extend as far down the body as do those of the largest child doll. She does not have a stocking groove on her legs, but she did come to Virginia with black Schoenhut stockings. Because of her sleep eyes, she dates to the 1921 to 1928 period. Her body is unmarked, and we have not removed her wig to check her pate for the patent mark, but she is undoubtedly a very special Schoenhut.

The final treat was when Virginia brought the doll to the 1991 Schoenhut Convention and allowed me to examine her. Her feet are wood, in the Schoenhut style, but are a little wider than the standard 22in (56cm) *Dolly*. They are beautifully carved with the toenails carefully indicated. She is clearly a factory product. Her well sculpted hands may be German composition hands finished by the Schoenhut factory.

Connie Mack

When I first showed pictures of this doll to an old time Philadelphia Athletics fan he laughed aloud and then said, "All he's missing is a copy of the *Daily News* tucked under his arm. He always had one at the game." This is indeed a wonderful portrait of a famous Philadelphian and captures his spirit as well as his physical likeness. This doll has always remained in the Schoenhut family so his history is easier to trace.

Cornelius McGillacuddy, known to everyone as Connie Mack, was manager and part owner of the Philadelphia Athletics (called "The Athle-etics" or the "A's" when I saw them play in Shibe Park, later renamed Connie Mack Stadium) for over 50 years. The Athletics were not the first baseball team in Philadelphia but they were early enough, having been founded in 1860. Mack's control of the team covered the entire first half of the 20th century. His "A's" won the world series in 1910, 1911 and 1913. After 1914 Mack decimated his team by trading many of the players. He apparently never said why, but it is generally believed by baseball historians that it was financially profitable, as the profitability of a team was much less connected with whether the team won or lost, which now helps to engender the great incomes produced by television rights and product endorsements. Connie Mack never lost the hearts of Philadelphians and slowly his team came back to the forefront, winning the World Series again in 1929, 1930 and 1931.

The Schoenhut family members were ardent fans. Although factory workers could not go to the daytime games, a young boy walked around the immense work spaces with the latest scores chalked on a board during championship time. Bill Schoenhut recalls that his mother actually took him and his sister Frieda out of school when important games were played so that they could attend them.

Apparently the doll *Connie Mack* was sculpted by Harry E. Schoenhut for his own pleasure. Harry, like a lot of today's doll artists, sculpted first in clay and then made a plaster of paris model on which he could refine the details with dental tools. *Connie Mack* never was made in wood. Harry painted the plaster head model and mounted it on a "Manikin" body. The doll was given Schoenhut stockings and lace-up boots (which have disintegrated with time) and was dressed in a replica of the real Connie Mack's well-known three-piece wool suit, which he wore on even the hottest days. Connie Mack never managed a game in a team uniform as other managers did, perhaps because he was an owner as well.

The doll itself is 19¼in (49cm). He has brown intaglio eyes with well modeled eyelid wrinkles and "laugh lines." He has bushy brown eyebrows and short hair of the same shade of reddish-brown. He is modeled with a broad grin and a mouth full of upper and lower teeth. He has detailed throat modeling as well. Like the "Mr. Common People" dolls, his wrinkles and ear folds are accented with paint. His coloring is realistic, and he has blush on his prominent, high cheek bones. His profile is wonderful, having a "hawk" nose, a distinct chin and lines on either side of his smile. He is a real portrait rather than a caricature. Photographs of

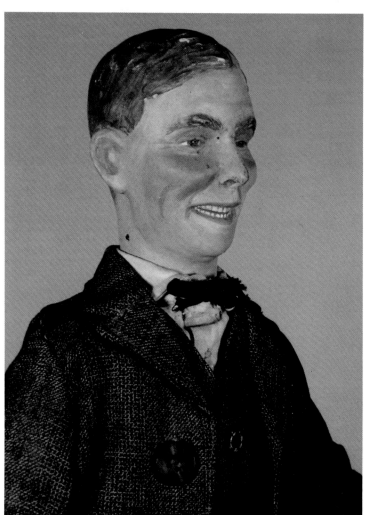

Illustration 413. 19¼in (49cm). This portrait of *Connie Mack*, owner-manager of the "A's" baseball team for over 50 years, is a remarkable likeness sculpted by Harry E. Schoenhut, perhaps in celebration of one of the six World Championships won by Philadelphia's American League team in the first third of the 20th century. It was never produced commercially. The head is plaster which shows the fine web lines around his eyes caused by a combination of laughter and middle age. The smile lines on either cheek show in all the photographs of Connie Mack. *William F. Schoenhut Collection.*

Illustration 414. *Connie Mack's* profile is much the way he looks in newspaper pictures taken while he is congratulating Jimmy Fox or Lefty Grove on a great game. He has a wonderful "hawk" nose, high cheekbones and long upper lip. The dolls ears are uncharacteristically small for a Schoenhut, but they are just right for *Connie Mack*. Note the eyelid creases and fine wrinkles. A metal bar runs through his neck from one side to the other to hold the head hook. The end of the bar shows in the sides of his neck. The back of his head has more hair modeling than that of the Stetson Hat Man. *William F. Schoenhut Collection.*

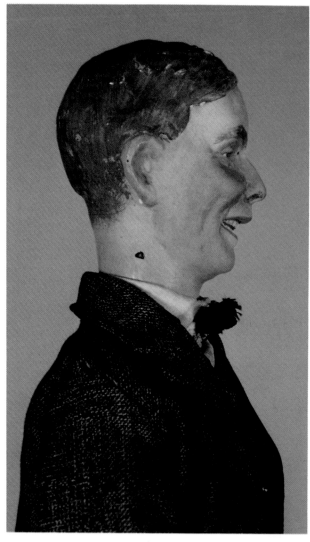

Connie Mack show how closely the doll resembles the man. Pictures of him taken before World War I show a man with fewer wrinkles than the doll has. Pictures taken in the mid to late 1930s show that his hair is turning gray. The doll probably dates to the 1920s.

Connie Mack is dressed in a three-piece salt-and-pepper fine wool suit. He has a white cotton full shirt with a separate finished cotton collar and a black bow tie. His outfit is carefully detailed. The vest is lined and the jacket has dark bone buttons. He has his original factory black stockings and a pair of replica shoes made for him as well as the pieces of his original boots.

William F. (Bill) Schoenhut remembers the doll standing in a workroom at the factory. It was evident that the company was losing its battle to survive the modernization of toy manufacture and the Depression, and he asked Harry if he could take it and give it to his mother, the ardent "A's" fan. Harry said he could. Bill gave it to his mother, who willed it to him after she died. Bill has kept it because Harry meant so much to him and because of the memory of his mother and the good times they had at games when he was a boy. The doll is yet another example of Harry Schoenhut's real artistic ability.

1. Factory Original Clothes

The vast majority of Schoenhut dolls were sold "undressed." Boy dolls were sold in a long-legged union suit which was often held in place at the ankle with a gummy ring (or some kind of light glue) on the bottom of the doll's leg. Stockings were rolled up over the union suit leg and shoes were added. Early in production the undressed boys were shown with dark (apparently black) stockings and white oxfords. The early dressed boys were shown with shoes and stockings that matched each other and "went with" the clothes. Starting in 1912 the boys were usually sold in shoes and stockings that matched. Examples have been found in white, light blue, red, brown and black.

The undressed girls were originally sold in a slip with white stockings and black oxfords. Frequently the dressed girls were also presented with white stockings and dark oxfords, but other combinations were shown as well. The undressed "Transition" girls were still in a slip until June of 1912 when the girls are first shown in a union suit in an advertisement in *Playthings*. At that point shoes and stockings were matched for girls as well. Examples have been found in white, light and darker shades of pink, light blue, light brown, black and occasionally red.

Four styles of shoes were offered in 1911 for either boy or girl dolls. They were sold in a variety of colors which are not specified in the catalogue. The styles were a lace-up boot which came above the ankle, a side button boot with two (and sometimes three) buttons, an oxford and a "slipper" with an ankle tie and a metal buckle with a leather "bow" threaded through it to trim the toe. This last shoe was identical to the typical leather doll shoe found on German and American dolls of the period. Schoenhut shoes had leather rather than the oilcloth soles and uppers that are found on many doll shoes of the period. The shoes had the two holes with grommets that matched the holes in the doll's feet and enabled the doll to hold a steady position on the stand.

Beginning in 1914 the child doll's shoe was made in two models, the slipper and the oxford. Examples of dolls in original factory dress from 1915 and 1916 have been found with button boots, but the boots were not offered separately by the company. From the beginning these styles were not assigned as boy and girl shoes, and all styles have been found on both boy and girl dolls. Separate "infant" shoes for undressed babies do not seem to have been available before 1919 and maybe not until 1921.

For the Graziano six months and the first bit of the "Transition Period," the stockings had a white cotton inset in the sole. This inset had two round unfinished holes in it which matched the holes in the doll's foot. The stocking also had a grommeted hole at the top rear which was hooked onto the nail which stuck out of the back of the doll's thigh. This held the stocking up. After the first year a groove was cut around the doll's thigh, just above the knee joint, and the stocking was tied up with a fine silk ribbon which matched the stocking in color. The inset was dropped from the sole of the stocking and a large oval opening, finished around its edge, took its place. The opening was large enough to expose both holes in the foot.

The dressed dolls were offered in miniatures of the typical well-dressed child of the period. The earliest dolls had more fabric in each outfit, like the bulky children's clothes of 1911. They became considerably more "streamlined" by the middle of 1912. The early cotton was not preshrunk, and girls in factory dress sometimes appear to be in a dress made for a smaller doll, which would shrink when washed in hot water. Union suits shrink a good deal even when washed carefully. Boy's union suits suddenly have legs that end at mid-calf leaving a bulge under the stocking where it ends, and girls are left with a gap between the top of the stocking and the lace trimming on their shorter and fuller union suit leg.

The details of presentation of undressed girl dolls are often quite nice. Silk hair ribbons were usually matched by a bow of the same color on the union suit. Sometimes pink, blue or white shoes and stockings also matched the ribbons. The pink and blue shoes (and the stockings) have sometimes faded so much that the only way one can verify the original color is by checking the rear seam inside the shoe (or the stocking where it has been protected from light by the shoe leather).

In the 1911 catalogue 18 different dresses and one "regulation blue serge gymnasium suit" are shown for girl dolls. Many of the outfits are similar to each other, sometimes with only color differences to distinguish one model from another. Most have natural or slightly lowered waistlines. Six of the dresses are either plaid or checked gingham. Pink and blue chambray and percale are also used. There is one figured dimity with a natural waist and a bertha edged with lace and three fine white lawn dresses, one trimmed in blue, one trimmed in pink with lace, and the most elaborate trimmed with "fancy val lace and colored ribbons." Most of the dresses had stand up collars.

There were also five hat styles available for girls. One was a white sailor hat to go with the white sailor dress. Others were braided straw or white horsehair trimmed with satin ribbons. The last was described as a "fine white embroidery mushroom Hat with colored satin ribbon trimming." These last sold for $1.75 a hat!

In 1911 an extensive line of 12 boys' suits and one "regulation gray flannel gymnasium suit" (which has occasionally been found on an early boy doll and thought to have been a baseball player's uniform) was offered. There was a wide variety of styles. Although most were typical of well-dressed American boys of the time, one was a royal blue velveteen "Fauntleroy" suit with a lace trimmed blouse. Two of the boy's suits were white sailor suits with long pants — one trimmed in red, the other in blue. Four other boy's suits had sailor-style tops with shields and ties. All four had baggy pants which were gathered just below the knee. One was a white "Norfolk Suit" with bloomer pants and a white cotton shirt. There was also an "Over-all Suit" with a percale shirt and a boy's "Fancy Masquerade Suit" in bright colors.

There were four different hat styles for boys in 1911. One was a flat round sailor hat with blue trimming. One was a simple braided straw, and two were the soft "linene" floppy, brimmed hats that have rarely survived to the present.

The early transition clothes were the same models offered in 1911, but the dolls shown wearing those clothes had changed.

In these earliest catalogues clothing was specified for "carved hair" and wigged dolls. The 500 Series was designated for "carved hair" girls. The 600 Series was for "carved hair" boys. 700s were designed for wigged girls and 800s for wigged boys. From the beginning any number clothing style could be purchased separately, so the distinction in series made little sense. The clothing in the 500 and 600 Series was less bulky so that it did not overwhelm the "carved haired" dolls, but customers could judge that for themselves. The Series' designation was changed after the first year with all girls' dresses renumbered to the 500 Series (with infant clothes having the 550s), and all boys' suits assigned to the 800 Series. For a brief period of time girls' hats took over the 700 Series, and boys' hats were given the 900 Series.

In 1912 advertisements dolls were shown in a new line of clothing which included coats as well as hats on a few girl models. The girls' dresses seem less bulky. Some dresses have no waist but may have a loose belt around the hips. Some dolls have natural waistlines in their clothes.

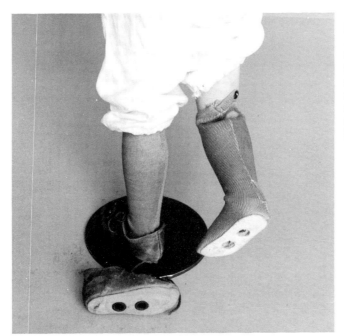

Illustration 416. The eyelet at the top 1911 stocking allowed it to be hung on the round headed nail on the back of the thigh. The doll's right stocking is unsupported as the nail has come out of her right thigh. These stockings have a separate inset white cotton sole with two small holes in it which match the holes in the doll's foot.

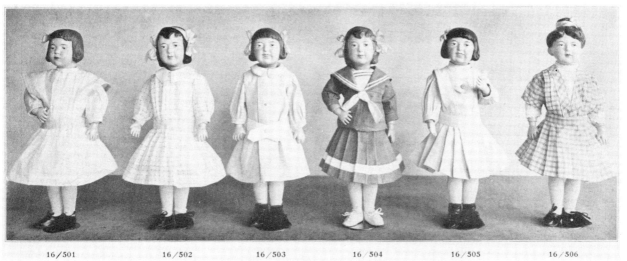

| 16/501 | 16/502 | 16/503 | 16/504 | 16/505 | 16/506 |

Illustration 417. When this group shot appeared in Eleanor St. George's book *Old Dolls* with the "dolls" attributed to a collection, one can imagine how collector's searched for them in later sales, but the pictures are really cuts taken from the original 1911 Schoenhut Doll Catalogue showing the variety of dressed dolls available. The size and model numbers have been left on to show how the company presented them. The number covered both the doll and its clothes. All child dolls were 16in (41cm) tall that year. Model 16/504 is shown as a real doll later in this chapter, as is dress 16/503.

| 16/601 | 16/602 | 16/603 | 16/604 | 16/605 | 16/606 |

Illustration 418. Here are the 1911 dressed "carved hair" boys, also shown in the St. George book. Outfits 601, 603, and variations of 605 and 606 are shown on real dolls in this chapter.

Illustration 419. These are the dressed dolls with simpler wigs. The second dress is a flowered dimity. Model 16/705 is shown as a real doll later in this chapter, as is the transition version of 16/706.

Illustration 420. The more expensive line of dressed wigged dolls from the 1911 catalog is shown here. The 1912 version of dress 707 is shown on a real 19/102 later in this chapter. An all original 16/708 is also shown. A version of 709 from 1912-1913 is also shown in a different color combination.

Illustration 421. The more expensive line of wigged, dressed boys in the 1911 catalogue. Outfits 802 and 803 are shown in this chapter on real dolls. Later versions of 801 and 805 are also shown. The 806 outfit is blue velvet with lots of lace and the doll has shoulder-length curls

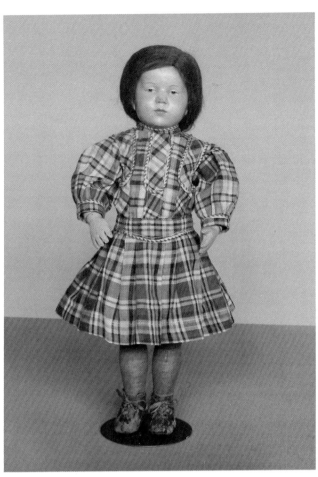

Illustration 422. Doll 16/708 as she appeared in the first *Illustrated Catalogue...Dolls the A. Schoenhut Company*. The dress is described as "Scotch Plaid Gingham, with fancy braid and button trimmings." Even her cranberry red stockings and high-laced matching boots are original. Underneath she has a full slip and matching white drawers. The doll also appears in the Graziano chapter. She is Doll 302 in her undressed form. Note the natural close fitting waist and the stand-up collar. This outfit also had a braided straw hat with a satin ribbon around the crown. The dress sold separately as 16/708GD (girl's dress); the hat as 16/708GH (girl's hat). *Dorothy Dixon Collection.*

BELOW LEFT:
Illustration 423. The doll in this outfit is called 16/603 in the 1911 first Doll Catalogue. The percale shirt has fine red stripes. He was posed this way to show off the pockets in his blue "Over-all Suit." He had a bow tie and straw hat at one time. The price of $56.00 a dozen was probably retail. To buy the suit without the doll one had to order 16/603BS (for Boys Suit).

BELOW RIGHT:
Illustration 424. This particular doll in this dress was simply called 16/504 in the first catalogue. The 500s were originally reserved for dressed "carved" hair girls. To buy the dress alone one ordered 16/504GD (for Girl's Dress). There was no hat for the "carved" hair girls and only half of the dressed "carved" hair boys had hats. The skirt should have pleats sharply pressed in. The blouse has shrunk over the years and is too close to lift over her head without slitting it below the lacing. It is the opposite color pattern from dress 707 which in 1911 was made for a wigged doll, although later it was featured on the "Classic" 102.

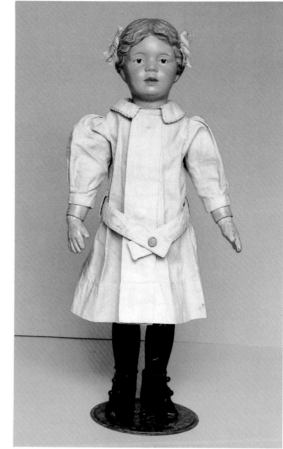

ABOVE LEFT:
Illustration 425. Boy's suit 16/803 is from the 1911 catalogue and is in excellent nonfaded condition. The 800 series was originally made for wigged boys, and all of them had hats. Only half the dressed "carved hair" boys came with hats. The star on his shield is red, and it is possible that his original tie was also red. This black tie is old but not original. The blue chambray blouse suit has buttons closing the front of the shirt and a gathered long-waist which is bloused over. His white boots have two buttons. Note the stitched-down pleats on the outside of the blouse sleeves. This detail is found on many Schoenhut boy's tops.

ABOVE RIGHT:
Illustration 426. From the first catalogue and the "Transition" folder, this is girl's dress number 16/503GD, described as "One-piece Russian dress made of light blue percale fancy braid edging, white belt." In this example the belt is made of the same light blue percale as the dress. The panel in the front has blue snap fasteners under it. The belt is fastened with a similar snap. These snaps, which appear to have a celluloid cover which yellows and changes color when exposed to light over a period of years, are colored to match the clothes and were used a great deal on early factory clothing. *Gail Hiatt Collection.*

RIGHT:
Illustration 427. This style doll in this particular outfit, including white stockings (which hang on nails protruding from the back of her thighs) and shiny black oxfords, was sold as 16/705 in the first catalogue. The only way to order this Kämmer and Reinhardt-based face was as a dressed doll in the Graziano period. The 700 series was reserved for wigged girls. After 1912 all the girls dresses became the 500 series, but by then this dress was gone from the line. Note the braid trim. It is a particularly nice finishing touch. Her yoke is embroidered eyelet. Originally her braids were arranged across the top of her head. Even her shredded bows are original. *Dorothy Dixon Collection.*

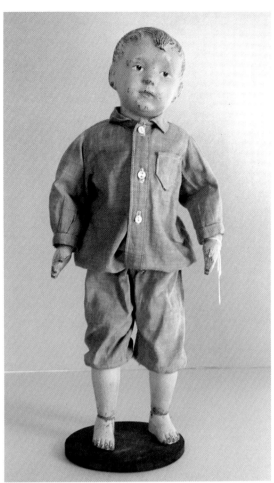

Illustration 428. This light blue "Chambray Boy's shirt-waist Suit with bloomer pants" was number 16/601 in the original 1911 catalogue. By 1913 its number had changed to 810. In 1911 the 600 digit meant that the outfit was for a "carved hair" boy and included the doll as well as the suit. By 1913 or earlier all boys suits were renumbered to the 800 series and the distinction between whether the suit was originally designed for a "carved hair" or a wigged boy was gone. He originally had a colored ribbon bow at his neck and a handkerchief in his pocket. *Bud and Dot Hutton Collection.*

BELOW LEFT:
Illustration 429. Doll 16/706, as she was presented in the "Transition" folder. The dress is pale "blue percale, with bias straps and edged with pink." The snaps are just decoration on the dress front. They were probably originally pink. Now they are almost white. The outfit is completed with brown stockings and lace-up boots.

BELOW:
Illustration 430. This is Doll 16/802 just as he appears in the "Transition" folder from November 1911 to April 1912. It is described as a "Boys white sailor suit, with red trimmings and tie; also white linene sailor hat to match." This suit first appeared in the original 1911 catalogue and probably was not available after 1912. The red braid has faded and the tie is an old silk ribbon replacement, but the rest of his suit including his red hat band ribbon, white button boots and stand are original. His shield buttons into his jacket which closes with hidden buttons. There was a similar suit with blue trimmings which came on a "carved hair" doll and was numbered 604.

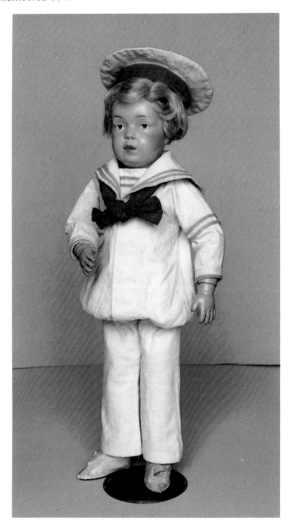

ABOVE:
Illustration 431. By 1912 this sailor dress, which was model 707 in the original catalogue, was made with a blouse that buttoned down the front under the plain blouse front. The buttons do not show so the plain front is neatly preserved, but the doll is much easier to dress and undress. This dress was shown on the 19in (48cm) model 102 in advertising and catalogues from 1912 to 1916 but was probably not sold after July 1913 when dress 530 appeared in advertising. The tie is as shown in 1912, but is not original. It is made from real middy braid that is as old as the dress. The shield buttons into the blouse front under the collar.

TOP RIGHT:
Illustration 432. In 1911 this outfit came in blue and white fine check gingham with blue chambray trim and a separate white guimpe and a straw hat. It was Doll 16/709 and the face of the doll was based on Kämmer and Reinhardt's 114. By 1912 the outfit came in four sizes, and as you can see, one variation had caramel tan, checked gingham with white embroidered trim. The guimpe was still separate and the part that fills the neck has a pattern of pulled threads giving a feeling of vertical stripes in it. This is doll 19/311, and her outfit was renumbered to the 500 series. It appears to be a variant of number 519. Her brown stockings and slippers are factory-original. Under her dress she wears a union suit and a cotton, fitted full-slip with factory trademark bone buttons.

RIGHT:
Illustration 433. This factory dress is a variation in color, but not in pattern, to one shown in June 1912 advertising in *Playthings*. The dress is a faded light blue. The trim is white, and there is embroidered braid around the edges of the yoke and lace at the neck and cuff edges. It is number 513.

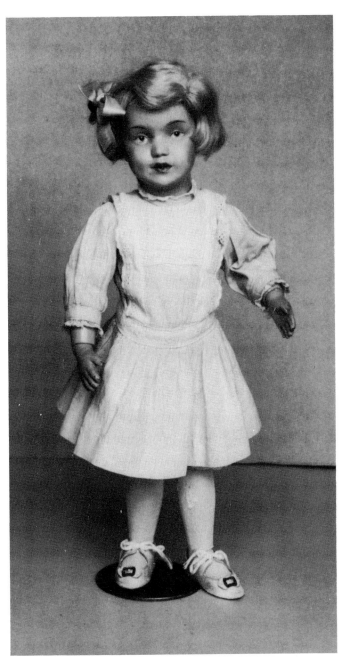

Illustration 434. The dress, original to this doll 16/311, is shown in early 1912 advertising. There is no model number given, but the dress is clearly the same. The light blue cotton has faded over the years and the white eyelet trim has considerable wear. This doll was played with gently, and she is in super shape. Her original shoes and stockings are white. Only her blue silk hairbow and shoelaces are replacements.

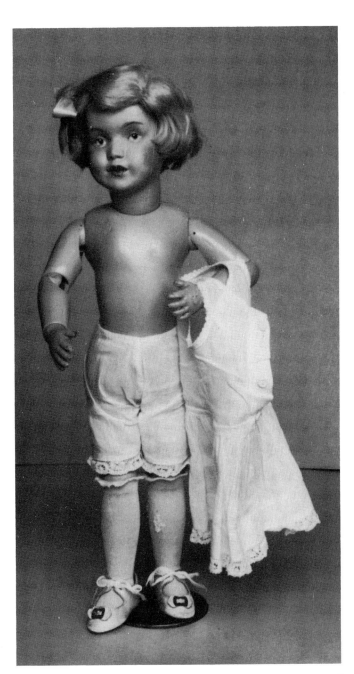

Illustration 435. Undressed, Doll 16/311 shows her slip and drawers of fine cotton. The drawers have a slit in the back from waist to crotch allowing the doll freedom of movement. The slip has a natural waist and the usual bone buttons. Girl dolls dressed in the factory originally had drawers and slips rather than union suits, according to the catalogues, but we have found some with union suits and slips as well.

The 1914 catalogue shows the largest line of girl doll dresses. Colored dresses came in 12 different styles, all of which were offered in two different color choices. Six styles had natural or slightly lowered waistlines, four had no waist line and had fabric belts around the hips, and one was "short waisted" with the gathered skirt attached to the yoke. The colors mentioned are pink, blue, red, brown and white. Fabrics were "figured lawn," plaid and striped gingham, chambray, white lawn, and "linene." Two of the dresses have separate guimpes. Eight of them have stand up collars. The "Peter Thompson suit" (which appeared in 1913 and continued through at least 1918) was offered in blue as well as white linene. There were also 12 white dresses. Two had natural or slightly lowered waists, one was "short waisted" and one had no waist but did have the cloth belt around the hips. Eight were clearly low-waisted. Fabrics used were lawn, "linene" (for the "Russian" dress with colored braid edging on the collar) and eyelet embroidery. Colored ribbons were inset in the trim of simpler dresses and tied in large, multi loop bows on the fancier ones. Eight of the white dresses had stand-up collars. Sleeves were elbow, three-quarter and wrist length. Lace of various widths (depending on the cost of the dress) trimmed most sleeves, necks yokes and hems.

Six boy doll suits were offered: The simple blue chambray "Boys Shirt Waist Suit with bloomer pants" and breast pocket; the "overall suit" with its separate percale shirt, tie and straw hat; the white "linene Russian Suit" with sailor collar, shield and white linene "outing" hat; the striped white and navy blue galetea Russian suit; and the boys' fancy suit with white linene bloomers, percale shirt, red coat and white linene floppy "outing" hat — all continued from 1911. These suits are more streamlined in appearance. The sixth suit was a striped gingham "Buster Brown" suit with a wide, white collar and large blue silk bow at the throat.

Six separate hats are shown, five of which are girls'. Two are braided straw with colored satin ribbon trim, one is covered with red mercerized poplin (and has a red quill), one is covered with blue velveteen with large matching velveteen rosettes, and one is an eyelet embroidered "mushroom" hat with colored satin ribbon trim. The boy's hat is the white linene outing hat with colored ribbon trim.

Infant doll clothes were rompers of pink and white plaid gingham or blue chambray, ankle-length white walking dresses and long white lawn dresses with matching caps.

By 1915 all of the girl's dresses had a dropped waistline or a loose belt around the hips of an otherwise waistless dress. Most of the sleeves were three-quarter length. Only one of the dresses had a stand-up collar, although three others had gathered lace trim around the neck. One-third of the 18 girl dress models came in fine white cotton trimmed with lace insertion and ribbons. The rest came in a variety of plaids and ginghams and solid chambrays, usually in pink or blue. A few models over the years were offered in tiny floral prints using a variety of colors. Braid trimmings in contrasting as well as complimentary colors were used. Some versions of a sailor (originally called a "Peter Thompson") dress was offered until the company stopped making its own clothes at the end of 1924.

Boys' clothes came in six styles in 1915 and 1916. There were two "Oliver Twist" suits, with either brown or blue pants; two "Russian Suits" with loose middy-type jackets; a striped seersucker (red and white or blue and white) "Buster Brown Suit;" and the "Fancy Suit" with white bloomer pants, shirt, tie and hat, and red double breasted coat. The two "Russian Suits" and the "Fancy Suit" were shown in the 1911 catalogue.

During the years 1915 and 1916 clothes were still made in layers. Dresses sometimes had an underskirt of colored chambray or percale and an overskirt of stripes or plaid. The layers were completely made, but sewed onto each other rather than being separate pieces as they had been earlier.

The clothing line was streamlined (as was the doll line) in 1917, and though the clothes did not change dramatically in appearance, the layers became indicated with bands of the fabrics sewn together instead of covering each other. This was a saving of fabric and gave the doll less bulk to carry. Besides the simplifying of the clothes, the variety offered was also cut in 1917. The girls' line was cut to nine dresses, three of which were white. The boys' line was cut from six to four models which kept the "Buster Brown" suit and the three that had been shown in the original 1911 catalogue. All clothing shown in 1917-1919 had appeared in 1915 with the simplification mentioned earlier.

In 1920 the line changed for the last time. There are still nine dresses offered for girls, three of which are white lawn, but the waists are mostly at natural level or slightly high (except for a white linen Middy blouse which is over a blue pleated skirt). There are three boy's suits. One is a Buster Brown suit, one a striped poplin blouse suit and the last is the "fancy suit" with the red coat. Pongee is mentioned for the first time as well as poplin and piqué. Pink and blue still dominate the colors, and striped and checked ginghams are also used. 1924 was the last year that dressed dolls or extra clothes were offered (except for the "Mamma Doll" and the Composition child which only came dressed). In that year the girl and boy dolls were sold undressed only, but the same clothes found in the previous four years were available separately. During this period the toddler's dress was a short white lawn with a high waist.

The infant clothes are further discussed in the chapter on infants. The baby with "Nature limbs" had its own soft leather "bootee" available from 1921 through 1926, and a button boot was offered for all three sizes of the toddler during the same period. The slipper was offered in the 11in (28cm) and 14in (36cm) sizes as well.

In an article in a July 1919 issue of *Playthings* about Katherine A. Rauser, a noted designer and manufacturer of clothes for higher priced dolls, the A. Schoenhut Company was listed as one of her customers. As Mrs. Rauser was known for her large factory as well as her design skills, and Schoenhut consistently said its dresses were made in their own factory (even featuring photographs of its wig and dressmaking departments in catalogues through 1916), there is some confusion about the role played by Katherine Rauser in relation to the Schoenhut Company. Did she make some of the infant dresses or even the boy's suits? The infant dresses seem more likely as they are very similar to those worn by other baby dolls of the period. The boy's suits, according to the catalogues, only fit Schoenhut boy dolls with their slimmer bodies. It is also possible that *Playthings* made a mistake listing a connection between the two companies.

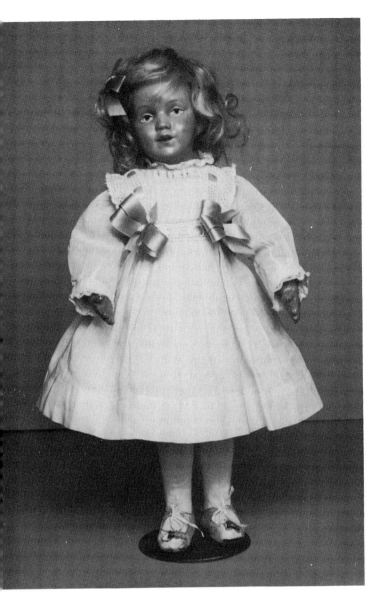

Illustration 436. Doll 14/311 is modeling factory dress 516/1 from the 1914 catalogue. This dress came in three color options: White with pink or blue silk ribbons, blue chambray with blue ribbons and, pink chambray with pink ribbons. The high waist right under the drawn-work yoke is not usually associated with Schoenhut, but they have surprised us again with the variety of their products. The silk ribbons are old but they are replacements.

507/1—2   525/2—3   526/2—3   527/2—3   528/2—3   513/1—3

Illustration 437. The 1914 catalogue showed 24 different dress styles for girl dolls. Most of the 12 "colored dresses" came in two color choices. The number after the slash indicates the colors offered — 2 indicates blue, 3 stands for pink or red depending on which was offered for that design and 4 indicates brown. Model 526 was offered in blue and brown plaid gingham with blue trim and tie or a striped gingham with red trim and tie. 527 came in blue or red. The other 3s stood for pink. Model 525 appears on its original doll in the following pages. 513's plaid was pink or blue. Another variation of 513 is also shown in this chapter.

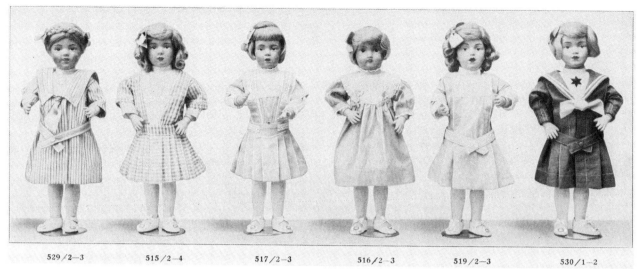

529/2—3   515/2—4   517/2—3   516/2—3   519/2—3   530/1—2

Illustration 438. More 1914 doll dresses. 529 came in red or blue, 515 came in blue or brown, 517 in pink or blue. The pink version is found on a real Doll 19/311 in this chapter. 516 and 519 came in pink or blue chambray. 519 had a separate guimpe. A brown and white checked version of this dress is shown on another 19/311 in this chapter. Dress 530 is shown in its blue version which was not made after this year. The white version of 530 continued to be made through 1918 and is shown in this chapter.

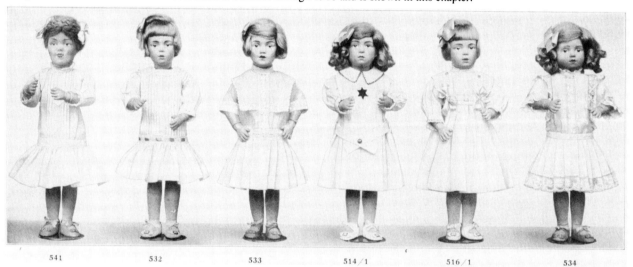

541   532   533   514/1   516/1   534

Illustration 439. From the 1914 Doll Catalogue — these dresses are white. As can be seen, 516/1 is the white version of a dress which also came in pink or blue chambray. It is also found on a real doll in the following pages. 514 came in a checked version in 1912.

535   536   537   538   539   540

Illustration 440. The fancier white dresses from the 1914 catalogue combine lace and eyelet embroidery. Dress 537, 538 and 539 all appear on real dolls in this chapter; 539 is even on the same model doll. Dress 540's suggested retail price was $3.00 in the 16in (38cm) size, while the undressed doll that wears it cost about $3.20 if the retailer decided to take his highest mark-up. The least expensive dress, 507, is suggested to sell at about 60 cents.

Illustration 441. These are the 1914 boys' styles. Some had hats included. Examples of 810, 811, 812, 813, and 818 are shown in this chapter.

Illustration 442. Hats shown for separate order in the 1914 Schoenhut Doll Catalogue. 716 is covered in red poplin; 717 in blue velveteen.

Illustration 443. There are similar dresses to this in the first catalogue, but this one is dress 517, described as "Plain blue or pink chambray with pleated shirt, lace and embroidery trimmings." It is found in *Playthings* advertising in 1913 and is modeled by Doll 19/311, which dates from the same period. The hat was found with the dress. The fabric is very similar but not identical. It may have been specially made to go with the dress in the home, or it may be factory-original.

Illustration 444. This factory dress, modeled by "Transition Doll" 103, dates circa 1912 to 1914. It is dress 537 as shown in 1914 catalogue.

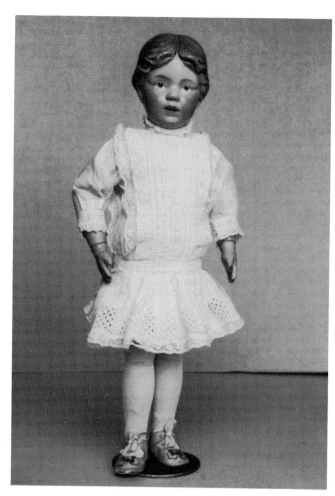

BOTTOM LEFT:
Illustration 445. The matching factory slip for Doll 103 has a natural waist and a tiered slip which fits fairly closely at the hips and flairs out nicely to support the dress skirt. The lace has the same clover pattern.

BOTTOM RIGHT:
Illustration 446. Doll 103's drawers have a drawstring through the waist. The rear opening and back slit drawers allow the doll great freedom of motion without tearing her clothes. The lace on the drawers matches the slip and the dress.

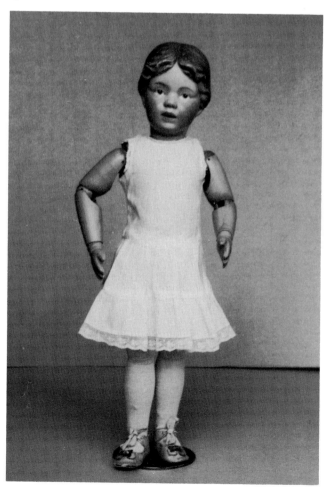

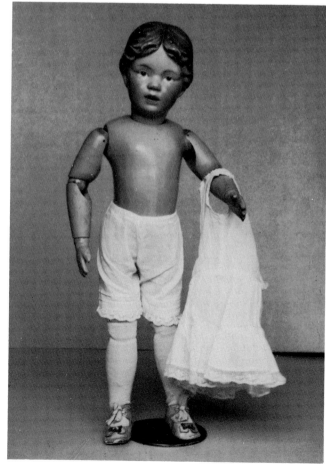

RIGHT:
Illustration 447. This 16/301 is all-original, complete to her stockings' ties. The dress has not yet been found in company literature, but it is very professional in its appearance. The blouse was made separately but is sewn into the dress. Its cuffs have pink edging. She has her original (although shredded) bright pink hairbow. Her stockings and shoes, though faded, are also pink.

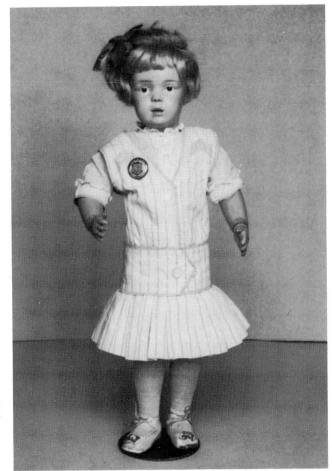

BOTTOM LEFT:
Illustration 448. The slip worn by Doll 16/301 is quite low-waisted and slim. It is similar to the slip under the 530 model "Peter Thompson" dress both in its line and mother-of-pearl buttons.

BOTTOM RIGHT:
Illustration 449. Even the union suit bow worn by Doll 16/301 is pink.

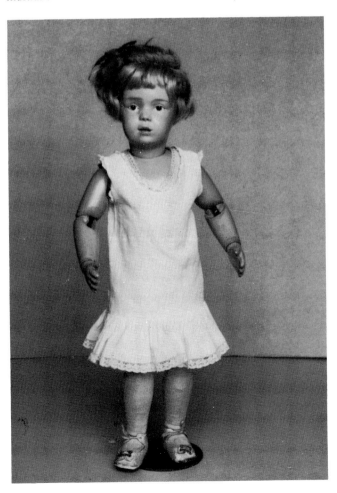

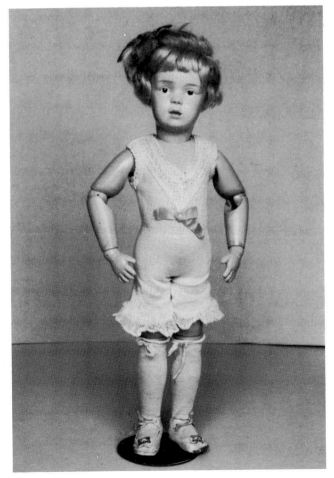

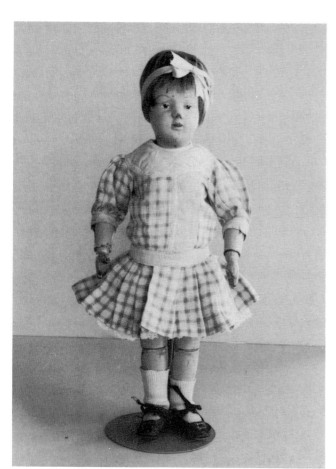

LEFT:
Illustration 450. This Doll 14/312/525 is in July 1913 advertising and is also shown in a 1914 catalogue. The dress is described as "plaid gingham with colored and white trimmings to match." The yoke band down the side front of the dress and waist band were all originally light blue but have faded almost completely over the years. There is a narrow white tape trim at the neck, the bottom edge of the round yoke, and at the inside edge of the band that goes down the front. The dress cuffs are also blue with white edges. *Regina A. Steele Collection.*

BOTTOM LEFT:
Illustration 451. This "White Linene Norfolk Suit" with its floppy white hat was shown in its double breasted form in the June 1912 edition of *Playthings*. Its catalogue number was 16/605. The hat was not shown as a part of this suit in advertising, but it could be bought separately as item 16/801. B.H. (for Boy's Hat at 34¢).

BELOW:
Illustration 452. By the time this boy 206 came on the market his "White Linene Russian Suit" with its blue collar, separate shield and belt were sold as number 812. In the original 1911 catalogue it was much fuller in cut and was listed as 801. It also came with the 801 B.H. hat. From circa 1912 to 1916 it had this shield. From 1916 through 1918 the suit was made with a shield that had a square cut neckline with the two stripes of braid across it. Note: This union suit has shrunk to shin level. This is one of the tops with stitched down pleats on the lower half of the sleeves. The catalogues show this outfit with a silk ribbon tie.

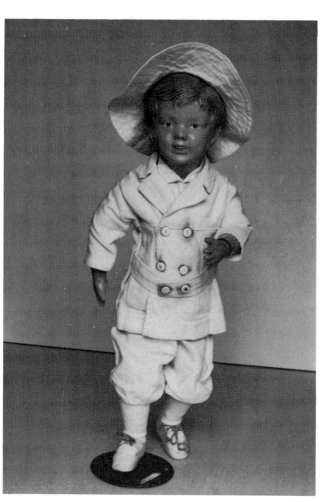

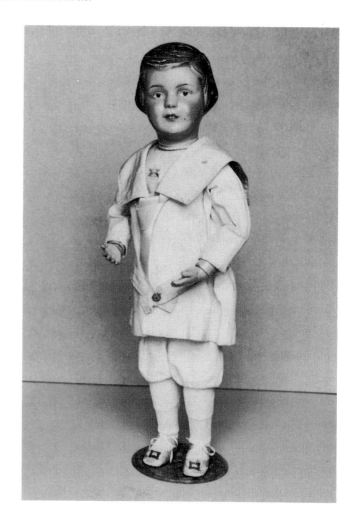

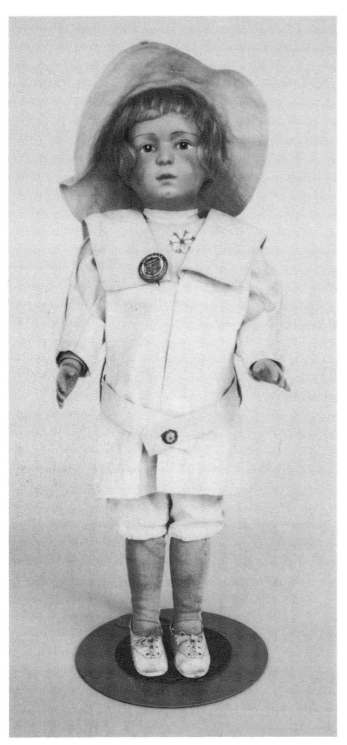

Illustration 453. Doll 16/403/812 Blue-Blonde. This variation has blue stockings and his oxfords were probably blue as well. Schoenhut shoes often fade to white, and the original pastel colors only show in the turned leather inside the heel seam. He also has pink stitches added to his star. He has his original white "Outing Hat." *Photograph by Monty Moncrief. Becky Moncrief Collection.*

Illustration 454. This factory outfit 812 Pink came in white linene and was described as a "White Linene Russian Suit," separate shield, belt and tie. It usually came with a wide floppy white linene hat with a silk ribbon. As he is in church, this ringbearer does not wear a hat. The suit was made with blue collar, shield and belt from at least 1911 to 1918. It could be ordered with pink accents from at least 1915 to 1918. He has no union suit and as he appears to have been made for a special occasion or display rather than to play with, he may never have had one. His stockings are replacements. His Schoenhut oxfords complete his outfit. *Becky and Jay Lowe Collection.*

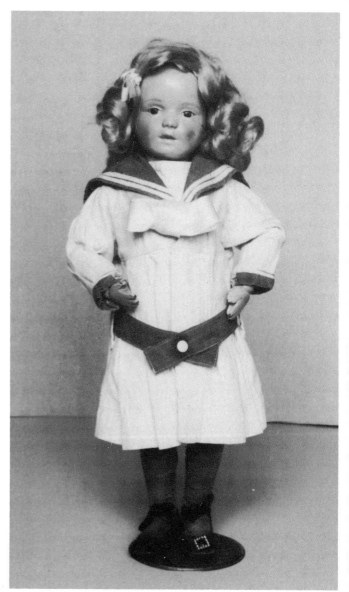

Illustration 456. This doll 14/313 is in her original factory model 530 dress. The doll was only made through 1916. The dress first appears in 1913 advertising with a blue shield and white star and continued to be made through 1918. The shield is old but does not appear to be original. The 1915 to 1918 shield was white and had a red star on it. The dress came with a white tie some years and a red tie after 1916. This doll probably was purchased undressed, and the dress and its underwear was bought separately, as she is wearing a union suit under her factory drawers and slip (one of the slips found with mother-of-pearl rather than bone buttons). Her blue collar has white stars in the back corners. Her blue stockings are replacements, but her black shoes are original.

Illustration 455. Doll 19/405/813 has a very dark blue striped Galetea Russian Suit. His belt is a replacement made from the hem of his jacket. The company made belts with vertical stripes in 1911 and 1912. His star is navy blue, his tie a black silk ribbon replacement. His black stockings and black slippers are Schoenhut original, as is his button. This suit also was shown with a white tie and sometimes came with white stockings and oxfords. Model 813 came out in the original 1911 catalogue and was made from 1911 to 1918. In this color variation it was originally presented for "carved haired" dolls and numbered 606. All boy's suits were renumbered to the 800 series in about 1913.

OPPOSITE PAGE:
Illustration 457. This dress is model 538 from the 1914 catalogue. Over the basic dress is a panel which starts in the back of the dress as a square yoke and comes forward and drops in a tapered rectangle down the front of the dress to its hem. The lace on the yoke and panel is the same as that on the rest of the dress. This is the flower girl from *The Wedding Party. Becky and Jay Lowe Collection.*

219

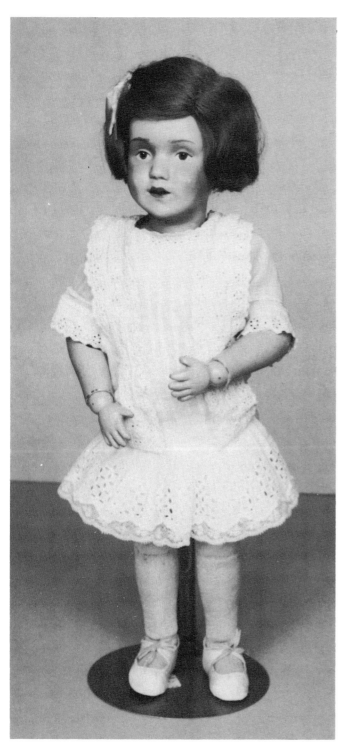

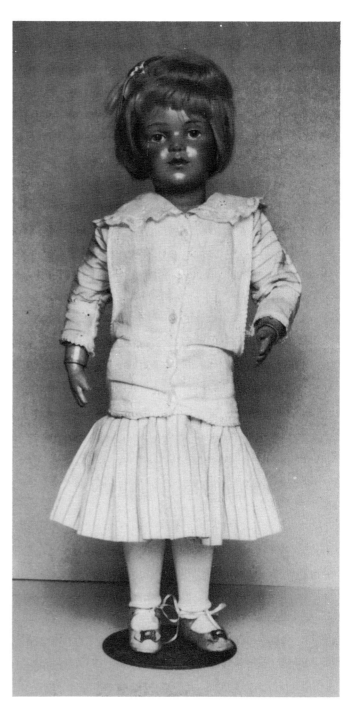

Illustration 458. The factory-original dress on this sweet 14/311 is Model 539 in the 1914 catalogue. In the catalogue a huge wide sash was tied around the low-waist with a fat bow in back. This dress has holders built into the embroidered eyelet shoulder straps that would hold a wide sash. Her factory shoes and stockings were originally pale blue. She is the trainbearer in *The Wedding Party. Becky and Jay Lowe Collection.*

Illustration 459. Doll 19/308X/568 as she appeared in the 1915 to 1916 catalogue and described as "made up in two assorted dresses of pink and fancy striped zephyr gingham with braid and embroidery trimming." This is the pink striped version. It has a "T-shaped" top with the sleeves not set in. The vest is white with embroidered eyelet, as are the collar and cuffs. The vest buttons in front, in this case with five buttons. Smaller dresses would have fewer buttons. It has a V-neck. The vest becomes a wide belt in the back of the dress and fastens around the back of the hips with two buttons. There is white-on-white twist braid at the edges of the vest and the 1½in (4cm) deep cuffs. The shawl collar is trimmed with lace. Dress from the *Gail Hiatt Collection.*

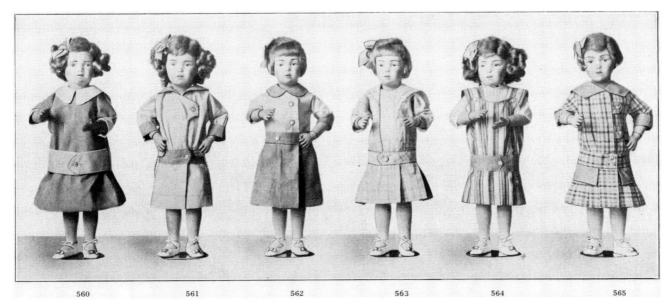

Illustration 460. These dresses are from the 1916 Company catalogue. The colors are usually pink and blue with white.

Illustration 461. These dresses are from the 1916 catalogue. Dress 530 is shown with a real doll in this chapter.

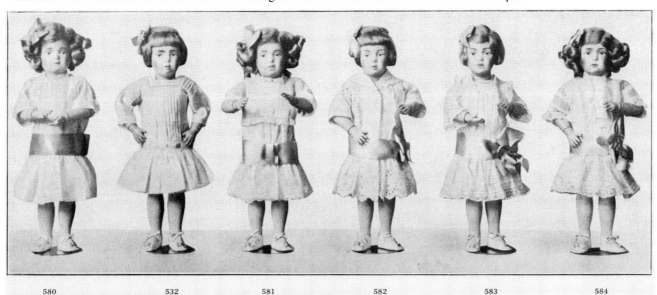

Illustration 462. Fully one-third of all the dresses in the 1915 and 1916 catalogues were white. All of these dresses are white with colored ribbon and lace and eyelet trim.

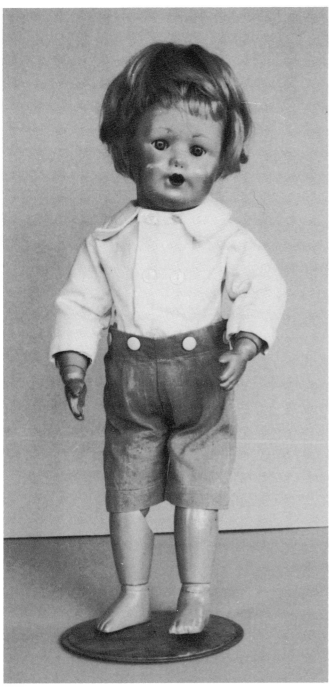

Illustration 463. This is factory outfit 821 described as an "Oliver Twist Suit" in the 1915 and 1916 catalogues. It came with either brown pants, as shown here, or with blue pants. The blue pants suit has a blouse with blue collar and cuffs. This is a 14in (36cm) early boy's suit, but has always been on this 14in (36cm) doll 109W because its young owner wanted a boy doll. The doll dates 1921 to 1923. *Phyllis Schoenhut O'Hare Collection.*

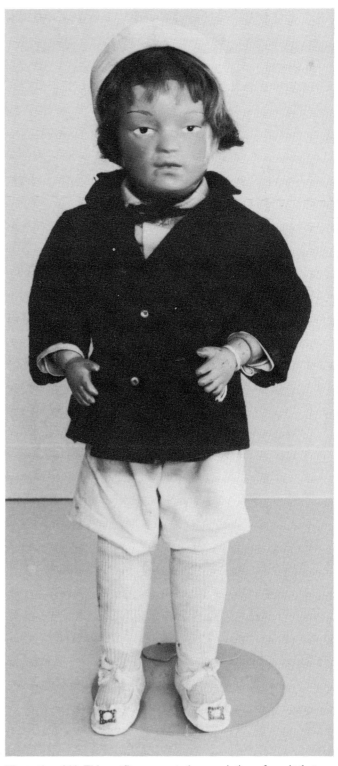

Illustration 464. This outfit appears to be a variation of a suit that was offered every year from 1911 to 1924 (the last year the company sold doll clothes). In 1911 it was numbered 805. By 1914 it had been renumbered 818. It is described as a "Fancy Suit; fine red coat, white pants, percale shirt, silk tie, white linene pants and hat to match." The hat shown in the catalogues with this suit is the floppy "outing hat," but this hat is made of the same linene as the bloomer pants. It also is shown in 1919 company advertising. The felt jacket may be a replacement, but it is old and follows the lines and descriptions of it given in catalogues. *Sara T. Kocher Collection.*

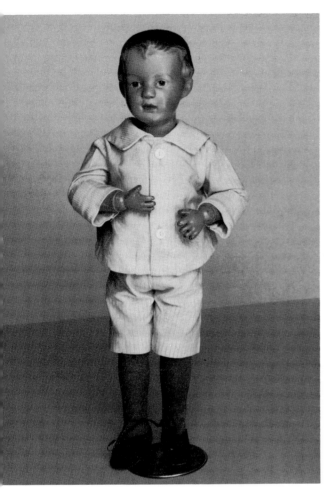

Illustration 465. With some unsureness, the author is placing this suit in the "factory made" section. It appears to be a variation of suit 820 made in the early 1920s. It is white cotton with a fine blue stripe through it. The collar and cuffs are piqué. The blouse has a close-fitting waistband at the bottom. The extra fabric blouses over it and the top of the simple short pants. The trousers are fastened with tiny bone buttons. A factory hallmark was using bone buttons on underwear and all areas of outer clothing that did not show. The shirt has mother-of-pearl buttons. It should have a short, silk ribbon tie. The suit is about five years younger than the doll. Apparently the doll was sent back to the factory to be refurbished, as its body is factory-repainted. The suit may have been bought as a separate item at that time. Boys' suits came without underwear, and this boy has none, but he does have his original brown socks. His shoes are modern replicas.

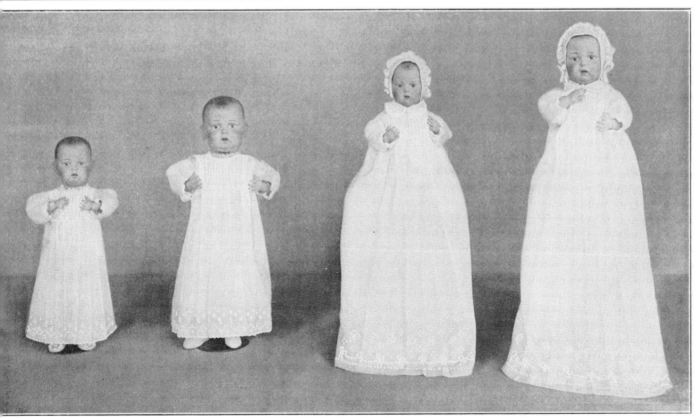

| 14/550 | 17/551 | 13/552 | 15/553 |

Illustration 466. The Schoenhut Infant Dolls designed by Harry E. Schoenhut, and known as "The Copyright Babies," were available undressed (in a simple chemise, no stockings or shoes) or dressed in this style from 1913 to about 1920 when the toddler's dress became a short white child's dress. The clothing could also be purchased separately. Original 1916 catalogue picture.

Illustration 467. This is the late "infants" dress model 551 sold from 1920 to 1924 for the fully-jointed toddler version of the infant. It is made of fine white lawn (as shear as organdy). The neck, three-quarter-length sleeves, high-waist and skirt, just above the hem, are all trimmed with lace. Her underwear is a full, white lawn slip with fitted bodice and separate drawers which fasten with a tape tie drawstring in the back. They have the rear slit which allows more movement. Her shoes are quite unusual. They are original to the doll and are made of oilcloth with nickel buckles like those of the Mamma Doll; however, they have grommeted holes in the bottom which appear to be original Schoenhut work. Phyllis Schoenhut O'Hare was not born until 1923 which was quite late in the company's doll production period. Many of her dolls have indications that they were specially assembled for her by a loving father. These shoes may have been specially adapted from late 1920 shoes just for her. *Phyllis Schoenhut O'Hare Collection.*

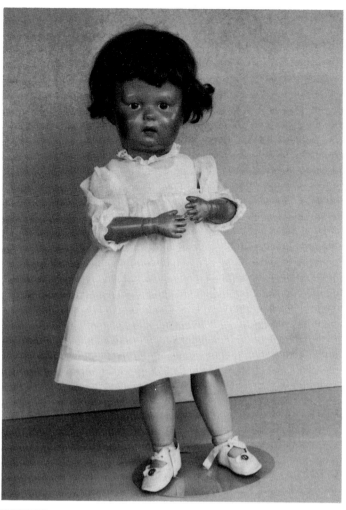

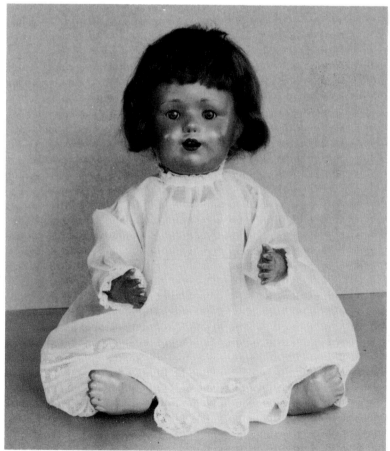

Illustration 468. This dress has not been found in catalogues so far; however, it is shown in company advertisements for the "Walkable Doll," being played with by a very young Doris Schoenhut, daughter of Otto. It has the factory traits of fine white lawn, with a factory slip and drawers. It may be in the 1919 and 1920 catalogues which I have not found. *Phyllis Schoenhut O'Hare Collection.*

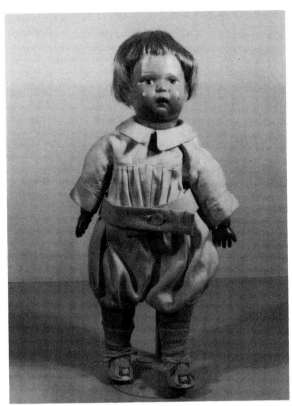

Illustration 469. This smaller sized "Mamma" doll has a yoke on her romper, no pocket but a belt instead. She is shown just this way and numbered 41/107W in the 1924 through 1928 catalogues.*Dot and Bud Hutton Collection.*

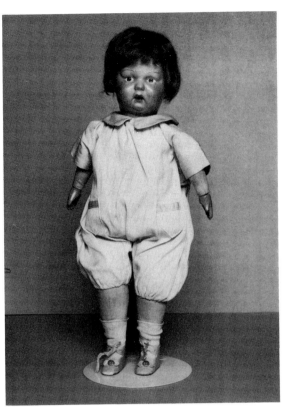

Illustration 470. The "Schoenhut Stuffed Doll with Mamma Voice" was only sold dressed. Examples have been found with blue and white rompers as well as pink and white. The field and trim colors may also be reversed. The larger doll is shown in the catalogue just like this with trimmed pockets and no belt. No number was given for the outfit, as it was part of the doll order and not available separately. The fabric shoes were colored to match the outfit. The entire doll with this outfit was numbered 61/108W in the 1924 through 1928 catalogues.

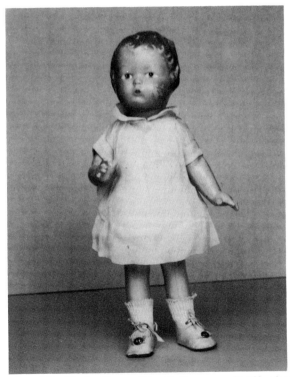

Illustration 471. All the Composition Dolls were sold "Handsomely Dressed." This series was numbered 13/21 through 13/28 with the "13" standing for the size. This is model 13/26. Her white organdy dress has a light mint-green collar and cuffs. Typical of Schoenhut's sense of detail, she has matching green stripes at the top of her socks. Her white shoes have nickel decorations, typical of dolls of this period. She is shown in this outfit in the 1930 catalogue.

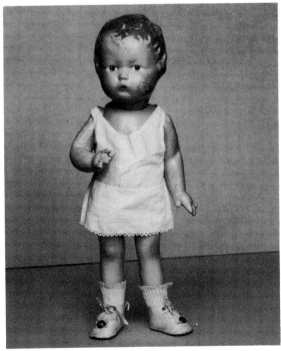

Illustration 472. A combination slip, with panties sewn in, was the factory underwear for the Composition Doll.

225

2. Other Original Clothes

The majority of dolls were sold "undressed," but they had other "original" clothes too. These were made at home by mothers, aunts, nannies, grandmothers and sometimes by professional dressmakers who dressed the doll as well as its young owner. The dolls were also dressed by children who were learning to sew. All these outfits were original to the doll for which they were made. Unfortunately, many homemade "originals" have been lost when the doll was "spruced up" (sometimes with new paint as well as new clothes) for a younger relative. They have also been lost when collectors decided to make the dolls look "more authentic" by redressing them in copies of clothes from the company catalogues. This section shows some of these precious homemade "originals." The dolls can sometimes be dated, within a range, from the clothing they wear. The clothes vary in the needlework skill they show. There is far more variety in colors and fabrics used in these "other than factory original" clothes. Some clothes in this section may actually have been made at the factory, but as they have not been found yet in company literature they are placed here. This does not make them less valuable than "factory" clothing if they are well made.

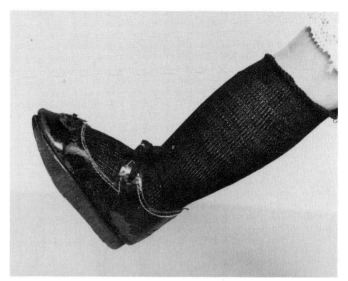

Illustration 473. The left leg of a large "Walkable Doll" is extended to show its shoe. The sole is soft wood, carved at a wedge angle to make the walking movement smooth. The shoe was available in black or white only (according to company catalogues). It was not sold as a separate item as were the rest of the Schoenhut shoes.

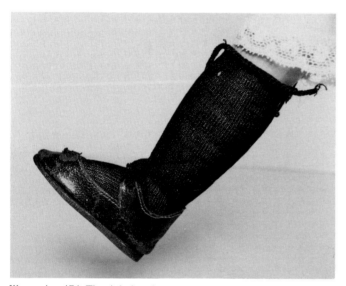

Illustration 474. The right leg shows a much less wedged-inside portion on the "Walkable shoe."

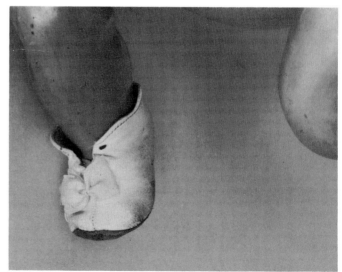

Illustration 475. This baby slipper was offered to fit the two sizes of "Nature Limb" bodies from about 1919 through 1926. There was a second ribbon which tied in a matching fat bow through the top lace holes. The lower bow is set permanently in place. The slipper had a soft tan sole which conformed to the baby's foot.

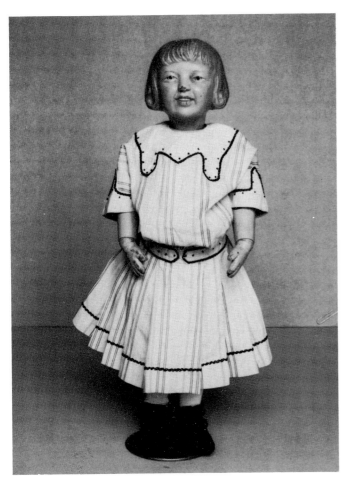

TOP LEFT:
Illustration 476. This nicely made dress is believed to be original to this Graziano Doll 16/101. It is bulky, as are the 1911 company dresses. It has stripes of black, pink and celery green on a white ground. The yoke cuffs and waist are white and are trimmed with black chain stitch and small French knots. The hem is also trimmed with chain stitch. She has original white Schoenhut stockings hung on a nail on the back of her thigh and black two-button boots.

TOP RIGHT:
Illustration 477. This is really an example of contemporary clothing that was probably originally on a Schoenhut, as the fit is so perfect. The dress is white cotton with a fine cross-pattern woven into it and lace at cuffs and neck. The waist is natural. Over the dress is a brown plaid pinafore which fastens in the back with a self belt. She wears white stockings and brown Schoenhut button boots.

LEFT:
Illustration 478. This is the very well-made dress from the McCall's pattern. It was made for doll 312 when she was new. There is no number on the pattern. It is simply called "Doll Special//14 inches long." There are six pieces in the pattern. The rever is made of the chambray trim color and has a button for trim. The plaid is green, red and caramel on white. The blouse part has five buttons in a diagonal row as trim to the left of the rever.

Illustration 479. This is the envelope of McCall pattern "Doll Special." The pattern was found with all six pieces intact.

Illustration 480. This sweet homemade dress appears to be original to the 16/310 and adds greatly to her appeal. The dress is cotton with tiny brick red dots and squares that are turned diagonally. It has pleated bodice which is joined to a pleated skirt at a natural waistline with no trim at the joining. It fastens with flat two-prong silver-colored hooks and white threads. It is completely machine sewn, including the hem. The apron falls from the shoulders and has two bands of commercially-made decorations of a repeated pattern with a girl feeding chickens. There is a decorative hem stitch around the bottom and down the front panel which ends with a flounce at the bottom. It fastens in the back with one hook and eye at the neck. The hook and thread eye are identical to those on the dress. Her union suit has a pink bow. Her Schoenhut stockings are black, as are her Schoenhut two-button boots.

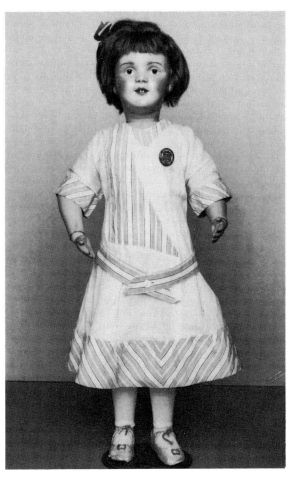

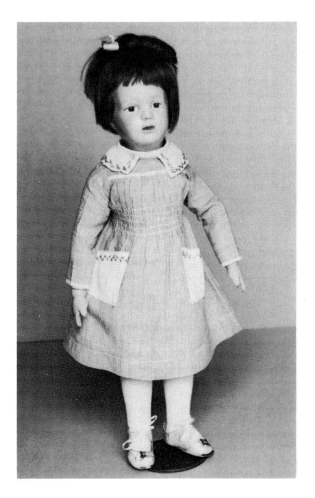

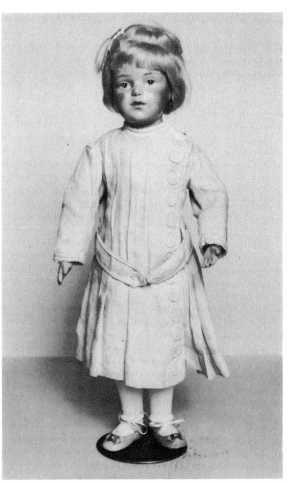

TOP LEFT:

Illustration 481. This is a great dress on a wonderful 21/309 doll. Her union suit slip, shoes and stockings are all factory-made, and her button appears to be original to her, but her dress has not been found in a company picture. The dress is fine white percale, trimmed with material striped in pink and white with fine black stripe accents. The material is cut and placed to form the patterns shown. I have tried placing the belt many different ways to fit the pattern, as a seam runs down the skirt from the lowest point on the quadrilateral front piece, but the hem trim and neck pattern are centrally oriented so this seems best.

TOP RIGHT:

Illustration 482. This light blue chambray is apparently original to this doll. It is entirely machine-stitched in white. There is white piping trimming the collar. The white pockets and collar are hand-trimmed in blue feather stitch. Her shoes are factory-made. The dress has a belt with buttons across the back. The white band on the yoke and sleeve edges is a clever use of the white selvedge edge on this chambray.

LEFT:

Illustration 483. This pink linen Russian dress dates about 1915. It is trimmed around the collar, cuffs, down the opening and belt, edged with plain bands of white soutache braid. Down the opening panel is soutache braid carefully stitched in large loops. Her original shoes are also pink.

RIGHT:
Illustration 484. Here "Miss Presbyterian Hospital" (typed on a small piece of paper and pinned under a purple rosette on the left side of her apron) has removed her navy cape and holds it by its sturdy black hanging loops so that the label shows. It reads, "C. D. Williams Co. 246 S Eleventh St. Philadelphia" in fine gold fancy script on a ½in by 2in (1cm by 5cm) black label. The cape lining is Scarlet. *Gail Hiatt Collection.*

BOTTOM LEFT:
Illustration 485. This pair has always been together and is presented this way as a record in the hopes that it will be kept together. These all-original 14in (36cm) "twins" wear quite charming examples of home made blue, white and brown plaid dresses. The brown-eyed doll has original brown stockings and shoes. Note her flounced skirt is cut on the bias. Her union suit bow is blue. Her blue-eyed sister has blue replaced stockings and somewhat faded blue original shoes. Her flounces are cut with the plaid running vertical and horizontal. Her union suit bow is blue. Neither doll wears a slip. Both dolls have their original stands.

BOTTOM RIGHT:
Illustration 486. Merilee's dress is a creamy white china silk with a fuschia silk overvest, trimmed with mother-of-pearl buttons. The fine ribbon that trims the neck and sleeves is a true bright red. Her stockings are not original Schoenhut, but are made of silk. Melvin has an Oliver Twist-style suit which is very similar, in lines, to two of the Schoenhut Factory models. The shirt is a cream linen-type material. The trousers, collar and cuffs are all a rougher beige linen-like material topstitched in fuschia. His fuschia tie is original and sewn to his shirt. It has faded considerably. The girl's shoe ribbons are old; the boy's are replacements for older shredded ones that he once had.

SCHOENUT COMPANY HISTORY PART II

Through the years that the company produced its dolls it was also turning out hundreds of different toy designs. It employed more than 400 workers during the height of production, in the first two and a half decades of the 20th century. It had separate catalogues for dolls through 1916, usually containing 28 pages full of the many different models offered. Another catalogue for the many designs of boats was kept until the late 1920s. The sail boats had a patented keel design which kept them from capsizing easily. At a time when most toy sailboats were produced in Germany with water base paint which dissolved in water, Albert and his family produced only oil base enameled boats that could sail for years, and did. They also produced mini canoes and lifeboats with tiny cast people to man them. A line of "Motor Boats" powered with rubber bands and spring-wound motors were also designed for water play. For a while Schoenhut even produced a pool to put in backyards for their boats.

Another catalogue was produced specifically for schools which contained many of the regular toy and doll line but also contained products designed just for group play. The most famous of these were the "Hill" Kindergarten Floor Blocks. These wonderful blocks were invented by Patty Smith Hill, Director of the Department of Kindergarten and Primary Grades at Columbia University's Teachers College (and author of the song "Happy Birthday"). They were designed to encourage the children to develop muscle coordination and strength. They allowed children to build two and even three story buildings which were stable enough for them to climb on and play in. Wheels, rods and pins were included in the sets allowing older children to make wagons and cars in which they could ride. Another special feature of their extra-large size was that children needed to work cooperatively in planning and building their projects. As any primary school teacher knows, cooperative work or play is not always instinctive with people and has to be carefully facilitated in a class group with a lot of work on the teacher's part. The largest blocks (up to 36in [92cm] in length by 3in [8cm] wide and 1-¼in [3cm] thick) were made of basswood. The smaller pieces were maple. The blocks came out in 1918 and seem to have been made until about 1930. Because they are so big, they necessarily take up a lot of classroom space. The set also used steel pipes and wire rods to stabilize buildings and make axles. Over the years new teachers came into rooms and worried that children would hurt themselves or each other with the heavy pieces. They opted for the cleaner, newer all-maple unit blocks preferred by many kindergartens today, and most of the old Hill blocks have been lost to us. Having seen building projects done with these and similarly designed blocks over the years, it is obvious why some teachers have guarded their sets as treasures, particularly in the schools that are limited financially and have learned to clean and refurbish old equipment. In the late 1920s a miniature set of the same blocks was available (sold under the name Schoenhut's Building Blocks, but giving Patty Hill credit for the design) for table top construction at home. Each block was exactly one-third the size of its school counterpart.

Of course, the largest catalogue continued to be the one for general toys. It is these catalogues, over the years, that show the fabulous wealth and variety of toys the Schoenhut company produced. The piano, in over 40 different models (not including the differences in paint finish), continued to be produced even beyond the company's life span. The Circus was a toy whose popularity covered 30 years. Added to the large size set was a smaller set specifically designed for younger children. This came out in 1924.

Doll houses entered the line beginning in 1917. Tiny furniture to go with them was not produced until 1928. A toy with a popularity that lasted over ten years consisted of a wooden toy Dreadnought and a submarine which shot tiny wooden torpedoes. The Dreadnought came in pieces with a mousetrap inside the body. The mousetrap was set, the Dreadnought's pieces lightly stacked together and the submarine was set a few feet away and aimed by the child at the red target on the Dreadnought. The child fired the torpedo. If it hit the target, the Dreadnought "blew up" in a most satisfying way. The Super Dreadnought set had two deck levels to explode, two targets and two submarines. There was also a version which had a sleekly designed German U-Boat and a U.S. submarine chaser which was popular during World War I and into the late 1920s.

Many factors affected the financial decline of the company, and it was not obvious at first what was happening. The five surviving Schoenhut brothers continued to produce fine quality wooden toys in the 1920s, convinced that there would always be a solid market for them. The world, however, was changing rapidly around their four-square-block empire. Electric and action toys were becoming popular. Airplanes, blimps and powered metal trains were becoming more popular. The company built dirigibles, planes and trains, but they were in kit form for the child to put together, and they did not "do" anything.

Labor had always been cheap, and the family counted on loyalty in its workers, as in the beginning they had been ahead of their time in the way they had established a more consistent level of work for their workers and a feeling that they genuinely cared for them. After World War I, however, men returned from Europe with a vision of a world that existed beyond Kensington. They wanted more money as well as paternal good will at the work place, and the company had difficulty adjusting to the growing labor movement.

Younger American toy companies were constantly updating their machinery and equipment. Other puzzle and doll house making companies were stamping out their products in one clean movement when Schoenhut was cutting out its puzzles and doll house windows individually on a jig saw, thus using far more labor time. In the early 1920s import restrictions were lifted from German goods and much cheaper German toys and dolls flooded the market.

The first recession hit in 1923 and the company, which had always produced "top of the line" toys felt it, as people had less to spend on non-necessities. The company tried to adjust by bringing out the small sized Circus, the Basswood Elastic Doll, and dropping the character dolls which took more time to produce as they required a variety of decorating details. These were all attempts to produce less expensive toys for the public.

Schoenhut also began to try to meet the changing public taste in toys. Cannons and toy guns, with the exception of target gun sets, were discontinued in the middle 1920s. Swords continued into the late 1920s. Many new toy designs were being produced each year. Doll-sized cribs, beds and kitchen cabinets were produced in the late 1920s, after the "heyday" of the dolls themselves. Doll house furniture was finally added to the doll house line which was doing well. The "Modlwood" kits were expanded to add planes and dirigibles to a line that already included various different trains, automobiles and trucks. The popular Rolly-Dolly toys were simplified in more modern and easily molded designs and included special designs for Easter to encourage year around sales. The "Alphies," a series of shaped alphabet blocks with delightful "googly" eyed children on one side and funny animals on the other was patented in 1916, but not brought out until 1920. Sets even included small balls with them so that children could bowl over their toys, after learning the clever alphabet poems that came with them. The Vocophones continued to be popular and a "Black Cat Jazz Band" version was added. The Schoenhut's Indoor Golf set came out in 1923 ("for adults and children over 14 years of age"), and a Kiddie-Golf set followed in 1924. Although popular with collectors and imitated years later in the "Arnold Palmer Golf Game," it was out of the line by 1927.

Musical instruments were also redesigned. Banjo Ukuleles, Hawaiian Ukuleles and "Mando-Ukes" were added. Pianos with music boxes inside of them were added to the regular pianos. The Trinity Chimes which had come out in 1900 was redesigned to sell at a cheaper price and Jazz Orchestra Bells, which appears to have been an adaptation of the old metallophone to meet the new taste for Jazz, came in three sizes ranging from eight to 22 notes. The pianos, xylophones and metallophones continued to be produced with some changes in decoration to make them look more modern.

During the mid and late 1920s Schoenhut also produced a line of jointed figures based on popular comic characters for George Borgfeldt & Co. Borgfeldt had been a partner in Strassburger, Pfeiffer, and Co. when Albert sold his first pianos to them in the 1870s. After Borgfeldt and Pfeiffer left to form the new company in 1880, the Schoenhuts maintained strong business ties with him. The comic characters carry no mark identifying them as Schoenhut and never appeared in the Schoenhut catalogues, but collectors who have been lucky enough to find them in their original boxes note that the labels have "Manufactured by the A. Schoenhut Co." in tiny print. (Even the wholesale lot boxes with a dozen 4in [10cm] models of *Felix the Cat* in them have this note on the label.) The characters were: Rube Goldberg's *Boob McNutt*, Pat Sullivan's *Felix The Movie Cat*, International Features Service Inc.'s *Happy Hooligan* as well as *Jiggs* and *Maggie*, Max Fleischer's *Ko-Ko* the *Inkwell Clown*, and King Features Syndicate's *Spark Plug and Barney Google*.

Then the Great Depression hit the American economy. Toys were the first thing to go. Many companies went under almost immediately. The A. Schoenhut Company did not die easily. There was tremendous family pride at stake. This was a family that had made it to the very top of their field through lots of hard work. The children and grandchildren had begun earning pennies for piece work after school at a young age, and naturally the boys became full-time workers at the company right after graduating from high school. If they needed additional education to make their work or the company more successful, they got that too, but education after high school was to answer a specific need. If dedication and hard work could have saved the company, it would have survived, but the willingness to work hard and the horror of not paying one's debts by going into bankruptcy could not change the fact that the vast majority of Americans simply could not afford to buy toys, particularly good toys.

Harry was the first brother to see how impossible it was. He left the company and went into the hosiery manufacturing business in 1930. While he had been the last son to leave the family home, continuing to live there with his unmarried sister Caroline after their mother died in 1915, he actually moved his family including his new wife and his sister just north of the city limits in about 1920. The other brothers followed the movement north that many of the wealthier manufacturers in Philadelphia made in the early 1920s. None of them, however, moved beyond the city limits. By 1922, Otto moved to 5129 North 15th Street, and William moved his family to the northeast corner of 7th and Chelten Avenue. Gustav followed William and settled at the corner of 6th and Chelten Avenue in 1924. Only Albert F. remained at 2355 Cumberland Street within two blocks walk to work. His son, Frederick Carl, was a clerk at the company.

The company responded to the deepening Depression by producing new designs to appeal to what little money was available and by borrowing from banks to "tide them over." A "Blox De-Luxe" set based on the Alphies came out. Other block sets were added and some were painted in bright primary colors to make them more appealing. They were also packaged in a variety of colorful wagons and pull toys. Nobby-Nobs were similar in design to Tinker Toys. A number of marble mazes, shooting and pin games were tried. A tiny bowling alley could be purchased both with and without return gutter. The Ski-Jumper Toy and the Run-Pig-Run Game also date to the early 1930s, as do clockwork driven Rodeo toys. The company had made clockwork toys originally in the last two decades of the 19th century. Probably the funniest name to the modern ear was "Shoot-The-Bull," a variation on the old target toys. The popularity of comedian Ed Wynn was capitalized on with a variety of Ed Wynn Fire Department Toys. Wardrobes, dressers and beds were added to the doll furniture line.

The milk and bread delivery wagons date from 1930 to 1933. They are small versions, 24in (61cm) long including the horse, of the wagons which brought bread or milk in glass bottles to homes early each morning. Some of the platform horses have "Made in Germany" stamped on them indicating that even Schoenhut had to use cheaper German products in their toy line. In the catalogues, the company displayed a generic "Fine Bread" wagon and two different designs for the Alderney Dairy wagon. They also sold drivers, bread crates with 12 tiny wooden loaves of bread in them and two sizes of milk crates with either six or 12 wooden bottles of milk (with cream at the top) in them separately. As they had throughout the company's history, they produced many special orders and examples have been found of Hoods Dairy, (Massachusetts); Western Maryland; Supplee, Wills, Jones Fairmount Farms, Bordon, and Abbotts (all Southeastern Pennsylvania); a dairy in St. Louis, Missouri; as well as Alderney, New Jersey. Most of these were probably ordered by the dairies themselves for advertising purposes. Bond Bread and Freihofers had their own wagons as well.

None of this worked. The toy market had even cheaper Japanese toys now available to it. The toy catalogue which was 85 pages in the late 1920s and 72 pages in 1933 contained 29 pages in 1934. The piano line was reduced to 13 models with a range of six to 37 keys. Three Metallophones and two xylophone models,

Illustration 487. A sailboat from 1930, two delivery wagons with horses and drivers (1930 to 1933) and an Ed Wynn fire house toy (1933) are among the transportation toys. Backgrounds for these unit displays were designed by Shirley Butson. *Photograph by Dorothy McGonagle.*

Illustration 488. A range of musical instruments from the years 1872 to 1934. *Photograph by Dorothy McGonagle.*

a banjo style and two Hawaiian style Ukuleles and two new "Junior Guitar" models were sold. Nine Rolly-Dolly designs, the Noah's Arks which had come out in the 1930s and the hooked rug kit were offered. Blocks included a new set of nested cardboard blocks with the same bright lithographed on each side as had been used on the Blox De-Luxe in 1933, the Little Tot's Building Blocks and four sets of the primary colored blocks in small wagons. There are only two sets of "Modlwood" type kits left and the cars and trains have a sleeker "thirties" look to their design. Four miniature boat sets with flat bottomed boats to be used on land or water replaced the once extensive flotilla of sail boats. The "Robuster," a coil spring driven variation on a rocking horse, was still in the line with a smaller version called "Pony Boy" for children under four. Small furniture included cribs, dressers, four-poster beds, a tea cart, and a wheel barrow. Doll house furniture was made in two sizes and doll houses came simply in knocked-down versions to assemble at home, or assembled by the company. The famed Humpty Dumpty Circus was sold in the small size only. The elephant and the donkey were offered separately in the large size with a note that other large size personnel, animals and accessories were available "on request."

In 1935 the company went into bankruptcy and the remaining brothers went their separate ways. Albert Frederick and his son Frederick Carl joined with Robert MacMillan to form the Schoenhut Manufacturing Company. They secured the rights to produce the Schoenhut piano from the creditors and moved into a shop at 2046 East Castor Avenue. MacMillan was a model

railroad buff, and the new company produced pieces for model railroads. It is not clear what these pieces were and whether they were scenery accessories or mechanical pieces.

Gustav moved into a smaller house and "fixed" things for other people. William remained to see the company through its final year and liquidation before he became a salesman for another company.

Otto joined with a friend, Stanley Osborn, who while working for Philco Manufacturing Company had invented a toy using scrap pieces from the manufacture of Philco products to copy pictures into perforated designs. He called it "Perf-O-Art." He, unlike Otto, had money to put into its manufacture. Together they formed O. Schoenhut Incorporated and invited Theodore's son, George Weber Schoenhut, who was then working at a theater in New Hampshire to join them and "help design new ideas,... in the manufacture and sales or wherever you would best fit in," as stated in a letter to George from Otto in summer of 1935. Otto planned to get lots of sound financial advice "to keep me straight on financial matters." To this end he convinced Stocton Mortimer who was an executive at Philco, first to give him advice, and then to invest in the company. They started out producing "Perf-O-Art and the Pinn Family Dolls designed by Emily T. Myers in September 1935 at the unheated, empty A. Schoenhut Company plant which had not yet been sold. They hired some of the woman who had worked for the original company, and Emily Myers came from St. Paul to teach them how to paint the faces and arrange the wool yarn hair. In the first few months they were forced to move

Illustration 489. Companion studio shot of a young boy with his Schoenhut clown, donkey and elephant, which were both the first and last produced personnel and animals in the famed Schoenhut Circus. *Courtesy Becky Moncrief.*

twice, first to seek heat and then because they could afford better space.

On February 26 to 28, 1936 the properties, few remaining toys, parts and all the machinery and equipment of the A. Schoenhut Company were sold at a three-day auction. The *Philadelphia Record* detailed the sale on the first page of the second section in an article headlined "Dream Factory Goes on The Block," accompanied by three photographs and an interview with William G. Schoenhut who had remained to oversee the long death of the company, which had continued to send out toys from stock through the Christmas season.

At about the same time a toy buyer for Gimbels showed Otto a simple version of an old spillikins or jack straws game that was popular in Europe at the time. The new set had thin wooden dowels with pointed ends that were painted in bright colors. They put the game out under the name "4-5-6 Pick Up Sticks" in a cleverly designed container with the directions illustrated by a well-known artist, Katherine Milhouse. The toy became very popular with both adults and children and remained so for almost 20 years. It was simple to make and therefore inexpensive and ensured the success of the new company.

When the Schoenhut Manufacturing Company went out of business in about 1940, O. Schoenhut Incorporated took over the Castor Avenue address and the rights to manufacture the Schoenhut piano. They also acquired the bookkeeper and the piano tuner from the original A. Schoenhut Company. The company continued to produce pianos and a few other products under the Schoenhut name until the mid 1980s.

In 1964 the huge building complex that had stretched from Sepviva to Trenton Avenues and York Street to East Adams (which had been renamed East Hagert in about 1912 but was erroneously reported to be changed *from* E. Hagert *to* E. Adams in the city directories for so long that the Schoenhut Company did not recognize the East Hagert address until 1924 when the correction was made in that directory) was demolished to make way for Hackett School, a Philadelphia Public Elementary School. Now children work and play every day on the spot where "Santa Claus" reigned. It somehow seems appropriate. Now 2215-2217 East Hagert (Adams), which extended back to Letterly Street, stands in abandoned and dilapidated state but is still recognizable with its two large bay windows at the second level and the huge entrance that allowed carts and later trucks to pick up the millions of toys that the company produced.

THE JOY OF SCHOENHUTS

Schoenhuts make a delightful addition to a doll collection. They are an example of the best of American dolls and the ingenuity that went into their design. People love the ones in perfect shape because they hold their own against the bisques and compositions of their periods. Schoenhuts, however, were made to be **played with**. If you have a beat up one, do not feel bad about it. Play with it! Schoenhuts can do hand springs. They stand on their heads for six weeks at a time. One can be interested for hours by searching for all of their points of balance. They are a toy as well as a doll and informal research in my classroom shows that boys as well as girls enjoy making them do tricks. Like the Schoenhut Circus they provide the stimulus for extended atten-tion, patience, imagination and perseverance for the person "play-ing" with them. This is the joy of Schoenhuts. A few have loose joints, but most have been played with for 70 years and are just as tight and well balanced as when they were new.

As collectors, we are only temporary custodians of these objects from the past and as such are responsible for their preser-vation. If, however, we simply line them up in glass cases, whether in our homes or in museums, or keep them "safe" wrapped up in drawers, we are denying the uniqueness of the Schoenhut Doll and thereby not "preserving" it at all. This last section of pictures is dedicated to the joy of Schoenhuts and the joy of play.

Illustration 490. This doll held his position for six weeks in the Delaware Art Museum. Schoenhuts are well-balanced and steady in play.

Illustration 491. *Schnickel-Fritz* is about to fire this small-sized Schoenhut Cannon (which is cocked and ready to go) while his 14/207 friend is sure the noise will be overpowering. The cannons were available as early as the 1890s and continued at least through 1914. At one time they were made in four sizes, the three larger could be purchased with a caisson. The doll stands allow full play value for the dolls. Fortunately, they are available in replica, as most of the originals have been separated from their dolls.

Illustration 492. This little girl (11/107W) is waiting for someone to give her a ride in her Schoenhut Bunny Riding a Carrot Cart. The rabbit's legs are attached to a simple movement under the cart, and when it is pulled, his legs appear to scoot the carrot along the floor. The cart has the same round sticker on the bottom as the composition child and probably dates from 1931 or 1932.

Illustration 493. *Fritz* and the Schoenhut bull-dog.

236

ORIGINAL PRICES

A note on prices seems necessary. Because people have studied Schoenhut Catalogues in the past and have known that these were wholesale catalogues for use within the trade the assumption has naturally been made that the prices listed in them were wholesale prices. This has lead to a series of misconceptions about the expensiveness of the Schoenhut Doll. The confusion has only been compounded by the discovery of a few retail store catalogues which carried the Schoenhut line of dolls and toys. The prices in these catalogues are similar to those of the so called "wholesale" prices. Sometimes the prices are even lower in the store catalogues!

The discovery of Schoenhut retail catalogues sent to people who otherwise had no access to stores selling the products of this prolific company along with a letter from the company enclosed in a 1927 catalogue has done something to ease this confusion.

The letter, which is dated February 5, 1927, was sent to the Lynn Sporting Goods Company in Lynn, Massachusetts. It offers the new catalogue and quotes "our best trade discounts, term etc." on an enclosed sheet. The discounts offered in 1927 were in three "classes." Class One offered a discount of 40% on any order amounting to less than $300.00 retail. Class Two gave a discount of 45% for any order amounting from $300.00 to $699.00 retail. Class Three offered a 50% discount on any order that totaled $700.00 or more. When any order, no matter how small, entitles one to a 40% discount, stores could afford to carry the line for their more affluent customers.

The other piece of ephemera that was particularly helpful in understanding original prices was the retail folder (which was really a complete doll catalogue) which dates before April of 1912. The price breakdown on each doll is exactly one-twelfth of the 1911 *Doll Catalogue*, in which the dolls were listed by the dozen as is typical of wholesale catalogues.

Thus the original "carved hair" children (undressed) were priced at $3.00 each retail. This was the price unless the store wanted to take a smaller profit on the doll. If a store wished to use the doll as a "loss leader" or simply as a customer grabber, they might sell the doll for considerably less.

The other main pressure on prices was what was going on in the economy of the time. The 1911 catalogue states:

> "In the manufacture of Dolls, our first aim was to make **a perfect indestructible doll**, regardless of price. ...Our next aim was to make a **popular price**, which we have done by adopting...only one size...but will produce this size in numerous ways. These will sell at different prices, according to the style and quality of dress, packing etc. We are not competing in **price** with other dolls in the market, but we are the strongest competitors for **Quality** that ever entered the field, therefore our Doll will be the **cheapest Doll** in the market of its class, and in class it stands **alone**."

This justification of price did not last long. The dolls went through several changes in their manufacture, including the heated molds used to finish the lathe carving and add detail to the features,

which allowed the prices to be dropped considerably after the initial season. The 14in (36cm) "carved hair" doll retailed for $2.00, and the 16in (41cm) doll for $2.35, or less, from 1912 to 1915. Over the years less hand work was needed and the clothes were also simplified. The quality of the painting remained consistently high, however.

Even with the dramatic rise in toy prices which occurred during the years 1914 through 1918 the dolls did not reach their original prices again until 1916, and in some models until 1917. Their prices rose sharply in the years 1917 and 1918 and then stayed stable through 1921. Prices rose again in 1922, stayed the same for 1923 and then dropped by nearly 20% on all models in 1924. These prices remained the same for as long as each model was made and were affected by several general economic factors. The price increases during World War I were general through the economy and not just confined to the toy industry which was experiencing a temporary lack of competition from the huge German share of the market. There was a post-war depression which affected prices as the previous inflation had done. The influx of German produced toys into the market in the 1920s had to have influenced prices as well. German imports still manufactured as a "cottage industry," which allowed them to be sold quite cheaply.

The last factor which eventually lead to the demise of the company (despite the blame laid on Japanese imports at the time of the bankruptcy auction) was the fact that the company never really changed its process of manufacture to make its products cheaper. William F. Schoenhut recalled that the company was still cutting out its wooden jigsaw puzzles and doll house windows on jigsaws when other companies were stamping them out with a die by a single movement of a heavy machine. By the time the company realized how far ahead of it other companies had grown in modernizing their plants, it was too late for Schoenhut to do the same, and a source of high quality toys was lost to the American market.

The last consideration of prices must be what these prices meant in the world of their time. Doll collectors are fond of speculating how many dolls they could own at the original prices, but the hard facts are that it seems unlikely that as a teacher I could have afforded a Schoenhut doll when they were manufactured. Teachers' salaries did not allow for an upper middle class doll for their children. Schoenhut dolls were most likely purchased for the children of doctors, company owners and managers, some lawyers, and people who had inherited wealth. They were more expensive than many German bisque dolls (but not all) and less expensive than the Jumeaus sold by John Wanamaker's Philadelphia store. They were popular with educated upper middle class Philadelphians and still show up occasionally in estate sales there. They were purchased by the same people who bought the dolls produced by Martha Jenks Chase in Pawtucket, Rhode Island, and the cloth dolls of Käthe Kruse. At that time people did not buy their children a large number of toys, but valued the educational and play value of certain quality toys.

BIBLIOGRAPHY

COMPANY CATALOGUES

Illustrated Catalogue and Price List for The A. Schoenhut Company for the years 1889, 1898, 1906, 1907 (Boats), 1910, 1911, 1914.

Illustrated Catalogue...Dolls The Schoenhut Company. (Marked in pen "1911." First doll catalog.)

Illustrated Price List "Schoenhut Dolls." (An oversized folio with additional inside sheet. Six pages from late 1911 or before April 1912. Dolls [retail].)

"Schoenhut Doll." (A 21-page digest booklet of the Schoenhut doll line which dates about 1913 or 1914.)

All Wood Perfection Art Doll, The Schoenhut Doll Catalogue, 1915. (26 pages including covers. Reprint.)

All Wood Perfection Art Doll, The Schoenhut Doll Catalogue 1916. (26 pages including covers.)

"Schoenhut Doll." (A 16-page digest booklet of the Schoenhut doll line which dates about 1919, as it includes the "Walkable" but not the sleep eye dolls.)

Schoenhut Toy and Doll Catalogue. 1917 and 1923. (Courtesy Zip's Toys to Go.)

Schoenhut Toy and Doll Catalogue. 1918 and 1926. (Courtesy Harry R. McKeon.)

1920 Catalogue fragment. (Courtesy Hutton Collection.)

Schoenhut Toy and Doll Catalogue. 1921, 1922, 1924 (Copy of doll sections), and research through 1928 and 1931 catalogues. (Courtesy Margaret Woodbury Strong Museum Library.)

Schoenhut Toy and Doll Catalogue. 1925, 1930. (Courtesy Bud and Dot Hutton Collection.)

Schoenhut Toy and Doll Catalogue. 1927.

Schoenhut's Celebrated Toys Catalog. 1933.

Schoenhut Toys. 1934.

All Wood Perfection Art Doll, The Schoenhut Doll Catalogue 1914, (28 pp).

OTHER COMPANY PUBLICATIONS

Pages from circus booklet, circa 1912, showing Graziano "infants" and Leslie (second style) child dolls. (Courtesy Blossom Abell.)

Illustrations of Schoenhut's Marvelous Toys The Humpty Dumpty Circus. (From 1913 copy with cover date of 1904 which introduces the copyright baby and states "Not made with Mohair Wigs.")

Forty Years Of Toy Making. (Reprint of original which was dated 1912.)

The Story of the Schoenhut All-Wood Perfection Art Doll. Circa 1918. (Courtesy Zip's Toys to Go.)

The Story of the Schoenhut All-Wood Perfection Art Doll. Revised edition, circa 1922.

COMPANY ADS FOUND IN:

Playthings. Numerous full-page ads ranging in date from 1903 through 1930. (Courtesy Geyer McCallister.)

Ladies' Home Journal, Women's Home Companion, Numerous ads, 1903-1930.

OTHER CONTEMPORARY SOURCES

Articles and political cartoons in *The North American*, Spring 1911 through Spring 1912.

Articles in *The Philadelphia Record*, Sunday, November 26, 1911, "Toymakers Busy For Santa Claus" with two pictures of the Schoenhut Company at work and February 26, 1936, "Dream Toy Factory Goes On Block."

OTHER PRIMARY SOURCE MATERIAL

Schoenhut Family dates and names provided by William F. Schoenhut from family records.

City Directories for Philadelphia. 1869-1935 on microfilm at The Free Library of Philadelphia, Logan Circle, for locations of the company and the family member's homes during these years.

Photographs from the Collection of the Historical Society of Pennsylvania.

Oral history and family photographs from William F. Schoenhut, Harry E. Schoenhut Jr., Phyllis Schoenhut O'Hare, and Eleanor P. Swanson

Schoenhut, George, "George Schoenhut Remembers" from *Schoenhut Newsletter*, February 1981, Volume VII, Issue I, for information on the end of the A. Schoenhut Co. and the formations of the Schoenhut Manufacturing Co. and O. Schoenhut Incorporated.

SECONDARY SOURCES

Ackerman, Evelyn and Keller, Fredrick. *Schoenhut's Humpty Dumpty Circus From A to Z.* ERA Industries Inc., 1975.

Buser, M. Elaine and Dan. *M. Elaine and Dan Buser's Guide to Schoenhut's Dolls, Toys and Circus.* Collector Books, 1976.

Coleman, Dorothy S., Elizabeth A. and Evelyn J. *The Collector's Encyclopedia of Dolls*, Crown Publishers, Inc. 1968, *The Collector's Book of Dolls' Clothes, Costumes in Miniature: 1700 - 1929.* Crown Publishers, Inc., 1975, *The Collector's Encyclopedia of Dolls, Volume Two*, Crown Publisher's Inc., 1986.

Manos, Susan. *Schoenhut Dolls and Toys: a Loving Legacy.* Collectors Books, 1976.

Poe, Marion Ball. "Schoenhut Treasures," an article which first appeared in the 1974 *Silver Anniversary Convention* souvenir book of the United Federation of Doll Clubs, Inc.

St. George, Eleanor. *Old Dolls.* Gramercy Publishing Co., New York, 1950. *The Dolls of Yesterday.* Bonanza Books, New York, 1948.

Wolf, Edwin, 2nd, *Philadelphia: Portrait of an American City.* Camino Books in cooperation with The Library Company of Philadelphia, 1990.

APPENDIX — Table of Contents

Comparative features aid the Schoenhut collector with identifying, dating, and authenticating their Schoenhut piece. These parts of the appendix will be of immense value to the reader.

A. Chart of the
Years of Manufacture of Schoenhut Doll Models

Doll	Designer	Description	Size	Years of Manufacture
THE GRAZIANO "YEAR"				
16/100	G	c.h. girl, sober	16in (41cm)	May 1911 - April 1912
16/101	G	c.h. grinning girl, outlined iris, squinting eyes	16in (41cm)	May - November 1911
16/102	G	c.h. girl, bun on top, outlined iris	16in (41cm) +	May - November 1911
16/103	G	c.h. girl, loose ringlets, outlined iris	16in (41cm)	May - November 1911
16/200	G	c.h. boy with short curls	16in (41cm)	May 1911 - April 1912
16/201	G	c.h. boy based on K*R 114, outlined iris	16in (41cm)	May 1911 - April 1912*
16/202	G	c.h. boy/forelock, outlined iris, first 6 mos.	16in (41cm)	May 1911 - April 1912
16/203	G	c.h. boy/grinning, smooth hair 3 mo., comb marks 3 mo., out-lined iris/squinting	16in (41cm)	May - November 1911
16/300	G	long curl wig, face of 102, outlined iris	16in (41cm)	May - November 1911
16/301	G	bobbed wig w/bangs, face of 300, outlined iris	16in (41cm)	May - November 1911
16/302	G	based on K*R 101, outlined iris	16in (41cm)	May 1911 - April 1912
16/303	G	short bob/no bangs, grinning girl, outlined iris, squinting eyes	16in (41cm)	May - November 1911
16/304	G	wig in braids, stick-out ears, outlined iris	16in (41cm)	May - November 1911

* = reissued briefly in 1930 as a blonde

G = Graziano   L = Leslie   L/G = Leslie based on Graziano
H.E.S. = Harry E. Schoenhut   c.h. = carved hair   N.L. = Nature Limb body

Doll	Designer	Description	Size	Years of Manufacture
16/305	G	"snail" braids, grinning girl, face of 303, outlined iris, squinting eyes	16in (41cm)	May - November 1911
16/306	G	long curls, face of 304, outlined iris	16in (41cm)	May - November 1911
16/307	G	short bob/no bangs, "Dolly" type, smooth eyeball	16in (41cm)	May 1911 - April 1912
16/400	G	short bob, K*R 101 face, outlined iris	16in (41cm)	May 1911 - April 1912
16/401	G	side part bob, face 300/301, outlined iris	16in (41cm)	May - November 1911
16/402	G	side part bob, grin (as 303), outlined iris, squinting eyes	16in (41cm)	May - November 1911
16/403	G	long curl boy, face of 304/306, outlined iris	16in (41cm)	May - November 1911

THE "TRANSITION" PERIOD

Doll	Designer	Description	Size	Years of Manufacture
16/100	G	same as before, no iris outline, stocking groove	16in (41cm)	May 1911 - April 1912
16/101	L	short c.h. bob/bow, round eyes/ smile, outlined iris	16in (41cm) +	November 1911 - April 1912
16/102	L	braids carved around head	16in (41cm)	November 1911 - 1923*
16/103	L	heavy c.h. in front/fine braids in back	16in (41cm)	November 1911 - April 1912
16/104	L	fine c.h. in front/fine braids in back	16in (41cm)	November 1911 - April 1912
16/200	G	same as before, no iris outline, stocking groove	16in (41cm)	May 1911 - April 1912
16/201	G	same as before, outlined iris, stocking groove	16in (41cm)	May 1911 - April 1912

* = reissued in 1930 as a blonde

G = Graziano   L = Leslie   L/G = Leslie based on Graziano
H.E.S. = Harry E. Schoenhut   c.h. = carved hair   N.L. = Nature Limb body

Doll	Designer	Description	Size	Years of Manufacture
16/202	G	same face, but smoother, no iris outline	16in (41cm)	May 1911 - April 1912
16/203	L/G	smiling boy, round eyes, no iris outline	16in (41cm)	November 1911 - 1916
16/204	L	serious boy, c.h. brushed forward	16in (41cm)	November 1911 - 1916
16/300	L	round face, chin dimple, long curl wig	16in (41cm)	November 1911 - 1923
16/301	L	face of 102, bob/wig girl	16in (41cm)	November 1911 - 1924
16/302	G	same as before on K*R 101, stocking groove	16in (41cm)	May 1911 - April 1912
16/303	L/G	based on 303 G, smiling girl, round eyes, short bob/no bangs	16in (41cm)	November 1911 - 1916
16/304	G	based on K*R 114 earlier sold — dressed only, no iris outline on "Transition" doll, braids	16in (41cm)	November 1911 - Summer 1912
16/305	L/G	face of 303, braided wig, round eyes/smile	16in (41cm)	November 1911 - 1916
16/306	G	same as 16/304, long curl wig, see 304 history	16in (41cm)	November 1911 - Summer 1912
16/307	G	based on 16/307 G, "Dolly" type, smooth eyeball	16in (41cm)	November 1911 - 1916
16/400	G	same as before on K*R 101, stocking groove, no iris outline	16in (41cm)	May 1911 - April 1912
16/401	G	based on K*R 114, see information on 304 above	16in (41cm)	November 1911 - Summer 1912
16/402	L/G	smiling boy, round eyes	16in (41cm)	November 1911 - End 1912
16/403	L	same as 300 during "Transition," had side part bob	16in (41cm)	November 1911 - 1924
14/404	L	same as 301, side part bob	16in (41cm)	November 1911 - 1916

* = reissued in 1930 as a blonde

G = Graziano
H.E.S. = Harry E. Schoenhut

L = Leslie
c.h. = carved hair

L/G = Leslie based on Graziano
N.L. = Nature Limb body

Doll	Designer	Description	Size	Years of Manufacture
THE CLASSIC DOLLS				
101	L	same as "Transition," no iris outline	14in (36cm) 16in (41cm)	April 1912 - 1923* November 1911 -1916
102	L	same as "Transition"	14in (36cm) 16in (41cm) 19in (48cm) 21in (53cm)	April 1912 - 1923* November 1911 - 1923* April 1912 - 1916
105	L	short c.h. bob, ribbon around hair	14in (36cm) 16in (41cm) 19in (48cm) 21in (54cm) +	April 1912 - 1923* April 1912 - 1923* April 1912 - 1916
106	L	bonnet on short hair	14in (36cm) 16in (41cm) 19in (48cm)	April 1912 - 1916
203	L	same as "Transition"	16in (41cm)	November 1911 - 1916
204	L	same as "Transition"	16in (41cm)	November 1911 - 1916*
205	L	boy c.h. — covers ears	14in (36cm) 16in (41cm) 19in (48cm) 21in (54cm) +	April 1912 - 1923* April 1912 - 1923 April 1912 - 1916
206	L	2 teeth, c.h. covers ears	19in (48cm)	April 1912 - 1916
207	L	short curly c.h., younger boy	14in (36cm)	April 1912 - 1916*?
300	L	same as "Transition"	16in (41cm)	November 1911 - 1923
301	L	same as "Transition"	16in (41cm)	November 1911 - 1924
303	L	same as "Transition" 305	16in (41cm)	November 1911 -1916
307	L/G	Dolly type, smooth eye, long curls	16in (41cm)	November 1911 - 1916
308	L	serious face, braided wig bobbed hair bob or curls	14in (36cm) 19in (48cm) 19in or 21in (55cm) +	April 1912 - 1916 April 1912 - 1924 1917 - 1924

* = reissued in 1930 as a blonde

G = Graziano   L = Leslie   L/G = Leslie based on Graziano
H.E.S. = Harry E. Schoenhut   c.h. = carved hair   N.L. = Nature Limb body

Doll	Designer	Description	Size	Years of Manufacture
309	L or H.E.S.	2 teeth, long curls, bobbed hair	16in (41cm) 19in (48cm) 21in (53cm)	April 1912 - 1913 April 1912 - 1916
310	L	105 face, long curls	14in (36cm) 16in (41cm) 19in (48cm) 21in (53cm)	April 1912 - 1916
311	L	heart shape face of 106, bob/no bangs	14in (36cm) 16in (41cm) 19in (48cm)	April 1912 - 1916 April 1912 - 1913?
312	L or H.E.S.	younger, bobbed hair bob or curls	14in (36cm)	April 1912 - 1924 1917 - 1924
313	L or H.E.S.	smooth eyeball, long curl wig, receding chin	14in (36cm) 16in (41cm) 19in (48cm) 21in (53cm)	April 1912 - 1916
314	L or H.E.S.	smooth eyeball, long curl wig, wide face	19in (48cm)	April 1912 - 1916
315	L or H.E.S.	triangular mouth, 4 teeth, long curl wig	21in (53cm)	April 1912 - 1916
403	L	same as "Transition," bob with bangs	16in (41cm)	November 1911 - 1924
404	L	same as "Transition"	16in (41cm)	November 1911 - 1916
405	L	face of 308, bobbed wig	14in (36cm) 19in (48cm)	1912 - 1924 1912 - 1924
406?	L?	face of 309 or 312?		1912 - 1913
407	L	face of 310, bobbed wig	19in (48cm) 21in (53cm)	1912 - 1916

* = reissued in 1930 as a blonde

G = Graziano
H.E.S. = Harry E. Schoenhut

L = Leslie
c.h. = carved hair

L/G = Leslie based on Graziano
N.L. = Nature Limb body

Doll	Designer	Description	Size	Years of Manufacture

THE MANIKIN

Doll	Designer	Description	Size	Years of Manufacture
175	H.E.S.	slim body w/ball jointed waist, adult male face	19in (48cm)	1914 - 1918 may be as early as 1912

MISS DOLLY

Doll	Designer	Description	Size	Years of Manufacture
316	H.E.S.	curls — all sizes painted eye — all sizes decal eye — all sizes bobbed hair — all sizes	15in (38cm) 17in (43cm) 19in (49cm) + 21in (54cm) +	1915 - 1924 1915 - 1920 1920 - 1924 1917 - 1924
317	H.E.S.	all sizes — sleep eye, long curls or bob	15in (38cm) 17in (43cm) 19in (49cm) + 21in (54cm) +	1921 - 1928
		above offered elastic strung		1924 - 1928

INFANTS

Doll	Designer	Description	Size	Years of Manufacture
Tootsie Wootsie	G	o/c mouth, 2 upper teeth	15in (38cm)	May 1911 - 1912
Schnickel-Fritz	G	o/c mouth, 4 teeth toddler	15in (38cm)	May 1911 - 1912
107/107W 107W	H.E.S.	N.L. baby toddler toddler the above — elastic strung with "Mamma" body	13in (33cm) 11in (28cm) 14in (36cm)	1913 - 1926 1917 - 1926 1913 - 1926 1924 - 1926 1924 - 1928
108/108W 108W	H.E.S.	N.L. baby toddler the above — elastic strung with "Mamma" body	15in (38cm) 17in (43cm)	1913 - 1926 1913 - 1926 1924 - 1926 1924 - 1928
109W	H.E.S.	sleep eye, open mouth, N.L. baby toddler	13in (33cm) 14in (36cm)	1921 - 1923
110W	H.E.S.	sleep eye, open mouth, N.L. baby toddler	15in (38cm) 17in (43cm)	1921 - 1923

* = reissued in 1930 as a blonde

G = Graziano
H.E.S. = Harry E. Schoenhut

L = Leslie
c.h. = carved hair

L/G = Leslie based on Graziano
N.L. = Nature Limb body

B. Schoenhut Doll Bodies

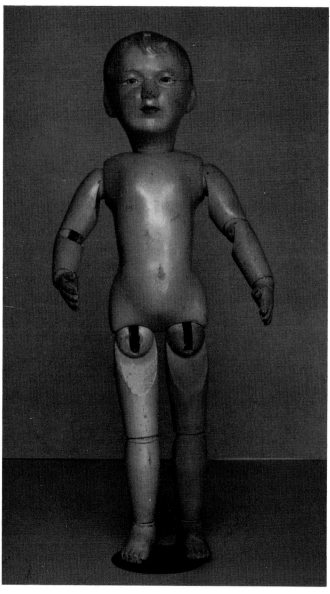

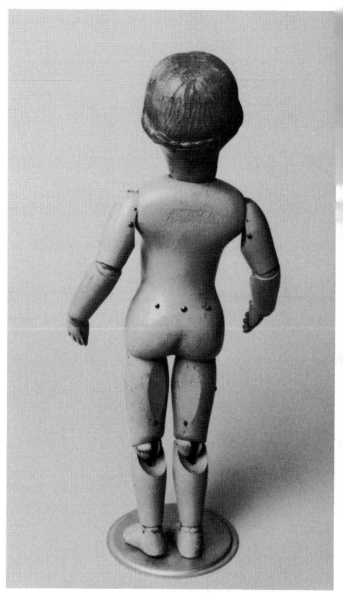

Illustration 494. The torso of the Graziano body is more detailed with slightly modeled breasts, abdomen and even a suggestion of a navel. This very early example of Doll 16/202 is also interesting because his entire left leg and foot have been replaced with a perfect hand-carved replica complete with handmade replacement springs. The work is by craftsman/collector Carl Hansen who took great care in detail work such as the carving of the toes. Carl never painted his work as he wanted it obvious that it was not original.

Illustration 495. The back of the torso is shapely as well. The bodies remained the same in their construction through the years. This is Doll 16/104. *Marianne Ripley Collection.*

Illustration 496. Elizabeth MacIntyre asked me about dovetailing in Schoenhut torsos when she discovered one with worn paint at the top of torso. We thought it might be a repair, but since then I have found salesmen's samples which are unpainted. They have a separate front to the torso which is jointed to the rest with dovetails. The jointing spots have been emphasized on this one with a pencil, but they show naturally as the wood is a different color. It does not break through for placement of the inside spring system, so it was probably done to allow more modeling. The dovetail pattern is not the same on different doll torsos.

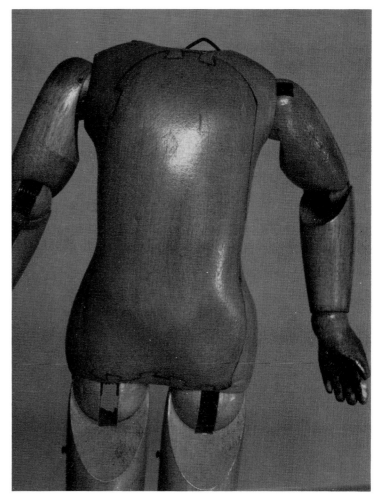

BELOW:
Illustration 497. This salesmen's sample body from circa World War I is posed to best show the doll's spring system. The springs are held in a taut position by a series of metal pins in the foot, thigh, hand, shoulder, and torso.

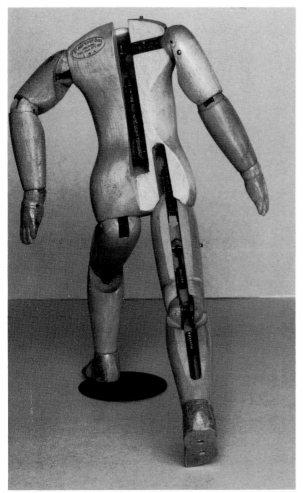

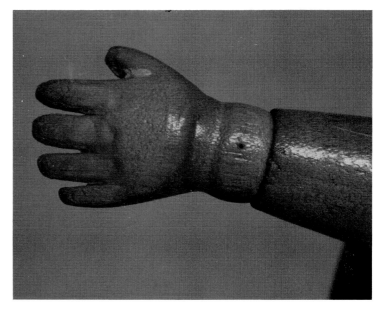

Illustration 498. The back of this hand has knuckle dimples and skin folds at the wrist. The palm shape and the finger joints are clearly indicated in the molding.

C. Schoenhut Eye Treatment

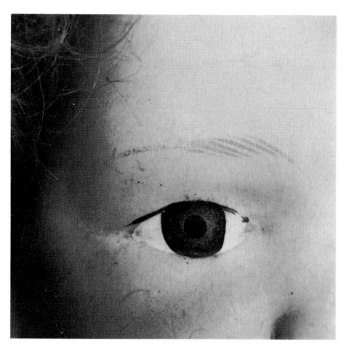

Illustration 499. Eye treatment, 1912 to 1916. The eye treatment of a smooth-eyed character 19/314 shows a wide, dark stippled ring around the lighter brown iris center. The pupil is black and the upper lid line is a red-brown. There is also a small pink tear duct as well as a lightly feathered brow.

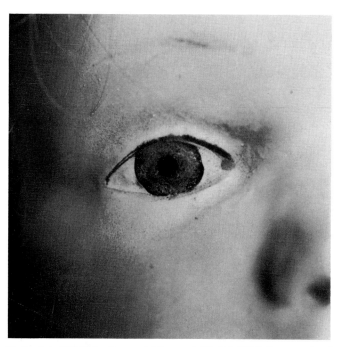

Illustration 500. This close-up of the eye of Doll 14/313 shows a mix of colors in the stippled iris which is outlined in black. The impression given is a golden-amber iris. Note the larger pink dot in the inside corner, brown lid line (eyelash line) and modeling of both upper and lower lids. (1912 to 1916.)

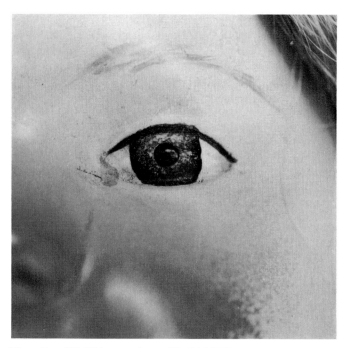

Illustration 501. This smooth-eyed Doll 14/313 has a lighter center and darker margin in its iris. The upper lid line is very dark and runs through the top of the iris. The pupil is black but because it is quite shiny, it is reflecting light back to the camera. The brows are blonde and feathered. Circa 1912 to 1916.

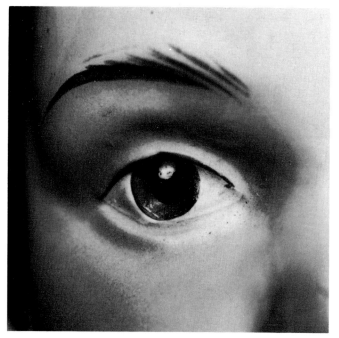

Illustration 502. The intaglio eye style has a natural depth caused by the fall of light on its incised (concave) iris and pupil. Paint can be applied smoothly as it needs no stippling to achieve depth. The white "reflection dot" at the top of the iris is raised, as are the eyelids. The brows of many of the "Classic" brunettes are strongly feathered. Circa 1912 to 1920.

248

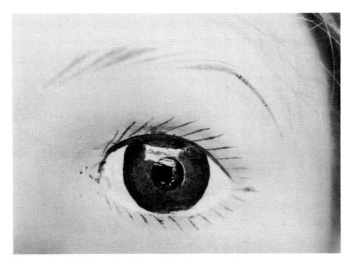

Illustration 503. Eye detail. The *Miss Dolly* eye from 1915 to 1919 was similar to the smooth-eyed characters, but then it was varnished over. It is shiny enough to reflect light from the window. This was done to make it look more like glass. Lashes were painted above and below the eye as well as the usual lid line.

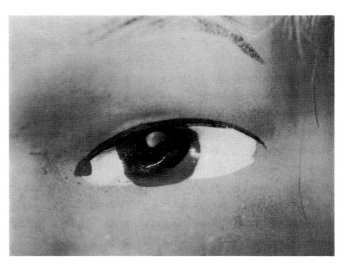

Illustration 504. Late intaglio eye detail from the early 1920s. The lower lid is completely gone so the bottom of the eye has no modeling to contain the paint. The eye is more concave than intaglio. The upper lid has a tiny crease over part of it. The tear duct spot is bright and fairly large.

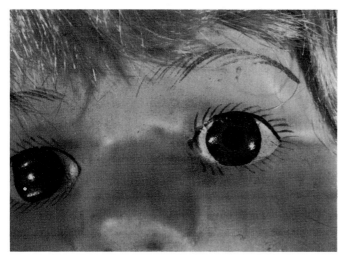

Illustration 505. Decal Eyes, 1920 to 1924. The brown decal eye has depth suggested by printing tiny black dots on the iris making them heavier and closer together near the edge. The decal eyes were designed by William George Schoenhut.

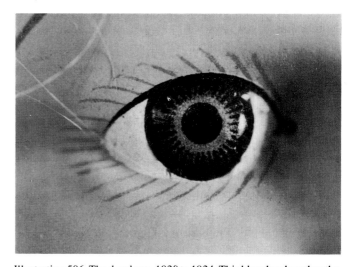

Illustration 506. The decal eye, 1920 to 1924. This blue decal eye has the bright blue applied as tiny dots printed on the film. The black threading lines in the eye make it look more like a glass eye. The eye is molded convex. The white of the eye sometimes does not match the lid line so it may have been applied separately. The lid line is part of the decal. The eyelashes and tear duct are added with paint. *Miss Dolly* and the sleep-eyed dolls are the only dolls with lashes painted around the eye. The characters all have their lashes indicated by a simple lid line on the edge of the upper lid.

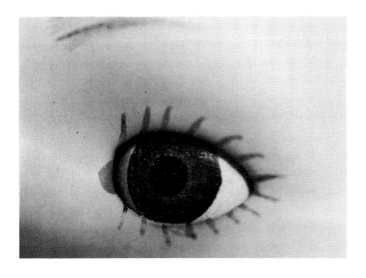

RIGHT:
Illustration 507. The "Sleep Eye," 1921 to 1928. The Schoenhut sleep eye was achieved with wooden eyeballs which had a lid painted on them and below that a decal eye. The patent for this eye, which was taken out by H.E. Schoenhut, is in the patent section. Apparently two patents were taken out by the company. The the one that covers this eye arrangement has two eyeballs on a rocker with a weight similar to that used in most sleep-eyed dolls, whether bisque, composition or other material. The other shows a separate lid that dropped over the eye. The latter patent apparently was never used.

D. Schoenhut Mouth Detail

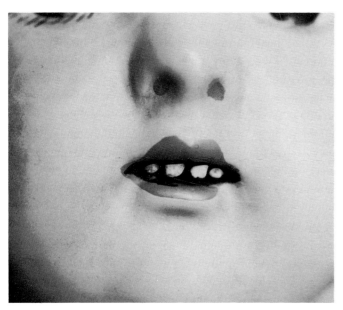

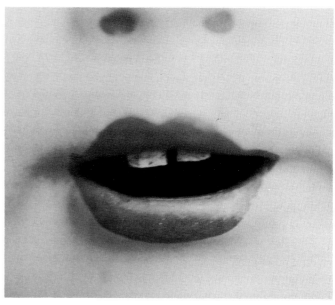

Illustration 508. Mouth Detail. This is the mouth of a very early *Miss Dolly*. The teeth are deeply "carved" so that a real space exists between them and the back of her mouth. The depth is accented with black paint to make her look more like an open-mouthed German bisque dolly.

Illustration 509. The sleep-eye baby has a truly open mouth. A light shown inside shows red felt on the plate that holds the eye mechanism in place on some of these dolls. The teeth are metal and are often set a little crookedly.

E. Schoenhut Marks

Illustration 510. The impressed mark was the earliest one. It usually appears on the back of the doll between its shoulders. It has been found stamped vertically on the torso of the *Manikin* under the arm. This mark first appeared in 1911. It appears to have been used through 1917 or 1918.

Illustration 511. The decal mark seems to date from 1916 on. It has been found on some dolls that were not offered after 1916 and is on most later characters, *Miss Dolly*, later babies, sleep-eyed dolls, and some walkable dolls. Its use appears to have overlapped that of the impressed mark from at least 1916 to 1918. It was placed on the same part of the back shoulders.

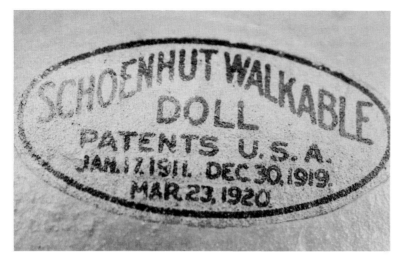

Illustration 512. This decal was a special one developed for the "Walkable Doll." The dates refer to the original doll patent with spring jointing, taken out by Albert Schoenhut; the walker joint patent taken out by William George Schoenhut; and the decal eye also patented by W.G. Schoenhut.

Illustrated 513. The body of these babies often had the impressed mark if they were toddler bodies. Baby bodies may be unmarked. The impressed mark was used briefly on the back of the neck of Harry E. Schoenhut's "Copyright Baby." As it did not impress clearly and completely very often, this method of marking was quickly replaced by the decal of the same design. Circa 1913 to 1914.

LEFT:
Illustration 514. This Harry E. Schoenhut copyright mark on the baby came shortly after production began. It appears to be a sticker rather than a decal and was an easier mark to put on a curved surface.

Illustrated 515. Sticker found on the composition child doll's back, as well as on later toys put out by the company.

Illustration 516. This mark also fits the naturally shaped body of the infant. It may also have been a sticker originally and later a decal.

F. Schoenhut Tags

Illustration 517. The obverse of the tag is light blue, yellow and red with a gold boarder. The top center of this tag is ripped off. This lightweight cardboard tag was used by the company during two periods of doll manufacture. It is shown in the earliest 1911 catalogue and appears to have been used through 1914. The metal button pin made its appearance on the new *Miss Dolly* in the 1915 catalogue. The tag has been found on late model dolls and sleep-eyed *Miss Dolly's* indicating that it came back into use around 1925 and was used through 1928, which was the last year that a regular doll line (the Mamma babies and the sleep-eyed Dollys only) were offered. These tags are harder to find than the pins because they are more perishable.

Illustration 518. Reverse of Illustration 517, which has further information about the Schoenhut dolls.

G. Schoenhut Pins

Illustration 519. At ⅞in (2cm) diameter, this is the pin that came on dolls beginning about 1915 and continuing through 1921 and possibly later. A sleep eye 317 with late decorating style has been found with the cardboard tag indicating that the company went back to using the tag in the last years, probably to save money. There are many modern copies of this pin being made. Most are either slightly larger (1in [3cm]) or slightly smaller (¾in [2cm]), but some are exactly the same size and only a slightly less sharp print may give them away.

Illustration 520. The inside of the pin has this label. At the present time this label is only found in original buttons.

252

H. Schoenhut Doll Box Labels

Illustration 521. This is a pre-1915 character doll box for model 16/300. Next to "color" is stamped "Blonde." Written in pencil is "Blue." Although the doll appears to have a white hair bow, shoes and stockings, in fact they are a very faded blue. The metal edges on the plain pasteboard boxes made them sturdy but they have dried out and become quite fragile with age.

Illustration 522. This label was placed on the top of the lid of both display boxes and plain pasteboard boxes.

Illustration 523. This is a box from 1915 or 1916, the only two years *Miss Dolly* (in this case 16/316) was offered without a "B" or "C" to indicate hairstyle. Note that the label simply says "ONE Schoenhut All-Wood Doll" without the reference to "Character Girl Doll" on the earlier label. Also the shield is now presented surrounded by a circle just like the Schoenhut pin. The fuzzy stamp next to the word color says "BROWN." This indicates the hair color. Before 1917 Brown means tosca. In pencil the words "Tan" and "Pink" are written below "No. 16/316." The doll inside has tan stockings and shoes and a pink hair ribbon. The trim at the top of this box bottom indicates that this is a display box. When the plain pasteboard lid is on the box, it shows no decoration on the outside. The display boxes unfolded at the corners, so they do not have metal edges.

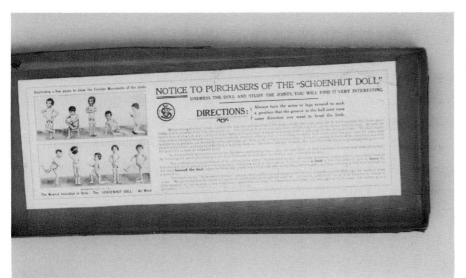

Illustration 524. Inside the box lids was this label. This one is printed in sepia. Some are printed in red. Note the green stamp at the bottom says "DO NOT SOAK THE DOLL IN WATER." This must have been added after people tried to "wash" the dolls more thoroughly than the company envisioned.

Illustration 525. Doll 16/300 "Blonde" with her stand. The plain pasteboard box predates, is contemporary with, and postdates the display box. This one predates it. The inside seems sponged with green.

Illustration 526. *Miss Dolly* still tied in her display box.

UNITED STATES PATENT OFFICE.

ALBERT SCHOENHUT, OF PHILADELPHIA, PENNSYLVANIA.

JOINTED FIGURE.

982,096. Specification of Letters Patent. **Patented Jan. 17, 1911.**

Application filed July 3, 1909. Serial No. 505,806.

To all whom it may concern:

Be it known that I, ALBERT SCHOENHUT, a citizen of the United States, residing in Philadelphia, Pennsylvania, have invented
5 certain Improvements in Jointed Figures, of which the following is a specification.

My invention relates to toy figures, manikins, jointed dolls, and the like, and the object of my invention is to provide a struc-
10 ture of this character with means serving to articulate the several members, such means being of a character as to insure the maximum degree of friction whereby the several limbs and portions of the same may be
15 turned and held in various positions assumed by such turning operations without danger of disarrangement except at the desire of the person using the toy, doll, or jointed figure. In addition, the means
20 which I have provided for articulating the structure are so arranged as to insure movement of the several limbs substantially in accord with the movement of the several limbs of the human body.

25 The essential feature of my invention is the character of the hinge joints between the body and limbs and between the sections of the several limbs.

My invention is fully shown in the ac-
30 companying drawings, in which:

Figure 1, represents a front elevation of a jointed doll made in accordance with one embodiment of my invention; such doll being shown partly in section; Fig. 2, is a
35 sectional view on the line a—a, Fig. 1; Figs. 3 and 4, are respectively a side elevation and a section of the thigh and leg of the figure shown in Fig. 1; the section being taken on the line a—a thereof; Fig. 5, is a
40 perspective view illustrating one form of my improved joint; Figs. 6 and 7, are views similar to Figs. 3 and 4, illustrating another form of joint, and Figs. 8, 9, 10, 11, 12 and 13 are views illustrating various
45 forms of joints embodying my invention.

In the drawings herewith, 1 represents the trunk of the figure; 2 the head; 3 the upper arm portions; 4 the lower arm portions; 5 the hands; 6 the thigh portions; 7
50 the leg portions, and 8 the feet.

The joint for use between the limbs and the trunk and between the several sections of the limbs of the figure shown in Fig. 1, is fully illustrated in Fig. 5, and comprises
55 a folded piece of material, preferably sheet metal indicated at 10, having enlarged bearing surfaces 11 at one end and a connecting portion 12 at the opposite end, such element being of a width to fit the recesses or slots 13 in the end of the several limbs and form-
60 ing a double walled metal structure adapted to lie against the walls of the same. To maintain the sides of said member 10 in contact with the walls of said recesses or slots, I provide a tension device, which may
65 be in the form of a coiled spring 14, or may be a section of rubber or other suitable resilient material, preferably encircling a pivot pin 14ᵃ passing through said member 10.

Carried by the member 10 is a swivel pin
70 or bar 15 having a spring 16 interposed between the end wall 12 of the joint member 10 and the head 17 of such swivel bar, and said swivel bar may be secured to the body or to the limbs, preferably by means of pins
75 or nails 18 passing through the walls of the trunk of the body and the walls of the several sections of the limbs.

The head, which may have the usual contracted neck portion, fits a suitable opening
80 in the upper portion of the body and may be provided with a loop 19 to which a link 20 may be connected, and the lower end of said link may be attached to a swivel pin or bar 15 carried by one of the elements 10 with
85 the usual spring 16; said element 10 being suitably anchored within the body by a pin 14ᵃ. The upper arm joint connections may be provided with swivel pins or bars with hooked ends 21 which may interlock with
90 each other. In the other instances, the swivel pins may be and preferably are secured by the nails or pins 18 passing through the walls of the figure or the limbs thereof.
95 The connection for the head is such as to permit said head to move in a complete circle. The connection for the upper arms is such as to permit complete rotary movement of the same; a ball and socket joint being
100 provided, and such arms are rabbeted at 22 so as to permit them to lie close to the body. The connection of the forearm with the upper arm, which is of the ball and socket type, is such as to permit movement of such
105 forearm toward and from the arm only, with its rotary movement limited by a pin or obstruction 23 carried by the upper arm and lying between the walls of the joint member 10. The connection of the thigh
110 with the lower portion of the body, also of the ball and socket type, permits movement

of the thigh toward and from the body in a substantially vertical direction with its rotary motion limited by a pin 23ᵃ passing through the body and extending into the space between the walls of the joint member 10. The movement of the knee joint is forward and back like the human knee joint; the rotary motion being limited by a pin or obstruction 23ᵇ extending into the space between the walls of the joint member 10 carried by the leg. The ankle joint between the leg and foot permits slight up and down movement of the foot and slight rotary motion limited by an obstruction 23ᶜ passing through the lower portion of the leg. In all instances, the joints are provided with tension means, preferably the springs 14 between the walls of the joint members 10, with swivel pins or bars permitting the slight rotary movement and with the springs 16 for insuring the holding of such parts in close connection with the rest of the figure. The tension means or springs 14 disposed between the side walls of the joint members hold the latter against the walls of the slots in the several sections of the limbs and thereby insure such an amount of friction as to cause said members to be held in the several positions to which they are moved.

In Figs. 6 and 7, I have shown a form of jointed limb structure in which the thigh portion 6 has a rounded end or ball to fit a socket in the leg portion. The joint connection for these sections is substantially the same as that shown in Figs. 1 to 5, inclusive, with the exception that the ends of said joint member between which the spring is disposed are slightly enlarged and provided with stops 25 and 26, with which a pin 27 carried by the thigh contacts when in the straight and bent positions respectively. In addition, the thigh portion of this limb structure has the slot for the joint connection with the body disposed diagonally with respect to the knee joint.

In Figs. 8 and 9, I have shown sectional views at right angles to each other of another form of joint, substantially the same as that indicated in Figs. 4 and 5, there being, however, no swivel tension connection between the sections. In Figs. 10 and 11, I have shown another slightly modified form of joint with a metal plate 28 at the bottom of the slot to resist any tendency of the folded metal member to wear the same. In Figs. 12 and 13, another form is shown, comprising a pair of folded members 10ᵃ, one of which lies within the other, and each of which is adapted to a slot in the respective leg and thigh portions. These members are held together by a pivot pin, with a spring disposed between the same and providing the necessary tension to secure the desired friction. In all instances, the purpose is to secure tension that will maintain a high degree of friction and insure sufficient resistance to bending or turning of each joint. In addition, the swivel connections with their springs provide for maintaining the several limbs in close frictional contact with the sockets of the body or trunk of the figure.

Although I have shown my improved form of joint and swivel connections for the head, trunk and limbs of a doll or manikin, it will be understood that it may be employed with all forms of animal toys having articulated joints.

I claim:

1. A joint for toy figures comprising a folded section of metal arranged to fit slotted portions of said figures, and having resilient tension means interposed between the side walls of said metal structure whereby the latter are held against the walls of the slot to increase the frictional resistance to turning, with a swivel pin connected to said joint, and a spring interposed between said swivel pin and joint.

2. The combination, in a toy figure structure, of means for joining the limbs and trunk of said structure, ball and socket joints for the limbs and trunk, friction producing means for said joints, and means for limiting rotative movement of the limbs at their ball and socket connections.

3. A joint for toy figures comprising a folded section of metal arranged to fit slotted portions of said figures, spring tension means interposed between the side walls of said metal structure whereby the latter are held against the walls of the slot to increase the frictional resistance to turning, a swivel pin connected to said joint, and tension means interposed between said swivel pin and joint.

4. The combination, in a toy, doll, or figure structure, comprising a trunk and articulated limbs, of means for joining the limbs and trunk of said structure, means combined with said joints for increasing the frictional resistance of said limbs to turning, and pins extending through the structure adjacent the joints for limiting rotative movement of the limbs.

5. A joint for toy figures and the like, comprising a folded section of material arranged to fit slotted portions in the limbs of said figures, and having resilient tension means interposed between the sides of said folded material whereby the latter are held against the walls of the slot to increase the frictional resistance of the joints to turning, with a swivel member connected to said joint, and tension means interposed between said swivel pin and joint.

6. The combination, in a jointed toy, doll, or figure structure, of means for connecting the limbs and trunk of said structure, means

for increasing the frictional resistance of the joints to turning, means for limiting their bending movement, and means for limiting rotative movement of the limbs of such structure.

7. A joint for toy figures and the like, comprising a folded section of material arranged to fit slotted portions of the limbs of said figures, a coiled spring interposed between the sides of said folded material whereby the latter are held against the walls of the slot to increase the frictional resistance of the joints to turning, a swivel member connected to said joint, and a spring interposed between said swivel pin and joint.

8. The combination, in a toy, doll, or figure structure, comprising a trunk and articulated limbs, of means for joining the limbs and trunk of said structure, means combined with said joints for increasing the frictional resistance of said limbs to turning, means for limiting the bending movement of the joints, and pins extending through the structure adjacent the joints for limiting the rotative movement of the limbs.

9. The combination, in a jointed figure, of a socketed trunk, limbs adapted to said sockets, anchors for said limbs, swivel connections between the anchors and the limbs, tension means for the swivel connections, joint members attached to said swivel connections, and means for directly applying tension to the pivot portions of said joints.

10. The combination, in a jointed toy, doll or the like, of a sectional limb, a swivel connection for the sections of said limb, tension means for said swivel connection, and a friction joint for said sections, said joint being attached to the swivel connection and engaging the walls of a slot in one section of said limb.

11. The combination, in a toy, doll, or figure structure, of ball and socket joints for the limbs and trunk of said structure, means for pivotally connecting the limbs and trunk at such ball and socket connections, means for increasing the frictional resistance to turning at said pivotal connections, and means for limiting rotative movement of the limbs at their ball and socket connections.

12. The combination, in a toy, doll, or figure structure, of ball and socket joints for the limbs and trunk of said structures,

means for pivotally connecting the limbs and trunk at such ball and socket connections, the limbs being slotted for such pivotal connections, means for increasing the frictional resistance to turning at said pivotal connections, and means carried by one limb member and entering the slotted portion of another for limiting rotative movement of the limbs at their ball and socket connections.

13. In a toy figure having elements with slotted portions pivotally connected therewith, a jointing element comprising a double-walled metal structure arranged to fit said slotted portions, the walls of said metal structure lying in engagement with the walls of said slotted portions, and resilient tension means interposed between the walls of said metal structure directly at its pivot point whereby said metal walls are held against the walls of the slotted portions to produce frictional resistance to turning.

14. In a toy figure having elements with slotted portions, a jointing element comprising a double-walled section of metal arranged to fit said slotted portion and engage the walls of the same, a pivot pin carried by said slotted portion, said pin passing through the walls of said metal structure to confine the same to the slotted portion, and tension means interposed between the side walls of said metal structure at the pivotal connection whereby said walls are held against the walls of the slotted portion to produce frictional resistance to turning.

15. In a toy figure having elements with slotted portions, a jointing element comprising a double-walled section of metal arranged to fit said slotted portions with its walls in engagement with the walls of said slotted portion, a pivot pin in said slotted portion passing through the walls of said metal structure to confine the same thereto, and a coiled spring interposed between the walls of said metal structure and surrounding the pivot pin whereby said walls are held against the walls of the slotted portion to produce frictional resistance to turning.

In testimony whereof, I have signed my name to this specification, in the presence of two subscribing witnesses.

ALBERT SCHOENHUT.

Witnesses:
MURRAY C. BOYER,
WM. A. BARR.

A. SCHOENHUT.
JOINTED FIGURE.
APPLICATION FILED JULY 2, 1909.

982,096.

Patented Jan. 17, 1911.

2 SHEETS—SHEET 1.

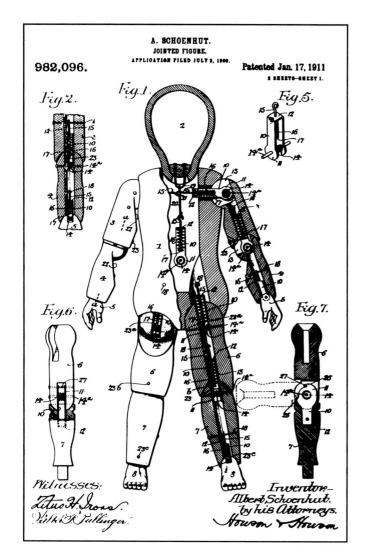

Witnesses:

Inventor
Albert Schoenhut.
by his Attorneys
Howson & Howson

A. SCHOENHUT.
JOINTED FIGURE.
APPLICATION FILED JULY 2, 1909.

982,096.

Patented Jan. 17, 1911.

2 SHEETS—SHEET 2.

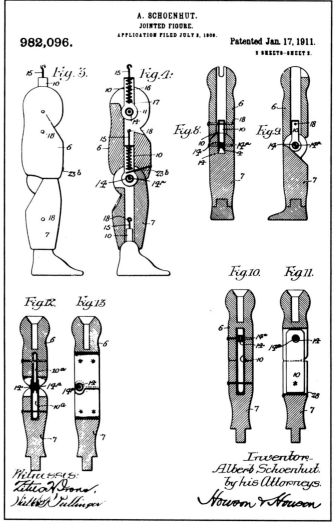

Witnesses:

Inventor
Albert Schoenhut.
by his Attorneys
Howson & Howson

UNITED STATES PATENT OFFICE.

WILLIAM G. SCHOENHUT, OF PHILADELPHIA, PENNSYLVANIA, ASSIGNOR TO THE A. SCHOENHUT COMPANY, OF PHILADELPHIA, PENNSYLVANIA, A CORPORATION OF PENNSYLVANIA.

JOINT FOR DOLLS.

1,326,790. Specification of Letters Patent. **Patented Dec. 30, 1919.**

Application filed September 18, 1919. Serial No. 324,343.

To all whom it may concern:

Be it known that I, WILLIAM G. SCHOENHUT, a citizen of the United States, residing in Philadelphia, Pennsylvania, have in
5 vented certain Improvements in Joints for Dolls, of which the following is a specification.

My invention relates to dolls; and the object of my invention is to provide that form
10 of mechanical dolls known as "walking dolls" with a special form of joint for connecting the legs to the body which, while sufficiently stiff to insure either leg maintaining the desired position or condition
15 when the doll is operated to simulate walking, may be turned on its pivotal connection with the body so that the doll may be caused to assume a sitting posture.

As is well known, dolls of the so-called
20 "walking" type are provided with spring tension means of some suitable character that will cause the legs to project forwardly a slight distance; the tension of such spring not being sufficient to prevent one leg being
25 held momentarily while the other is projected forward by the spring, and these acts being carried out alternately, the walking effect is produced. In the former constructions, however, the joints between the legs
30 and the body have been of such a character that the doll cannot be placed in a sitting posture, and the essential object of my invention is to provide means that will permit this condition and at the same time
35 provide a structure that may be operated as a "walking" doll.

These and other features of my invention are more fully described hereinafter, reference being had to the accompanying draw
40 ings, in which:

Figure 1, is a side elevation showing a form of doll to which my invention has been applied.

Fig. 2, is a front elevation of sufficient of
45 the doll's body and the legs thereof to illustrate the joint structure connecting these parts and forming the subject of my invention.

Fig. 3, is a side elevation, partly in sec
50 tion, showing the position of the joint structure in the so-called "walking" position, in full lines, and showing in dotted lines the position of the joint structure when the doll is in the sitting posture.

Fig. 4, is a perspective view of the form 55 of joint block shown in Figs. 1, 2 and 3.

Fig. 5, is an edge view of another form of joint block within the scope of my invention, and

Figs. 6 and 7, are sectional views of the 60 joint member shown in Fig. 5, taken on the lines VI—VI and VII—VII, respectively.

In the drawings, 1 represents the body of the doll, and 2, the legs. These parts are shown in the present instance as connected 65 by joint blocks 3; the latter having a pivotal connection with the body, and a pivotal connection with the legs; pins 4 and 5, respectively, being employed for this purpose.

The connection of these joint-blocks with 70 the body should be quite tight, and to produce the desired friction and maintain a relatively stiff joint at this point which will require some effort to effect movement of the same with respect to the body, I may 75 provide a structure such as illustrated in the accompanying drawings.

The joint block 3 shown in Figs. 1, 2, *et. seq.*, may be of compressed fiber, hard rubber, or other suitable material, and com- 80 prises the part 3^a which is in engagement with the body, and the part 3^b engaging the leg; said part 3^a being relatively larger than the part 3^b and having very tight frictional engagement with the body, which is slotted 85 at 1^a to receive the same. The legs are slotted at 2^a to receive the ends 3^b of the joint blocks.

The opposite end of the joint block, indicated at 3^b and pivotally connected to 90 the leg by the pin 5, is provided with a slot or groove 6 for the reception of a spring member 7, which may be of wire and which is employed with the leg-joint to keep the leg or body projected forward with respect 95 to each other, and the free movement of such part 3^b with respect to the leg is only restrained by said spring. The position of the spring, which is a light affair preferably of round wire, is clearly shown in Fig. 100 3; one end may be caught in the joint block as indicated, while the other end may hook over the back of the leg in the slot 2^a. The tension of the springs is such that it will not prevent movement of the doll on one leg 105 against the force or power of the spring carried by the other leg, and then when the leg which has been first held is released, the spring of the same will throw it forward to the extent of its movement with respect to the joint, and a repetition of these acts will simulate walking, when the doll is held by the hand and moved along, with the feet alternately contacting with the ground.

The smaller projection 3ᵇ of the joint block, therefore, while lying in the slot 2ᵃ at the upper end of the leg is not in frictional contact therewith, and is free to move to the extent permitted by the wall of the slot 2ᵃ. The larger projection 3ᵃ, however, is in definite frictional engagement with the walls of the slot 1ᵃ in the body; the frictional engagement being such that while no movement with respect thereto can take place while the doll is simulating walking, such joint block 3 can be moved upon its pivot pin 4 with respect to the body when it is desired to place the doll in a sitting posture.

In Figs. 5, 6 and 7, I have shown another form of joint block of the same shape as that shown in Figs. 1, 2, *et seq.*, which joint block may be of wood and may comprise the part 33ᵃ for engagement with the body, and the part 33ᵇ for engagement with the leg; said part 33ᵃ being relatively larger than the part 33ᵇ as in the other structure, and being provided with grooves 8ᵃ and 8ᵇ, which may be essentially narrow saw kerfs. The abutments or end walls of these saw kerfs may lie at an angle with respect to each other, as clearly shown in Figs. 6 and 7, an arrangement which gives the block the desired compressibility and resiliency and avoids danger of the material, usually wood, splitting.

While I have shown a joint structure involving a joint-block of solid material, one form being of wood, with saw kerfs therein to provide the desired resiliency to insure proper frictional engagement with the walls of the recesses 1ᵃ formed in the body of the doll, I do not wish to be limited to the precise construction shown since any suitable means; a metal structure, solid or otherwise, or a combination structure including metal parts, having a portion or portions for engagement with the body and insuring the desired frictional engagement therewith may be employed, such modified forms of joint structures having in all instances means that will additionally provide the desired spring supported pivotal connection with the leg; the joint structure or joint block being so held to the body as to prevent movement with respect to the same until it is desired to place the doll in the sitting posture.

I claim:

1. In a joint for the legs of dolls, the combination with the body and a leg, of a member connecting the leg and body, means providing for frictional engagement of said member with the body to prevent movement of the same under normal conditions but permit movement under other conditions, and a pivotal connection for said member with the leg free to have limited movement with respect to the latter under all conditions.

2. In a joint for the legs of dolls, the combination with the body and a leg, of an intermediate joint member connecting the leg and body; said member having such frictional engagement with the body as to prevent movement of the same under normal conditions and permit movement under other conditions and a pivotal connection with the leg free to have limited movement with respect to the latter under all conditions, and tension means between said joint member and the leg.

3. In a joint for the legs of dolls, the combination with the body and a leg, of an intermediate joint member, and pivotal connections between the same and the leg and body; said joint member tightly fitting the body whereby movement of the same under normal conditions is prevented while the pivotal connection of said joint member with the leg is free to have limited movement with respect to the latter under all conditions.

4. In a joint for the legs of dolls, the combination with the body and a leg, of an intermediate joint member comprising a block connecting the leg and body, and pivot pins securing said joint member to the leg and body; said block having such frictional engagement with the body as to prevent movement of the same under normal conditions but permit movement under other conditions; the pivotal connection of said joint member with the leg being free to have limited movement with respect to the latter under all conditions.

5. In a joint for the legs of walking dolls, the combination with a body and a leg thereof, of a joint section connecting the leg and body and pivotally attached to each of the same, means insuring close engagement of said joint section with the body to maintain the leg of the doll in the walking position but permitting movement of the leg to a sitting posture; the pivotal connection of said joint section with the leg being relatively free to have limited movement with respect to the latter, and tension means between the joint section and leg.

6. In a joint for the legs of walking dolls, the combination with a body and a leg thereof, of a joint section connecting the leg and body and pivotally attached to each of the same; the body being slotted to receive the joint section and the latter being held in tight engagement with the body to maintain the leg in the walking position but permit-

ting movement to a sitting posture with respect to the body, and the pivotal connection of said joint section with the leg being relatively free for limited movement with respect to the latter, and a spring interposed between the joint section and the leg for effecting movement of the latter with respect to said joint section.

7. In a joint for the legs of walking dolls, the combination with a body and a leg thereof, of a block forming a joint section, pins connecting the leg and body thereto; the connection with the body being stiff and the connection with the leg being loose, and tension means at the connection between the joint section and the leg for effecting movement of said leg with respect to the joint section.

8. In a joint for the legs of walking dolls, the combination with a body and a leg thereof, of a block forming a joint section, pins connecting the leg and body thereto; the connection with the body being stiff and the connection with the leg being loose, and a spring interposed between the joint section and the leg for effecting movement of the latter with respect to said joint section.

9. In a joint for the limbs of dolls, the combination with the body and a limb, of a member mounted for movement with respect to the body and normally in tight frictional engagement therewith; said member having a pivotal connection with the limb free to have limited movement with respect to the latter under all conditions.

10. In a joint for the limbs of dolls, the combination with the body and a limb, of an intermediate joint block member mounted for movement with respect to the body and normally in tight frictional engagement therewith; said member having a pivotal connection with the limb free to have limited movement with respect to the latter under all conditions, and tension means between said joint member and the limb.

11. In a joint for the legs of walking dolls, the combination with a body and a leg thereof, of a block mounted for movement with respect to the body and leg and having tight engagement with the body; the connection with the leg being relatively loose, and tension means at the connection between the joint block and the leg for effecting movement of said leg with respect to the joint block.

12. In a joint for the legs of walking dolls, the combination with a body and a leg thereof, of a block mounted for movement with respect to the leg and body and having tight engagement with the body; the connection with the leg being relatively loose, and a spring interposed between the joint block and the leg for effecting movement of the latter with respect to said joint block.

WM. G. SCHOENHUT.

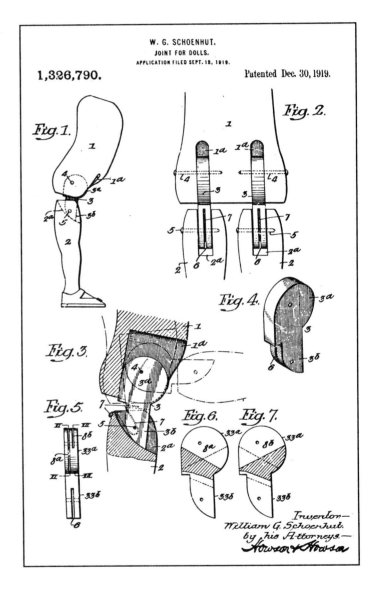

W. G. SCHOENHUT.
JOINT FOR DOLLS.
APPLICATION FILED SEPT. 18, 1919.

1,326,790.   Patented Dec. 30, 1919.

Fig. 1.

Fig. 2.

Fig. 3.

Fig. 4.

Fig. 5.

Fig. 6.   Fig. 7.

Inventor—
William G. Schoenhut.
by his Attorneys—
Howson & Howson

UNITED STATES PATENT OFFICE.

WILLIAM G. SCHOENHUT, OF PHILADELPHIA, PENNSYLVANIA, ASSIGNOR TO THE A. SCHOENHUT COMPANY, OF PHILADELPHIA, PENNSYLVANIA, A CORPORATION OF PENNSYLVANIA.

DOLL.

1,358,470.   Specification of Letters Patent.   **Patented Nov. 9, 1920.**

Application filed March 18, 1919.   Serial No. 283,344.

To all whom it may concern:

Be it known that I, WILLIAM G. SCHOENHUT, a citizen of the United States, residing in Philadelphia, Pennsylvania, have invented certain Improvements in Dolls, of which the following is a specification.

My invention relates to dolls, more particularly to the facial features of the heads of the same, and the object of my invention is to provide an improved form of eye representation. While my invention has been applied more particularly to the heads of wooden dolls of well known construction and with which I am very familiar, it may be applied to other forms of dolls' heads; such heads, including the wooden heads, being suitably shaped to the desired contour and being provided with eye sockets. After shaping, of course, the faces of such heads must receive the features—the eyes, the eyebrows and eyelashes, nostril indications, lips, &c.

Heretofore, in the delineation of the facial features of these wooden heads, as well as other forms of dolls' heads, the eyes have usually been painted in, and this method of delineation has produced a highly satisfactory result, excepting that it is a very tiresome and tedious operation and very hard upon the eyes of the artist. Difficulties attendant upon such method of procedure and the necessity for artistic accuracy have drawn my attention to the desirability of providing other means for effecting the placing of the eye that would be more or less mechanical, and yet would require considerable dexterity and accuracy of adjustment to secure the desired effect.

These and other features of my invention are more fully described hereinafter, reference being had to the accompanying drawings, in which:

Figure 1, is a front elevation of a doll's head, which may be of any type and of any material, wood, plastic composition, vitreous material, papier-mâché or the like; the same being shown in a finished condition, except for the eyes.

Fig. 2, is a similar view showing the eyes in position, and

Fig. 3, is an enlarged view of a film upon which the eye is printed, which film is subsequently applied to an eye socket in the head of the doll.

In Fig. 1, the head 1 is shown with the shaped eye sockets 2, ready to receive the eye representation constituting the subject of my invention. This eye representation is in the form of a decalcomania film 3 of the shape of the eye socket; such film having printed or otherwise mechanically produced thereon, by any process, a representation of the complete eye, constituting the ball, pupil, iris, cornea, &c. Such showing may be in any desired color normal to human eyes, and it may include the pink surface of the *caruncula lacrymalis*, adjacent the nose, displayed by the human eye.

The films 3 so prepared are carried upon a supporting medium—a sheet of paper 4, or the like—with a suitable adhesive body between the same and the film, preferably water-soluble.

In practice, in applying such eye representations, one of the eye films with a small portion of its support or backing is separated from a sheet of the same, then dipped in water, allowed to stand for a short while, and then applied to the eye socket of the doll's head and held in proper place by the finger while the paper or other support is slipped or pulled from beneath the same, whereupon the finger can press down the eye film upon the rounded surface of the eye socket, and the moistened adhesive previously holding the film to its backing will hold the same securely in place on the eye socket surface. The film, which is flexible, is then smoothed into position over the shaped ball by any suitable means; a camel's hair brush, for instance, and it may be subsequently varnished if desired; the varnish having the further effect of protecting the eye film and waterproofing the surface of the same.

It will be understood, of course, that the eye representations are made in rights and lefts; the single eye representation shown in Fig. 3, being the left eye.

I claim:

1. A doll's head having an eye member provided with a film of gelatinous character permanently affixed thereto and having thereon a printed finished simulation of the human eye.

2. A doll's head having a shaped eye member and a flexible transfer member of stretchable consistency readily conformable to said eye member and permanently attached thereto and bearing a printed finished representation of an eye.

3. A doll's head having a shaped eye member and a decalcomania film thereon of substantially the shape of the eye and having a printed simulation of the human eye.

4. A doll's head having its eyes each formed of an adhesively-supplied gelatinous film of oblong form having a printed representation of the human eye.

5. The method herein described of apply-

ing an eye to a doll's head, said method consisting, essentially, in previously preparing and adhesively attaching to a backing sheet, a film bearing a printed simulation of an eye; moistening the sheet to soften the adhesive which unites the film thereto; positioning the sheet with its loosened film relatively to a previously shaped eye member; separating the loosened film from its backing by a movement of one of these parts relatively to the other and applying the removed film to a previously shaped eye member by pressure.

6. The method herein described of applying an eye to a doll's head, said method consisting, essentially, in positioning relatively to a previously shaped eye member, an adhesively mounted backed and moistened transfer-film bearing a simulation of the human eye, and then removing the backing and directly affixing the moistened film to the previously shaped eye member by pressure.

7. The process of indicating eyes in dolls' heads, which consists in shaping the head with an eyeball socket having a suitable surface, providing a film of the shape of such socket and having the representation of an eye; said film being mounted upon a support or backing and secured thereto by a water soluble adhesive, wetting the backing to permit removal of the film therefrom, applying such film and backing in proper position over the surface of the eyeball socket, slipping the backing from beneath the film whereby the latter will be left in position over the surface of the eyeball socket, and smoothing the same into place; the adhesive originally connecting the film to its backing serving as the means whereby the film is attached in position in the doll's head.

8. The process of indicating eyes in dolls' heads, which consists in shaping the head with an eyeball socket having a suitable convex surface, providing a flexible film of the shape of such socket and having the representation of an eye printed thereon; said film being mounted upon a support or backing and secured thereto by a water soluble adhesive, wetting the backing to permit removal of the film therefrom, applying such film and backing in proper position over the convex surface of the eyeball socket, slipping the backing from beneath the film whereby the latter will be left in position over the surface of the eyeball socket, and smoothing the same into place; the adhesive originally connecting the film to its backing serving as the means whereby the film is attached in position in the doll's head.

9. The process of indicating eyes in dolls' heads, which consists in shaping the head with an eyeball socket having a suitable surface, providing a film of the shape of such socket and having the representation of an eye; said film being mounted upon a support or backing and secured thereto by

a water soluble adhesive, wetting the backing to permit removal of the film therefrom, applying such film and backing in proper position over the surface of the eyeball socket, slipping the backing from beneath the film whereby the latter will be left in position over the surface of the eyeball socket, smoothing the same into place; the adhesive originally connecting the film to its backing serving as the means whereby the film is attached in position in the doll's head, and subsequently varnishing such film.

10. The process of indicating eyes in dolls' heads, which consists in shaping the head with an eyeball socket having a suitable convex surface, providing a flexible film of the shape of such socket and having the representation of an eye printed thereon; said film being mounted upon a support or backing and secured thereto by a water soluble adhesive, wetting the backing to permit removal of the film therefrom, applying such film and backing in proper position over the convex surface of the eyeball socket, slipping the backing from beneath the film whereby the latter will be left in position over the surface of the eyeball socket, smoothing the same into place; the adhesive originally connecting the film to its backing serving as the means whereby the film is attached in position in the doll's head, and subsequently varnishing such film.

11. The combination of a doll's head having an eye socket with shaped surface, of an eye representation in the form of a flexible film applied to such socket.

12. The combination of a doll's head having an eye socket with shaped surface, of an eye representation in the form of a flexible printed film applied to such socket.

WILLIAM G. SCHOENHUT.

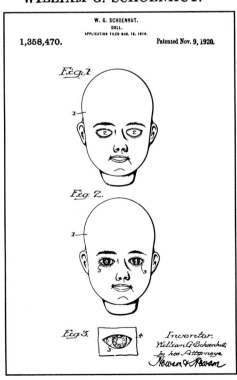

W. G. SCHOENHUT.
DOLL.
APPLICATION FILED MAR. 18, 1919.

1,358,470.   Patented Nov. 9, 1920.

Fig. 1

Fig. 2.

Fig. 3.

Inventor:
William G. Schoenhut,
by his Attorneys,
Howson & Howson

UNITED STATES PATENT OFFICE.

HARRY E. SCHOENHUT, OF PHILADELPHIA, PENNSYLVANIA, ASSIGNOR TO THE A. SCHOENHUT COMPANY, OF PHILADELPHIA, PENNSYLVANIA, A CORPORATION OF PENNSYLVANIA.

DOLL.

1,387,317. Specification of Letters Patent. **Patented Aug. 9, 1921.**

Application filed March 26, 1920. Serial No. 368,863.

To all whom it may concern:

Be it known that I, HARRY E. SCHOENHUT, a citizen of the United States, residing in Philadelphia, Pennsylvania, have invented 5 certain Improvements in Dolls, of which the following is a specification.

One object of my invention is to improve the construction of dolls by making the eyes in a fixed position and providing movable 10 eyelids, which will move to the open position when the doll is erect, and will cover the eyes when the doll is in a recumbent position.

A further object of the invention is to de-15 sign the doll so that the eyes are carried by a removable section.

A still further object of the invention is to design the doll so that the weighted member carrying the eyelids is pivoted to the re-20 movable eye section.

In the accompanying drawings:

Figure 1, is a side view of a doll's head, partly in section, the section being taken on the line 1—1, Fig. 4;

25 Fig. 2, is a sectional view on the line 2—2, Fig. 4;

Fig. 3, is a rear view of the head with the back section removed and the eye section also removed;

30 Fig. 4, is a view similar to Fig. 3 with the eye section in place;

Fig. 5, is a sectional view similar to Fig. 2, showing the head when the doll is in a recumbent position;

35 Fig. 6, is a detached perspective view of the eye section;

Fig. 7, is a detached perspective view illustrating the weighted lids;

Fig. 8, is a rear view with the back section 40 removed, showing a modification in which the lid section for each eye is operated independently, and

Fig. 9, is a detached perspective view of one of the eye sections illustrated in Fig. 8, 45 the lid being attached thereto.

Referring to the drawings, 1 is the head of a doll, which, in the present instance, is made of wood. The head is recessed at the back, as at 2. Connecting with this main 50 recess 2 is a deeper recess 3 of the shape clearly shown in Fig. 3, and having eye sockets 5, 5 therein. 4, 4, are the eye openings in the head. The deep recess 3 has a portion 3ª which extends below the sockets 55 to allow a weight to swing freely therein.

6 is an eye section, having a body portion 7 and two cylindrical extensions 8 in the present instance which fit the curved sides of the recess. At the ends of the extensions are ball portions 9 forming the eye balls on 60 which the eyes 10 are indicated in any suitable manner. This eye section is forced into the recess 3 and can be held therein by friction, by a brad, or other suitable fastenings. The eye section, when in position, is station-65 ary, and is so located that there is a space between each socket and a ball as indicated in Fig. 1, and pivoted to the eye section at 11 is an eyelid member 12 having a weight 13 and bent portions 14, which form the 70 eyelids so that when the parts are in position, as illustrated in Figs. 1 and 2, the eyelids are raised above the eyes within the sockets 5 and the eyes 10 are exposed through the openings 4, but when the doll is moved 75 to the recumbent position, as in Fig. 5, the weight holds the eyelids in the vertical position so that they cover the eyes.

In Figs. 8 and 9, I have illustrated a modification in which the eye section is made in 80 two disconnected parts 8ª, each fitting a cylindrical recess in the head. Pivoted to each section is the lid section 12ª consisting of a weight 13ª and a lid portion 14ª. In this instance, while the lids are mounted 85 independently, they close simultaneously when the doll is moved into the recumbent position.

The constructions above described are exceedingly simple and are especially adapted 90 for use in connection with heads of dolls made of wood. When the eye section is placed in position, the back section 15 is secured in place covering the recess at the back of the head. If, for any reason, the 95 eyelids will not act properly, all that is necessary is to remove the back section and withdraw the eye section with the lid section attached thereto. The repair can be readily made, or, if necessary, a new lid 100 section can be substituted, and the parts reassembled.

I claim:

1. The combination of a doll's head having a recess at the back, a socket extending 105 from said recess toward the front of the head, said socket having an eye opening at its forward end; an eye section having a ball portion at one end, said ball portion being located in the socket; and a lid be- 110

tween the ball portion and the socket and adapted to move so as to close the eye opening when the doll is in a recumbent position.

2. The combination of a doll's head having a recess at the back; two sockets extending from said recess toward the front of the head, said sockets having eye openings at their forward ends; an eye section having a ball portion adapted to the sockets; and a weighted lid section pivoted to the ball portion of the eye section.

3. The combination of a doll's head having a recess at the back terminating in two sockets spaced apart, and having an eye opening in each socket; an eye section having a body portion fitting the recess and having two extensions; a ball at the end of each extension forming an eye; and a lid section pivoted to the ball section and consisting of two laterally curved portions forming the lids and a weight connected to said curved portions adapted to swing freely in the recess in the head.

4. The combination of a doll's head having a recess at the back with curved sides; sockets at the end of the recess; an eye opening in each socket; an eye section having a body portion; and two cylindrical extensions fitting the curved sides of the recess in the head, said extensions having eye balls at their outer ends fitting the sockets, and an eyelid section pivoted to the balls and having a weight.

HARRY E. SCHOENHUT.

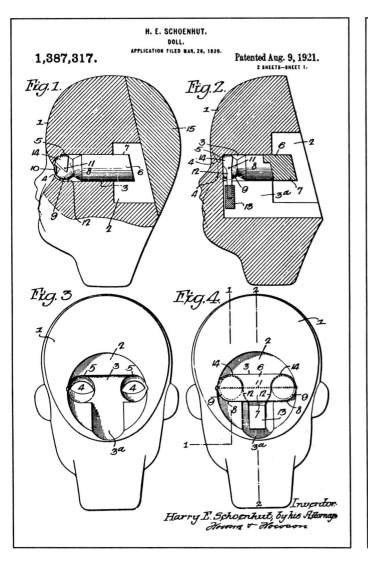

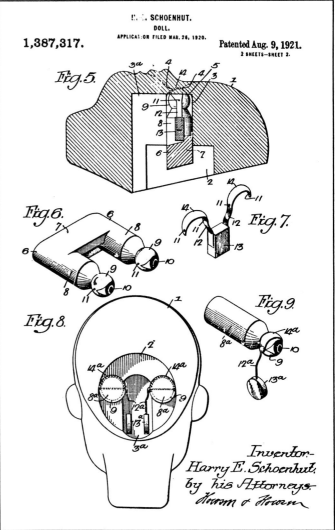

UNITED STATES PATENT OFFICE.

HARRY E. SCHOENHUT, OF PHILADELPHIA, PENNSYLVANIA, ASSIGNOR TO THE A. SCHOENHUT COMPANY, OF PHILADELPHIA, PENNSYLVANIA, A CORPORATION OF PENNSYLVANIA.

DOLL.

1,390,820. Specification of Letters Patent. **Patented Sept. 13, 1921.**

Application filed March 22, 1920. Serial No. 367,960.

To all whom it may concern:

Be it known that I, HARRY E. SCHOENHUT, a citizen of the United States, residing in Philadelphia, Pennsylvania, have invented 5 certain Improvements in Dolls, of which the following is a specification.

One object of my invention is to improve the construction of the movable eyes of dolls so that they can be mounted to rotate freely 10 in sockets without pivot pins.

A further object of the invention is to provide an eye member for a doll, which can be readily assembled in a solid head.

This invention is especially adapted for 15 use in connection with heads made of a solid piece of wood in which a cavity is formed for the reception of the eye member, which is allowed to turn freely therein.

In the accompanying drawings:

20 Figure 1 is a sectional view of a portion of a doll's head illustrating my invention, the section being on the line 1—1, Fig. 3;

Fig. 2 is a sectional view on the line 2—2, Fig. 3;

25 Fig. 3 is a rear view with the back section of the head removed, and showing the eye member in place;

Fig. 4 is a view, similar to Fig. 3, showing the sockets for the eye member;

30 Fig. 5 is a perspective view of the eye member; and

Fig. 6 is a perspective view of the disk, which holds the eye member in the sockets.

Referring to the drawings, 1 is the head 35 of a doll made of a solid block of wood, in the present instance, having a recess 2 at the back, closed by a back section 1ª of the head, as shown in Fig. 1. This recess extends well toward the front of the doll's head, and in 40 the recess are two sockets 4. The front walls of the sockets have openings 3, similar to the natural eye openings. Mounted in the sockets are the ball sections 5 of the eye member 6, made as shown in Fig. 5. 45 These two ball sections are connected together by a bar 7 to which is attached a wire 8 having a weight 9, forming a pendulum. Representations of eyes are formed on the ball sections 5 by painting, decalco- 50 mania, or other means. The sockets 4 are shaped to conform to the shape of the balls

of the eye member, as clearly shown in Fig. 1. The ball sections of the eye member are held in the sockets by a disk 10 of any suitable material, preferably flexible, and in the 55 present instance, this material is cardboard which is secured in place by tacks 11, or other suitable fastenings. The cardboard disk is slotted at 12 to allow free movement of the weighted wire or pendulum 8. 60

While the balls 5 of the eye member fit snugly in the sockets they are free to turn therein and the representations of eyes are so placed in relation to the pendulum that when the face of the doll is in an upright 65 position, the eyes are exposed, but when the doll is in a recumbent position the representation of the eyelids, which are above the eyes, are exposed, simulating sleep.

By this construction, all pivot pins are 70 dispensed with and the eye members can be readily assembled and secured in position without expert manipulation, and the eye section can be removed and repaired or replaced without difficulty. 75

I claim:—

1. The combination of a substantially solid doll's head having a recess at the back, eye sockets spaced apart and extending from said recess toward the front of the head, said 80 sockets having eye openings at their forward ends; an eye member consisting of a cross bar having a ball at each end; a representation of an eye on each ball member; a pendulum depending from the cross bar; 85 and a disk holding the balls in the sockets so that they will turn freely therein.

2. The combination of a doll's head having a recess at the back, two sockets connected to the recess; an eye member having 90 a cross bar; a ball at each end of the cross bar, the front portions of the sockets conforming to the shape of the ball members; a pendulum depending from the cross member; a weight at the end of the pendulum; 95 and a flexible disk secured to the head of the doll at the inner end of the recess and retaining the eye balls in their sockets, the disk being slotted for the free movement of the pendulum.

HARRY E. SCHOENHUT.

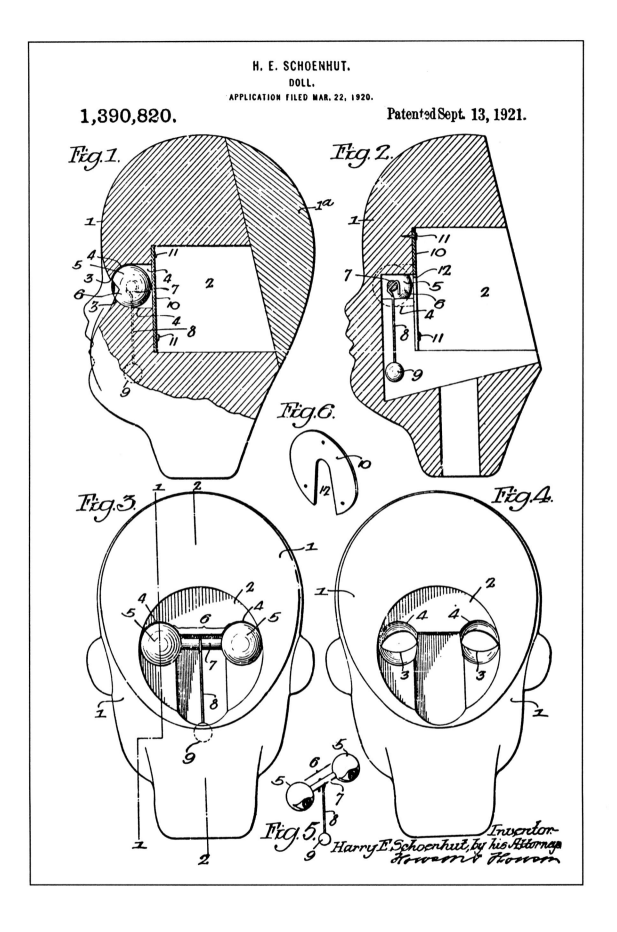

H. E. SCHOENHUT.

DOLL.

APPLICATION FILED MAR. 22, 1920.

1,390,820.

Patented Sept. 13, 1921.

Fig.1.

Fig.2.

Fig.6.

Fig.3.

Fig.4.

Fig.5.

Inventor

Harry E. Schoenhut, by his Attorney

Howson & Howson

Index

(Illustration page numbers listed in Bold Italics)

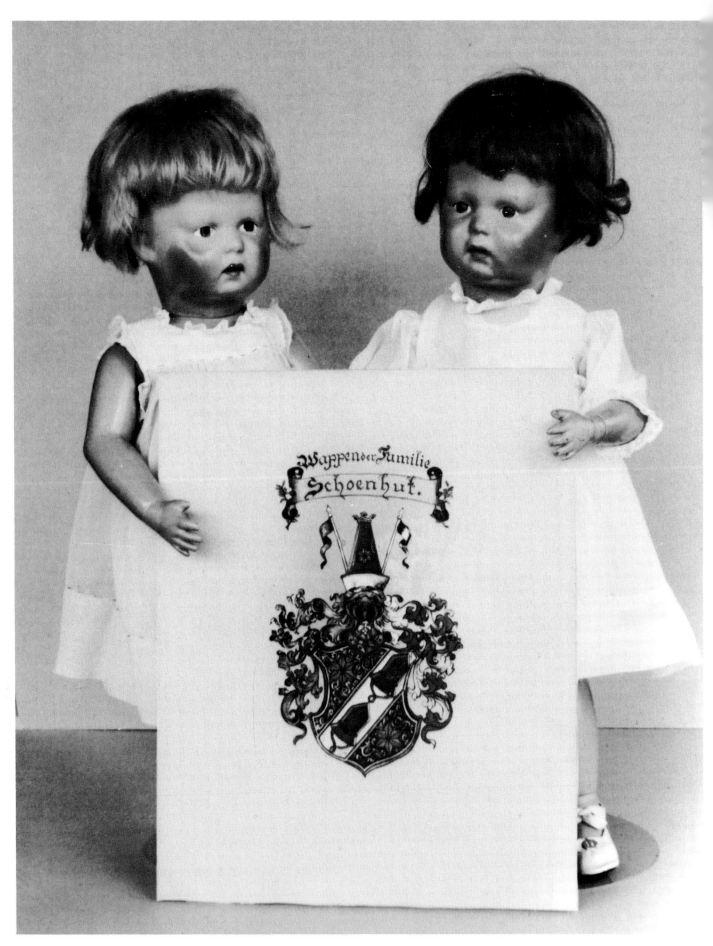

Illustration 517. The dolls 17/108W, named Dorothy and Doris by their owner, were made by Harry Schoenhut for his daughter, Phyllis. They are showing the family Coat of Arms. Schoenhut means "beautiful hat" in German and the crest is a hat. There are also two hats on the bar. *Phyllis Schoenhut O'Hare Collection.*